eVeryDay eBay

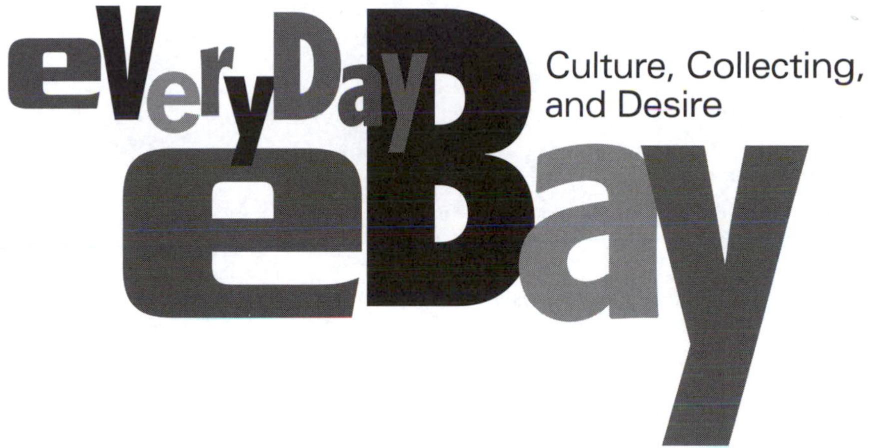

Culture, Collecting, and Desire

Edited by
Ken Hillis and **Michael Petit**
with **Nathan Scott Epley**

Routledge is an imprint of the
Taylor & Francis Group, an informa business

Grateful acknowledgment is made to the following for permission to reprint previously published material: "My Obsession: I Thought I Was Immune to the Net. Then I Got Bitten by eBay." by William Gibson was originally published in *Wired* 7, no. 1 (January 1999). Copyright © 1999 by William Gibson. Reprinted by permission of the author and Condé Nast Publicatons.

Published in 2006 by
Routledge
Taylor & Francis Group
270 Madison Avenue
New York, NY 10016

Published in Great Britain by
Routledge
Taylor & Francis Group
2 Park Square
Milton Park, Abingdon
Oxon OX14 4RN

Routledge is an imprint of Taylor & Francis Group

Printed in the United States of America on acid-free paper
10 9 8 7 6 5 4 3 2 1

International Standard Book Number-10: 0-415-97435-6 (Hardcover) 0-415-97436-4 (Softcover)
International Standard Book Number-13: 978-0-415-97435-6 (Hardcover) 978-0-415-97436-3 (Softcover)
Library of Congress Card Number 2005029547

Library of Congress Cataloging-in-Publication Data

Everyday eBay : culture, collecting, and desire / edited by Ken Hillis, Michael Petit, and Nathan Epley.
p. cm.
Includes bibliographical references and index.
ISBN 0-415-97435-6 (hardback : alk. paper) -- ISBN 0-415-97436-4 (pbk. : alk. paper)
1.eBay (Firm) 2. Internet auctions. I. Hillis, Ken. II. Petit, Michael, 1956- III. Epley, Nathan, 1968-

HF5478.E84 2006
381'.177--dc22 2005029547

Taylor & Francis Group
is the Academic Division of Informa plc.

Visit the Taylor & Francis Web site at
http://www.taylorandfrancis.com

and the Routledge Web site at
http://www.routledge-ny.com

CONTENTS

List of Illustrations ix

Introducing *Everyday eBay*
KEN HILLIS, MICHAEL PETIT, AND NATHAN SCOTT EPLEY 1

1 My Obsession: I Thought I Was Immune to the Net. Then I Got Bitten by eBay.
WILLIAM GIBSON 19

2 Ephemeral Culture/eBay Culture: Film Collectibles and Fan Investments
MARY DESJARDINS 31

3 Virtual_radiophile (163☆): eBay and the Changing Collecting Practices of the U.K. Vintage Radio Community
REBECCA M. ELLIS AND ANNA HAYWOOD 45

4 Fortune-Telling on eBay: Early African American Textual Artifacts and the Marketplace
ERIC GARDNER 63

5 Reading eBay: Hidden Stores, Subjective Stories, and a People's History of the Archive
ZOE TRODD 77

6 Immaterial Labor in the eBay Community: The Work of Consumption in the "Network Society"
JON LILLIE 91

7 The Perfect Community: Disciplining the eBay User
KYLIE JARRETT 107

❑ 8 "Black Friday" and Feedback Bombing: An Examination of Trust and Online Community in eBay's Early History
LAURA ROBINSON 123

❑ 9 Return of the Town Square: Reputational Gossip and Trust on eBay
LYN M. VAN SWOL 137

❑ 10 Of PEZ and Perfect Price: Sniping, Collecting Cultures, and Democracy on eBay
NATHAN SCOTT EPLEY 151

❑ 📷 11 Auctioning the Authentic: eBay, Narrative Effect, and the Superfluity of Memory
KEN HILLIS 167

❑ 📷 12 Between the Archive and the Image-Repertoire: Amateur Commercial Still Life Photography on eBay
JAMES LEO CAHILL 185

❑ 📷 13 "Virgin Mary In Grilled Cheese NOT A HOAX! LOOK & SEE!": Sublime Kitsch on eBay
SUSANNA PAASONEN 201

❑ 📷 14 eBay and the Traveling Museum: Elvis Richardson's *Slide Show Land*
DANIEL MUDIE CUNNINGHAM 217

❑ 15 The Contradictory Circulation of Fine Art and Antiques on eBay
LISA BLOOM 231

❑ 📷 16 My Queer eBay: "Gay Interest" Photographs and the Visual Culture of Buying
MICHELE WHITE 245

❑ 17 "Cleaned to eBay Standards": Sex Panic, eBay, and the Moral Economy of Underwear
MICHAEL PETIT 267

❑ 18 **Playing Dress-Up: eBay's Vintage Clothing-Land**
KATALIN LOVÁSZ 283

❑ **Contributors** 295

❑ **Index** 301

LIST OF ILLUSTRATIONS

Figure I.1 "Blackness for Sale," 2001. Courtesy of Mendi and Keith Obadike.
Figure 3.1 U.K. vintage radio repair and restoration discussion forum.
Figure 3.2 "40s/50s bakelite radio."
Figure 5.1 *Carte-de-visite* vintage photograph of girls holding books. Courtesy of Zoe Trodd.
Figure 11.1 "Size 12 Wedding Dress/Gown No Reserve."
Figure 12.1 Examples of amateur commercial still life photography.
Figure 13.1 Virgin Mary grilled cheese sandwich in plastic display case.
Figure 13.2 "Virgin Eating Grilled Cheese" and "Virgin Mary Grilled Cheese Rotating Holy Shrine."
Figure 14.1 *Slide Show Land* by Elvis Richardson, 2002. Courtesy of the artist.
Figure 14.2 eBay remediates the slide.
Figure 16.1 "Vintage Photo Gay Brothers Double Date In Wagons 1916."
Figure 16.2 "gay int tintype 6 affectionate men overthetop."
Figure 18.1 Katalin Lovász in a 1930s dress. Photograph by Andrew Moore.

❑ INTRODUCING *EVERYDAY EBAY*

❑ KEN HILLIS, MICHAEL PETIT,
AND NATHAN SCOTT EPLEY

From its inauspicious launch on Labor Day 1995 as AuctionWeb, a free auction website designed by computer programmer Pierre Omidyar, eBay has evolved into a global economic, social, and cultural phenomenon. Wildly profitable since it began charging listing fees in early 1996, the company has benefited from exponential growth in registered users and sales volume. Even as it faces the maturation and potential saturation of its U.S. market, it is aggressively expanding globally, in part to meet the expectations of the stock market.[1] During the second quarter of 2005 alone, eBay had over 440 million listings and 157.3 million registered users worldwide (of whom eBay counts 64.6 million as "active," having bid on, bought, or listed an item within the previous twelve-month period).[2] In 2004, the website facilitated international gross sales of more than 34 billion USD in merchandise, and in 2005 was on target to facilitate over 40 billion. Each day, sellers list 4.89 million items organized across more than 40,000 main and subcategories that continually expand in number. Five hundred thousand Americans, eBay estimates, made all or part of their living from selling on its site in 2005; other business analysts project that hundreds of thousands more sellers worldwide make their living through eBay. As the *Economist* noted, "Never before has there been a market with such abundant dimensions."[3]

The world's largest online market, eBay is a virtual setting where capital, desire, and identity converge. A crucial component of eBay's success, both economic and cultural, is its organization of the site as a series of stages allowing sellers to design, perform, and sell memorable experiences, thematically linked to goods, for which purchasers are willing to pay a premium. These performances, and the willingness to pay, exceed commonsense understandings of eBay as a giant garage sale or the old-fashioned auction house writ virtual. The final price—the winning bid—paid on eBay is the outcome of negotiations among buyers and sellers over value, and these negotiations, as the essays collected in this volume demonstrate, are influenced by many factors, including users' Feedback Forum ratings; the elaborate histories frequently accompanying items listed; how users interpret ambiguous images and perceive relationships among various strata of "lowbrow" collectibles, kitsch, and "high" art objects; and the building, performing, and maintaining of online personae. Value also depends on an object's association with authenticity, memory, and experience. These, too, are up for auction, available to the highest bidder.

Drawing on the work of the volume's contributors, we identify eBay as an important component of the contemporary "experience economy." *Work Is Theatre and Every Business a Stage* is the subtitle of Joseph Pine and James Gilmore's 1999 book, *The Experience Economy*.[4] It is also an apt description of eBay and how staged performances and experiences are integral to the merchandising and trading of goods and services on the site. In the experience economy, individuals willingly pay a premium for a sense of experience, the exchange of which is at once prior to and part of the sale. Such marketing of experience joins service to entertainment, thus taking part in the increased commodification of services more generally.

To participate fully in the experience economy, Pine and Gilmore suggest that businesses should imagine charging admission and then reconfigure the entertainment value of their services to match the added fee. The more that people associate the activity of purchasing with pleasure (and not just desire for objects), the more they find worthy the objects they desire and the commodity experience itself. Pleasure still comes from actually possessing the object, but also from closer association with the channels of desire urging its acquisition. Pleasurable advertising and its promotion are hardly new; however, convincing people to pay more for an object linked to an enhanced experience that is itself designed to promote the sale helps to cement affect—the emotional responses sparked in consumers—to the serialized commodification of their desires. Desire for an object and pleasure in purchasing it coalesce; individuals literally "buy into" the hegemonizing logic of their own commodification at an earlier stage in the cycle of consumption.[5]

Consuming a pleasurable experience that increases perceptions of value also helps foster brand loyalty. On eBay, each seller's listing can be seen as a mini-site that participates in the aura of the eBay™ brand. Media accounts of spectacular eBay phenomena and of buyers' and sellers' noteworthy performances always refer back to the global brand—eBay—even as such coverage ostensibly focuses on the singularity and affect of the specific listing itself. Even the most banal listing participates in this dynamic.

Auctions, we suggest, are models for the experience economy and long predate Pine and Gilmore's identification of its rise. The excitement auctions generate through the bidding process can itself be seen as a form of added value and has long contributed to increasing price—as any successful bidder later chagrined at having paid too much due to "auction fever" can attest. In designing an online auction site, therefore, Omidyar provided a blueprint for the experience economy and the four themes that drive it: entertainment, education, aesthetics, and escapism. The riches, Pine and Gilmore dryly note, belong to those whose offerings combine all four, and, as the essays in *Everyday eBay* collectively show, eBay provides a venue for each.

Some first-generation new media scholars, writing in the 1990s, offered utopian visions of the internet's future. Some predicted the expansion of democracy through widespread, networked online democratic participation; others emphasized the technology's potential for fostering self-publishing, especially through personal Web pages; yet others promoted the personal empowerment purportedly available through the performance of multiple and fluid identities within the anonymity of cyberspace. Increasingly, however, democratic participation and online self-expression take place on commercial sites such as eBay, which offers free space for creativity but only within the context of the site's willing embrace of experience-based consumption. The genius of eBay is that even art practices and performances on the site calling critical attention to issues of consumption themselves become part of "the eBay experience." John Freyer, for example, achieved notoriety by auctioning on eBay most everything he owned (beginning with a .99 USD bid on each item) to explore "our relationship to the concept of identity, as well as the emerging commercial systems of the Internet." Freyer's documented art project, www.allmylifeforsale.com, is now owned by the University of Iowa, Museum of Art. Keith Obadike's 2001 listing, "Blackness for Sale" (the narrative portion of which we reproduce in Figure I.1), explored intersections among race, identity, and their commodification, and it perhaps achieved greater saliency when eBay canceled the auction as a violation of its policies. The 2005–2006 exhibit *Spinning the Web: The eBay Connection* at the Museum für Moderne Kunst, Frankfurt am Main, Germany, presented objects purchased on eBay over a period of several months and juxtaposed them with artworks in the permanent collection. Posing the question "how does a museum change things that are placed within its walls?" the exhibit examined the intersections between a museum of modern art and the market place and how new forms of signification and meaning arise within individual contexts.[6]

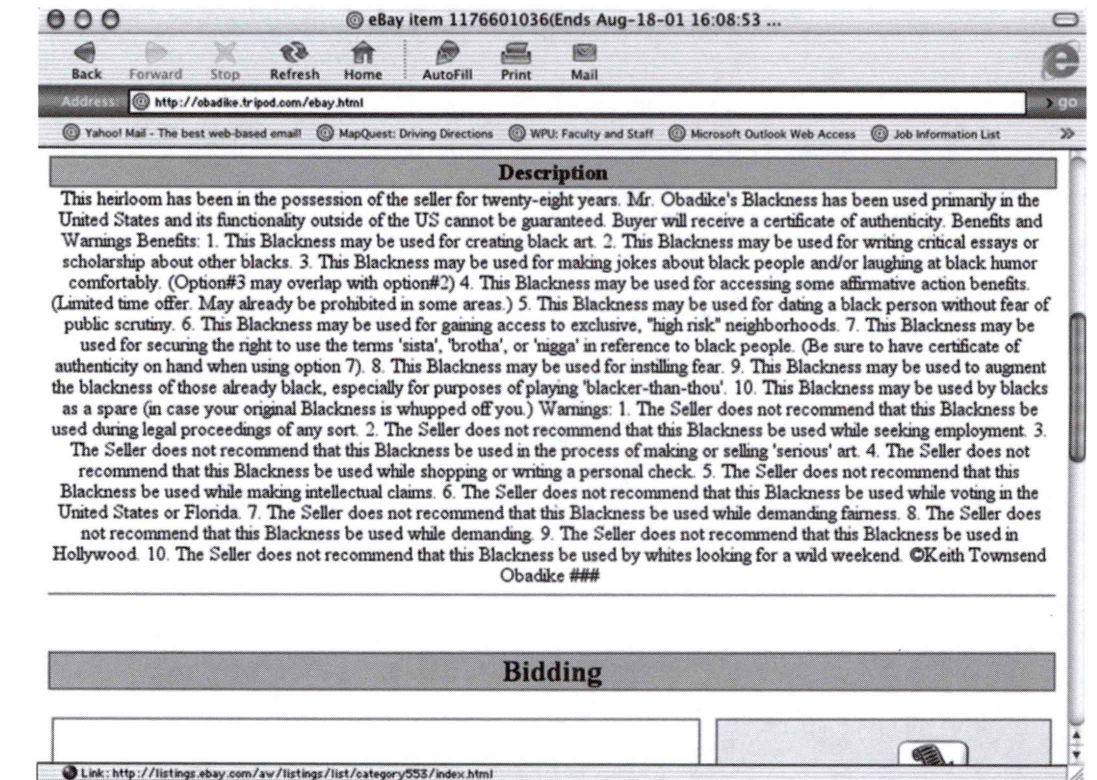

Figure I.1 "Blackness for Sale," 2001. Courtesy of Mendi and Keith Obadike.

The potential to perform multiple and fluid identities online has been influential in postmodern understandings of human culture. However, because of the need to establish trust when trading with strangers who one likely will never meet, identity on eBay is necessarily much more fixed than this, and the social utility of the site's Feedback Forum depends on such stability. To trade effectively on eBay, one must seem to possess a stable identity, verified through a user ID and password, a permanent address, and a credit card. While most users understand that this requirement applies to everyone, except for shill bidders who use multiple identities to fraudulently drive up prices, they are more likely to maintain a single eBay identity because, as it accumulates positive feedback, it constitutes a key component of their eBay brand. A stable identity, as several contributors demonstrate, adds value over time.

The insistence on stable online identity is increasingly the dominant paradigm of an ever more commercial Web that itself, with its high level of interactivity, helps drive the experience economy. It is not that there are fewer opportunities for identity fluidity than previously. Rather, sites such as eBay take part in a trend in which the internet and most other digital technologies increasingly warrant and fix identity in specific bodies in specific places. This occurs in part because of the dramatic proliferation of always-on, always-connected, high-speed internet service. The understanding of "going online" itself is disappearing, and eBay is less and less a separate or "parallel" virtual space to which buyers and sellers, donning cloaks of anonymity, might repair. Rather, eBay is always on, and each user's reputation is on the line with each transaction undertaken. If we take seriously critical assertions that the internet is a postmodern space that opens up possibilities for creative identity fluidity, it would now seem that, especially on eBay and the commercial Web, there has been a reassertion of a fixed, stable, and very modern identity formation. Arguably, most of us, particularly late adopters of new technologies, were never as enamored of identity fluidity as were techies and early internet enthusiasts. In the name of security and "safe trading"—to get on with business—most individuals willingly consent to the kinds of unitary self-representations required on eBay, just as they willingly consent to the enjoyment of an experience they know is designed to inveigle them to purchase and to produce brand loyalty. Our understanding of hegemony is that everyone has to get something out of any ideological system to which they consent, even though that "something" may be distributed in a wildly uneven fashion. Strongly articulated to the commercial necessity of identity verification are larger moral panics: who, discourses of security ask, would want to hide or disguise their identity anyway, except for thieves, child molesters, terrorists, and disaffected hacker criminals from former Soviet states such as Romania?

Reasserting and maintaining a stable identity in the name of fair trade and transparency dovetail with eBay's promotion of its site as a place to collect objects that remind one of those treasured in the past. As one eBay TV ad asks, "What if nothing was ever forgotten? What if nothing was ever lost?" In a culture of superfluity and short attention spans, yet one increasingly concerned that nothing be forgotten or discarded, the culture of collecting that eBay promotes implies that rather than seeing identity polyvalency as a freedom, people hold value in crafting a past and the continuity it represents. eBay, then, can be seen as organizing a popular refusal of postmodern understandings of multiple identities as a means to combat a pervasive sense in highly mediated cultures that the past has slipped away, and along with it individual personal control over one's everyday future. This dynamic of retrieving and reclaiming one's past through acquiring fetishized objects dovetails with the neoliberal ideological assertion that competent subjects should reject the state's organization of social welfare as patriarchal and inefficient, and instead take charge of as many aspects of their own lives as possible. In so doing, it comes to make "perfect sense" to them to never throw anything away, to become a collector, for in a do-it-yourself world, one never knows just when an almost forgotten object might once again be of benefit. In such a way does eBay mesh with ways that collecting increasingly constitutes the everyday.

WHY *EVERYDAY*?

Each of us experiences and performs certain acts and encounters daily. Habituation, repetition, and the rhythms of the everyday are part of who we are, part of how we make meaning. The contributors to *Everyday eBay* seek to understand and explain eBay as part of the everyday lives of its many users. Examining the everyday does not dismiss the products of the culture industries or their importance to people. Nor does it dismiss the insights of critical theory. At times, the repetitive practices of everyday life (such as browsing on eBay) are thought of as mundane. "Mundane" refers to the ordinary, and it encapsulates a sense of belonging to or being in the world. Lodged within the mundane, however, is also an idea of the cosmic, and an examination of the everyday speaks to the "organization of coincidences" that eBay draws together for its users: the unexpected and the ephemeral, the sublime and the kitsch, the economic and the cultural, the sacred and the profane.

Only now are academics beginning to examine new digital media as mundane and everyday objects rather than as extraordinary and revolutionary.

eBay is an excellent example of the mundane nature of the internet; critical analysis of its digital ephemerality as central to many everyday lives helps situate eBay within the cultural valence of the internet and the broader field of contemporary culture. Karl Marx noted that people make history even as they rarely control the contexts within which they make this history. The examinations of eBay collected here indicate how humans make do with and against everyday forces frequently more powerful than themselves. The idea of everyday life takes seriously all forms of human agency. Begging to differ with the Borg of *Star Trek*, we understand that resistance is not futile, even as we also recognize that everyday practices can be wholly consistent with and help secure consent to a variety of different forms of discipline, management, and control.

WHY *EBAY*?

eBay is a living part of culture, and many of the contributors to this volume are fans and users of the site. For most contributors, eBay is not the focus of scholarly research, yet for all of us, writing about eBay has been a labor of love. We take a critical perspective on the site but refuse to cast eBay as a fiend. Instead, we approach it as an object and link insights gleaned from our various disciplinary perspectives to both the site itself and the ways it extends itself into the broader lived world around us. This volume, in short, investigates those practices that distinguish eBay and why eBay matters both everyday and globally.[7]

Perhaps the single perspective that most unites us as authors is our commitment to simultaneously consider the economic, social, and cultural constructions and the specific technological form of the site. Such assertions are more frequent in current academic criticism of digital media and technologies than was the case a decade ago, but we believe it is important to stress our refusal of either social constructionist or technological determinist approaches to thinking about an object such as eBay. The volume as a whole owes a debt to critical cultural studies, but the authors refer sparingly to the canon of Karl Marx, Antonio Gramsci, Michel Foucault, or Gilles Deleuze and Félix Guattari. Instead, the specific contexts investigated in different chapters lead authors to specific detours through theory. The practices of buying, selling, and shopping on eBay direct several authors to consider Walter Benjamin's work on collecting. Those authors who deal with eBay images find that critics such as Roland Barthes and Susan Sontag enrich their understandings of eBay iconography. Others draw on the work of Russell Belk in analyzing eBay collecting practices. Consistently, eBay is the object of study, the organizing context that grounds and justifies each author's theoretical discussions.

As editors, our intention has been to produce a collection of essays that models collaborative interdisciplinary scholarship in the humanities and social sciences. We identified a range of practices on eBay calling for analysis, and we assembled a group of authors committed to producing not only a set of original accounts but also ones accessible to a wide range of interested readers. We sought a diversity of approaches and theories in order to provide both academic case studies and a historical record of eBay practices during the site's first decade of operation. The essays focus on eBay in complementary, overlapping, and, at times, contradictory ways. Where essays link at key points, we provide references within the text. We invite readers to engage the essays in the order presented or to browse the collection and, as on eBay, follow the links where they lead. Diverse and thorough, *Everyday eBay* by necessity must remain incomplete, for an exhaustive account of the myriad and divergent practices eBay organizes is beyond the range of any one anthology. Given its scale, diversity, and continuing growth as a global online virtual stage and new form of communication, eBay will continue to inspire humanities and social science academic research.

VOLUME OVERVIEW

eBay has a history. More than a decade has passed since its inception, and to historicize the company, community, and various practices we open with a reprint of novelist William Gibson's 1999 rumination on eBay and personal obsession. Gibson recounts how the Web held little personal fascination until he encountered eBay, a setting that stimulated his interest in replacing *the* watch: the Rolex Oyster Precision model he had sold for quick cash in his younger days. Gibson observes that "the main driving force in the tidying of the world's attic … is information technology," and he suggests that the sheer volume of things listed for sale on eBay reveals how information technology has worked to invert the modern understanding of the relationship between a map and the territory it represents. Gibson identifies eBay as "this territory the map became."

Gibson's obsession points to eBay as the place where collectors turn when seeking to acquire objects from the past, whether the personal past or the more mediated past of movie ephemera of interest to Mary Desjardins. Desjardins provides a case study of her use of eBay to acquire film-related materials important to her academic research. Searching eBay to locate these materials, however, leads her into direct competition with fans determined to acquire film star ephemera at virtually any price. She shows how buyers and sellers communicate their self-identity by announcing their fandom and fan authority through engaging in rituals of possession and divestment. These rituals are organized around the film-related objects that fans sometimes sell and for which they also compete with one another to acquire. Desjardins concludes by assessing how ephemera—objects that are meant to be thrown away but have become collectibles—are indicative of a wider cultural sensibility whereby everything is disposable *and* needs to be preserved. In both instances, eBay is there to help.

eBay organizes and helps produce a vast range of collecting communities of which Hollywood ephemera fans are but one. Like Desjardins, Rebecca Ellis and Anna Haywood focus on collectors—in this case, U.K. collectors of vintage radio sets—and the ritual practices they employ as part of acquiring and divesting themselves of radios and radio-related objects. The collectors who Ellis and Haywood interview provide, in their own words, a wealth of detail concerning the influence of eBay on traditional forms of radio collecting such as rummaging through car boot sales, attending swap meets, and relying on professional resellers. While considerable attention has been paid to the numismatic and philatelic communities' use of eBay, Ellis and Haywood contend that the practices of virtual radiophiles are more revealing still of the ways eBay influences collecting cultures: radio sets, they observe, unlike coins and stamps, come in many sizes. Collectors list smaller, easier-to-ship sets on eBay while retaining bulkier (though no less valuable) ones for material venues of exchange. Negotiating this divide can be tricky, and successful collectors develop new forms of knowledge. Ellis and Haywood show how vintage radio collectors have learned to traverse the intersections among the internet, geography, demographics, computer skills, and community networks. While eBay is unlikely to completely replace the material geographies of collecting cultures, it has already reworked their meanings.

Academics increasingly use eBay as a research tool. Eric Gardner's contribution may be read as a case study in using eBay to locate early and rare African American texts. It also shows how eBay democratizes traditional book collecting. Gardner, successful in acquiring a hitherto unknown chapbook published in the 1820s, offers something of an eBay primer for developing research skills necessary to locate "lost" materials. Their owners may have listed them without fully comprehending their value and, therefore, fail to describe them so as to realize this value. Such texts escape easy categorization on eBay and are therefore difficult to find. The racism built into many relevant listings means that the researcher at times must use the nineteenth-century language of race and racism in order to search the site. More troubling still, as Gardner notes, the auction's competitive process resonates uncannily with the history and actual mechanisms of the American antebellum slave auction.

Like Eric Gardner, Zoe Trodd uses eBay to acquire artifacts from the past that are important to her research. Trodd focuses on nineteenth-century *cartes-de-visite*. Cheap, mass-produced photographs often archived in personal albums, *cartes-de-visite* were used as calling cards and took the form of the individual bearer's photographic portrait mounted on cardboard stock. Trodd shows how these images, often of women reading singly or in groups, constitute a people's history in images. The descriptions of these images provided by eBay sellers, moreover, participate in and renew this form of popular history; sellers who speculate about the women in these images, and who invite viewers to imagine new links with the past and the women who look out at them from these cards, themselves now write and depict new online forms of people's history. Trodd, then, identifies eBay as a people's archive, an ephemeral one to be sure, but one that reveals the American archival imagination to be as organized through images as it is through writing. The stories that sellers tell about these images operate in a similar fashion to the books the women hold in these images—they introduce personal narratives into the archive. They help reclaim the secret histories of women dismissed by the dominant collecting impulse to taxonomize and typologize the past.

Trodd's work points to the relationships among eBay, the archive, the fabrication of history, past collections, and the importance of retrieving such collections for making meaning today. With Jon Lillie's contribution, the volume moves to examine political-economic issues. Lillie details how eBay organizes its users' labor practices to accord with the precepts of neoliberal economic theory. He demonstrates how eBay is at the vanguard of technological and management practices seeking to produce neoliberal subjects. For example, services that would, in a traditional retail organization, be performed by paid customer service employees are, on eBay, performed voluntarily by community members. Lillie identifies this kind of work as affective labor—work intended to shift or transform those for whom it is performed. eBay's discourse of community encourages users to believe that the kind of "network citizenship" on offer will be incredibly robust, as it is associated with the technological power to connect with millions of other people. In the seventeenth century, European nations developed notions of citizenship based on emerging requirements that merchants interact freely in the marketplace. eBay, argues Lillie, in developing and fostering the technologies and rules that enable peer-to-peer e-commerce to take place, fulfills a similar role today in articulating new concepts of citizenship consonant with the needs of contemporary capital.

Maintaining the focus on neoliberal strategies, Kylie Jarrett delves into the ways that eBay's success depends upon the construction of community norms that effectively police the activities and transactions on the eBay site at little cost to the firm. She argues that a key element of the globally hegemonic model of neoliberal governance is the reconfiguring of individual citizens as fully responsible for their own conduct. Bringing together the insights of sociolinguistics and political economy, Jarrett shows how eBay's discourse of community is critical in achieving this goal on the site, and she interrogates the nature of eBay's mobilization of community as a means to discipline users into compliance with its corporate agenda. Across its entire platform, she argues, eBay represents itself through forms of discourse in ways that seem to minimize its authority over users. The apparent absence of eBay's direct intervention in the day-to-day aspects of trade-related issues such as fraud and trust, Jarrett argues, also promotes users' acceptance that they are fully responsible for their success or failure on the site. The Feedback Forum, eBay's chief mechanism for tying the individually responsible user to the established norms of the community, distributes the power of surveillance to all buyers and sellers. Users, conscious of the possibility of censure for conduct inconsistent with community values, willingly police their own conduct, not only from fear of reprisal but also because of the success the site associates with adherence.

The Feedback Forum, as Jarrett observes, is a brilliant neoliberal invention pivotal to eBay's success. Laura Robinson's contribution maintains the focus on feedback. An important objective of this volume is to bring together humanities and social science approaches, to gather different ways of thinking about eBay and its users. Robinson examines an important historical moment on eBay from the perspective of qualitative sociology. In August 1999, soon after the company became a publicly traded company and not long before the dot.com crash, eBay, without consulting its members, implemented new reserve auction policies particularly troubling to committed sellers emotionally and economically invested in eBay. Defiant and disenchanted, some members organized a boycott of the site in response to what they called "Black Friday." For some, the change in policy constituted a breach in institutional trust that was the culmination of long-standing grievances, many of which related to eBay's inability or refusal to police the Feedback Forum against malicious, vindictive feedback. Allowing members to speak in their own voices, Robinson provides a glimpse into the networked dynamics of collective and interpersonal trust, as well as reputation on eBay, in a moment of systemic crisis. Her work takes advantage of eBay's unique setting to examine the linkages between economic risks and payoffs and the social gratifications that flow from computer-mediated interactions in online communities.

Lyn Van Swol's contribution maintains Jarrett's and Robinson's emphasis on feedback. Social scientists have studied eBay extensively, and Van Swol provides readers with a useful summary of their research relating to online trust and reputation. She also examines the relationships among vulnerability, trust, and buyers' and sellers' concern for reputation with eBay's feedback system. Although one can learn quite a bit about a person's trading history through researching his or her feedback profile, one probably does not actually know that person. Therefore, Van Swol argues, because of this anonymity, one need not feel obligated to maintain a relationship with that person, and one would have few qualms about being promiscuous among sellers to capitalize on a seller with the best reputation. This promiscuousness drives the need to maintain a good reputation to prevent other eBay users from moving onto greener pastures. Trust, therefore, drives commerce on eBay but also forms part of the site's identity and brand. Van Swol contrasts this dynamic to social trends that obscure trust in favor of mechanisms such as insurance or regulation. With the use of technology, eBay operates by using a distinctly old-fashioned method to develop trust: reputational gossip.

Nathan Epley provides a concise account of how auctions work and the ways that eBay's standard auction format is an amalgam of different kinds of auctions adapted to the realities of internet trading. Epley resists eBay's move to establish itself as the arbiter of an object's "perfect price." Auctions, he shows, are efficient mechanisms for establishing price only when an object's value is difficult to determine in advance. The idea of perfect price, he argues, represents a desire to actualize the utopian theories of neoclassical economics. Yet eBay is not some latter-day "hidden hand" directing the perfect elucidation of any object's price at any time, and the idea of perfect price, Epley shows, fails to account for the complexity of factors (the uniqueness of eBay's auction format included) influencing exchanges between real individuals in real situations. For example, it is not possible for a buyer to completely know in advance what the quality of a secondhand item won on eBay might be. Social science refers to this as "information asymmetry" between buyer and seller, and Epley, also drawing from ethnographic interviews with collectors, shows how this asymmetry influences different price outcomes across various and constantly evolving market conditions.

As Epley indicates, producing value on eBay entails complex interrelationships among buyers, sellers, and the website itself. Ken Hillis examines the ways that some eBay listings also serve to perform the sellers' claims to authenticity. Extending C. S. Peirce's idea of the index, Hillis argues that a widespread, if implicit, belief that the Web constitutes a space allows eBay viewers buying into this belief to experience a trace of the seller online. Such an experience, in part also constituted through consuming the elaborate textual histories and images that form part of the listings Hillis examines, contributes to new forms of value negotiated among eBayers. The narrative effects that such listings induce constitute one of the principal "goods" exchanged in advance of any actual sale, yet one also freely available to any viewer. Indeed, Hillis argues, while such listings suggest that authenticity itself is transferable, an exchange value available to the highest bidder, it is an experientially credible trace of the seller that "exchanges" or passes between her or his listing and all viewers. This trace—credible, memorable, and at times, therefore, also fantastical—can be understood as part of an evolving strategy of online selling that allows purchasers to consume "something" in advance or in addition to any actual items up for auction.

With James Cahill's essay, the volume turns to examine more centrally a range of art and aesthetic practices on eBay. Cahill examines the practices of photo-imaging developed by eBay sellers. Self-produced images of secondhand items constitute the site's dominant set of photographic conventions, and Cahill identifies an emergent genre of photography on the site—what he terms "amateur commercial still life photography." At the interface of the amateur and the professional, the individual and the corporation, a screen-based aesthetic has developed that minimizes, without entirely expunging, characteristics of amateur photography such as poor focus, eccentric framing, indifferent lighting, and shadows. In this way, Cahill argues, self-produced images appeal to viewers' sensual and even tactile apprehension. The supposed lack (of quality) ascribed to amateur photography therefore converts into a surplus on the site. It helps induce desire in the viewer to bid on what comes to seem a more authentic or "truthful" object. The "look" of such images, then, helps decommodify objects for sale even as it also recommodifies them as objects awaiting exchange. Drawing on Jacques Derrida and Roland Barthes, Cahill thinks through eBay's relation to the archive and the image-repertoire.

On November 22, 2004, bidding closed on an eBay auction titled "Virgin Mary In Grilled Cheese." According to the seller, this partially eaten sandwich, miraculously, had not molded in a decade and had helped her win considerable amounts of money at a nearby casino. Susanna Paasonen's essay approaches this well-publicized auction as exemplifying a fusion of categories generally assumed incompatible: the sublime and the banal, the sacred and the commercial, the reverential and the parodic. To understand this fusion, Paasonen addresses the mutability of commodity value from three intertwining perspectives: the cultural history of commodified Christian iconography, the categories of the sublime and the banal, and the act of interpretation where a mundane snack is read as a divine sign. She brings to her assessment questions of class and cultural hierarchies, of high and low. While artworks such as Andres Serrano's *Piss Christ* (1989) or Chris Ofili's *Holy Virgin Mary* (1996) have provoked fury in the United States over the intactness of religious iconography, the links of half-eaten processed foods, apparitions, gambling, and internet auctions in the realm of kitsch fail to inspire similar outrage. The description of the Virgin Mary sandwich declared faith in the authenticity of the apparition and its powers. Paasonen shows that, situated in the realm of the banal, the listing successfully communicated a textual innocence void of sacrilegious intentions or critical agendas, and in so doing the sandwich and its mass mediation achieved a quality of the sublime.

Daniel Cunningham's essay theorizes the work of Australian artist Elvis Richardson, who has created an installation project, *Welcome to Slide Show Land*. Richardson conceives of her work as an archive and uses eBay to buy the 35mm slide photographs featured in her installation. These slides comprise personal visual records of travel, family life, and landscapes. For Cunningham, that eBay "users" discard such evidence of their families' personal histories in an online global trading environment makes for interesting questions about the value (or nonvalue) of personal history. Do such histories, he asks, become irrelevant, too difficult to preserve and comprehend when the formats on which they are archived, in this case the slide, become redundant? For Cunningham, what makes eBay unique as a secondhand marketplace is the way it remediates past technologies and secures them in the digital archives of the present. eBay itself, he argues, through its strategies of display, remediates slide technology. That the slide's formal constraints endure on eBay is also ironic, Cunningham finds, given that eBay positions the slide as a "collectible" due to its status as a dying media format.

Lisa Bloom, an eBay Power Seller, discusses how eBay has democratized the fine art and antiques sector of the economy. She argues that the greater access to information that eBay provides, along with the anonymity and global reach permitted by internet-mediated communication, have opened up possibilities for women and younger traders in this historically hierarchical and patriarchal trading community. Bloom further assesses the failure of high-end firms such as Sotheby's and Christie's to establish themselves as successful Web presences. She also details the painstaking work required of online art and antiques sellers to overcome the resistance of prospective purchasers who cannot physically examine objects prior to their purchase. For the low- to mid-range art objects constituting the majority of items in this sector traded online, sellers must produce much more detailed information about the objects for sale than would have been available from bricks-and-mortar auction houses.

With Michele White's essay, the volume turns to consider ways that identity and eBay intersect. eBay provides no separate categories for the sale of items that might appeal to gay and lesbian identity formations. In response, sellers have developed the search term "gay interest" to provide another viewing structure within eBay's heteronormative category system. White focuses on vintage photography sellers including "gay interest" in their listings to designate objects they think gay people might want. In so doing, such sellers acknowledge the diverse sexualities of collectors; produce gay, lesbian, queer, transgendered, and bisexual histories for individuals once photographed; and queer the past by describing same-sex duos and groups as "gay." Gay interest photography sellers, White argues, integrate gay politics and desires into the eBay site by making their listings visible and by suggesting that vernacular vintage photography has gay content. She also notes, they undermine eBay's normalizing discourses about heterosexuality, romance, and gendered expectations.

If White's essay indicates that not all collecting communities are equally welcomed into eBay's catalog structure, Michael Petit further exposes the myth of eBay as a perfect market in which individuals trade freely with one another. He recounts how eBay banned auctions for used underwear as part of a systematic "cleanup" of its "Adult Only" listing category just before the company's pending business alliance with Disney in November 2000. Extending Gayle Rubin's arguments, Petit discusses how eBay's actions update the dynamics of "sex panic," a form of moral crusade producing crackdowns on sexual outsiders. Petit's historicization of eBay's scapegoating of used underwear sellers and buyers also interrogates utopian claims that the Web and information technology more generally offer a supposed salvation from unequal and vexed embodied social and political relations in favor of an idealized model of "friction-free capitalism." Such claims, he argues, actually reinforce hegemonic understandings of sexuality while simultaneously suppressing meaningful discussion of the social and political issues raised by these understandings.

Like William Gibson's opening essay, the volume's final contribution is a meditation on eBay's role in influencing the relationship between oneself and the objects one seeks. Katalin Lovász's academic research examines representations of female identity in 1930s Hollywood screwball comedies. Lovász allows her academic research into her daily life by wearing the 1930s clothing that she purchases on eBay and uses in her research. She celebrates this act as working to counter the unproductive and patriarchal dichotomizing belief that a researcher's thought-life should be distinct from her lived and felt experiences. Lovász reveals that her ability to experience bodily movement while wearing the vintage clothing allowed her to more fully comprehend how clothing acts as a screen to hide behind and as a set of constraints that strongly influence how one moves through social and public space. Wearing clothing purchased on eBay allowed her to develop the theory at the heart of her research: that women in the 1930s encountered themselves in the bodily motion of the actresses on the screen, actresses wearing clothes similar to their own in a way that broke down the barrier between these women's imaginary and experiential lives. For Lovász, then, eBay allows for a similar set of crossings between the imaginary and the experiential, and a personal union with history and the past.

NOTES

1. While the American site remains the most heavily trafficked of all eBay national sites, the company has embarked on an aggressive campaign to extend its brand globally. There were twenty-seven national eBays in 2005, the first year when more people living outside the United States used eBay than those living within its borders. Keenly aware of a slowing down in the rate of its U.S. growth, eBay has stated its vision to be "a global online trading platform where practically anyone can trade practically anything." Most eBay national sites are portals for First World Western countries, but producing and consuming citizens of almost all Newly Industrializing Countries now have access to their own eBay experiences, including those in India and Malaysia, South Korea, the Philippines and Taiwan, Singapore, Brazil, Argentina, and Mexico. The firm is investing heavily in eBay China. Japan is the only country where eBay was unable to penetrate the market and has ceased operations. On the difficulties eBay faces in maintaining its growth, see Gary Rivlin, "EBay's Joy Ride: Going Once … a Seller's Rebellion May Be the Least of Its Worries," *New York Times*, March 6, 2005, sec. 3.
2. Figures are provided by eBay and are the latest available as of this writing. See eBay, "Metrics," http://investor.ebay.com/downloads/Metrics.pdf (accessed August 17, 2005).

3. "Anniversary Lessons from eBay," *Economist* 375, no. 8430 (June 11, 2005): 9.
4. Joseph Pine and James Gilmore, *The Experience Economy: Work Is Theatre and Every Business a Stage* (Cambridge, MA: Harvard Business School Press, 1999). On the importance of entertainment to this economy, see also Michael J. Wolf, *The Entertainment Economy* (New York: Times Books, 1999).
5. Roland Barthes argues that in desiring an object through its representation, we are also aware of its absence. However, the experience economy foregrounds the production of pleasure in the very production of desire for the object, a move that, at least for some, temporarily occludes experiencing this absence and thus inverts Barthes's proposition that although consumer culture is all about desiring, desire itself is the absence of pleasure. See Roland Barthes, *The Pleasure of the Text*, trans. Richard Miller (1975; New York: Noonday Press, 1980).
6. Museum für Moderne Kunst, http://www.mmk-frankfurt.de/# (accessed November 27, 2005).
7. A multidisciplinary academic conference on eBay, organized by two of *Everyday eBay*'s contributors, Rebecca M. Ellis and Anna Haywood, occurred at the University of Essex, Colchester, United Kingdom, in August 2005. *Cultures of eBay: Making Sense of Social and Economic Aspects of the eBay "Phenomenon"* brought together academics, business industry specialists, and eBay practitioners to explore the cultural, social, and economic aspects of eBay. *Cultures of eBay* was the United Kingdom's first academic conference on eBay and e-commerce. See Chimera, http://www.essex.ac.uk/chimera/culturesofebay.html (accessed November 28, 2005).

1

My Obsession

I Thought I Was Immune to the Net. Then I Got Bitten by eBay.

WILLIAM GIBSON

When I was a young man, traversing the '70s in whatever post-hippie, pre-slacker mode I could manage, I made a substantial part of my living, such as it was, in a myriad of minuscule supply-and-demand gaps that have now largely closed. I was what antique dealers call a "picker," a semi-savvy haunter of Salvation Army thrift shops, from which I would extract objects of obscure desire that I knew were up-marketable to specialist dealers, who sold in turn to collectors. To this day I am often unable to resist a professionally quick, carefully dis-passionate scan over the contents of any thrift shop, though I almost never buy anything there. Mainly because the cut-rate treasures, the "scores" of legend, are long gone. The market has been rationalized. We have become a nation, a world, of pickers. There are several reasons for this. One has to do with boomer demographics and the cult of nostalgia. There are now more fifty-somethings than there are primo childhood artifacts of a similar vintage. Most of our toys, unlike the wood and pot-metal of yore, were extrusion-molded ephemera, fragile styrene simulacra, highly unlikely to survive the random insults of time. A great deal of the boomers' remembered world has been melted down, or crushed into unreadable fragments in forgotten strata of landfill. What remains, particularly if it's "mint in box," becomes increasingly rarefied.

Another reason, and this one is more mysterious, has to do with an ongoing democratization of connoisseurship, in which curatorial privilege is available at every level of society. Whether one collects Warhol prints or Beanie Babies becomes, well, a matter of taste.

The idea of the Collectible is everywhere today, and sometimes strikes me as some desperate instinctive reconfiguring of the postindustrial flow, some basic mammalian response to the bewildering flood of sheer *stuff* we produce.

But the main driving force in the tidying of the world's attic, the drying up of random, "innocent" sources of rarities, is information technology. We are mapping literally *everything*, from the human genome to Jaeger two-register chronographs, and our search engines grind increasingly fine.

"Surely *you* haven't been bitten by the eBay bug," said my publishing friend Patrick. We were in the lobby of a particularly bland hotel somewhere within the confines of a New England technology park, and I was in fact feeling twinges of withdrawal. eBay, which bills itself as Your Personal Trading Community™, is a site that hosts well over 800,000 online auctions per day, in 1,086 categories. eBay gets around 140 million hits per week, and, for the previous few months, a certain number of those hits had been from me.

And, in the process of adding to eBay's gargantuan hit-pile, several days before, I had gotten myself in trouble. In Uruguay. How this happened: I'm home in Vancouver, midway through that first cup of morning coffee, in front of the computer, ready to work straight from the dream-state.

I am deep into eBay, half-awake, staring at a scan of this huge-ass Zenith diver's watch. And I am, mind you, a practicing ectomorph. I have wrists like pipestems. I am not going to get too much wear out of a watch that's actually wider than my wrist.

But a little knowledge is a dangerous thing, and I know, having already become a habitué of eBay's Clocks, Timepieces, and Wrist Watches, that the movement in this particular Zenith is the very one Rolex installs in the big-ticket Daytona. Making this both a precision timepiece and possibly an undervalued one—the identical thing having sold on eBay, the week before, albeit in better cosmetic condition, for around two grand.

"I didn't even know you had Web access," Patrick said. "You mean you've overcome your infamous resistance to using the Net, but only in order to service an eBay addiction?"

Well, yes. Sort of. Not exactly.

eBay is simply the only thing I've found on the Web that keeps me coming back. It is, for me anyway, the first "real" virtual place.

In Patrick's hotel room, we used his laptop to get onto eBay, where I discovered that, yes, I was *still* high bidder for the damned Zenith: $500 American. This bid, you see, was the result of Fiddling Around. I'd sat there in my office, not quite awake yet, and had poked around with modest but increasingly higher bids, assuming that the seller's hidden "reserve," the lowest bid he'd accept, would be quite high. But no, at $500 I hit it, and suddenly I was listed there as high bidder. This had happened before, and I had always been outbid later. So I didn't worry.

But I didn't really want to have to buy this very large watch. Which was in Uruguay. And now I was still high bidder, and the auction would be run off before I got back to Vancouver. I thought about having to resell the Zenith.

When I did get back, though, I discovered, to mixed emotions, that I'd been "sniped." Someone, or rather their automated bidding software, had swooped in, in the last few seconds, and scooped the Zenith for only the least allowable increment over my bid.

How did I get into this, anyway?

I went happily along for years, smugly avoiding anything that involved a modem. Email address? Sorry. Don't have one.

And then I got a Web site. Had one foisted upon me, actually, and quite brilliantly, by Christopher Halcrow, who created William Gibson's Yardshow, an "official" home page. So I kept having to go into my kids' bedrooms and beg for Web access to look at it, which bugged them.

Then Chris, who knows a bargain when he sees one, happened to buy this Performa 5200CD from someone who was leaving town. He passed the Performa on to me for what he'd paid for it, and suddenly I had this video-ready machine I could look at my site on, and the video-ready part brought cable into the office, so I got a cable modem, because it was faster, and I already had a hole drilled in the wall, and then I discovered that, damn, I had an email address. It was part of the deal. So email, over the course of about 15 minutes, replaced the faxes I'd been using to keep in touch with certain people.

In the way of things, very shortly, I no longer had a Web site, Chris having found it necessary to get a life. But there was the rest of the Web, waiting to be explored. And I did, and promptly got bored. It was fun, at first, but then gradually I found that there wasn't really anywhere in particular I wanted to go. I went a lot of places, but I seldom went back.

Then I found eBay. And I wanted to go back. Because eBay is, basically, just a whole bunch of *stuff*. Stuff you can look at and wonder if you want—or let yourself want and then bid on.

Mechanical watches are so brilliantly unnecessary.

Any Swatch or Casio keeps better time, and high-end contemporary Swiss watches are priced like small cars. But mechanical watches partake of what my friend John Clute calls the Tamagotchi Gesture. They're pointless in a peculiarly needful way; they're comforting precisely because they require tending. And vintage mechanical watches are among the very finest fossils of the predigital age. Each one is a miniature world unto itself, a tiny functioning *mechanism*, a congeries of minute and mysterious *moving parts*. Moving parts! And consequently these watches are, in a sense, alive. They have heartbeats. They seem to respond, Tamagotchi-like, to "love," in the form, usually, of the expensive ministrations of specialist technicians. Like ancient steam-tractors or Vincent motorcycles, they can be painstakingly restored from virtually any stage of ruin.

And, as with the rest of the contents of the world's attic, most of the really good ones are already in someone's collection. But the best of what's still available, below the spookily expensive level of a Sotheby's watch auction, can still be had for a few thousand dollars at most. At the time of this writing, the most desirable vintage Rolex on one New York dealer's website, a stainless steel "bubble back" automatic, is priced at $3,800, a fraction of the cost of many contemporary watches by the same maker. (And it's so much cooler, possesses so much more *virtu*, than one of those gold-and-diamond Pimpomatic numbers!)

My father bought a stainless steel Rolex Oyster with a stainless band at a duty-free in Bermuda in the early '50s.

After his death, not very long after, my mother put it away in a bank vault, from whence I wheedled it when I was 18 or so. I had a Rolex dealer in Tucson replace its white dial with a black one, so that it would be more like the one James Bond wore in Fleming's novels. I loved it, and, one very sad night a few years later, I sold it for very little to a classmate of mine, in order to pay for a hotel room in which to enjoy, if that's the word, a final bitter tryst with my high school sweetheart. It was one of those dumb-ass, basically self-destructive gestures, and I actually don't regret it. I needed that hotel room. But I've always missed that watch, that Rolex Oyster Precision, and have always had it in the back of my mind to replace it one day with another of similar vintage. I had never done anything about it, though, and made do quite happily with quartz. My last quartz watch was a French faux-military job I bought at the airport in Cannes, on my way home from the film festival. Cost about a hundred dollars. Perfectly adequate for everything—everything except the Tamagotchi Gesture.

Last year, for some reason, I was struck by an ad, one that ran repeatedly in the British men's fashion magazines, for the Oris "Big Crown Commander." It was just a very good-looking watch, I thought, and it was Swiss, and mechanical, and not terribly expensive as such things go. Driven in part by my then brand-new Web access, I used a search engine to determine that Oris had no Canadian distributor. This made the watch seem even cooler, so I went on, via the Web, to locate a Seattle retailer who carried what a sarcastic friend had taken to calling the Big Dick Commando. (The crown, the bit you twist to set it, see, is rather more than usually prominent, so that you can do it without removing your whacking great RAF pilot's gloves.)

And I was and am quite happy with it.

Except that, though I didn't know it at the time, my search for the Big Crown Commander had inadvertently exposed me to the eBay bug.

I got a little compulsive, eventually.

I found myself coming down to my basement office every morning and going straight to that one particular bookmark. New auctions are posted daily on eBay, so there was always something new to look at.

The first watch I bought was a Croton "Aquamedico," a rare—or obscure, depending on how you look at it—Swiss manual-wind from the late '40s or early '50s, black dial with a white medical chapter ring. (Getting the terminology down was a big part of the kick, for me; a medical chapter ring is an outer, 60-second set of graduations that facilitate taking a patient's pulse.) It had been listed by a seller who didn't seem to be particularly into watches; the language of the listing was casual, nonspecialist, and not much mention was made of the watch's condition. Email to the seller elicited the opinion that the watch looked as though "it hadn't been worn very often," which I liked. The scan was intriguingly low-res, but I really liked the design of the numerals. And I really liked its name, "Aquamedico," which for some reason evoked for me the back pages, circa 1956, of *Field & Stream* and *True*.

Tentatively (but compulsively), I placed a low bid and waited to see if the Aquamedico attracted much attention from the eBay watch buffs. It didn't.

In the meantime, I determined that Croton was a long-established Swiss maker whose watches had been a lot more prominent in the United States in the '40s and '50s. Full-page ads in wartime *Fortune*.

I decided to go for it. To try and buy this thing. To import a unique object, physically, out of cyberspace. Well, out of Pennsylvania, actually, but I did experience this peculiar yearning to turn the not-so-clear scan on my screen into a physical object on my desk. And for all I knew, it might be the only Croton Aquamedico left, anywhere. (And in fact I've only ever seen one other Aquamedico since on eBay, and it was gold-filled with a white dial, neither of which I liked as much.) On the night of the auction, after having carefully considered bidding strategy (and this with no prior experience of bidding in any kind of auction), I placed a bid for considerably less than the $200 limit I'd set for myself.

That put me in high-bidder position. And then I sat there. What if, it occurred to me, someone noticed my Croton in the auction's last few minutes and decided to grab it? eBay's system of proxy bidding encourages buyers to offer the most they're willing to pay for an item—their "maximum" bid. My maximum bid was $140. But on eBay you don't necessarily end up having to pay your maximum bid. In an auction house, if you raised your hand to bid $200 on a watch, you'd be on the hook for that amount. But on eBay, each auction has a set "bid increment"—with some as little as 5 cents. With a $2 set bid increment, a rival could bid $200 on my watch, beat me out, and end up having to pay only $142, or $2 over my maximum.

I started to get nervous. (And this, mind you, was before I even knew about sniping software and autobid bots.) What if someone else got this watch, this watch I'd never seen but which I now, somehow, was emotionally invested in winning? I began to have some sense of the power of the psychology of auctions, something I hadn't really experienced before. I'm not a gambler. I've never put money on a horse, bought a lottery ticket, or bet on a hand of cards. Just doesn't do it for me. I've engaged in compulsive risk-taking behavior, certainly, but not the kind involving games of chance. But here, I recognized, I was starting to experience a buzz that I suspected was very much like a gambling buzz.

And what if, I asked myself, the Croton was really not all that desirable an object, a lemon, something a serious watch-nerd would find laughable?

What if the seller simply cashed my money order and did a runner? But I'd already checked his profile in the Feedback Forum, and there were lots of people on record there as saying he was honest, prompt, goods as described, and pleasant to deal with. (All of which turned out to be true.)

Meanwhile, with less than an hour to go before the auction closed, I was robotically punching the Netscape Reload button like a bandit-cranking Vegas granny, in case somebody outbid me. I knew how long it would take me to counterbid (not long), but I didn't know how quickly I could expect the server to process my bid.

Into the final countdown, nobody else showing up, when one more click on the Reload button produced … a new high bidder! Galvanized, I scrambled frantically through the bid process, and hit Bid. Real heart-in-mouth stuff, this. And, I must say, really fun.

Reload. And I was back, reinstated.

The auction closed.

The Aquamedico was mine.

I examined the address of the buyer who'd tried to outbid me at the last minute. An "hk" suggested that he was out of Hong Kong, which I already knew to be a hotbed of serious vintage-watch action. (The day before, I had found a wonderfully bizarre site in Taiwan, a sort of micro wrecker's yard, exclusively devoted to selling parts of Rolex watches: cases, dials, hands, et cetera.) I loved it that this Hong Kong bidder had popped in at the last minute, hoping to scoop what he, with his no doubt very considerable watch-savvy, knew to be an extremely desirable piece. But I had been there, ready, and I had prevailed.

I emailed the seller, sending my physical address and asking for his.

In the morning, I went out to buy a postal money order, the standard medium of exchange on eBay.

When the Aquamedico arrived, however, I was dismayed to find that it was peculiarly small, probably a "boy's" watch. I went back to its page on eBay and noted that, yes, it was indeed described as being a 30-mm watch. But the scan was larger than the watch itself, and I had assumed that 30 mm was standard (36 mm is actually closer to the contemporary men's standard). And while the steel case was very nearly mint, even better than the description, the crystal was in such rough shape that it was impossible to get a clear idea of the condition of the dial and hands. It had arrived from cyberspace, but it didn't really look like the scan. It looked as though it had been sitting in a sock drawer, somewhere in Pennsylvania, for 40-some years. Which it probably had.

But the seller's performance had been excellent, so I added my own note of positive feedback to his profile, and he gave me one in turn.

I took the Aquamedico to Otto Friedl, élite specialist in the care of vintage Swiss Tamagotchis, down in the lower lobby of the Hotel Vancouver, and asked to have it cleaned, lubricated, and the crystal replaced. When I went back for it, I discovered that it was a beautiful object indeed, the black dial immaculate, *virtu* intact.

But it wasn't *the* watch.

I told myself that there wasn't any *the* watch, and that I had simply found my own way, after avoiding it for years, of compulsively wasting time on the Net.

But I kept doing it. Opening that same bookmark and clicking down through pages and pages of watches. Learning to read a restricted code. And there was everything there, really: Swatches (which are collected like Barbies), the same battered Gruens you would see gathering dust in a Kansas City pawnshop, every sort and vintage of Rolex, wartime Omegas with the British broad arrow stamped into the caseback, German Sinn chronographs that you aren't really supposed to be able to buy here, Spiro Agnew campaign watches… .

And bidding. I'd bid a few times per week and was usually content to let myself be outbid. But I did buy another watch, from London, an oddly named Tweka with a two-tone copper dial. It went for around $150 and had been listed as "NOS," which means new old stock, something that supposedly has sat in the back of a jeweler's drawer since 1952. Very nice, after a trip to Otto, but still not *the* watch… .

eBay is a cross between a swap meet in cyberspace and a country auction with computer-driven proxy bidding. The auctioneer is one of eBay's servers.

Buyers don't pay anything to eBay; they just pay sellers for the items they buy. Sellers, however, pay a fee on each item they list, and another fee if it sells. You can set this up so that your eBay seller's account comes off your credit card. I doubt if anyone's seller account amounts to much in a given month, but eBay moves a lot of items.

There's a sense of taking part in an evolving system, here. I suspect that eBay is evolving in much the way the Net did. I started visiting eBay just as user IDs were coming in. You can opt to do business on eBay under a handle. I think that this was introduced in order to foil spam-miners, who were sending bots into eBay to scoop up email addresses. And I actually did get spam, my very first, after my initial foray into eBay. But then I got a user ID and the spam stopped.

Looking over the Announcement Board recently, I saw that eBay now requires credit card information before allowing users into such categories as firearms and X-rated adult material: an age-checking strategy.

One thing I can imagine changing on eBay is the current requirement that sellers who want to display scans of their items find an off-site page on which to host their HTML. eBay links to tutorials on how to do this, but it's just enough of a learning curve to discourage some people. Myself included. If it were possible to send a scan directly to eBay, I think selling would take a major step toward becoming a ubiquitous activity.

I find clutter, in my personal environment, oppressive. But crazed environments of dead tech and poignant rubbish turn up in my fiction on a regular basis, where they are usually presented as being at once comforting, evocative, and somehow magical. The future as flea market. I really do tend to see the future that way, though not exclusively. My first impulse, when presented with any spanking-new piece of computer hardware, is to imagine how it will look in 10 years' time, gathering dust under a card table in a thrift shop. And it probably will.

The pleasure afforded by browsing eBay is the pleasure afforded by any flea market or garage sale. Something ruminative, but with an underlying acuity, as though some old hunter-gatherer module were activated. It's a lot like beachcombing.

Where eBay departs from the traditional pleasure of a flea market, though, is in its sheer scale and its searchability. If you can think of a thing, you can search it on eBay. And, very probably, you can find it.

If randomness is what you're after, though, there are ways to surf eBay, rather than search it. Modes of sheer drift. Every item offers you a chance to peruse Seller's Other Auctions, which can take you off into categories of merchandise you wouldn't have thought of. A search for Hopi silver, for instance, brought up other kinds of Native American artifacts, much older ones, so that a series of clicks through stone adzes and Clovis points led to an obscure monograph on mound-excavation in Florida in the 1930s.

But it was the watches that kept me coming back.

And I started to get sniped.

I'd find a watch I wanted, work my way up to high-bidder position, check my position regularly (eBay regularly informs you of your bidding status, and outbid notices arrive promptly, but it's still fun to check), and find, as the auction ran off, that I'd been zapped, in the last five minutes of bidding, by someone offering just one increment more than I had bid. I began to smell a rat.

The nature of the rat became apparent when I started checking out "Dutch" (multiple buyer) auctions of eBay-specific software, and discovered that one could buy plug-ins that automated the bidding process.

This bothered me. I thought about it. It bothered me more. The idea of this software ran entirely counter to the peculiar psychology of bidding at auction. The software-driven sniper isn't really bidding; he's shopping. Skimming an existing situation. The sniper (or his software package) is able to look at the final minutes of any auction as a done deal, then decide whether or not to purchase that item at the fixed price, plus one bid increment. Which pissed me off, and took some of the fun away.

A friend's hacker boyfriend, in Chicago, offered to write me a piece of software that would out-snipe anything on the market. Tempting, but not very. Instead, I sent eBay a message to the effect that allowing auto-bid software detracted from the eBay experience. That it spoiled the chemistry of the thing, which in my view was a large part of what they offered as a venue. I also suspected, though I couldn't think of a convincing way to put it, that sufficient proliferation of sniping software could eventually, theoretically, bring the whole community to a halt.

I got no reply, and I hadn't expected to, but the problem seems in the meantime to have been resolved. Entirely to my satisfaction, and in a way that illustrates exactly how things have a way of finding their own uses for the street.

Text of a message sent to all vendors of third-party bidding software at eBay, 8/13/98:

> eBay bid system change: Yesterday, through the help of an eBay user, we detected and disarmed a "bid bot" which had placed bids on hundreds of items. A bid bot is a program which bids on many items or the same item over and over again. Our SafeHarbour team is tracking down the source of the bot, and will be working with our lawyers and the authorities to take appropriate action. In an effort to prevent this type of system attack in the future, eBay plans to make an internal change to the bidding process. Most of you will not notice this change. It will NOT affect the interface you use at all. All bidding processes will remain the same as they were before. Unfortunately, the change may disable most, if not all "automated bidding programs" (aka sniping programs). We apologize for this, but it's important that we make eBay safe from robots of this kind.

I'd love to know what that bot was bidding on. Beanie Babies, probably. (A follow-up message partially reversed course: eBay would not outlaw bid bots but would require that they conform to sign-on procedures.)

With a level playing field restored, I decided to kick this eBay watch-buying habit in the head.

Addictive personality that I am, I decided that the best way to do that was to binge: to do a whole bunch of it at one time and get it out of my system. To that end, I decided to buy a couple of fairly serious watches. Keepers.

I bid on, and won, a late-'40s Jaeger two-register chronograph in Hong Kong. The idea of sending a check off to Causeway Bay for more than a thousand dollars to someone I'd never heard of, let alone met, seemed to be stretching it a little. But Eric So, a B Tech (Mech) at the Hong Kong Water Supplies Department and an avid watch fancier, was so evidently honest, so helpful, and responded to email so readily, that I soon had no reservations whatever. Once the check had cleared, the Jaeger arrived with blinding speed and was even nicer than described.

And I did have one authentic auction-frisson over the Jaeger when, very near the end of the auction, someone bidding "by hand" topped me. This gentleman, when I checked his profile, appeared to be a European collector of some seriousness. After I bid again, I waited nervously, but he never came back. My other binge watch was a Vulcain Cricket, an alarm-watch introduced in the late '40s, which sounds like a very large, very mechanical *cricket*. I wanted one of these because the older ones look terrific, and because "Vulcain Cricket" is one of the finest pieces of found poetry I've ever stumbled across.

I found the best one I'd ever seen, offered by Vince and Laura of Good Timing, who, by virtue of tagging all their items "(GOOD TIMING)," have built themselves the equivalent of a stall in cyberspace. Most sellers' goods on eBay are spread, as it were, on the same huge blanket, but Vince and Laura's tag allows them an edge in rep-building.

I think it worked, the binge cure. Possibly because getting serious about choosing serious watches made the shuffling of pages a chore rather than a pleasure. Whereas before I'd been able to veg out, in the style of watching some version of the Shopping Channel that actually interested me, I now felt as though I were buying real estate. Investing. Collecting.

I'd always hoped that I wouldn't turn into the sort of person who collected anything.

I no longer open to watches on eBay first thing in the morning. Days go by without my contributing so much as a single hit.

Or maybe I just have enough wristwatches.

I wonder, though, at the extent to which eBay facilitated my passage through this particular consumer obsession. Into it and out the other side in a little under a year. How long would it have taken me to get up to speed on vintage watches without eBay? Would I have started attending watch shows? Would I have had to travel? Would it have taken years? Would I have gotten into it at all?

Probably not.

In Istanbul, one chill misty morning in 1970, I stood in Kapali Carsi, the grand bazaar, under a Sony sign bristling with alien futurity, and stared deep into a cube of plate glass filled with tiny, ancient, fascinating things.

Hanging in that ancient venue, a place whose on-site café, I was told, had been open 24 hours a day, 365 days a year, literally for centuries, the Sony sign—very large, very proto-*Blade Runner*, illuminated in some way I hadn't seen before—made a deep impression. I'd been living on a Greek island, an archaeological protectorate where cars were prohibited, vacationing in the past.

The glass cube was one man's shop. He was a dealer in curios, and from within it he would reluctantly fetch, like the human equivalent of those robotic cranes in amusement arcades, objects I indicated that I wished to examine. He used a long pair of spring-loaded faux-ivory chopsticks, antiques themselves, their warped tips lent traction by wrappings of rubber bands.

And with these he plucked up, and I purchased, a single stone bead of great beauty, the color of apricot, with bright mineral blood at its core, to make a necklace for the girl I'd later marry, and an excessively mechanical Swiss cigarette lighter, circa 1911 or so, broken, its hallmarked silver case crudely soldered with strange, Eastern, aftermarket sigils.

And in that moment, I think, were all the elements of a real futurity: all the elements of the world toward which we were heading—an emerging technology, a map that was about to evert, to swallow the territory it represented. The technology that sign foreshadowed would become the venue, the city itself. And the bazaar within it.

But I'm glad we still have a place for things to change hands.

Even here, in this territory the map became.

2

Ephemeral Culture/eBay Culture
Film Collectibles and Fan Investments

MARY DESJARDINS

Many articles about eBay dispel readers' presumed impressions that eBay is a virtual swap meet, successful because it is a site for auctions of collectible items. Inevitably, they point out that although eBay may have started as such a forum, it quickly became a site for a subeconomy of small businesses—liquidators, wholesalers, small retail shops, and stay-at-home entrepreneurs who use eBay to conduct a major portion of their trade. While businesses selling toys, jewelry, computers, sporting goods, cars, real estate, appliances, and so on may constitute only 10 percent of eBay sellers, they are responsible for 80 percent of its sales and thus form the core of eBay's profitability.

Yet such articles frequently include quotes from or discussions with eBay CEO Meg Whitman, who tends to emphasize that the sellers and buyers of collectibles are the heart of eBay: "Collectibles may not be the largest portion of gross merchandise sales," says Whitman, but they "will still be the essence of the community."[1] Whitman sees the buyers and sellers of collectibles as eBay's "essence" because they come together over a shared interest. However, even the business seller who seeks to unload an overstock of stereo equipment comes together with a buyer over a shared interest in exchanging a bargain turntable, and it is significant that Whitman does not choose this kind of exchange for her example. Her rhetoric makes for a powerful and efficient advertising and public relations construction that appears not only in articles quoting her or other company officers, but also in the firm's public relations page, www.thepowerofallofus.com, and its employment information page, http://ebaycareers.com.[2]

As a group, buyers of collectibles (who may also be sellers of collectibles) express their desires for material objects serially (they keep adding to their collections) and personally (they keep adding particular kinds of items because their collections relate to self-identity). As historians of collecting have argued, there is a widespread assumption that collectors' motivations originate and express themselves in affective contexts.[3] Not surprisingly, then, Whitman and others at eBay conceive of collectors as constituting a community, the members of which buy and sell not just for utilitarian purposes but also because *something more than the sale matters to them.* eBay mobilizes this conception to define the site as a whole and thereby brands eBay as a site for financial transactions that are also affectively bound community interactions.[4] This "humanizes" eBay's broader marketplace, a move encapsulated in Whitman's claim that eBay provides a "small-town feel on a global scale."

Lisa Long has argued that only traditional auctions have the capacity for such humanization. At embodied auctions, she suggests, only the actual presence of bidders and objects in the same place can give bidders a more realistic sense of the objects for auction. In addition, the auction's unfolding, during which the entirety (or large part) of a household's material effects is up for sale, provides a history of the objects in the life of that household and the specific community of which it forms a part. For Long, cyberauctions make objects a secondary consideration and focus instead on the production of narratives and images that function on the level of the "imaginary," offering, following Baudrillard, a "procession of simulacra."[5] Nevertheless, eBay attempts to humanize its virtual marketplace via its advertising and publicity, and in its design of user protocols. Its publicity and advertising strategies do this in part through an appeal to the imaginary, where sellers are conceptualized as enabling buyers to have reconciliation with the past via their shared interest in certain kinds of objects. The question remains, however, how sellers and buyers of collectibles negotiate eBay's expectations, and this chapter therefore focuses on the buying and selling protocols, behaviors, and practices of a specific collecting community—those interested in Hollywood-related ephemera from the pre-1960 studio system—because such objects accrue greater market value and affective resonance over time as ephemeral traces of past experiences of earlier commodified American popular culture.

In the world of antiques and collecting, "ephemera" is a category of material objects that are, paradoxically, throwaways not thrown away. Usually paper, collectible ephemera includes items produced to accompany or promote passing events such as the printed programs of plays and concerts, ticket stubs, movie posters, and lobby placards; items meant to be consumed serially, such as a newspaper or magazine, in which each issue supposedly replaces or supersedes the previous; and the packaging of products. Theories of the ephemeral, including those originating from the insights of ancient theologies and those from continental philosophies responding to changes wrought by modernity in the early twentieth century, refer to the fleeting aspects of material reality as detritus that also represents the exchange, passing, and vanity of civilizations. How fitting, then, that ephemera connected to studio-era Hollywood film production is a major collectible category on eBay. This period of Hollywood history is a popular signifier of the ephemeral nature of the mythic rise to and fall from fame in American culture. Many of these tie-ins are available on eBay for recirculation as images and, for successful bidders, as objects of exchange. eBay's structure not only makes the category of ephemeral film-related objects available as imaged (and as purchasable or winnable) collectibles but also is itself based on ephemeral moments of viewing, ephemeral interactions based on exchanges between sellers and buyers, and the often frenzied time-based activity of bidding during the final seconds of a listed item's availability. I focus on the relationships among theoretical concepts of material culture, film-fan practices around film- and star-related commodity tie-ins, the way eBay conceptualizes collectors as similar to fans, and how the selling and buying protocols and behaviors on the site encourage performances of fan practices that illustrate how eBay constructs the notion on an affectively bound community as a way to humanize the marketplace. This study contributes to understandings of how various fandoms manifest themselves in relation to cultural identity and technologies (in this case, Web-based technologies) at certain times (in this case, between 1999 and 2002, the period from which the examples discussed below are drawn).[6]

EBAY: EPHEMERAL COMMUNITY

While eBay offers a site for those interested in Hollywood-related ephemera to come together, its ephemeral temporal structure and its competitive set of interactions and transactions work against some of the constituent elements of fan communities. Fans typically come together over shared interests in objects, texts, and figures—both real and fictional—that matter to them, and doing so is a major pleasure and function of fandom, if not always a conscious motivation. Coming together may also produce repeatable, enduring community relations, such as fans getting together for annual conventions or a fan club that meets locally in a home, in a public space, or as an online chat group. On eBay, however, the community that comes together is usually ephemeral, often based on individuals temporarily competing with one another as bidders, and in positions of judgment as sellers and buyers expected to leave feedback about one another regarding promptness, courtesy, and credibility. In addition, eBay overdetermines the ephemeral aspects of ephemera. Rendered as images and seemingly no longer produced material objects subject to the decay of age, items are made available to fans as visual spectacle and potential purchase, but only in a strictly determined time-based fashion. Sellers choose how long items will be displayed—three, five, seven, or ten days—and the collector-viewer-fan-buyer often purchases them through frenzied bidding in the last moments of their availability. Such competitive and fleeting interactions are not foreign to collectors, and so the fans who come to eBay probably come expecting not communal experiences but collecting opportunities. Nevertheless, sellers of film-related ephemera often adopt the rhetoric of affective-bound community interactions and construct pitches for their commodities on the assumption that the seller and buyer are members of a community coming together to share fan investment in the ephemeral object.[7]

LIFE IN THE HUMANIZED MARKET: FAN PRACTICES ON EBAY

Scholars of material culture have inquired into the central role that material objects play in the formation and maintenance of selfhood in modern life, and many of their observations illuminate the trading practices of film-fan buyers and sellers on eBay. Psychologist Mihaly Csikszentmihalyi argues that the self, a "fragile construction of the mind," is constantly threatened by psychic entropy. Human consciousness, in his view, is characterized by a tendency to fade into unfocused, chaotic activity. However, "artifacts invest the human self with a degree of objectivity" and sustain fleeting aspects of this self by displaying power and social status; securing the continuity of the self over time in terms of focal points in the present, traces of the past, and indications of future expectations; and providing material evidence of one's self in the web of social relations.[8] Jean Baudrillard argues that the passion we invest in the personal possession of objects, best expressed in our collecting of them, keeps the "lives of the individual subject or of the collectivity on an even footing, and [has a role] in supporting our very project of survival."[9] Other scholars examine fandom by looking at the ways that fans deploy material culture production and consumption practices often involving commodity objects to construct, maintain, and communicate self-identity to others.[10]

My analysis of a variety of listings for studio-era Hollywood ephemera on eBay shows how buyers and sellers communicate self-identity by announcing their fandom and fan authority while engaging in possession and/or divestment rituals organized around film-related material culture. A potential buyer of a 1950 Nabisco photo card of Barbara Stanwyck (eBay item #1126216162), for example, announces his or her identity as a fan in selecting the eBay user ID luvsbarbara. In acquiring fan magazines from the 1930s and 1940s over a period of several months, I continually bid against and was often outbid by eBay user ID blanchehudson (Blanche Hudson is the character played by Joan Crawford in Robert Aldrich's 1963 cult classic *Whatever Happened to Baby Jane?*). At the time, my acquisitions primarily supported my research into Hollywood studios' promotions of stars. Although I also consider myself a fan of many of the stars featured in these magazines, I was not primarily bidding *as a fan*, with an interest focused on just one star or on the excellent condition of cover artwork. However, a Joan Crawford fan had a vested interest that the focus of his or her affection be showcased in a mint condition object, and was willing to bid more than I was on magazines featuring the star on their covers. My criterion for bidding on a magazine—that it was a good example of a certain kind of star promotion I might write about in my critical work—was "trumped" by a fan whose interest and criteria for the object were likely more specific and more important to his or her conception of the object's place within a larger collection of specific star-related ephemera. eBay IDs such as luvsbarbara announce fan identification and are also forms of "possession rituals" over the objects on display. Grant McCracken suggests there are rituals around material objects that represent constructions of the self in relation to social networks. Possession rituals make the object part of the self and function as a way to communicate to others.[11] Fans who chose eBay IDs such as luvsbarbara, blanchehudson, or ilovestuffretro suggest they are already engaging in possession rituals to claim the objects on sale even though they have not yet won them. This claim could also be made about bidders who immediately bid on an object just after it is listed; if they are habitual eBay customers, they know that bids are usually won and lost in the final moments of an object's availability.[12] As my interaction with blanchehudson suggests, possession rituals are also about control, both over objects and others who compete for their possession.

Some sellers appeal to buyers on the basis of anticipating such buyer possession rituals: the seller of a Bergel Perfume Punch Card with images of 1940s movie stars (eBay item #1125362895) begs buyers to "bookmark" his or her site, in a sense asking bidders to possess him or her as well as the object. The seller repeats the order "bookmark me" three times, adding the plea, "[M]ake me your fafourite [*sic*]," revealing an almost desperate eroticization of the hoped-for financial exchange. This suggests that the exchange of objects can also involve the seller in self-constructions formed in relation to social networks. In this case, the seller constructs his or her persona through a conflation of that self with his or her eBay listings. John Fiske argues that fans use commercial texts and objects to amass popular cultural capital that gives them pleasure and the esteem of their peers in a community of taste.[13] This is reflected in eBay sellers' desire for the network of film-fan viewers and potential buyers to make this page ("me") their "favorite" and to "bookmark" it ("me") for quick "double-click" returns in the future.[14] The seller desires to be more accessible to buyers and to engage them in further viewing experiences or commodity transactions. In the process the seller also exposes how the "community" experience on eBay is, like some experiences among fans and collectors in embodied situations, part longing for communication with and attention from others, part commodity exchange that confers status on seller and buyer alike, and part eroticization of the display and exchange of objects that relate to self-identity. These practices, contrary to Long's argument that only traditional auctions have the capacity for humanization, suggest that affectively bound community interactions can and do take place on eBay.

Moreover, many sellers of ephemera engage in wistful, even nostalgic, performances of divestment. These performances, which suggest the seller's disengagement from personal meanings associated with or invested in the object, cannot be reduced to a single motivation or effect. A performance of divestment could be a seller's strategy to make potential buyers believe he or she has undervalued the object (and consequently, has set the opening bid too low), or it could signal to a buyer that the seller's distance from the object—which the buyer, in her or his status as fan, may not have—allows the seller to drive a hard bargain. Performances of divestment can also be ritualistic practices. Such rituals allow the owner to divest the object of personal meaning in preparation for giving it up and, as with possession rituals, allow the self to control the objects rather than be controlled by them.

Divestment rituals conducted through eBay listings often necessitate more narrative about an item's history than do possession rituals. For example, the Vintage 1942 Party Game on Movie Star Trivia (eBay item #572220896) is an object that the seller tries to sell for his eighty-eight-year-old mother, who used to be the "social director at partys [*sic*] way back when." The son indicates that his mother is trying to "clean house." The reader or potential buyer may imagine an elderly lady preparing to move to an assisted living facility, or to make life simpler as she moves closer to death; the narrative suggests a poignant letting go of an object that defined a life now drawing to a close. In another listing, a seller guarantees that a 1940s Warner Brothers scarf (with photos of four major male stars on it) is genuine because the seller knows the original buyer who has owned it since the 1940s (eBay item #1536770010). I won this item and discovered through correspondence with the seller that the owner is her mother. I also have won fan magazines listed for auction by people helping elderly neighbors. After even a cursory viewing and buying of film-related objects from the studio era on eBay, one learns that some film-related ephemera sales are part of a divestment process for elderly movie fans or for younger people with affective ties to such fans.

Such divestment performances are distinct from, though often conjoined to, appeals to potential buyers on the basis of an object's "mint condition," such as in the Bergel Perfume Punch Card; an object's scarcity, as in the "extremely rare" original press book for Karl Freund's 1932 *The Mummy* (eBay item #1533287749); or, in the case of the 1940s Warner Brothers movie star scarf, its status as "genuine," in "perfect condition," and an "unusual movie relic." Such descriptors signal the object's potential monetary value on the antique or collectors' market, and one might assume it would appeal, at least in part, as a financial investment to any collector of movie memorabilia. Russell Belk suggests that financial investment is commonly believed to be one of the main motivations of collecting. He argues, however, that this is rarely the only, or even the most important, motivation for most collectors. In his history of collecting, Belk places the medieval practice of collecting relics, which were believed to carry a manifestation of the power of the person with whom they were affiliated (splinters from Christ's cross or the bones of a saint, for example), as having a contemporary counterpart in the way collectibles are sometimes conceptualized as fetishes, and he suggests that this usually has nothing to do with their monetary value.[15] The fetishistic quality of the "movie relic" resides in its physical proximity to a star from the studio era of production. Examples of this dynamic occur in listings that suggest, for example, that jewelry might have been touched by Audrey Hepburn (eBay item #1126216162) or a book might have been signed by Peter Stackpool, a professional photographer who captured images of daily life at the Hollywood studios (eBay item #1535407122). The Warner Brothers scarf has the fetishistic quality of a relic because photos of stars comprise its design; photographs have often been theorized as possessing an indexical trace of the person (or object) photographed (see chapter 11).

Collecting does involve a financial investment; however, as with Belk and other theorists referenced here, Susan Stewart further emphasizes the importance of the psychic investment in collecting by arguing that collectors have a psychic investment in seriality.[16] Adding a rare object to a collection is a serial process moving toward completion of the collection. Yet, in a dynamic akin to the logic of fetishism, since completion would mean a kind of death, indefinite seriality is the modus operandi here. On eBay, this mode of object-self relations is signaled by the number after an eBay user ID, which in announcing how many objects the buyer has successfully bid for on eBay, designates a quantity to the serialized collecting in process. Further, the appearance of the bidder's name and number on the bidding page also attests to his or her continual collecting, to the fact that seriality's end is indefinitely postponed. Such an investment in seriality and the object's "mint condition" also exposes the degree to which collecting, as Stewart argues, removes an object from history—an object in mint or perfect condition erases the history of the object's use and place in the past.

Yet it is possible that the object's perfect condition might also allow a buyer to fantasize him or herself as the object's first "user," and its appeal to the buyer then would not inevitably mean that the object would lose all historical meaning—it might provide the buyer the opportunity to project herself into the past as if she were the first to encounter the object (see chapter 18 for a particularly striking account). Listings for objects are often accompanied by testaments to or speculations about the authenticity of the object in question, which suggests that the object's status as souvenir—its trace of an authentic past elsewhere—can trump any erasure of history afforded by its pristine condition.

The way an object's souvenir status or the way possession and divestment rituals around it are performed and displayed on eBay are especially interesting in regard to established assumptions about how commodified objects are positioned in capitalist culture to be superseded by other, newer, commodified objects.[17] According to McCracken, such rituals attest to the mobility of meaning via the object from culturally constituted world to individual consumer. An understanding of these rituals suggests that the insatiable consumption cycle that leads from pleasurable anticipation to disappointment, which is then restimulated by pleasurable anticipation of new objects, is not fully participated in by fan-consumers, or at least not without a great deal of enunciative activity that articulates the meaning of the objects for these individuals.[18] The performative and enunciative activities of taking possession or divesting of a fan-related object prolong the life span and perhaps even reject the continual abandonment of objects in commodity culture, thereby also attesting to the sustaining of a self-identity crafted, in part, through association with objects. Divestment rituals on eBay, which are attempts to divest the object of personal meaning so it can be given up or so the owner can control the terms and cost of its reinvestment, can be seen as attempts to prolong the life span of an object. Divestment narratives—"Memories of this belonged to my mother"; "I know who owned this and why she collected it"—are offered as the terms by which a new owner will be able to find a similar, meaningful possession. Such narratives also point to how affectively bound interactions among film fans on eBay call on memories associated with Hollywood-related ephemera and the collecting experience itself.

EBAY: MEMORY MACHINE

Virtual market sites such as eBay contribute to the construction of a popular memory of filmgoing and star-worshipping experiences from a period that many eBay sellers designate as a "bygone era." For those growing up during the studio era of Hollywood production (the late 1910s to 1960) or during the initial recycling of its films on television, in repertory exhibition sites, and in college film societies (1950s–1980s), these old "pictures" and their stars were a taken-for-granted part of everyday experience. Film theorists and historians are studying the role of past cinematic experiences in the "memory work" of certain generations. Annette Kuhn explores how the "everydayness" of Hollywood films for an elderly British population (old enough to have attended films in the 1930s) lingers in memories and narratives of self-identity. Kuhn's theory of popular memory is underpinned by a belief that "it is important to attend to the ways in which memory is produced in the activity of telling stories about the past, personal or shared; to the construction and narration of these memory stories; and in the present instance to the ways in which cinema figures in and shapes these memories."[19]

Despite the concerns of theorists who posit a loss of history in postmodernity, my research into movie-related ephemera on eBay, including seller performances of fandom together with their assumptions about buyers as fans, suggests that neither they nor eBay evacuate history from objects, their own pasts, or the pasts of the community of which they presume or hope the buyer is a part (see also chapters 5 and 16 for separate accounts of how sellers use eBay to claim histories). For instance, even seller narratives not necessarily narrativizing possession or divesting often attempt to appeal to the buyer on the basis of a presumed shared interest in prolonging the meanings attached to objects from the past and what they have signified about a habitual, taken-for-granted appreciation for moviegoing and stargazing as components of constructing and maintaining self-identity. eBay sellers of movie-related objects often start or end descriptions of these objects by suggesting that an object will allow the buyer a pleasurable return to a bygone era, the only remaining material traces of which may be ephemeral. This return will conjoin ephemeral, material objects and similarly ephemeral performative activities on the part of the collector who sees and enacts "a microscopic victory over the fate dwelling within the commodified object; a tiny anticipation of reconciliation."[20]

eBay's own advertising strategies seemingly clue into this theoretical insight about the affective nature of self-object relations. In a 2004 U.S. television commercial for eBay, a young boy loses his toy boat at the seashore. Years later, fishermen catch the boat in their net and list it on eBay. The boy, now in his thirties, sits mesmerized before the computer screen, gazing at the image of the boat he lost so long ago. A voice-over asks, "What if nothing was ever forgotten? What if nothing was ever lost?"

In her dismissal of the value of cyberauctions, Long speculates that one day perhaps we will buy only virtual collections, that maybe cyberauctions will make us believe we don't need to physically possess the object. I would not foreclose this possibility, including that it might offer its own pleasures, drawbacks, and contradictions. Yet the question asked by the narrative of the toy boat is a good one—good on one level for its appeal to the affective longings of most adults for retrieval of some of the lost pleasures of childhood as symbolized by the little tug, but also on another level. What if material objects and our memories of them are never lost? Is it possible that new technologies and the economic forces that frame their use now allow us to believe that, like ephemera—throwaways not thrown away—everything today is both disposable *and* needs to be preserved? While such a contradictory project (disposal and preservation) could be a response to a fear of loss of history in the postmodern world, it also forces the fan-consumer to ponder and perhaps resist the temporal cycles by which objects and identities are defined by economic powers, even as they create new cycles (the set bidding period for an object on eBay, for instance). The pressure from the contradictory project of disposal and preservation also exposes the degree to which the self is a historical project, and when we define selves in relation to objects produced from various temporal moments, we are at least implicitly admitting that no identity comes from a ground zero.

eBay, of course, is offered up as a testament that nothing is ever lost and that anticipation of reconciliation is possible and pleasurable. The pleasure comes from the possibility that both memories and objects are enduring, and that they mutually sustain one another. In addition, the company has fostered the idea of a community of users who not only never forget but also help others do the same. "The power of all of us" is a phrase used repeatedly in eBay public relations and promotion. In actuality, eBay users may never forget, but "the power of all of us" involves displays of power that have multiple motivations and effects. Exchanges among eBay users are characterized by self-conscious performances and ambivalent expressions—of competitiveness, exhibitionism, control, possession, nostalgia, and divestment—that suggest that in the communal remembering via the online marketplace, when one person is reconciled, another is always outbid.

NOTES

1. Miguel Helft, "What Makes eBay Unstoppable?" *Industry Standard*, August 6–13, 2001, 35. See also Jerry Adler, "The eBay Way of Life," *Newsweek*, June 17, 2002, 50–60; and Lisa Guernsey, "The Powers behind the Auctions," *New York Times*, August 20, 2000, sec. 3.
2. thepowerofallofus.com reiterates eBay users are "establishing personal connections with like-minded strangers, discovering the things they love… . They're joining a community where anything is possible if all put our mind to it, and believe. EBay. The Power of All of Us." Readers and viewers are treated to sentimental text and images testifying to the "goodness" of people. eBay's employment information site states that "what we've done at eBay is promote the growth of community where people can share similar interests about things they have or want."
3. See Russell W. Belk, *Collecting in a Consumer Society* (London: Routledge, 1995) for histories not only of collecting itself but also of popular and theoretical assumptions about collecting.
4. Helft, 37.
5. Lisa Long, "All Buy Ourselves at Household Auctions," in *Acts of Possession: Collecting in America*, ed. Leah Dilworth (New Brunswick, NJ: Rutgers University Press, 2002), 250. Sharon Zukin has a similar take on cyberauctions, although Zukin embeds her discussion of eBay in a history of shopping in its many forms (not just auctions). Both Long and Zukin are disturbed by cyberauctions' participation in the suggestion that everything is up for sale in contemporary culture, which is a valid criticism (especially from scholars who admit to the pleasures of buying). However, both assume cyberauctions have monolithic effects. Zukin believes that eBay makes all buyers into sellers, and neglects the affective relations that fans might have with objects that prevent some from becoming sellers. Neither acknowledges the possibility that the circulation and selling of "everything" might make available new access to knowledge about the past for both fan-consumers and scholar-consumers. See Sharon Zukin, *Point of Purchase: How Shopping Changed American Culture* (New York: Routledge, 2005), 244–51.
6. See Matt Hills, *Fan Cultures* (London: Routledge, 2002) for a discussion of the relation of various fandoms to cultural identity at certain moments.

7. To discern if the kinds of seller and buyer expressions I collected from listings of film-related ephemera were similar to or different from those expressed on listings of other kinds of objects, I looked at pages auctioning collectible retro china (Fiestaware, Hall, etc.) and noncollectible objects such as stereo equipment. With these latter listings I found the seller discourse to be, without exception, functional and purely descriptive, offering no commentary about the potential meanings of the objects for bidders.
8. Mihaly Csikszentmihalyi, quoted in David Morgan, *Visual Piety: A History and Theory of Popular Religious Images* (Berkeley: University of California Press, 1998), 5.
9. Jean Baudrillard, "The System of Collecting," in *The Cultures of Collecting*, ed. John Elsner and Roger Cardinal (London: Reaktion Books, 1997), 7. An event concurrent with the revision of this essay in June 2005 would seem to confirm Baudrillard's insight. Brennan Hawkins, an eleven-year-old boy, was lost in the Utah wilderness for four days. His mother told the press that one of the first things he asked about upon his rescue was whether the Pokemon cards he bought on eBay the week before had arrived. Mrs. Hawkins, convinced the boy's anticipation of the arrival of his cards sustained him, told the press, "that's what got him off the mountain." This was reported widely in a variety of press venues. The Yahoo! News site reporting the boy's rescue sold advertising space to eBay next to the article. Paul Foy, "Parents: Scout's Survival 'Like a Dream,'" http://news.yahoo.com/s/ap/20050622.
10. Henry Jenkins, for example, describes how fans use the raw materials of commercial culture to create a folklore community and enunciate fandom through dress, display, and the production of their own texts about favorite media artifacts. Jackie Stacey discusses how female fans use images and commodities tied to 1940s and 1950s female film stars to enunciate an identity tied to feminine cultural competence and thereby potentially transform themselves into the embodiment of an idealized femininity. See Henry Jenkins, *Textual Poachers: Television Fans and Participatory Culture* (New York: Routledge, 1992); and Jackie Stacey, *Star-Gazing: Hollywood and Female Spectatorship* (London: Routledge, 1994).
11. Grant McCracken, *Culture and Consumption: New Approaches to the Symbolic Character of Consumer Goods and Activities* (Bloomington: Indiana University Press, 1988), 85–86.
12. Some sellers engage in early bidding under a second eBay ID to inflate the price beyond the starting amount.
13. John Fiske, "The Cultural Economy of Fandom," in *The Adoring Audience: Fan Culture and Popular Media*, ed. Lisa A. Lewis (London: Routledge, 1992), 30–49.
14. Internet Explorer uses the term "Favorites," while Netscape and its successor Mozilla use "Bookmarks" to indicate a user's list of frequently viewed sites.
15. Belk, 56, 94–96.

16. Fans of media texts, such as television programs, also engage with their object of fandom in serialized ways. This has interesting implications for how they communicate with other fans on websites that allow fans to post queries and commentaries on the nature of the program's serialization, anticipated closure, and so forth. See Matt Hills for a discussion of this engagement and of how other theorists of fandom have examined it.
17. See Colin Campbell, *The Romantic Ethic and the Spirit of Modern Consumerism* (London: Blackwell, 1989); and Susan Buck-Morss, "Dream World of Mass Culture: Walter Benjamin's Theory of Modernity and the Dialectics of Seeing," in *Modernity and the Hegemony of Vision*, ed. David Michael Levin (Berkley: University of California Press, 1993) for theories on consumption cycles.
18. Pleasure in anticipation of consumption, and what some theorists such as Campbell suggest is the inevitable disappointment following consumption, can be understood in relation to psychoanalytic notions of desire that always emphasize the incommensurability of desire with its object.
19. Annette Kuhn, *Everyday Magic: Cinema and Cultural Memory* (London: I. B. Tauris, 2002), 9.
20. Max Pensky, *Melancholy Dialectics: Walter Benjamin and the Play of Mourning* (Amherst, MA: University of Amherst Press, 1993), 242.

3

Virtual_radiophile (163☆)

eBay and the Changing Collecting Practices of the U.K. Vintage Radio Community

REBECCA M. ELLIS AND ANNA HAYWOOD

> The Internet has changed the world for collectors. It makes it easier to find people who share your interest, simpler to photograph and display your collection, and, if you log on to the auction site eBay.com, you can acquire almost anything.
>
> **Brian Jenner, *Men and Collections*, referring to Jeremy, a vintage radio collector**[1]

This chapter explores U.K. vintage radio collectors and their relationships to eBay. Drawing on ethnographic data gathered over a two-year period, including participant observation material, qualitative interviews with radio collectors, and postings from an online vintage radio forum,[2] we contend that the very nature of eBay and the ways that goods are exchanged on the site make for a qualitatively new space of productive consumption that challenges the traditional practices, rituals, and geographies of collecting familiar to those individuals who frequent boot (trunk) sales, swap meets, and collectors' fairs.

Collections are assemblages of goods that project the taste, discernment, and knowledge of their owners, and intrinsic to the act of collecting and the performance of this "knowledge" is that objects should be geographically scattered and retrieved from spaces of "unknowingness" such as boot sales, swap meets, and junk shops. Recognizing "unknowingness"—spotting a bargain when an object's contemporary exchange value remains unknown or hidden to others—is important in collecting and demonstrates being "in the know" at community collecting events. For collectors, the difficulty of acquisition—the time and effort involved in searching for collectibles located across scattered geographies—forms part of the ritual of collecting. Collecting on eBay, however, challenges this ritual by making formerly "private" or "hidden" objects public and readily accessible to anyone with an internet connection and the ability to conduct online research. The widespread use of eBay has meant that many of the most desirable collectibles increasingly gravitate toward the site. Prices have moved upward partially because of the vast market eBay organizes, and in part by virtue of the competitive auction process and the seductive virtual packaging of goods on the site.

While eBay challenges traditional practices and established collecting rituals, as our discussion of the U.K. vintage radio community indicates, it also opens possibilities for new forms of ritual practice related to online trading among collectors. Vintage radio collectors are a strong community and hold numerous face-to-face events during which radios are bought and sold. The community is also one of contrasts. Radiophiles tend to collect based on a radio set's technical or aesthetic merits. The community includes a high percentage of electronics engineers and those in technical occupations or with an interest in design. These attributes account for a largely computer-literate membership, yet there is resistance to internet collecting from some older members who do not own computers or who prefer to collect the "traditional" (noninternet) way. The community has its own society or collectors' club, the British Vintage Wireless Society (BVWS), founded in 1976. Membership allows entry to a number of trading events or swap meets held across the United Kingdom. In 2004, active membership totaled 1,553 individuals and was fairly stable. A radio collectors' magazine, *The Radiophile*, also sponsors its own "expositions." BVWS and *Radiophile* swap meets, which mostly take place inside village or town halls, are characterized by stallholders and a traditional afternoon auction. These events, however, are increasingly supplemented and, at times, "hollowed out" by collectors who also maintain e-commerce Web pages and trade online using eBay's active vintage radio category.

To date, much of the discussion about eBay's influence on collecting practices is found on collector groups' Web pages, yet this discussion has been limited to items easy to post or mail, particularly coins and stamps.[3] Collector Jim Stoutjesdyk discusses the internet's influence on coin dealers and suggests that internet sales are likely to diminish dealers' attendance at coin shows and lead to closure of marginally profitable coin shops.[4] Collector Brian Schneider comments on his increased ability to find coins necessary to complete collecting sets, noting a particular acceleration in the ability to research older, less common coins.[5] He also mentions that constructed "unknowingness" and misrepresentation are problems, with sellers cleaning coins and representing them as being in "mint" condition, and online dealers claiming to know nothing about grading so as to avoid responsibility for items they sell. Stamp collecting websites describe the internet as a revolution for philately;

a stamps.net newsletter terms it the "central clearing house" for hobbyists, a mechanism by which one can buy stamps effortlessly without fruitless visits to shows and dealers.[6] The newsletter also notes that while selling opportunities have increased, problems abound online, including inflated prices for stamps and covers considered ordinary, a lack of sociality in chat rooms relative to traditional events and the face-to-face meetings they facilitate, and photographic misrepresentation of stamps listed for sale. The vintage radio community faces parallel issues. However, the very materiality—the size and weight—of radio-related items contributes to an even more complex picture of changed collecting practices in an internet era, and how eBay, in particular, challenges associated collecting rituals. While coins and stamps are easy to post (mail), the size and weight of many radios require sellers to decide which are sold on eBay (smaller, lighter ones) and which are taken to physical events (heavier, bulkier ones). Items are listed on eBay because they have specific eBay potential or are of uncertain value but may fetch a high price. Our discussion of the vintage radio-collecting community highlights the changing geographies of collecting—from its globalization, to negotiating the use of eBay versus swap meets, to the evolving distribution networks for collectibles.

VIRTUAL RADIOPHILES AND CHANGING COLLECTING PRACTICES

One of the most tangible ways in which eBay is changing the collections and practices of radiophiles is by rapidly accelerating the speed at which they accumulate collections. Jason, a Pye radio collector, when asked if eBay was changing the nature of his collection, responded, "Dramatically … I wouldn't have half of the radios that I've got if it weren't for eBay." Collectors describe eBay as publicly "outing" radios that would require many visits to physical venues to find. As Philip, a hi-fi collector, notes, "It will unearth the things that you might have to wait for years to find." eBay's central role in rapidly accelerating collecting, however, itself causes problems. Russell Belk argues that collections concern acquiring a set of things bounded, in part, by what is appropriate for the collection or not,[7] and the increased possibilities for acquisition afforded by eBay allow collectors to buy radio sets they may later deem inappropriate for their collection. Some collectors describe eBay as addictive (see chapter 1),[8] and some bid on items they do not need or cannot afford. Relisting "inappropriate items" on eBay is an acceptable way to continue collecting and "police" one's collection.

In the absence of a comprehensive U.K. radio price guide, eBay also changes radiophiles' collecting practices in providing up-to-the-minute values for items traded on the site, along with a searchable database of completed transactions. As Peter, a radio collector, says, "It's now much easier to value something … because … now anybody, with very little knowledge, can now go and have a look." John, however, believes that price on eBay is not always a reliable indicator of value. He finds eBay a setting of dangerous price unpredictability. However, eBay does afford users gaining other kinds of knowledge,[9] including what is available. "I've seen products that I didn't know existed" (Philip, hi-fi collector). At times, having more information also promotes acquiring greater knowledge: "I've occasionally seen things for sale and gone off and researched them … just to see what they are" (Martin, radio collector).

In addition to allowing for knowledge formation through interested browsing, eBay has also changed collecting practices by enabling information and knowledge to be publicly offered and relationally performed. Asking a question is regarded as the mark of the genuinely "unknowing" eBay seller:

> There are some … people who genuinely *don't know* anything about radios, but you find that most of those will ask—"if there's anybody can help me here identify the date of this set," or something like that, they often say: "please send me an email." … If people *don't* ask for that now, you think either they don't understand that process or more likely they *know very well what they've got*. (Arthur, radio collector)

The false "unknowingness" of unscrupulous sellers entails no knowledge giving—such individuals provide limited or wrong information to obfuscate while also appearing naïve.[10] Unlike discussions among collectors at a swap meet, knowledge formation on eBay, if accepted by the buyer, can become a highly public performance. Sellers often publicly acknowledge advice received about their revised eBay descriptions: "I said, 'Look, I do work for [the company]… . I'll get the approximate date of manufacture.' … So I was able to pass it on to him and say, 'Look that was 19--,' and he put it on the description, he said 'Thanks to [Philip], we've narrowed it down to these two years'" (Philip, hi-fi collector).

Public displays of knowledge on eBay are also common on the U.K. Vintage Radio Repair and Restoration online discussion forum, a site for radio, hi-fi, and TV collectors. The forum's knowledgeable collectors, who are also eBay participants, publicly deconstruct eBay descriptions for their assumed lack of knowledge (see Figure 3.1). Through these postings, members learn that the original eBay listing (see Figure 3.2) contained a number of faux pas, including listing a manufacturer's name as "Echo" instead of "Ekco," after E.K. Cole, or misspelling Bakelite, a trade name for thermo-setting plastic, as

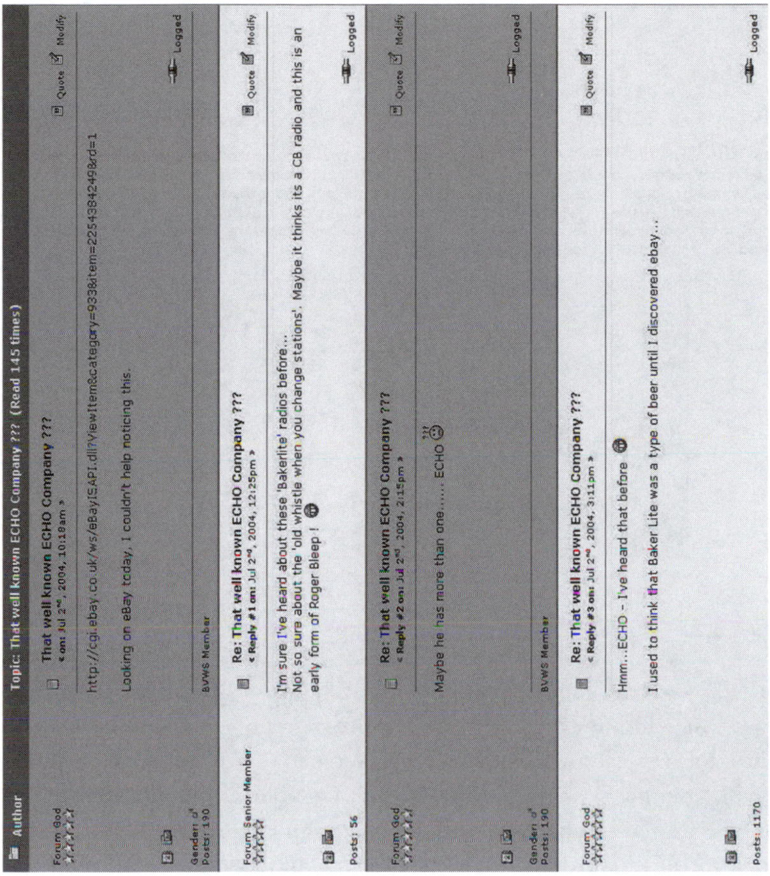

Virtual_radiophile (163☆)

Author | Topic: That well known ECHO Company ??? (Read 145 times)

Forum God ☆☆☆☆☆
Gender: ♂
Posts: 190

That well known ECHO Company ???
« on: Jul 2nd, 2004, 10:18am »
Quote Modify

http://cgi.ebay.co.uk/ws/eBayISAPI.dll?ViewItem&category=933&item=2254384249&rd=1

Looking on eBay today, I couldn't help noticing this.

Logged

BVWS Member

Forum Senior Member ☆☆☆☆
Posts: 56

Re: That well known ECHO Company ???
« Reply #1 on: Jul 2nd, 2004, 12:25pm »
Quote Modify

I'm sure I've heard about these 'Bakerlite' radios before...
Not so sure about the 'old whistle when you change stations'. Maybe it thinks its a CB radio and this is an early form of Roger Bleep !

Logged

Forum God ☆☆☆☆☆
Gender: ♂
Posts: 190

Re: That well known ECHO Company ???
« Reply #2 on: Jul 2nd, 2004, 2:15pm »
Quote Modify

Maybe he has more than one...... ECHO

Logged

BVWS Member

Forum God ☆☆☆☆☆
Posts: 1170

Re: That well known ECHO Company ???
« Reply #3 on: Jul 2nd, 2004, 3:11pm »
Quote Modify

Hmm...ECHO - I've heard that before

I used to think that Baker Lite was a type of beer until I discovered ebay...

Logged

Figure 3.1 U.K. vintage radio repair and restoration discussion forum.

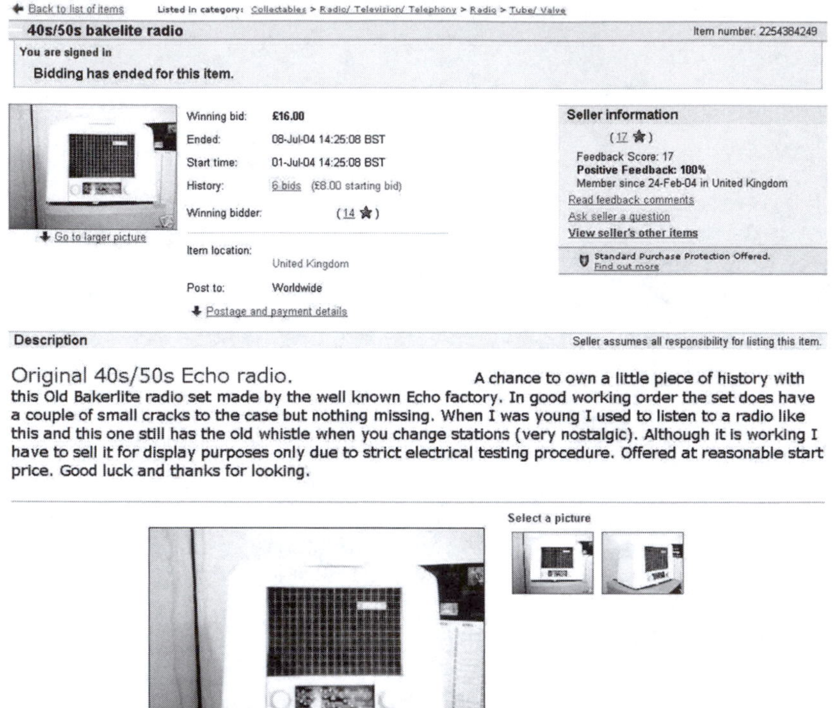

Figure 3.2 "40s/50s bakelite radio."

"Bakerlite." Such spelling errors are one of the forum's principal means for identifying the "unknowing." Members calling attention to such errors perform their collecting knowledges. Although some may view the snide responses as classic "flaming," we argue, after Steven Vrooman,[11] that this mockery is more the performative enactment of an elite group identity based on "knowing" collectors distinguishing themselves from "unknowing others."

EBAY'S CHALLENGE TO COLLECTING RITUALS

> It's very hard work, it's very thin pickings … every antique shop you go round or antiques market, you spend a load of time and your chance of finding anything is *minimal.*
>
> **Jason, Pye Radio collector**

Collecting rituals are instances of symbolic action through which collectors give objects new meanings that evoke, affirm, or revise the existing meanings of objects. Collecting rituals make objects "worthy" of a collection; through the process of meaning making, the ordinary becomes special and worth collecting.[12] Grant McCracken identifies collecting rituals associated with consumer goods—rituals of exchange, possession, grooming, and divestment. Rituals of exchange, for example, involve the movement of meaningful properties—such as "collectible" or "rare"—between the trading parties. Acquisition rituals are also vital to traditional ways of collecting.[13] In general, collectors value genuine rarity; acquiring rare items is a challenge and confers a sense of accomplishment and accompanying kudos. Finding rare items is part of an acquisition ritual entailing extensive searching in many places over a lengthy time period.

eBay challenges these rituals. Buying on eBay means anyone may acquire a rare radio, if prepared to pay the eBay price. Additionally, many common radio sets are listed as "rare" to fetch higher prices. This disrupts traditional exchange rituals and makes it more difficult to transfer the meaning of an object's rarity: "Everyone is so full of how wonderful everything is, you know … and incredibly rare, and the only one in the universe and all the rest of it" (John, radio dealer). Overpraising of items by sellers is common. The term "rare" may inflate an object's presale value, and increasingly "nonexperts" (not "trusted" parties such as known collectors or dealers) are listing radios on eBay. Evaluating the rarity of an eBay item remains difficult even for knowledgeable collectors, as listings frequently disrupt the social construction of rarity established by collecting communities. For example, an eBay listing of a truly rare radio may spark a number of listings of similar rare sets. Therefore, eBay contributes to altering perceptions of rarity with sudden "peaks" in supply, and prices, consequently, may fall in such situations (even though, as we noted above, the vast marketplace influences an overall trending upward in price). As Peter, a radio collector, says, "It indicates that things people say are very rare, aren't actually that rare. Because obviously once something appears on eBay, somebody says: 'Oh I've got one of those,' and conversely, of course, the value goes down." When prices fall it becomes less attractive to sell such items but, over time, their absence reestablishes conceptions of rarity. Overheard conversations during fieldwork pointed to dealers' concerns that "too many" rare sets were appearing on eBay: "SW is heard voicing concern about the market for round Ekcos being flooded by eBay—making prices fall. He suggests that there should be collusion between sellers to let out round Ekcos in a controlled way" (ethnographic diary, May 2003).

Buying radio sets on eBay and other internet sites also challenges the importance of and pleasure in recalling how an item was acquired—a component of acquisition rituals that helps make an object special. Philip, the hi-fi collector, believes that buying through eBay is "clinical":

> I mean, I picked up a Revox tape recorder that was in a pile of dustbin bags outside a house (laughs)… . And there you are, you've got it for nothing so, but you got more of a buzz out of that than you did with anything on eBay… . And I think with eBay that's sometimes the bit that's missing is the excitement of finding things… . You know, you're seeing pictures and you're bidding over it, for a period of days or hours, depending on when you've found it, it can be a bit of a clinical process. Whereas the swap meets, it's the excitement.

It is true, however, that eBay listings, particularly of collectibles, often feature narratives about the item and its historical provenance. As Sharon Zukin comments, when you buy on eBay you buy someone's story about an object (see also chapter 11 of this volume).[14] Such stories may be rejected as inauthentic—there are only so many family heirlooms in the loft forgotten until "rediscovered" for eBay. Again, we see here how eBay can disrupt exchange rituals during which cultural meaning is passed between the old and new owners. The virtual aspect of the exchange makes it harder for collectors to evaluate a provenance (for example, assessing the veracity of the story through asking face-to-face questions and evaluating body language and voice), and thus the "story" of the object is often uncertain and less a part of making it "special," unless backed up with incontrovertible documentary evidence.

For collectors such as Philip, eBay does not offer adequate gratification in purchase and possession because it cannot provide the excitement of accidentally stumbling across things in physical, material geographies. This interruption of traditional ritualized pleasures relates strongly to eBay's final challenge to traditional rituals of acquisition—that collecting should be an "organization of coincidences."[15] What items will look like, how and where they will be acquired, and whether they can be purchased at a bargain price—all are intrinsic to collecting rituals relying on the organization of coincidences. On eBay, the how and where are obvious (purchased through the site), but this is not necessarily the case for knowing what will turn up and when. Additionally, while false claims of rarity may deflate some prices, in general prices may be inflated by a large market and the competition of the auction.

In allowing for the "outing" of formerly "hidden" objects and making them accessible to all, trading collectibles online potentially challenges rituals of acquisition and their organization of coincidences. For some radio collectors, using eBay proves uncontentious. Martin, a radio collector, doesn't subscribe to formalized distinctions against collecting on eBay as his focus is on possession through "armchair collecting" rather than the "hunt" of acquisition: "If you want something specific, you'll try any means you can to get it." For some collectors, finding radios in scattered geographical locations is too much effort. According to Gregory, another collector, "I once put an advert in a local paper, in my early days. Oh, that was a disaster, really… . You just spent ages of time driving round seeing late fifties square boxes… . It was just too much like hard work… . It's just easier to sit in front of the computer … while you are waiting for dinner to be cooked."

Most virtual radiophiles choose to complement eBay collecting by frequenting, for example, swap meets that, with their choice of radios and possibilities for embodied social interaction, allow them to perform aspects of collecting rituals not possible on eBay. Attending car boot sales has also been made very fashionable in the United Kingdom by television programs such as BBC 1's *The Antiques Roadshow* and ITV's *Boot Sale Challenge* as well as *BBC News*'s reports on people making a living through buying at boot sales and reselling on eBay. For Peter, a radio collector:

> It's a habit, and it's a very sociable activity. I meet friends there and by 9 o'clock we go and have a cup of coffee. It's a nice interaction with other collectors; it's a bit of exercise. It's very enjoyable, you know, and it's always the thrill of you don't know what's going to turn up next. I mean last weekend I bought a *fantastic* Toshiba early '60s little record player, Japanese, with *beautiful* green plastic, classic '60s look … along with a lovely 625, 405 line tiny Sony television, with the original instructions. And I bought the two for £20, which really is, you know, and that was at the car boot sale.

The car boot sale is a place of serendipity where the "traditional" organization of coincidences still comes to pass, including negotiating prices downward. As long as traditional face-to-face sociality and forms of collecting rituals remain important, eBay is unlikely to completely replace physical venues.

Yet it would be simplistic to suggest that eBay is an undifferentiated collecting space. Virtual radiophiles are reformulating some of their rituals of collecting, particularly the "organization of coincidences," through searching relatively "unknown spaces" on eBay where the potentially serendipitous item may await. Karl located a highly desirable yellow and black Bakelite Kolster-Brandes BM20 by making the effort to find out more information than the set's listing provided: "I just emailed the guy and said sort of casually, as you do, 'Could you tell me what color the Bakelite is, under that cream paint.' 'cause, the next day, I got an email back from him: 'Yeah,' he said, 'it looks kinda black and yellow.' And I thought: 'Oh God, it's one of *them*.'" Hi-fi collector Philip sums up this corollary between material geographies and eBay's virtual geographies:

> This thing I bidded on last ... someone had advertised I think it was a Quad ... unit ... and I looked at it and I started scanning though the pictures, and he'd taken pictures of the equipment and on the back of the tuner is a stereo decoder unit, and I looked at it and I thought, "He hasn't put it on the description but it's on the back there" ... well he knew what he had, but obviously on the description he hadn't done it very well, and hadn't only put it in on the main headings ... so yeah, sometimes you might find that someone has done a cock up on the description, spelt it wrong, or they didn't really know what they've got, you can maybe get a bargain ... it's akin to us like at swap meets going through boxes on the floor, it's the trawling through eBay looking through boxes on the floor for things that have fallen between the stalls, you know, in the wrong category.

Finding eBay's unknown spaces requires research skills and personal labor (see chapter 6 for a discussion of how eBay disguises labor). Bidders must carefully study photographs and listing descriptions, request additional information from sellers as deemed necessary, and also search outside of the object's usual categories and search terms. And there is always the risk that experienced "eBay lookers" may pounce on or "snipe" the item at the last minute.

EBAY AND THE CHANGING GEOGRAPHIES OF COLLECTING

Before internet collecting, it was relatively difficult for collectors to acquire radio sets from abroad on their own; these were usually imported by specialist dealers. The advent of eBay has allowed peer-to-peer exchange among strangers living anywhere; buyers can purchase directly from sellers regardless of national borders. Globalized collecting has increased in tandem with greater individual knowledge about what is available—a knowledge fostered by studying the specifics of eBay's many listings. Often, buying from abroad is another way to exploit eBay's "unknown" or "unknowing" spaces. Jason, the Pye collector, comments, "My best buys have been from abroad … because obviously people are less knowledgeable about English radios abroad.… One thing I got from the States was a Chinese lacquer-work painted record player for a £100 plus a £100 postage, and in this country they'd cost you £500." U.K. radio collectors also take advantage of eBay's increasingly global reach though bidding strategically on different eBay national sites: "Initially things on New Zealand eBay were quite a reasonable price, and I bought a couple of nice little radios there at hardly any … you know, stupid money… . But the prices have gone up as they got bigger and bigger … so you're not likely to repeat that again" (Gregory, radio collector).

Other collectors have become pure virtual radiophiles, either due to reduced mobility or because they are driven by motives of possession and convenience, rather than ritual: "You can sit there in your front room bidding on all this stuff, and it comes in boxes, you've not had the fun of driving halfway across the country … it could be seen as a bit of a cheat… . It's not doing it for real" (Philip, hi-fi collector). Despite Philip's assertion, we find no evidence that collectors who avoid eBay do so because they regard eBay buying as not "real collecting." While a number of collectors' practices are rooted in tradition, these individuals are often uncomfortable with new technologies. They eschew digital photography and refuse to have a computer; however, this is not the same as refusing eBay because it is not "real." At times eBay nonparticipation does reflect fears of purchasing something of dubious quality. Mostly, however, radiophiles are both virtual and non-virtual; the internet complements swap meets and other physical arenas, and collectors have learned what tactics of buying and selling work best in each setting.

As the place where vintage radio collectors expect to find "nuggets"—rare finds, often at bargain prices—the swap meet is still *the* place to go: "I think if you're patient enough and you wait around, there's always the nuggets there hidden away" (Peter, radio collector). Unlike an eBay auction, finding a "nugget" at a swap meet means that purchase is immediate and the item is removed posthaste to the car, away from other collectors' prying eyes. Compared to eBay's individual listing of each item, swap meet items often come bundled with a "job lot" of other items. eBay's format, therefore, helps render ordinary objects individually desirable by organizing them as separate pages and thereby allows viewers to infer that each object is a "*serious* object."[16] eBay items are often heavily virtually "packaged" through the seller's social construction of the object. Item descriptions often offer "opinions" about the importance of the object (for example, a Brimar ECC83 valve recently sold as "the best valve money can buy"), and objects are nicely photographed (see chapter 12) in expensive domestic interiors (we noted an incredibly rare green round Ekco included in the background of an Art Deco listing).[17] In contrast, items at swap meets may be in bits and pieces, covered in dust in a tatty box, or jumbled with unknown ancillary items.

Typically, radiophiles see eBay as the setting where higher prices are achieved: "Most people *know* they can get better money by selling it on eBay. And so that's what they do" (Arthur, radio collector). eBay adds value through the packaging and "spin" that form part of most listings for collectibles, and also by providing access to a worldwide market. Radio collector Gregory believes eBay is a completely different market than the swap meet: "If you put it on eBay, you're reaching a much bigger audience—an audience of people that, you know, may be not members of BVWS at all … and would like an old radio for whatever reason, and it's been restored and it's working." Most radio collectors who sell try eBay first, potentially "hollowing out" the swap meet in terms of the quality of items offered. Peter recounts a conversation with an American radio collector: "An American guy who came over to the N.E.C. [a very large swap meet event], he said eBay's just changed swap meets completely. There's often not the point of doing them for some people. The prices achieved on eBay are much higher… . Even things like garage sales, you just don't see anything interesting because people say: 'That's interesting, I'll put it on eBay.'" Peter predicts that hollowing out will happen in the United Kingdom, and eBay prices do seem to influence swap meet prices. Radio collectors believe eBay pushes prices up, with eBay prices becoming "list prices" for some items. Swap meet sellers often hold out for the price they want, and if they don't get it, they list on eBay. Many items that are swap meet nuggets, sold in bulk at bargain prices, remain so because sellers altruistically decide that other collectors who are BVWS members should have their unwanted items, or they either are non-eBay users or choose not to expend effort on "packaging" their items in multiple eBay listings.

Not everything is migrating to eBay, and swap meets still materialize particular sorts of collectibles. Despite "rarity" on eBay, the rarest items still turn up at swap meets, perhaps because it takes a hall full of knowledgeable enthusiasts to achieve the highest price for a very rare item. Additionally, swap meets often feature rare items from the estates of deceased collectors. Swap meet items, moreover, seem polarized into "very good" and "very bad" categories. Many collectors believe swap meets are where "castoffs" are sold, but eBay is thought to make this worse as the best items often are cherry-picked beforehand for the site. Finally, an item's size matters. As Peter says, "I think maybe one should put high value on small items on eBay, and then bulky things you take to the N.E.C. You know, big heavy radio sets [laughter]." Derek, selling off his collection, sold small sets on eBay and took big, hard-to-ship, console radios to a swap meet.

Swap meets are unlikely to disappear, mainly because collectors enjoy their sociality. Jason, the Pye collector, says his attendance has not waned "because it's a very different environment. It's slightly more human. You *meet* people." Jason also considers swap meets an experiential part of collecting: "There still [is] something about queuing up on a Sunday morning … I don't know, it's the fun of it, it's the event… . That feeling of community." Collectors also enjoy finding items by wandering through the physical collecting space, rather than searching online, because they feel they can see everything: "I mean, obviously with eBay you can only see so much … there's a hell of a lot of information out there and you're sort of wandering up to it with a little spoon trying to catch it all … you can't and I think things do slip through your finger[s] on eBay, whereas at a swap meet you can wander round" (Philip, hi-fi collector).

Some buyers purchase items with "eBay potential" at swap meets where prices are lower and resell them on eBay. This redistribution through the postal system and other private delivery services is one of the principal ways eBay has changed collectible networks. As Jason, the Pye collector, notes, "I'm sure there are an awful number of people who will go and buy at swap meets and sell on eBay… . I've seen a chap there with a wheelbarrow collecting small transistor radios, and he certainly wasn't buying them for a *collection* [laughter]." At swap meets, car boot sales, and traditional auctions, collectors purchase items brought together in one place from disparate geographical locations, each of which may have a market limited by its geographic boundaries, to resell them on eBay where they believe selling prices are higher. Some BVWS members, however, find reselling items from swap meets ethically troublesome. Philip, the hi-fi collector, disagrees strongly with such reselling, because society membership should not be held to make a profit, according to its rules. Much of this eBay reselling is done through fairly anonymous user names. Some collectors believe that people's "faceless" eBay presence renders such reselling less guilt ridden.

The ease of selling via eBay is also "outing" rare radios sold by collectors to raise funds. Such radios will have traveled along internal distribution networks of collectors, who come to swap meets from disparate geographical locations. Ironically, swap meets are important nodes in the unseen networks that channel rare radios onto internet trading spaces such as eBay: "Evidence here of the distribution networks which are going on with internet trading. Key sets are gravitating towards John [a dealer using eBay and the internet] via complex distribution networks of collectors from all over the country. Two Champion Venus sets and an M78F from a Welsh collector arrived [at the Harpenden swap meet] via [Charles] (Birmingham) to go north with John" (ethnographic diary, March 2003). Although informal networks to transport sets countrywide as favors for other collectors have always been in place, the internet has increased their use. The reverse is also true, with U.K. eBay descriptions offering the possibility of taking items to the N.E.C. or Harpenden events.

Although eBay and the internet are producing new collecting networks and greater utilization of existing ones, they potentially truncate others. Radio dealer John fears eBay will lead to his marginalization:

> There is a kind of food chain that there's always been in … collectibles … that you get sort of somebody whose aunty has died and they're clearing the house out … they ring some bloke up who'll come round with a transit van and says, "I'll give you 50 quid for the whole lot"… . And then, you know, and somewhere in the chain I buy it and then I sell it to somebody else who may be a collector, may be another dealer… . And then, you know, and they'll sell it onto somebody else and eventually it ends up with, you know, Mr., you know, International Financier in his loft apartment in… like New York who pays, you know, $10,000 for it after it's gone through about 20 people's hands and they've all made a few bob out of it along the way… . The danger is … that in the future when everybody has got internet access and everybody understands eBay … is that Billy Smith that clears the houses will just put an item on eBay and say "An old radio I don't know what it is, but it's got valves sticking out of the top," you know, 5 quid reserve, and it'll fetch $10,000 because, you know, like Mr. Big Businessman … will be bidding on it… . And all the other people won't be getting a look in on the way up.

John fears eBay will mean the elimination of intermediate dealers as items go straight to eBay. Networks between house clearance dealers and specialists who buy from them would gradually fade away.

NEITHER VIRTUAL CAR BOOT SALE NOR VIRTUAL SWAP MEET …

The very nature of eBay makes it a qualitatively new alternative consumption space that changes and challenges the collecting practices, rituals, and geographies of collecting that we are familiar with from attending boot sales, swap meets, and collectors' fairs. The analogy that eBay is a virtual car boot sale fails on close analysis. eBay is a particular type of continually reconstituted collecting space, a 24/7 global exchange venue that, unlike the swap meet, doesn't require getting up early on a Sunday morning. At physical collecting spaces, an organization of coincidences remains important, including geographies of serendipity and retrieving items from geographically scattered spaces of unknowingness. It is simplistic, moreover, to suggest that eBay is an undifferentiated collecting space that merely challenges collecting rituals rather than enabling their reformulation and performance in new and productive ways. Some radio collectors find spaces of unknowingness on the eBay site. Although eBay is qualitatively different from the swap meet or boot sale, U.K. radio collectors project back onto eBay analogies between finding virtual spaces of unknowingness and finding them physically in the geographic "hunt." Poor descriptions, misspellings, and wrong categorizations on eBay are the virtual equivalents of the liminal items that fall between swap meet stalls and the boxes on the floor. Radio collectors mirror the physical effort of acquisition in virtual spaces by finding the spaces less *viewed*, and by being critical and knowledgeable consumers of eBay item descriptions and photographs, in order to uncouple misrepresentations from the actual objects. Such collectors achieve an online organization of coincidences through their knowledge of other users' varied eBay practices and their increasing experience of eBay as collectors.

NOTES

1. Brian Jenner, *Men and Collections* (London: New Holland Publishers, 2004), 73.
2. To gain a more holistic picture of eBay's influence on radiophiles, our ethnography comprised a multimethod approach, with interviews and participant observation in offline and online spaces. Lurkers have traditionally failed to matter in internet "ethnography" (see Christine Hine, *Virtual Ethnography* [London: Sage, 2000]), and there have been few attempts to adjust methodologies to recover them (see Blair Nonnecke and Jenny Preece, "Lurker Demographics: Counting the Silent," in *Proceedings of the Annual ACM SIGCHI Conference on Human Factors in Computing Systems [CHI 2000]* [The Hague, the Netherlands: ACM Press, 2000], 73–80). Both eBay and the Vintage Radio Repair and Restoration forum have a large percentage of lurkers. On eBay, these may be people who watch or browse, rather than bid, and the forum attracts people who read others' comments but do not themselves post. All these people are lost in an internet-only ethnography, as are those collectors reluctant or unable to use the internet for collecting or communicating.

To offset these biases, we sought out a potentially different set of people taking part in swap meets. We also relied on online data to supplement information gained offline, as this gives greater insight into individuals' actions rather than relying only on textual or narrative accounts of what they do; see Chris Mann and Fiona Stewart, *Internet Communication and Qualitative Research* (London: Sage, 2000). Participants recruited through online spaces were also either interviewed on the phone or sent questionnaires to overcome the relative difficulty associated with conducting interviews online.

3. See, for example, Lloyd A. de Vries, "Vol. 1—Synergy," *Stamp Collecting and the Internet*, Virtual Stamp Club, 2001, www.virtualstampclub.com/synergy.html (accessed August 3, 2004).
4. Jim Stoutjesdyk, "The Future of Numismatics on the Internet," *Heritage Insider Magazine* 2, no. 2 (April 1999): http://apps.heritagecoin.com/features/insider/heritageInsider.php?issue=2_2_collectors_corner (accessed July 22, 2004).
5. Brian Schneider, "Coin Collecting and the Internet: A Look at Their Evolution," *Heritage Galleries and Auctioneers*, 2004, http://apps.heritagecoin.com/features/numisarticles.php?id=159 (accessed July 22, 2004).
6. "The Internet's Influence on Stamp Collecting Is Expanding Quickly," *Stamps on the Internet*, www.stamps.net/Newslett.htm (accessed July 22, 2004).
7. Russell W. Belk, *Collecting in a Consumer Society* (London: Routledge, 1995). See also Marina Bianchi, "Collecting as a Paradigm of Consumption," *Journal of Cultural Economics* 21 (1997): 275–89.
8. Laura J. Gurak, *Cyberliteracy: Navigating the Internet with Awareness* (New Haven, CT: Yale University Press, 2001).
9. See Sharon Zukin, *Point of Purchase: How Shopping Changed American Culture* (London: Routledge, 2004).
10. See Laura Robinson and David Halle, "Digitization, the Internet, and the Arts: eBay, Napster, SAG, and e-Books," *Qualitative Sociology* 25, no. 3 (Fall 2002): 359–83. Robinson and Halle's consideration of a painting listed on eBay that appeared to be an original by California artist Richard Diebenkorn illustrates these issues. The eBay seller who Robinson and Halle discuss constructs an air of naïveté that allows others to infer he had limited knowledge when, actually, the item was a clever fake. The seller provided subtle allusions to Diebenkorn, such as noting the painting's color palette. Essentially, bidders on the item hoped to take advantage of his supposed "lack of sophistication" and acquire a very valuable item at a bargain price. On "knowingness" as a performance of taste and discernment for knowing audiences and others "in the know," see Nicky Gregson, Kate Brooks, and Louise Crewe, "Bjorn Again? Rethinking 70s Revivalism through the Reappropriation of 70s Clothing," *Fashion Theory* 5, no. 1 (2001): 3–28.
11. Steven S. Vrooman, "The Art of Invective: Performing Identity in Cyberspace," *New Media and Society* 4, no. 1 (2002): 51–70.

12. See Grant McCracken, *Culture and Consumption: New Approaches to the Symbolic Character of Consumer Goods and Activities* (Bloomington, Indiana University Press), 83–89; and Belk, 74.
13. Walter Benjamin, "The Work of Art in the Age of Mechanical Reproduction," cited in Belk, 61.
14. Zukin, 247.
15. Walter Grasskamp, "Les Artistes et les Autres Collectioneurs," cited in Belk, 63.
16. Zukin, 246.
17. Item descriptions, or virtual packaging, of collectible items such as radios on eBay also aim to "singularize" the objects. Igor Kopytoff describes the process whereby ordinary objects are "singularized" or "decommoditized" through incorporation into cultural or personal frameworks of meaning. Item descriptions often describe objects as collectibles or personal items for which a new home is sought—to singularize them. Yet, as a part of what is essentially an advertisement, the item remains highly commoditized and only truly "singularized" when bought by a collector and incorporated into his or her collection. See Igor Kopytoff, "The Cultural Biography of Things: Commoditization as Process," in *The Social Life of Things: Commodities in Cultural Perspective*, ed. Arjun Appadurai (Cambridge: Cambridge University Press, 1986), 80; and Belk, 61–62.

4

Fortune-Telling on eBay

Early African American Textual Artifacts and the Marketplace

ERIC GARDNER

> Fortune—To make a sudden fortune in your dream is a bad omen.
>
> Paper—To dream of white paper, denotes respect; if scribbled or printed, you will do some mean or unjust action.
>
> **Chloe Russel, *The Complete Fortune Teller* (1824), 8, 10; eBay item #1982259838, ended on December 22, 2002**

In late 2002, after perhaps three years of using eBay to collect early editions of texts by nineteenth-century women and African Americans, I discovered one of only four extant copies of a hitherto unknown piece of Afro-Americana: Chloe Russel's twenty-page booklet (called a "chapbook"), *The Complete Fortune Teller and Dream Book*. The "dream book" portion, a list of items paired with explanations of what the presence of those items in a dream portends for the dreamer, is the source of this chapter's epigraph—a chilling prediction for any book collector. The volume was produced in the 1820s by Exeter, New Hampshire, publisher Abel Brown and notes on its title page that Russel was "A Woman of Colour in the State of Massachusetts."[1] Subsequent research has documented a free African American woman named Chloe Russel (c.1770–c.1835), who worked as a laundress and then a cook in Boston, owned property, and seems to have been a seer of some repute.[2] While *The Complete Fortune Teller* is certainly *about* Russel—and uses her exoticism to promote its sales—it may or may not be *by* Russel.[3] Nonetheless, as one of the earliest American texts to take an African American woman and African American divination as subjects, it is a find of some importance to the scholarly community—as evinced by its recent republication, with my introduction, in the *New England Quarterly*.[4]

The recovery of *The Complete Fortune Teller* through eBay foregrounds a number of questions that swirl around not only the collection and dissemination of rare Afro-Americana in an electronic age, but also, perhaps more pointedly, the ways in which race and "recovery" function in light of the socioeconomic, cultural, and political practices engendered by eBay's structure and user base. After briefly examining the "high-toned" world of serious book collecting and the ways in which Afro-Americana and African American collectors have begun to challenge this world, this chapter describes functional approaches to collecting Afro-Americana through eBay, and then steps back to critically examine the language of any such "how-to" guide. While it recognizes democratizing tendencies in such work, this chapter also suggests that this very language, which is full of racist undertones as well as metaphors of hunting (and so also of hegemonic power over racial artifacts), causes the overdetermined space of the marketplace (and specifically of eBay) to enact, given the place of the slave market in African American history, a set of curious revisions of those early sales of human beings. In this, the act of collecting Afro-Americana on eBay functions in complex dialogue with the language surrounding the entry of Afro-Americana into the traditionally "genteel" world of upper-class book dealers and collectors, academics, and librarians.

For decades, the representative book collector looked much like the massively wealthy Percy Gryce of Edith Wharton's *The House of Mirth*, whose sole purpose in life seemed to be a conservation of both his family name and a famous collection of rare Americana. Far from a figment of Wharton's imagination, this scion of the upper-class patriarchy of book collecting—the rich man who deigns to indulge in a passion for books (as opposed to more ostentatious modes of consumption)—is still celebrated in a range of contemporary texts on book collecting. For such collectors, fortunes and printed paper would seem far from the bad omens promised by Chloe Russel's fortune-telling guide and dream book. Consider, for example, the posh coffee table book *At Home with Books: How Booklovers Live with and Care for Their Libraries*, which retailed for 50 USD when released in 1995. Loaded with lush illustrations of private book collections, it features informative sections on "Library Lighting" and "The Art of the Bookshelf" and could stand alongside most contemporary design magazines.[5] The collectors profiled here are the financial elite: Paul Getty talks about his "thermostatically controlled" library, built because "[b]ooks, like wine, need to be kept at a regular, unfluctuating temperature," and Andrew, eleventh duke of Devonshire, whose library is "a mixture between an illustrated manuscript and a French restaurant."[6]

The entry of Afro-Americana into this (very white) world is a much more recent phenomenon: many books about books say little—when anything—about black books, and few have nonwhite faces among their sometimes posh illustrations. Arthur Schomburg and Charles Blockson, for example, *combined* get ten pages in Nicholas Basbanes's 638-page memoir-like study of book collecting and collectors entitled *A Gentle Madness*. Both entries focus on "the need to document black history"—rather than, say, Lincoln collector Louise Taper's claim that "I enjoy it. I love it, actually; I am driven by it."[7] Basbanes is correct that most major early black bibliophiles collected for reasons beyond personal obsession—and so also often left the genteel world of high-end dealers to "pick" among society's refuse in hopes of preserving a rare piece of an oppressed past.[8]

The end of the twentieth century saw some melding of these two discursive fields—passion and preservation—embodied in some ways in Henry Louis Gates's discussion of finding Hannah Crafts's manuscript of *The Bondwoman's Narrative* in 2001:

> Each year, Swann Galleries conducts an auction of "Printed & Manuscript African Americana"… . I have the pleasure of receiving Swann's annual mailing of the catalog … [which] consists of descriptions of … artifacts that have managed, somehow, to surface from the depths of the black past… . [T]o me, there is a certain poignancy to the fact that these artifacts, created by the disenfranchised, have managed to survive … and have found their way … to a place where they can be preserved and made available to scholars, students, researchers, and passionate readers… .
>
> I made my way through [the catalog] leisurely, keeping my precious copy on the reading stand next to my bed, turning to it each evening to fall asleep in wonder at the astonishing myriad array of artifacts that surface, so very mysteriously, from the discarded depths of the black past.[9]

The thickness of the language of gentility here—Gates's comments on both poignancy and passion—masks some of the marks of socioeconomic power: most Swann catalogs cost about 30 USD, and items are priced at a premium; Gates has the leisure to read the catalog and find the manuscript—as well as the somewhat rarefied knowledge necessary to mark its importance; and Gates speaks of his "modest cap" for bidding on the manuscript, which was actually 8,500 USD, a figure not discussed in most treatments of Crafts's novel.[10]

Still, if Gates's financial flexing seems akin to that of the collectors in *At Home with Books*, it actually signifies quite differently. Rhetorically, Gates is demonstrating that some African Americans are now able both to, in essence, join the country club and change it. His rhetoric and his actions suggest the less consumeristic goals of collectors like Schomburg and Blockson. Indeed, instead of keeping the rare manuscript after he got it, he engineered the publication of Crafts's novel (which brought it into the popular sphere—and so rescued it from obscurity) and then donated the manuscript, which had increased exponentially in monetary value, to a university library where it could be both preserved and ensured a place in American cultural remembrance.[11]

If Gates's work within the formerly white world of high-end book collectors offers these radical elements, then, because eBay in essence removes the country club walls surrounding serious book collecting, it would be easy to say that eBay democratizes such collecting much more fully. And it does. Both book collectors and booksellers took to eBay early, and eBay has long had a thriving market in Afro-Americana that extends far beyond the reach of the Swann Gallery catalogs.[12] Early editions of important texts such as Frederick Douglass's *Narrative* and even Olaudah Equiano's *Interesting Narrative* come up for auction with some regularity, and occasionally much rarer texts also appear—including two first editions (of perhaps only one hundred extant) of Harriet Jacobs's *Incidents in the Life of a Slave Girl*.[13]

The immediate surface difference between eBay and the more rarefied sense of collecting embodied in the Swann catalogs and, even more, Percy Gryce, is hierarchical: while eBay certainly features some of the most respected high-end dealers, it also brings in wares from original sources and "pickers" who canvas estate sales, flea markets, and library discard sales.[14] For decades among the more genteel collectors, the book dealer served as a skilled middle link in the chain of consumption. He (and occasionally she) purchased books from other dealers and from pickers, and then presented the artifacts (often cleaned up and prefaced by the obligatory brief textual description of content, context, condition, and price) to the collector in the "safety" of the bookshop (often open only by appointment), the general catalog, or the auction catalog—or even a private showing. (Though they focus on a field other that book collecting, Rebecca Ellis and Anna Haywood's chapter in this volume also demonstrates that eBay's inclusion of original sources and pickers in the same marketplace has exploded traditional senses of where and how artifacts circulate and are collected.)

Within this realm, "finding" on eBay is not—at least not primarily—simply finding the obvious, complete with a detailed description written by an expert and trustworthy dealer who articulates the object's significance and value. Rather, "finding" is about getting as close as possible to the estate sales and attics where objects have been "lost" and then about being able to recognize and articulate hidden value. As such, both finding and acquiring objects are, by nature, competitive—and dependent on some sellers listing objects the value of which they do not fully understand (and thus cannot articulate).[15]

In part for these reasons, by necessity eBay searches combine features of contemporary information technology (using Boolean logic and truncation to find variations of key words) and echoes of the nineteenth-century language of race and racism. Because Afro-Americana is not a separate eBay category (and not all sellers would list merchandise in that category even if it were), narrowing searches to a small set of categories limits the scope of the buyer's task. In addition to the obvious "Books: Antiquarian and Collectible" and, less so, "Antiques: Books, Manuscripts: American" subcategories, objects can occasionally be found in "Collectibles: Ethnic and Cultural" among racist memorabilia such as Mammy cookie jars and Little Black Sambo dolls. Searching both titles and descriptions is essential, as many sellers unfamiliar with Afro-Americana (and race studies in general) use idiosyncratic terminology in listing titles. The obvious search terms, "Black" and "African American," have notable problems on eBay. "Black" comes up much more often as a color—e.g., "black and white illustrations"—than as a racial signifier. ("Color," "colour," "colored," and "coloured," while certainly the terms of choice for many antebellum African Americans, are ineffective for the same reasons as "Black.") Adding "American"—for example, searching for "Black American"—improves searching with such terms, but, much like "African American," is usually only effective in finding items with descriptions by sellers who know what they have—and ask a premium for it.[16]

This means that terms common in early titles and book texts are often more usable for searching. Entering the truncated search term "slave*," which also hits "slavery," and the truncated "abol*," which brings up "abolitionism," "abolitionist," and so on, is often somewhat effective, though it can bring up a range of twentieth-century historical texts as well as other kinds of collectibles. The term "negro" finds texts dating from the late nineteenth century and early twentieth century; in addition to appearing in early titles, the term is used by sellers out of touch with the development of terminology like "African American." Combining search terms with truncated dates often narrows the search field further; for example, "slave* 185*," though not foolproof, generally brings up a number of items tied to slave narratives, antislavery texts, and proslavery texts because it hits a common term in early texts and a set of publication dates (which is common even in the most basic of book descriptions).

Still, to find the truly "lost" artifact, collectors look for texts without clear racial markers—texts not labeled by any term that obviously suggests a piece of Afro-Americana. Again, searching for terms common to nineteenth-century authors—yet unfamiliar to many twenty-first-century readers—offers some potential; the truncated "coloniz*," for example, brings up variants of texts by and about colonization societies. Searching by gender using nineteenth-century constructions of authorial names also offers possibilities: narrowing the focus to the category "Books: Antiquarian and Collectible" and searching for "mrs* 187*," for example, often finds a range of texts by women writers of the 1870s (including, once, an 1879 edition of Julia Foote's slave narrative *A Brand Plucked from the Fire*, the seller of which was almost certainly unaware of Foote's race, as the description was silent on the issue).

Finally, searching by eBay user ID can be useful to those buyers familiar with the relatively small circle of bidders most skilled at finding such texts; often, though, such bidders attempt to keep other buyers from doing this kind of searching by resorting to "sniper bidding" or, at least, holding their bids until late in auctions (see chapter 10 for a discussion of "why we snipe"). Still, the fact that eBay maintains a sixty-day history of items bid on by each user, as well as complete lists of current bids and bidders for most items, means that users can track bidding patterns, examine titles and descriptions for items initially missed and so learn more effective search strategies, and get a rough sense of the amounts a given bidder is willing to pay for an item.

Within this framework, *The Complete Fortune Teller* was not an ideal find; its seller was aware of the byline and so titled the listing "1824 Black Fortune Teller Freemasons, Irish"—with the last two words noting other chapbooks included in the bound volume. Further, he both quoted the byline and noted, "If Chloe Russel was real, she must have been one of the earliest black American women to be published." Still, the identifying terms here—"Black" and "color"—are not those most friendly to (or used by) most collectors of Afro-Americana, and no other commonly searched and used terms—abolition, slavery, negro, and so on—appeared. This must have limited the number of bidders. A counter placed in the description—marking the total number of hits to the listing rather than different users—showed only a few hundred by the end of the auction, perhaps forty of which (including refreshes) were made by myself.[17]

Nonetheless, it was clear, when the item turned up in a search for "Black America* 18*," that the seller was aware of at least the potential that the text was black-authored and was fully aware that the text had black subject matter, and so put something of a premium (100 USD) as an opening bid. The seller did not, though, have the knowledge of Russel's identity or the potential importance and rarity of the text. Between finding the item and placing a bid close to the auction's end, I was able to check for other copies using WorldCat, to use an extensive range of genealogical and historical sources including Ancestry.com to find the initial proof that there was an African American named Chloe Russel, and to do initial research on the links between African Americans and divination in early national New England. Probably few potential bidders were able to do such work, and few bid on the text. And thus a piece of rare Afro-Americana came to a middle-class professor who can't justify spending the 30 USD for the luxury of a Swann catalog—much less actually bidding on something in it.

The tone in the above—like that in much collecting literature (and even some of the high-end books on books)—is, of course, mingled pride in a successful hunt and excitement about a win in a competitive process.[18] Again, however, it was not the ideal find; it might have been had it simply been advertised as an early fortune-telling text with an opening bid of, say, 20 USD, and some clue that only I had caught.

The problems with such a tone, though, are myriad. Of course, my narrative is full of class markers—albeit not the level of markers in *At Home with Books*. My eBay acquisition might have been more "democratic" than the Swann auction, but… .

In some ways, the quality of gentility found in the Swann catalog is almost lost amidst the racist language that marks the discursive field of Afro-Americana on eBay. Indeed, racist items and/or descriptions turn up much more often in the searches described above (which are themselves dependent upon using racist terminology). Consider the early 2005 sales of the 1896 and 1897 picture book *Ten Little Niggers* by eBay ID rebel_soldier, who specializes in Civil War material; the book's backward counting in racist rhyme ("Seven Little Niggers chopping up sticks. One chopped himself in halves, and then there were Six") is accompanied by gruesome illustrations—several of which were reproduced in the item description.[19] In the first auction, which offered the 1896 edition, the seller quoted eBay's policy on "Offensive Items," which allows sellers to use such language "provided that the offensive words are actually part of the title of the listed item" and that their own language "shows appropriate sensitivity to those in the Community that might view it." In the second auction, in which the 1897 edition was presented in similarly great detail, the seller expanded the quotation from the policy to note, "Artists occasionally use offensive words and phrases such as 'Nigger' and 'Jap' in the titles of media items" and that, nonetheless, "eBay urges all of its community members to treat others as they themselves would like to be treated." The second auction was also a "private listing"; that is, bidder identification was visible only to the seller. Thus, though its policy statements suggest otherwise, eBay not only allows but even authenticates racist discourse.[20] Finding such texts, only a step from finding The *Complete Fortune Teller*, thus involves support of eBay's mixed message and direct use of racist language.

Perhaps more troubling still, all aspects of auctions of early Afro-Americana call to mind the most common auctions in African American history. The flipness of my narrative of acquisition—for example, wishing I could have bought the text for 20 USD instead of 200—frankly, insults: while we are not bidding on bodies, we are bidding on memories.[21] While many of the attributes of this narrative—the ascribing of monetary value to the invaluable, the sense of "knowledgeable" bidders, the contest between seller and bidder to get the "best price," and the bragging surrounding a "good find" and a "good buy"—echo most capitalist exchanges, the use of racist language to identify and mark racial objects and the subject matter and purposes of these texts call to mind a specific nexus of capitalism and racism, the antebellum slave market.[22]

While purchasing an antebellum text and purchasing a slave are obviously very different activities, the collector of Afro-Americana may certainly be buying the text—as slaves were bought—for both its use value and exchange value in all their complex shadings. As a collector, or, in Walter Benjamin's words, "a real collector, a collector as he ought to be," "ownership is the most intimate relationship that one can have to objects. Not that they come alive in him; it is he who lives in them."[23] I may want ownership of the text—as so many slave buyers seem to have wanted ownership of slaves—to articulate myself. Further, while the discovery of Chloe Russel certainly adds to our sense of African American history and literature, discovering and sharing that text will likely advance my academic career (Gates's discovery of *Our Nig* certainly advanced his).[24] I am also, frankly, using Chloe Russel's text in different ways than it was intended—including the making of specific arguments about the landscape of early African American literature. Such appropriation is complicated by the fact that *The Complete Fortune Teller* may well have been written by someone other than Chloe Russel, someone who hoped to capitalize on her name and race to sell books. If I am not fully akin to a buyer at a slave market, I may have more in common with the tradition of (sometimes well-meaning) whites—one thinks of the editors with whom African Americans such as Frederick

Douglass and Harriet Jacobs struggled over control of their stories—who have appropriated the texts and the stories of African Americans.

It would be easier—and, in the end, hopefully more true—to say that my own purposes were not pecuniary or oppressive, but better, higher, like those I ascribe to Gates and others who hope to rescue a piece of the black past. In explaining why he collects racist memorabilia, for example, David Pilgrim, founder of the Jim Crow Museum, says,

> I am a garbage collector, racist garbage. For three decades I have collected items that defame and belittle Africans and their American descendants … 4,000 … items that portray blacks as Coons, Toms, Sambos, Mammies, Picaninnies, and other dehumanizing racial caricatures. I collect this garbage because I believe, and know to be true, that items of intolerance can be used to teach tolerance.[25]

If even *this* material—and the approaches demanded by collecting it—can be redeemed, then perhaps my ends can in part justify the means I employed—the eBay requirement to use racist language in searching, the form of the auction, and the reenactment of scenes of racism. Were it not for these means, I submit, we would not today be able to remember Harriet Wilson, Hannah Crafts, Chloe Russel… .

But collectors of Afro-Americana cannot simply "dream" of clean and easy resolution, of "white paper," as Russel notes, and assume that such dreams portend respect. Just as slave narrators from Frederick Douglass to Harriet Jacobs, in speaking of how their friends purchased them with the express intent of freeing them, mingle gratitude with painful questions about participating in the slave economy, so too must we recognize that the quality of democratic openness fostered by eBay often opens the barely healing scars of racism. In short, the paper is already scribbled upon. And so when we dream of great fortunes based on printed pages, when we engage with Jim Crow language and the auctioning of memories, the cautionary fortune-telling of Chloe Russel's dream guide—embodied in this chapter's epigraph—and the cautionary tale of how Chloe Russel has come back to us via eBay may remind us of the complex terrain and the ironic series of trade-offs necessary to study slavery's remembrance in a capitalist society.

NOTES

The author wishes to thank Jodie Gardner for her comments.

1. Chloe Russel, *The Complete Fortune Teller and Dream Book* (Exeter, NH: Abel Brown, 1824), in *The Amusing Bud[get]* (Exeter, NH: Abel Brown, 1827). The

other copies of Russel's text include an 1824 chapbook not bound with *The Amusing Budget*, a partial copy that is owned by the American Antiquarian Society; a circa 1800 edition by Boston printer Tom Hazard, owned by the Boston Athenaeum; and an undated partial copy of another (perhaps earlier) edition owned by the Library Company of Philadelphia. The Library Company edition contains what purports to be an autobiography of Russel—which narrates a birth in Africa, years as a slave in Virginia, and the gaining of the "gift" of the powers of divination.

2. On Russel, see my introduction to "The Complete Fortune Teller and Dream Book: An Antebellum Text 'By Chloe Russel, a Woman of Colour,'" *New England Quarterly* 78, no. 2 (June 2005): 259–88.
3. Errors in the narrative included in the copy at the Library Company of Philadelphia, paired with what may well be incidents of plagiarism in the text, yield serious questions about its authenticity as a black-authored text. I posit three possible scenarios: that Russel wrote the text, that a white publisher (possibly Hazard) wrote it and hoped to capitalize on her name, or that they collaborated. Research following the republication of the text hopefully will help us make better guesses at just which scenario is true. It should also be noted that the seeming plagiarism in *The Complete Fortune Teller* echoes issues raised about *The Bondwoman's Narrative*, which borrows liberally from Charles Dickens even as it constructs a unique tale around such borrowings. See, for example, Hollis Robbins, "Blackening Bleak House: Hannah Crafts' The Bondwoman's Narrative," in *In Search of Hannah Crafts: Critical Essays*, ed. Henry Louis Gates Jr. and Hollis Robbins (New York: Basic Civitas, 2004).
4. Scholars have found only a small bookshelf full of texts written by nineteenth-century black women; few of these date to before 1830. The number of texts about African American women and divination is similarly small.
5. Estelle Ellis et al., *At Home with Books: How Booklovers Live with and Care for Their Libraries* (New York: Carol Southern Books, 1995), 132–35, 136–37. All of the coauthors have design backgrounds—including Ellis's tenure at *House and Garden*.
6. Ibid., 37 and 21. The books of Nicholas A. Basbanes, the dean of writers about bibliophilia (which he terms "a gentle madness"), often parallel such treatment, though at times they have less of the country club feel. See Basbanes, *A Gentle Madness: Bibliophiles, Bibliomanes, and the Eternal Passion for Books* (New York: Henry Holt, 1995). See also Nicholas A. Basbanes, *Among the Gently Mad: Perspectives and Strategies for the Book Hunter in the Twenty-First Century* (New York: Henry Holt, 2002); Lawrence and Nancy Goldstone, *Slightly Chipped: Footnotes in Booklore* (New York: St. Martin's Griffin, 2000); and Lawrence and Nancy Goldstone, *Used and Rare: Travels in the Book World* (New York: St. Martin's Griffin, 1997).
7. Basbanes, *A Gentle Madness*, 394–404, 427.

8. Robert Adger's collecting (which resulted in one of the most important collections of early Afro-Americana, now at Wellesley)—as well as the book collections created for the early World's Fairs and the now-famous efforts of librarians at historically black colleges (Howard's Dorothy Porter Wesley stands most notable here)—focused on preserving cultural memory because, as librarian and historian Tony Martin notes, "In the book-collecting world, books dealing with blacks have been treated with casual regard." See Wendy Ball and Tony Martin, *Rare Afro-Americana: A Reconstruction of the Adger Library* (Boston: G. K. Hall, 1981).
9. Henry Louis Gates Jr., "Introduction," in Hannah Crafts, *The Bondwoman's Narrative*, ed. Henry Louis Gates Jr. (New York: Warner Books, 2003), xxi–xxii.
10. The purchase reportedly totaled 9,775 USD (8,500 USD plus the commission), which was actually below the 10,000 USD price set by Swann. Gates's was the only bid, and Swann accepted it; see Alexander J. Blenkinsopp, "Gates Acquires Slave's Novel," *Harvard Crimson*, November 14, 2001. For Swann Gallery catalog information, see their website, www.swanngalleries.com.
11. On the donation, see "Henry Louis Gates Donates Slave Novel to Yale University," *Black Issues in Higher Education* 20, no. 9 (June 19, 2003): 12. The manuscript's monetary value is now reportedly assessed at well over 100,000 USD, thanks in part to the place of Gates's edition on the *New York Times* Bestseller List. Thus, Gates is far different from the curiously conservative sense articulated by Walter Benjamin (and, one would assume, espoused by the collectors in *At Home with Books*) that "[t]o a book collector, you see, the true freedom of all books is somewhere on his shelves"; see Walter Benjamin, "Unpacking My Library: A Talk about Book Collecting" in *Illuminations*, ed. Hannah Arendt (London: Fontana Collings, 1973), 64.
12. On most days in early 2005, at least seventy-five items came up on a search of the "Books: Antiquarian and Collectible" category using the very specific phrase "African American"; given what is said below about searching—as well as about other categories—the volume of Afro-Americana available on eBay in a month is probably larger than that of many small auction catalogs.
13. The most recent auction of a first edition of *Incidents* ended with a last-second bid of over 2,000 USD on June 26, 2005 (item number 6540838524).
14. My discussion of collecting here and throughout the essay owes much to Russell W. Belk, *Collecting in a Consumer Society* (New York: Routledge, 1995), especially his sense of late-twentieth-century collecting as a partially democratic phenomenon enabled by the rise of the industrial and postindustrial capitalist state. See also Werner Muensterberger, *Collecting: An Unruly Passion* (Princeton, NJ: Princeton University Press, 1994). Books on books privilege the traditional sense of the book dealer. Basbanes, for example, quotes historian and bibliographer Katharine Kyes Leab: "Bookselling is theater, and that is something the Internet cannot duplicate. It cannot create the drama that the

dealer of the auction fires up in a collector's mind" (*Among the Gently Mad*, 89). Basbanes also notes, "Another difficulty some professionals have with online auctions, especially those mounted on www.eBay.com, is the total absence of accountability on the part of the auction house" (ibid., 89).

15. In fascinating ways, Swann Galleries clearly knew what it had yet did not, at all, know what it had. Central to Gates's decision to bid on the Crafts manuscript, for example, was the Swann catalog's notation that it came from the collection of black bibliophile Dorothy Porter Wesley (Gates, "Introduction," xxiv). Still, the gallery was unable to pursue authentication as far as Gates eventually did—including conversations with several rare book librarians and, with the backing of Lawrence Kirshbaum, the CEO of the AOL Time Warner Book Group (*The Bondwoman's Narrative* was published by Warner), an extensive examination by historical documents dealer Kenneth Rendell and manuscripts expert Joe Nickell.
16. Such sellers may not be dealers—or even knowledgeable about the field of Afro-Americana, per se—but may simply recognize that an object's exoticism or connections to the well-publicized collecting of "Black Americana" artifacts should call for a premium price. See David Pilgrim, "The Garbage Man: Why I Collect Racist Objects," *The Jim Crow Museum of Racist Memorabilia*, www.ferris.edu/news/jimcrow/collect/.
17. Though I hopefully never became the "bandit-cranking Vegas granny" continually hitting the Reload button who William Gibson describes in chapter 1 of this book, I was also far from the "reflective" and "beachcombing" browser Gibson comparatively notes. In essence, the moment when the "hunt"—the capitalist struggle—begins is marked by such obsessive behavior.
18. Belk, 93, as well as 61–101 generally.
19. eBay item numbers 6954160399, ended April 9, 2005, and 6950967178, ended March 19, 2005, respectively.
20. For the full policy, see http://pages.ebay.com/help/policies/offensive.html. A full study of eBay's policy is beyond the scope of this essay—though such certainly needs to be done. Several users play on eBay's policy to specifically sell items; rebel_soldier, for example, in an auction for the collection of supposedly "true stories about 'Hill-billies' and 'Negroes,'" Carl Carmer's 1934 *Stars Fell on Alabama*, noted that the sale was "ALMOST BANNED FROM eBAY!!!" See eBay item number 6950874224, ending on March 19, 2005.
21. On the conflicts surrounding racialized memories in the marketplace, consider, for example, the recent coverage of the discovery by Holly Jackson that Emma Dunham Kelley-Hawkins, long thought to be one of the earliest African American woman novelists, may have been white—including her summary dismissal from inclusion in future editions of the Schomburg Library of Nineteenth Century Black Women Writers. These changes to the construction of the scholarly memory of her race will undoubtedly shape the prices demanded for original editions of her books, which, in the hands of high-end,

specialized dealers, were, just prior to the announcement of the discovery, upward of 1,000 USD—with the rare *Four Girls at Cottage City* at 8,500 USD on abebooks.com by Between the Covers Rare Books, Inc. See Holly Jackson, "A Case of Mistaken Identity," *Boston Globe*, February 20, 2005; and David Mehegan, "Correcting a Case of Mistaken Identity," *Boston Globe*, March 5, 2005. There has even been some internet debate on just who has claim to this discovery—and how memory should be presented. Katherine Flynn, a well-known genealogist who had been researching Kelley and was ready to publish her findings in a peer-reviewed journal when Jackson's newspaper accounts came out, is quoted on one site as saying, "I think that with all that is at stake here it is time to stop publishing in the *Boston Globe* as if it was now the new premiere journal in English lit or AA lit studies without any references to census records or any systematic study of the whole record"; see www.plastic.com/article.html;sid=05/03/02/10155368;cmt=11.

22. The best work on the rhetoric—and the history—of the slave market is Walter Johnson, *Soul by Soul: Life inside the Antebellum Slave Market* (Cambridge, MA: Harvard University Press, 1999). Johnson's discussion on "Marking Race," 136–61, particularly influences my comments here.
23. Benjamin, 69.
24. In part hoping to balance the mercenary with the community oriented, I am in the process of donating my copy of *The Complete Fortune Teller* to a university library.
25. www.ferris.edu/news/jimcrow/collect/.

5

Reading eBay

Hidden Stores, Subjective Stories, and a People's History of the Archive

ZOE TRODD

On my final day at one of Cambridge University's all-women colleges, I rummaged through a hallway cabinet outside my room. Full of old papers, knick-knacks, and photographs, the cabinet had a storied past: in 1938, the then-occupant of my room departed suddenly under mysterious circumstances, and college authorities placed her belongings in the cabinet, where they remained undisturbed for the next half-century. Now I, who had dressed like Virginia Woolf for my college interview and lived in Sylvia Plath's room in my freshman year, sought in the cabinet more fragments of instant female ancestry. Deep in this cabinet of curiosities, I found a photograph of a young woman reading. Seemingly unaware of the photographer, she held a book, her face bent toward its pages. I kept the image.

INSTANT ANCESTRY AND EBAY'S ANTECEDENTS

The photograph was to be the first in a large collection: years later I discovered eBay, our latter-day cabinet of curiosities, and dozens of *cartes-de-visite* (CDVs) from 1840 to 1900, all of women holding or reading books. The first cheap, mass-produced photograph, with portrait studios located in the premises of hairdressers, butchers, and dentists, CDVs took the form of an individual bearer's photographic portrait mounted on sturdy cardboard stock (Figure 5.1).[1] Exchanged between people, CDVs were mementos of the giver; they were produced to be collected in albums and were also referred to as "album portraits." Collecting these images in albums was so widespread a practice that by 1866 Edward L. Wilson observed in the fall issue of the *Philadelphia Photographer*, "Everyone is surfeited with [the CDV] … everybody has exchanged with everybody."[2]

Figure 5.1 *Carte-de-visite* vintage photograph of girls holding books. Courtesy of Zoe Trodd.

As I rummaged through eBay's categories, the site reminded me of these album collections but also of the Renaissance *Wunderkammern*. eBay called to mind Thomas Platter's 1599 itemization of Walter Cope's cabinet: "a Madonna made of feathers, a chain made of monkey teeth, stone shears, a back-scratcher … an appartment stuffed with queer foreign objects in every corner."[3] eBay describes its "collectibles" category in similar terms: "Mickey Mouse and Tinkerbell items … a vintage Star Wars lunchbox … Napoleon Dynamite button or a Popeye bobble head … rare and one of a kind candle holders … Pez Dispensers, Keychains, and Promo Glasses."[4] eBay offers a melange of "anything that is strange," as a 1625 letter by Tradescant the Elder described the *Wunderkammer*, that "world of wonders in one cabinet shut."[5]

What Francis Bacon called "the shuffle of things" again passes through a "goodly huge cabinet," arranged and rearranged like a kaleidoscopic encyclopedia by eBay buyers with their Sort By and Customize Display options. Purchased items ship out like Renaissance collectors' New World curios, gathered for their *Wunderkammern*.[6]

Over time the Renaissance *Wunderkammer* evolved into the eighteenth-century American cabinet of curiosities; the nineteenth-century art studio and trompe l'oeil tradition; the dime museum with its freaks, waxworks, and relics; and, in the case of P. T. Barnum, *people* as curiosities. One of Barnum's pamphlets describes a woman as the "greatest natural and national curiosity in the world … [the] most astonishing and interesting curiosity."[7] Nineteenth-century freak shows often included such pamphlets chronicling the subjects' life stories: people became cabinet curiosities, and curious stories were central to the cabinet. Then, in the late nineteenth century, the *carte-de-visite* composite card, which sometimes featured up to a thousand tiny faces on one card, was advertised as a "photographic curiosity." *Cartes-de-visite* of people with unusual physical features were popular by the 1860s, and collectors made annotated albums in which they placed images of Renaissance artworks alongside those of celebrities, relatives, and natural wonders—creating in the form of the photo album their own personal cabinets of curiosities.

The fluid, chaotic cabinet of curiosities resurfaces as eBay, where one seller promises, "I have a little of everything." The *Wunderkammer*, the cabinet of curiosities, and my Cambridge cabinet seem to have new life online. Like all collectors who practice what Hayden White calls a "feverish rummaging of the past,"[8] I rummaged once again—in eBay's virtual "cabinet of curiosities." I found a listing for a CDV image about which the seller asked, "Wouldn't she make a great instant ancestor?" A different seller described the woman reader in a photograph as "a nice instant ancestor," and a third suggested of yet another image, "Recognize this as an image of your own past." eBay sellers of such images frequently invoke the instant ancestry of eBay collecting, as though suggesting we might make someone else's history our own and give these images the new context of our own stories, and seek the imagined identity and community *also* sought by nineteenth-century women readers photographed holding books.

To recollect these images on eBay fulfils the prophecy of one writer, who wrote of CDVs in 1862, "If a box or two … were to be sealed up and buried deep in the ground, to be dug up two or three centuries hence, what a prize they would be to the fortunate finder."[9] eBay's fortunate finders need not possess a fortune: just as the CDV was the everyperson's nineteenth-century portrait, so it can be the everyperson's collectible today. And just as the CDV could be a form of people's self-history, its twenty-first-century historians in the form of eBay sellers sustain its roots in people's history. As an online form of people's history, eBay remediates this popular form of earlier history making—one without a paper trail that challenged not only the nineteenth century's newly professionalizing historians with their focus on documents and disinterest in objects, but also its museum movement, and faith in the importance of classification and order within society and the archive. eBay's archive itself echoes the nineteenth-century CDVs of women with books included in its vast listings for auction. These images, initially collected into albums, were motley archives telling tales and narrating people's history, *themselves* exploring the storying of women, their stored yet story-like interior lives.

Allan Sekula argues that archives are "torn between narration and categorization, between chronology and inventory."[10] The story of the United States is equally "torn and between," and eBay-the-archive continues the saga. Archives "constitute a territory of images,"[11] and in eBay and its CDV listings we encounter the transient archive as a social as well as a physical place, and see women's history made and unmade by the archive and the auction house. eBay allows for a revisiting of gendered nineteenth-century tensions between objects and subjects, objective histories and subjective stories, archives and narratives, production and consumption. The site indicates how hidden stores or images may become stories, how the "I" enters eBay's sellers' "stores" to make "stor*i*es"—stories that narrate the individual "I" of the collectible little women in these images, consumed as art objects and storied as subjects by cameras, CDV albums, and eBay photographic thumbnails.

Much like my Cambridge rummaging, eBay's visitors repeat, if only virtually, nineteenth-century tours that exhumed relics from old family garrets. Yet it also reverses that era's tendency to bury unwanted history deep in its national cabinet. In 1863 Oliver Wendell Holmes wrote of burying war photographs in the recesses of a cabinet as one would the "mutilated remains of the dead they too vividly represented," the scenes "strewed with rags and wrecks" best archived, then forgotten.[12] eBay, however, unearths the fragments buried in the recesses of nineteenth-century America's cabinet; history appears where storied object meets seller's narrative, and where, as the eBay bulletin board "Collectible? or junk? Not sure what this is!" posits, story turns junk into collectible. Sekula further suggests that archives "maintain a hidden connection between knowledge and power," that they should be "read from below, from a position of solidarity with those displaced, deformed, silenced, or made invisible by the machineries of profit and progress."[13] To examine eBay listings for CDVs of women readers is to read the archive from below, to encounter a people's history, a suppressed countermemory, disjectia without a paper trail once deemed unworthy of the museum.

THE DIN OF SMALL VOICES

In the ebb and flow of eBay's memory machine, a people's history emerges: of the people and by the people, for the internet "era vibrat[es] with the din of small voices."[14] Part of a popular tradition maintained by "bards and story-tellers and minstrels … soothsayers and priests," eBay sellers are the opposite of certain "historians of the [nineteenth] century who found some special magic in the word 'scientific.'"[15] As unofficial historians, eBay sellers provide open-ended history, literary background on the books the women hold, and visual analyses ("there's a lot going on in this image," claims one seller). Anyone with internet access and a potentially collectible item can be a popular historian on eBay: one seller spots a note on the back of an image "that says S. Shattuck, 19 Central St., Lowell," and explains, "I looked him up and found the following," then invites other eBayers to contribute further information. eBay's bulletin boards for the "collectibles" community frequently contain requests from individuals seeking help identifying an item or its era, and many replies. The "Official Collectibles 'What IS it????' Thread," active since June 2002, even echoes Barnum's 1860s series "What is it?" similarly offering, unlike the museum, possibilities without definitive answers.

In 1847 Honoré de Balzac claimed that "the joy of buying bric-a-brac is a secondary delight: in the give-and-take of barter lies the joy of joys."[16] eBay's online forms of give-and-take and communal search for information make any histories mounted on the site less official than subjective and locate historical value in the eye of the individual. After speculating about a CDV, one seller adds, "Who knows? Buy it for what you think." Another concludes, "[B]ut you make up your own mind as to what this photo is all about." A third emphasizes, "This is only my opinion." Another states, "I'll call this Preacher Woman. I'll put my best guess forward, I would say … a female minister or perhaps a travelling preacher maybe with a sideshow … she has left clues … if I were on CSI or something like that I'd say she was a faith healer … it is a great image with tremendous potential." A popular historian reading "clues," referencing a tradition of popular detection that runs from Sherlock Holmes to *CSI*, the seller nonetheless concludes with an appeal to the open, fluid zone of potentiality.

Sellers develop plots around the women in these images, such as this Preacher Woman narrative.[17] They seek stories in the open books and the empty containers that often figure in the images too. One seller even imagines that an urn holds a "dear, departed loved one and [the figure] is in mourning." Sellers variously imagine the women to be "lively" or "austere," and give the images titles ("Her Favorite Book"), thereby echoing Paul Auster's description of a junk collector who sifts the city's "inexhaustible storehouse of shattered things … from the chipped to the smashed, from the dented to the squashed," and then "give[s] them names."[18] Sellers speculate as to whether the women might be sisters, or remark upon a "show of family closeness and affection." Making the histories of these nineteenth-century women readers their own, sellers speculate about the women's hidden stories: "[T]he way she seems to be resting her arm on her stomach, maybe she is pregnant," notes one. "The girl has an 'experienced' look which may indicate that she is an actress," says another, or a different seller comments that she "looks like she travelled some so may have been an actress."

eBay's CDV sellers imagine and give new meanings to the lives of these long-deceased women beyond the moment of pose: "I'm sure their mother dressed them alike a lot," says one seller of a CDV featuring two sisters. "You might think she grew up a spinster and the other one had 10 kids but I think the girl with glasses probably was more confident and happy with a great disposition," says another of two girls. At times sellers also imagine the moment of the photograph, rendering its production a drama complete with dialect: "[I]t's like the photographer just said 'you two just pretend like you wuz havin a conversation,'" writes one seller. Others point out unusual postures that might suggest a familiar relationship with the photographer, and one speculates that a woman's "wonderfully expressive face" shows "trepidation about the photo process." Yet another writes, "I'm not certain what her body language says. Maybe, I hate this stupid hat!"

History adds value to the collectible, stories help these items sell, and sellers consequently give the listed objects their own stories across time. Their descriptions include accounts of how and where they discovered the images: "found in attic of farm estate," for example. Sellers trace the passage from then to now, offering what Walter Benjamin calls "the testimony to the history which [the work of art] has experienced," without which "the aura" of the work of art "withers."[19] One describes the "edge-wear and soil" on an image (figure 1; as mentioned in note 1, this and all subsequent cited figures are available at www.people.fas.harvard.edu/~trodd/eBay/), adding that "someone along the way drew marks through the women's faces," encapsulating the storied status of both the CDV and the subjects it depicts.

The marks on the faces in this image might suggest age lines, traces of a lived life, as well as the photograph's own damaging passage through time. At times sellers even offer their own family history for sale: one image "is of a distant relative and his wife," another is "special for family reasons." Many sellers have acquired the images through years of Civil War reenacting, collecting them as souvenirs of a history they *made* their own through active and collective repetition of stories. They offer what Carl Becker calls the "impressions and images, out of which [Mr. Everyman] somehow manages ... to fashion a history, a patterned picture" that might not be "complete or completely true" but is relevant to "his idea of himself."[20] The commodity fetish for unstoried objects without paper trails becomes memory collection via souvenirs and storied relics, an ephemeral bric-a-brac collage of "impressions and images," stored and storied.

The narrativizing of objects is important in the context of online auctions. Narrative and stories counter the inability of viewers to touch the items for sale, and some sellers take pains to imitate the experience of a nonvirtual auction, describing, for example, the "bit of paper" that "adheres to the back from a time when the tintype was in its original cardboard frame." The site itself uses the click-to-enlarge device, which emulates the action of physically lifting an image closer, and sellers often photograph CDVs with their fingers visible at the edges, inserting an image of physicality much like the women readers with fingers tightly wedged between book pages (see figure 2). The women's physical contact with the books in the images is notable: even when tables are nearby for the book to rest upon, they still reach out to touch them, and one seller observes about an 1866 image that a girl's fingers are so insistently resting upon the page that "I suspect she's blind and reading Braille" (see figure 3; the United States actually adopted Braille later in the nineteenth century). As with the book in the image, sellers' gestures toward tactility work to insert material traces of history into the archive. Observing the physical connection between a woman and her book, one seller suggests this is the entryway to her story: "I wonder why she has her thumb in the book. I like it when these tell stories."

READING A WOMAN READING

The stories the sellers tell about the images have the same function as the books within the CDVs they sell: they introduce *narrative* into the archive. Burying their faces in books, the women readers are curious in the *other* sense of the word. The women readers often sit in front of cabinets (figure 4), and out of eBay's latter-day cabinet of curiosities emerge curious women readers who seek knowledge alongside their curious historians. Telling the story of one 1860s CDV, a seller comments about its four young women readers, "I found them to be curious." Here we see how these women readers resisted the dominant strain of nineteenth-century collecting culture organized by taxonomy, typology, and the archivist-curator who sought to classify and rationalize. Within these CDV images, it is the book that symbolizes the individual and storied life—the narratable self renarrated by eBay sellers today. The nineteenth-century physiognomical and art-historical search for truth revealed by external forms, and the Victorian attempt to read and classify the body, pushed interior life to the background. But the presence of books in collectible CDV images reclaims the secret histories dismissed by the dominant collecting impulse. The CDV women used the book lodged within the photograph to challenge the politics of collecting and surveillance and the nineteenth-century parlor and archive. The images are, as one eBay seller points out, a "social statement being made."

The *specific* books these women hold restore their history beyond the parlor: African American women hold books about abolition, postbellum women hold medical books to indicate their role as nurses during the Civil War, and women read suffragette volumes together. In one image a woman reader holds a whip, and its seller notes of the whip "that she appears to be using it to point to a passage in the book." For this seller, the woman might be a church worker, the book "a Bible, indicating the verse of 'spare the rod, spoil the child.'" Often the women's postures suggest the unreadable nature of closed books in the images—the women resist readability when the books are unreadable too (figure 5). Some women, photographed with men, stare at their books while the men look at them, and so invert the "ways of seeing" described by John Berger: "Men look at women," and "women watch themselves being looked at" and turn themselves "into an object … a sight."[21] In these CDVs women make their faces unreadable, averting their gaze toward the pages of the books they read: one seller describes "a photo of a lady who appears to be lost in thought with a book and her little dog, with a bow around its neck, looks at the camera." This seller adds, "I like this photo because so often the subject is looking into the camera, but here, she is reading."

Other CDV women readers insist on the presence of ongoing stories, events in time: in many images the only blur is that of the pages as they turn, or, if photographed with a man, a women often holds a book at the same angle as his fob-watch, or places it against her body at the same place as the watch, suggesting a life in time. Again suggesting the presence of a living story, one image positions two girls with books on either side of a third girl in white, seated and surrounded by flowers. As its seller points out, she is as pale as death, might *be* dead were it not that she is seated upright without obvious rigor mortis (figure 6). Bookless, storyless, hers is a kind of social death, while the standing girls hold their books at the same angle and wear the same dress. They're connected readers, part of a living community.

The blur of moving pages even appears in images where a solitary woman is interrupted in her reading and looks up from the book. Though interrupted, her story persists (figure 7). As one seller says of an image, "It looks for all the world like the photographer interrupted her reading and she responded by putting her book down but marking the page with her finger." In another image an interrupted reader stands directly above a stuffed dog. A second, bookless woman in the image faces to the left, mirrored by the right-facing dog that parallels her in a storyless state while the interrupted reader resists object status through the book (figure 8). This tradition of interrupted reading extends from the famous Gabriel Metsu painting of a woman being interrupted in her reading to a 1999 photograph by Joel Peter Witkin called *Interrupted Reading*, where a woman reader fragments into separate body parts as her reading is interrupted (figures 9 and 10). She keeps a finger between the pages of her book, as do most of the nineteenth-century interrupted CDV women readers, in resistance to the fragmentation of self through the interrupting, objectifying, classifying eye. Often posed next to small statue heads that sit, disembodied, at the same angle as their own heads, the CDV women readers on eBay have books to make them whole. The book stands for the *whole* story of the individual, as opposed to the story of *holes* and separated, cataloged parts (figure 11). Surrounded by empty vessels (urns, teapots, and boxes), women touch and hold the book, an open zone, and *whole* story.

As Benjamin points out, "[C]ollecting is a primal phenomenon of study: the student collects knowledge."[22] Though collected, the women readers are also collectors themselves—as the principal consumers of novels in this period, they are also consumers in these images, even while consumed as curious art objects. Collected within albums that had botanically themed surrounds, the women often hold their books beneath vases of flowers, or hanging vines, so that nature seems to explode from within the books' covers, spilling out like the loose pages of several books in other images (figure 12). In so doing they challenge—like the imaginative fiction of Victorian culture—the confined spaces of parlor, national archive, legible female body, and natural history museum. In one 1870s CDV, a woman holding a book also looks through binoculars, metaphorically connecting the book to the outside world. She is likely a bird-watcher and therefore a reader, gazer, and collector of bird sightings (figure 13). Using a taxonomical text, she inverts the usual dynamic of woman-as-collectible within dominant systems of classification. The object of her gaze lies beyond the photograph's edge, and the contents of her book remain invisible to the viewer. The book is a full but open potentiality of meaning, her mind a hidden store.

This woman is connected to the world via her reading, and in numerous other images women connect to one another *physically* through their books: groups of women touch one another and a book, sometimes with eyes connecting on the book's open pages. If only one woman touches the book, she tends to put her other hand on her friend's shoulder, so connecting her friend to the book via her intermediary body (figures 14–16). If several women in one image each hold a book, the *books* often touch each other, overlapping slightly on the table. The book, then, is a symbol of imagined community and a portal to an interactive realm: in one CDV a group of twelve women face in different directions, entirely disconnected as they wind yarn, knit, and play instruments. The sole connection is between two women in the background who gaze together at a book (figure 17).

In 1857 Lady Elizabeth Eastlake wrote of photography as a "new form of communication ... which now happily fills up the space between [people]."[23] Photography, like the novel before it, was a precursor to virtual communities of the internet and the eBay community that relies on this technology. Siegfried Kracauer writes that "photography tends to suggest endlessness" and probes into "an inexhaustible universe,"[24] and the book within the photograph within the eBay listing connects the women readers to that universe: it's a symbol like that of the key hanging on the blank wall in Nicolaes Maes's *An Old Woman Dozing over a Book* (1655), where the woman reader dreams herself into the inexhaustible universe of the imagination (figure 18).[25]

DYNAMIC DEBRIS AND HISTORY'S DUSTBIN

The concepts of inexhaustibility and renewability recur in discussions of photography, the archive, the auction, and eBay. Countering a static, taxonomized, and hierarchical archive with the model of narrative and story, CDVs of women with books are part of a tradition of biodegradable or replenishing history; this is echoed in form by eBay, a site of recovery, reinterpretation, and exchange. "If it isn't on eBay it doesn't exist," the slogan goes, echoing a nineteenth-century *Punch* parody of CDV albums: if your image is "not in the book it's because you're not wanted."[26] In exchanging the CDVs of women reading, eBay buyers and sellers give space to those whose real stories purportedly didn't "exist" because they weren't "wanted" as part of the Victorian national archive. A 2004 eBay TV ad asks, "What if nothing was ever forgotten? What if nothing was ever lost?" The "collectibles" section of eBay is a kind of archeological dig where forgotten and lost things are re-membered and re-collected. eBay inscribes the opposite impulse to that of Michael Landy, the installation artist who in 2001 destroyed all his possessions after making a full inventory; the eBayer-collector is instead like Charles Baudelaire's man who in 1860 "collects and catalogs everything the great city has cast off, everything it has lost, and discarded, and broken … collects the garbage that will become objects of utility or pleasure when refurbished by Industrial magic."[27]

During the nineteenth century, CDVs were understood as biodegradable history. "How long are card pictures to be the rage?" asked one critic in 1862. "In a few months or years at the most, our good patrons will have their albums full of dirty and yellow and faded pictures. Will they replace them with new ones?"[28] Even the albums were shifting narratives, with a first page inviting each viewer to add her or his own image after viewing, and so replenish the collection. As symbols of the inner lives of women, the books in the CDVs, like eBay, are archives of used and storied fragments. Collected into the parlor and taxonomized by late Victorian society, women found their stories consigned as fragments of what Leon Trotsky would later call the "dustbin of history," or what Benjamin would imagine as "aborted and broken-down matter."[29] eBay buyers who re-collect these stories *as* fragments adapt Henry Ford's famous statement, so that history becomes not bunk but *junk*; a collection of castoffs and a storehouse of relics become, on eBay, the auction house too.[30]

While the Victorian home was an archive of women as art objects and consumable goods, eBay and the internet bring the archive and auction into the home. The auction site breaks the boundaries that the CDV women also sought to transcend through reading and shatters the walls of the museum and the archive. Indeed, not the museum but rather the auction house creates the potential for an antitotalizing and biodegradable history. "My wish is that … my Curiosities … shall not be consigned to the cold tomb of a museum, and subjected to the stupid glance of the passer-by; but I require that they shall all be dispersed under the hammer of the Auctioneer, so that the pleasure which the acquiring of each one of them has given me shall be given again, in each case, to some inheritor," wrote Edmond de Goncourt in his 1896 will.[31] eBay wields this auctioneer's hammer and, with its different systems of archiving items (by price, date, and seller), even puts some auctioneer's tools in the hands of those bidding. And, while some sellers photograph their images alongside measuring sticks to indicate size, so echoing the rigid classification systems of the late nineteenth-century archive, many compare the image instead to miscellaneous objects: "Dimensions, approximately a little bigger then [*sic*] a pack of cigarettes," writes one seller about a CDV listed for auction.

eBay's renewable history has deep associations with the nineteenth-century women featured in the many CDVs listed on the site. In 1835 Lydia Maria Child favored "gathering up all the fragments, so that nothing is lost.... Nothing should be thrown away so long as it is possible to make any use of it," and in Laura Ingalls Wilder's *Little House* series, set in the 1870s and 1880s, Ma's scrap bag regenerates objects so that nothing is lost.[32] We also see this aesthetic in Louisa May Alcott's *Aunt Jo's Scrap Bag* anthologies, the March girls' quilt sewing in *Little Women*, Catherine Sloper's "morsel of fancy-work" at the end of Henry James's *Washington Square*, and Sethe's patchwork wedding dress and Sixo's friend of whom he says, "The pieces I am, she gather them and give them back to me" in Toni Morrison's *Beloved* (set in the late nineteenth century).[33] Scraps and junk are redeemed through story, and given new meanings and use values, just as the chaos of collectible items for sale on eBay is storied by these item's sellers and the fragments of women's stories are redeemed by the books depicted in CDVs. eBay's 2005 "One of a Kind Scrapbook Design Contest" continues the tradition: the winner and four of the five finalists were women who made stories out of scraps bought on eBay.[34]

Junk becomes a counterhistory, a potentiality. eBay, like women's nineteenth-century scrap bags, can be a site of alternate history making. Its shifting and dynamic archive is a storied store that renews the old cabinet of curiosities' archival tradition and rewrites the nineteenth-century gendered politics of the archive. One strain of the nineteenth-century archival imagination had sought a permanent totality, but as moving, shifting stories in time, the books within the CDVs instead anticipate a movable archive such as eBay's, where the "pile of debris" that famously "grows skyward" before Benjamin's angel of history is sifted, replenished, and also ceaselessly replaced in a real-time auction countdown reminiscent of Benjamin's "alarm clock that rouses the kitsch of the previous century to 'assembly.'"[35] Similarly, Susan Sontag's observation that photography is the "ceaseless replacement of the new"[36] in American society also applies to eBay's historical memory of sixty days, to the frequent comments by sellers that they're disposing of objects because their collections are full and need renewing, and to the idea that the internet more generally is "history's hugest living glossed manuscript, still and indefinitely in the process of production."[37]

Cartes-de-visite of women readers listed for auction on eBay emerge from the margins of that Web-based manuscript, their stories indefinitely renewed by eBay sellers and buyers, their books asserting their own gloss on history. While Benjamin glimpsed nineteenth-century photographs emerging "from the darkness of our grandfathers' days,"[38] the CDVs emerge from those days when the American woman reached, as Abba Goold Woolson put it in 1873, "the transition period of her history … midway between the fixed limitations of the past and the revealed possibilities of the future,"[39] and from the period that Benjamin also called "the era of the curio."[40] They emerge on eBay from the unofficial darkness of our grandmothers' days, like my instant Cambridge ancestor, unearthed from the darkness of her curious cabinet.

NOTES

1. Space only allows for this one image (Figure 5.1), but I have mounted a website with the other images discussed in this essay at www.people.fas.harvard.edu/~trodd/eBay/.
2. Edward L. Wilson in the *Philadelphia Photographer* (1866), cited in George Gilbert, *Photography: The Early Years* (New York: Harper & Row, 1980), 96.
3. Thomas Platter, *Thomas Platter's Travels in England 1599*, trans. Clare Williams (London: Jonathan Cape, 1937), 171–73.
4. http://collectibles.ebay.com.
5. Cited in Arthur MacGregor, ed., *Tradescant's Rarities* (Oxford: Clarendon, 1983), 15.
6. Francis Bacon, 1594, cited in Fulton Anderson, *Francis Bacon, His Career and Thought* (Los Angeles: University of Southern California Press, 1962), 24–71.
7. As described in an advertisement in the *New York Sun*, August 21, 1835. For a description of this particular "curiosity," see Phineas T. Barnum, *Barnum's Own Story*, ed. Waldo R. Browne (Boston: Peter Smith, 1972), 49.
8. Hayden White, "The Burden of History," *History and Theory* 5 (1966): 119.
9. "*Cartes-de-Visite*," *American Journal of Photography* (April 1862): 78.
10. Allan Sekula, "Reading an Archive," in *Blasted Allegories*, ed. Brian Wallis (New York: New Museum of Contemporary Art, 1987), 116.
11. Ibid., 118.
12. Oliver Wendell Holmes, "Doings of the Sunbeam," *Atlantic Monthly*, July 1863, 12.
13. Sekula, 119, 127.

14. Matt Drudge of *Drudge Report*, address to National Press Club, Washington, 1998. As reported by David T. Z. Mindich, *Wall Street Journal*, July 15, 1999, A18.
15. Carl Becker, *Everyman His Own Historian* (New York: F. S. Crofts, 1935), 247, 249.
16. Honoré de Balzac, *Cousin Pons* (1847; reprint, Boston: Dana Estes, 1901), 9.
17. See Michele White, chapter 16, for an account of how "gay interest" eBay sellers deploy similar narrative effects.
18. Paul Auster, *City of Glass* (Los Angeles: Sun & Moon, 1985), 76.
19. Walter Benjamin, "The Work of Art in the Age of Mechanical Reproduction," in *Illuminations*, ed. Hannah Arendt (New York: Harcourt, 1968), 271.
20. Becker, 245.
21. John Berger, *Ways of Seeing* (Harmondsworth, U.K.: Penguin, 1990, 1972), 46–47.
22. Walter Benjamin, *The Arcades Project* (Cambridge, MA: Harvard University Press, 1999), 210.
23. Lady Elizabeth Eastlake, "Photography" (1857), in *Classic Essays on Photography*, ed. Alan Trachtenberg (New Haven, CT: Leete's Island Books, 1980), 65.
24. Siegfried Kracauer, "Photography" (1927), in Trachtenberg, 264.
25. See figures 19–20 for comparable images.
26. T. Taylor, *Punch*, March 4, 1895.
27. Charles Baudelaire, *Artificial Paradise* (1860; reprint, New York: Herder and Herder, 1971), 7–8.
28. *Humphrey's Journal* 13 (1861–1862): 292.
29. Benjamin, *Arcades*, 203.
30. See figures 21–23 for nineteenth-century paintings that also figure history as junk.
31. Quoted in translation; B. Max Mehl catalog, *Catalog of the R. Taylor Sale*, November 8 (Fort Worth, TX: B. Max Mehl, 1932), rear cover.
32. Lydia Maria Child (1835), cited in Lynn Oshins, *Quilt Collections* (Washington: Acropolis, 1987), 3.
33. Henry James, *Washington Square* (1880; reprint, Harmondsworth, U.K.: Penguin, 1986), 220; and Toni Morrison, *Beloved* (New York: Penguin, 1987), 272.
34. http://pages.ebay.com/expowinner/.
35. Benjamin, "Theses," in *Illuminations*, 258; and Benjamin, *Arcades*, 205.
36. Susan Sontag, *On Photography* (New York: Doubleday, 1977), 68.
37. Thomas R. Martin, "Propagating Classics," paper presented at the annual meeting of the American Philological Association, December 28, 1997.
38. Benjamin, "A Short History of Photography," in Trachtenberg, 215.
39. Abba Goold Woolson, *Woman in American Society* (Boston: Roberts, 1873), v.
40. *Arcades*, 206.

6

Immaterial Labor in the eBay Community

The Work of Consumption in the "Network Society"

JON LILLIE

In the late 1990s, dot.com startups and multinational corporations worked to shift the culture and discourse of the World Wide Web from eclectic communitarianism and geek libertarianism to commercial media and e-commerce. eBay was a major player in this transformation. The company was one of the first to successfully apply the principles and technologies of online community toward the dominant regime of commerce and consumption. A key element of eBay's neoliberal business model is to attract networked individuals and train them in the precepts of eBay community members who do much of the company's work, from marketing and selling merchandise to customer service. eBay is a hybrid commercial entity that facilitates person-to-person (P2P) commerce with minimal infrastructure and relatively few employees, and its management understands and relies on the cultural sensibilities and technical labor power of its millions of active members. As a "community" of workers and a business, eBay is a prime example of the new commercial nodes that Manuel Castells describes as characteristic of the "network society."[1]

In this chapter, I discuss what eBay's community and its business model indicate about people's relationship to marketplace commodities in contemporary societies that are increasingly mediated and connected by information and communication technologies (ICTs). New ICTs offer individuation, choice, and a sense of autonomy in exchange for the work required by technology-mediated consumption practices.[2] I argue that predominant technology discourses, such as that of "virtual community" and arguments that progress is best actualized through ICTs, obscure the labor requirements and neoliberal politics of e-consumption. These discourses help to bring and then keep consumers and consumption online and, just as importantly, to keep e-business costs low by having consumers do the kinds of work once expected of a firm's employees and by using technology to match consumers with the goods they want or believe they need. eBay's significant influence therefore is primarily in its very successful extending of the culture and technologies of consumption. Although many progressive political and artistic groups use ICTs to expand social interaction and collective knowledge, the dominant discursive and technological regime of eBay champions a limited neoliberal version of the network society where the isolated yet purportedly savvy individual labors to engage the vast marketplace of consumable things.

EBAY'S LABORING COMMUNITY

In 2004, eBay U.S. contracted a new TV ad campaign for the winter holiday shopping season. Dubbed "The Power of All of Us," it moved away from the 2003 campaign's use of "My Way" performed by Frank Sinatra to laud the diversity of products available on eBay and instead returned to the narrative of online community. This narrative is central to the company's creation myth, just as it is central to the glory days of the noncommercial internet. "Belief," one of four television spots in the 2004 campaign, shows people picking up trash and holding open an elevator door as they help each other. The ad's voice-over intones, "We began with the belief that people are good. You proved it." "Belief" suggests that eBay's success relies on the kindness of strangers who come together on the site, and it was indeed eBayers' willingness to help each other that allowed the company to grow in its early days. eBay's founder, Pierre Omidyar, grounded AuctionWeb (eBay's precursor site) in the libertarian communitarian spirit of the early internet. Soon after AuctionWeb's first auctions in autumn 1995, Omidyar posted an open letter to users that established eBay's "fundamental values."[3] The first is "We believe people are basically good." The second privileges individual community participation: "We believe everyone has something to contribute."[4]

Internet researcher Jan Fernback has analyzed Omidyar's principles, noting that while eBay's narrative is communitarian, it also operates within a larger commercial discourse beyond which the community as a whole never moves. The community values statement "is steeped within the notion of organic solidarity. Terms such as 'honest, respect, open, good, members, and honor' connote a mood of unity, [yet] these values are delineated within the context of 'buying' and 'selling' so that the community is situated lexically and practically within the discourse of business."[5] Fernback's concern is that eBay members sacrifice privacy for social and commercial gratifications. He recognizes that the community offers benefits for some users other than commerce, but these come at the cost of being used by eBay for marketing and the value the firm extracts from user profile data.

All communities are created within a collective imaginary with which individuals and groups may or may not identify, and eBay's online community is experienced and defined differently by each member. Shared notions and experiences of community, however, are influenced by community narratives, geography, public spaces, and social interaction. No community is ever static or complete,[6] and individual identity, therefore, is always complex and conflicted, produced in the intersections between multiple imagined communities with which individuals identify variously and unequally. Online communities powered by ICTs promote specific forms of identification, and research shows that text-based computer-mediated communication encourages perceptions of equitable and horizontally organized dialogue that facilitates new members joining and feeling part of the group.[7] On eBay, one must be a member to buy or sell merchandise or to post to community forums. "Membership" thus invites identification with eBay, as does the social interaction that takes place in member forums.

Soon after AuctionWeb began to attract users, Omidyar introduced two important features that allowed users to contribute to the community beyond buying, selling, and communicating via email.[8] The first feature, the Feedback Forum, freed Omidyar from having to settle disputes between users. The technology (also discussed in chapters 7–9) allows buyers and sellers to rate each other cumulatively and to comment on each other's performance. The community is thus responsible for publicizing each member's reliability, and eBay administration acts on the community's feedback by suspending members with low ratings and excessive complaints.[9] The second feature introduced by Omidyar, the Bulletin Board, compensated for the fledgling company's lack of adequate customer support; users were encouraged to use the board to help each other learn how to use the site, and eBay's multiple public forums remain members' first and best option for most customer service and technical support questions. The company relied so heavily on the community acting effectively as customer service and technical support that it recruited one of its most active members, Jim Griffith, to answer customer emails. Using "Uncle Griff" to post as a community member on the Bulletin Board and a separate identity as an eBay employee for formal customer service emails, Griffith was the company's first paid customer service representative. Today the company's presence on community discussion boards is more transparent. eBay employees are identified by their pink-colored user names when they post on the boards, which they rarely do. Community members refer to them as "the pinks."

eBay community dialogue mostly takes place in the "Community" section of the site, which is divided into four sections: "Talk," "News," "Events," and "People." Most social interaction takes place in Talk, where members can read and post messages within several "Discussion Boards," engage in real-time text conversations in several "Chat" forums, or receive answers to technical questions in the "Answer Center." When eBay users enter the Answer Center, they first encounter the center's revealing title: "Member-to-Member Question & Answer Boards." All twenty-two Answer Center boards deal with eBay-related services, such as "Tools-Turbo Lister," "PayPal," and "Technical Issues." Pinks rarely post in Answer Center forums. Similarly, most topics on eBay's sixty-plus discussion boards relate to buying and selling on eBay. Several forums support general socializing, some with names that recall the techno-libertarian electronic-frontier manifestos of Howard Rheingold and John Perry Barlow: "The eBay Town Square," "The Homestead," "The Front Porch," and "The Park."[10] The eBay Town Square was created early on by Omidyar when members complained that there was no forum designated for noncommercial dialogue.[11] Topics within non-commerce-focused forums range from rants and babbling, to personal holiday rituals, to pleas for advice from members facing personal crises. These boards, however, the Town Square included, also feature continual discussions about using the eBay website and other auction-related topics.

"Business talk" is prohibited on several chat forums, but this only means that members cannot make deals directly with each other or conduct ad hoc auctions there. In eBay's chat rooms, users' posts load to one continuous scrolling page, with older messages at the bottom, as opposed to eBay's discussion forums, where posts are categorized by separate discussion threads. Still, most of the chat rooms are hobby or collectibles related, such as "Comics," "Dolls," "Elvis," and so on. New members are limited to ten chat postings and ten discussion postings per day until they amass at least ten feedback entries in their profile. This means that members must be at least somewhat active buyers or sellers. Although eBay's technology allows for several forms of interaction (email lists, discussion forums, photo albums, event calendars, and polls), it largely facilitates discussions and meetings related to buying and selling on eBay.

Although there are regionally specific forums on eBay, the community in general is not organized according to specific geographic places. The *eu topos* or "no place" of cyberspace and networked ICTs spans geographic, political, and social barriers, and the communities they make possible are predicated on a meeting of like-minded individuals in virtual environments where individual privacy, anonymity, and physical safety are more easily ensured than in many participants' real-world communities and lives. Cyberspace is based on liberating the subject from the limitations, inconveniences, inconstancies, dangers, and offenses of the places of the world outside the home or workplace, producing a discourse of social, economic, cultural, and public exchange devoid of place. Susan Leigh Star identifies the concerted, multifaceted, and overdetermined push "to make us live our lives on line, to abandon living and working in a particular locale."[12] One outcome of this discursive restructuring has been "the loss of urban communal space (eroded by privatization and replaced by 'pseudo-public space')—and it is this lost aspect of the city which has been replaced by cyberspace's 'virtual public sphere.'"[13] Significantly, the 1990s cyberflight of affluent American individuals to the internet occurred during a time of much suburban growth and urban decay. One irony of the eBay community, then, is that this "no place" created for exchange revolves around the trade of *material* goods that are contextualized and given meaning within actual geographic places and communities. Thus, eBay is a virtual community predicated on recirculation and reconfiguration of the material objects that form part of and signify place-based communities.

BUSINESS AND WORK THE EBAY WAY

While the company's television ads celebrate eBay's community structure and ethos, business and financial industries widely herald eBay for its innovative application of ICT. The company is a perfect example of a hybrid new economy enterprise. A profile compiled for potential investors by *Datamonitor* lists the firm's business model as one of its "biggest strengths."[14] Under this model, eBay has no inventory, low capital expenditures, and a global reach that tends to minimize the importance of political and geographic boundaries. Always open for business, eBay allows for real-time response among members; potential clientele includes internet users everywhere. eBay relies on its community to manage member personalities and questions so that paid employees can focus on maintaining and building eBay's most important asset: its website interface and auction software. As the market leader for online auctions and by far the Web's most visited e-commerce site, eBay has achieved a virtuous circle that explains its size and success: the larger it gets, the more items listed, the greater the likelihood buyers find interesting items worth their effort to acquire, the more sellers are attracted. Growth and profit, based largely but not exclusively on listing and transactional fees, depend on driving new users to the site. To increase traffic, eBay advertises extensively through traditional media, bulk mailings, and keyword-linked searches on Google and other internet search engines, and has forged marketing deals with AOL, MSN, and Yahoo!. A "Company Overview" available on eBay's site emphasizes global expansion; the company is spending upward of 100 million USD developing its Chinese site.

In his discussion of the network society, Castells identifies Cisco Systems as an example of a company well designed to thrive in the informational environment of the new economy, and his observations apply to eBay. Cisco uses its main website as a portal through which to manage commercial transactions (the site is the main mediator for sales), and information flows to and from customers. Cisco, like eBay, also utilizes a large intranet to maintain communication among employees. "By networking its operation internally and externally, Cisco Systems epitomizes the virtuous circle of the information technology revolution: the use of information technologies to enhance the technology of information, on the basis of organizational networking powered by information networks."[15] Castells also identifies Cisco and other technology companies as entities that have applied the "network logic" embodied in the technologies they design and sell to their own business and knowledge organization. For Castells, the new global economy is based on real-time management, flow, and the free exchange of information previously impeded by the vertical integration typifying twentieth-century corporate enterprises. Entities aligning themselves as networked nodes allowing for the free flow of information, knowledge, capital, and labor are more likely to adapt to the rapid pace of change in this global environment. This conclusion leads Castells to proclaim, "Networks are the fundamental stuff of which new organizations are and will be made."[16]

eBay is a better exemplar of Castells's argument than even Cisco Systems: the product that eBay sells is the website itself, including the Web-based transaction services enabled by eBay's software and that of subsidiary sites such as PayPal. The site facilitates online auctions by organizing information in the form of auction and product details to flow efficiently among the firm's customers. eBay's social interaction technology, combined with actual community participants, maintains and manages a vast amount of information about how eBay works and about current market conditions for an equally vast range of merchandise. eBay members function as network nodes, filtering and processing information and capital as it flows through the network. The many hobby- and collectibles-focused community forums, for example, channel cultural capital shared by members, archived by the website, and then actively applied by other members to gauge auction prices and product quality. In this sense, community members perform much of the work necessary for the everyday functioning and ongoing success of the website and the company that owns it.

Work done by eBay members organized as buyers, sellers, and community forum participants constitutes something of a textbook example of the labor increasingly required of consumers in contemporary capitalist society. Extending Michael Hardt, I characterize the type of work performed by eBayers as "immaterial labor," labor that creates an immaterial good—for example, communicating knowledge or providing a service.[17] Hardt delineates two types of immaterial labor. The first, which draws from Robert Reich, is composed of "symbolic-analytical services … tasks that involve 'problem-solving, problem identifying, and strategic brokering activities.'"[18] Many companies rely heavily on this type of labor through word processing, data entry, website maintenance, customer service through email, and so forth. This type of immaterial labor also recalls Antonio Negri's concept of the "social factory,"[19] a recognition that machine-like efficiency has transitioned from the industrial factory floor to the postindustrial service industries and consumer society as a whole; and Hardt suggests that its communication practices require impoverished, computer-like information processing even in face-to-face interactions. On eBay, this type of immaterial labor is performed by the millions of buyers, browsers, and sellers who visit eBay daily to troll, bid on, and interact with numerous auction listings. Such work is machine-like yet skilled; it requires proficiency in using computer hardware and Web software. Successful eBayers must acquire detailed knowledge of how online auctions work. In addition, sellers must package and ship items. In certain contexts, buyers too must engage in significant postauction labor. For example, individuals purchasing a car through eBay Motors are typically responsible for picking it up from the seller, which often means traveling by automobile or airplane to the pickup point and then driving the vehicle home. This skilled yet machine-like labor serves to construct the individual as a monad, a single node in the network who interacts with screen-based data more than people, even when the data are created by other people.

The second type of immaterial labor is "affective labor." Many service industry jobs produce affective labor—their "in-person" aspect is really the creation and manipulation of affects within customers and/or audiences with whom the laborers directly, virtually, or symbolically interact.[20] Although forms of immaterial labor predate the rise of capitalism (for example, caregiving, parenting, teaching, and forms of service performed by religious workers), Hardt notes they have been increasingly absorbed into the economy with the rise of postindustrial forms of production in areas such as sales, marketing, and customer service. Affective labor, in particular, garners high-value returns in the health industries (for example, nurses and therapists), service industries (for example, event organizers and employees working directly with customers in restaurants, clubs, and other entertainment venues), and cultural industries (for example, performers, artists, and sales and marketing personnel). Hardt argues that at its most productive, "what affective labor produces are social networks, forms of community, [and] biopower."[21] While human interaction in online auctions entails an instrumentalized form of immaterial labor, interaction on eBay community forums constitutes affective labor. Unlike the immaterial labor of symbolic-analytical services, affective labor seeks to produce positive results and lasting change in people. In the eBay community, the affective labor of members may assist those trying to complete commercial transactions, but such work is not solely directed toward commercial ends.[22] For some, everyday offers of assistance exemplify Omidyar's community values, yet such affective labor always takes place within the dominant commercial discourse. The content of community forums indicates that the vast majority of community labor directly supports (for example, auction troubleshooting) or indirectly supports (for example, discussions about collectibles) the auctions. With notable exceptions, it's ultimately all about the sale, arguably as it should be for an e-commerce website. However, the great influence that the eBay model has had in driving many ways of thinking about and using ICTs, along with its community narrative, open the company and its techno-libertarian neoliberal discourse to critique for how they constrain rather than enable human social, cultural, and political possibilities.

eBay's discursive production of social interaction and community obscures the work that members must do to participate in eBay commerce. When I go to a bricks-and-mortar store, I am at times aware of the work required to drive to the store, find parking, walk through the metal and concrete landscape, enter the store, find products, wait in the checkout line, make a return through customer service, and so forth. The labor in the e-commerce experience, however, remains strangely hidden, as much through the communitarian discourse as through the "magic" of technology and the related and sustained hype inviting users to experience ICTs according to the logic of a game. Kevin Robins has coined the term "techno-communitarianism" to describe the prevailing narrative of virtual community and how it takes place in the progress myth:

> These virtual ideologies are perpetuating the age-old idea of a communications utopia. Immediacy of communication is associated with the achievement of shared consciousness and mutual understanding. The illusion of transparency and consensus sustains the communitarian myth, now imagined at the scale of global electronic *Gemeinschaft*. It is an Edenic myth.[23]

Robins and Frank Webster argue elsewhere that the political philosophy of techno-communitarianism "represents the attempt to reconcile political idealism with the corporate reality principle. The new electronic communities that seem to promise the re-enchantment of social and political life are, in fact, the functional products of network capitalism, and are in no way contrary to its interests."[24] The traditional values and logic of Enlightenment liberalism, bound up in Western forms of modern citizenship cast, in part, in terms of marketplace rights and responsibilities, lurk behind techno-communitarian hype. eBay provides an excellent example of this dynamic at work—its community is both the master narrative and the glue that encourage member-citizens to participate in its marketplace.

The ideals of eBay as the "perfect store" and "perfect market" implicitly acknowledge eBayers as perfect citizen-consumers. Omidyar's vision for eBay is essentially about using technology to actualize the utopian ideal of the modern liberal subject—fully empowered without regard to class, race, gender, or economic background. eBay leverages ICTs and immaterial labor to empower the individual to find, obtain, and consume objects of desire. "If you come from a democratic, libertarian point of view, having a corporation just cram more and more products down your throat doesn't seem like a lot of fun," recounts Omidyar. "I wanted to do something different, to give the individual the power to be a producer as well as a consumer."[25] A key factor in explaining eBay's ongoing success is its success in communicating or branding itself as a collective of savvy, entrepreneurial, yet caring individuals; and in Omidyar's assertions, we see the belief that the free flow of affective labor in the eBay forums is partially fueled by a sense of joint participation in human social and economic evolution. Unlike some AOL volunteers, the majority of eBayers do not consider their labor to be *for* eBay; instead, they believe that they work for themselves. In this sense, eBay as a community functions somewhat like a co-op enterprise—by helping the common cause, for example by participating in community forums, members help maintain a commercial project in which they have established a stake. For Omidyar, technology as a mediator for social and economic transactions, and as a source and archive of knowledge and knowledge labor, can liberate the individual stakeholder to explore new depths in work and play, production and consumption.

eBay's discourses of individualism and community, articulated to the techno-utopic ideologies of ICTs, serve to insulate the company from certain critiques within the eBay community. The majority of anti-eBay sentiment is aimed at the existing "bugs" of online auctions, such as site navigation, billing software, and fraud protection.[26] Some eBayers lament the company's growth and arbitrary fee increases, as well as the influx of inexperienced newcomers to the site, but they never critique the scale of the online auctions themselves. They rarely, if ever, consider the consequences for place-based communities of the huge shift in volume of commercial transactions to online settings such as eBay. In contrast, while part of Wal-Mart's negative corporate image in the United States stems from its policy of expansion without community input, its glass-ceiling employment practices, and its abandonment of its promise to "always" sell American-made products, its status as the world's largest bricks-and-mortar retailer renders it a prime target for anticonsumption sentiments. The dominant discourse of the internet and ICTs obscures the very concrete and material connections between online commerce, culture, and community and the "offline" world. Many eBayers see computer-mediated P2P e-commerce as superior to the industrial-corporate culture and geographic inconveniences of large bricks-and-mortar retailers without acknowledging the hyphen or the bridge between *e* and *commerce* and therefore the necessary connections between purportedly utopian e-commerce contexts and the purportedly outmoded social, cultural, and political contexts informing "outdated" place-based retailing.

Stories of the middle-class family attic and the pack rat's garage bolster the eBay community narrative, but while some online auctions actualize the trash-to-treasure myth, eBay's broader success, ironically, depends on bricks-and-mortar retailers. Many items resold on the site were purchased at bricks-and-mortar retail outlets, a phenomenon critiqued by one eBay watcher: "[H]ey, a sucker born every minute you know. i saw lamps that were bought at walmart for 5 bucks get sold on ebay for 40 bucks. i would like to watch this auction and see who takes the bait."[27] My sister-in-law made a 900 USD profit by selling twenty wooden Advent calendars on eBay that she had bought at Costco, the giant North American membership-based retailer. Powerful bricks-and-mortars, such as Costco and Wal-Mart, leverage economies of scale, buying large quantities for a low per-item price, often from manufacturers taking advantage of cheap labor in newly industrializing countries.

Rather than circumnavigating the retail sector, then, eBay should be seen as actually extending their reach. The reality of eBay as a setting for real labor gets occluded by technotopian discoures of ease even as immaterial labor on eBay also depends upon the material labor exerted to produce these commodities in the first place. The macro- and micropolitical economic circumstances affecting the laboring bodies of producers vis-à-vis eBay traders can be quite different, but all their bodies are obscured through eBay's abstraction of exchange.

PERFECT STORE, PERFECT COMMUNITY, PERFECT CONSUMER

The mass of auction items, as well as the wealth of pop culture knowledge accessible via the eBay community boards, offer the individual consumer much more than a bricks-and-mortar store ever could. In this sense, the work of consumption is also at times the play of consumption. For the advanced consumer, eBay can be what Toys-R-Us is to a North American child. The immaterial labor of browsing, gathering knowledge, and making informed bids can be the play of consumption. Many people work for hours online and later play for hours online too. Like television, the Web in its current state facilitates both cultural and material consumption. Training for both modes of e-consumption takes place in many schools, workplaces, and homes in industrialized and wealthy areas of the world. The information society policy initiatives of several Western countries stress the need for ICT literacy so that citizens can be trained to be simultaneous e-workers and e-consumers.[28] The industrialized world has deployed the network-computer apparatus so that the modern demarcation between work and play—and increasingly among work, play, and consumption—is blurred.

By building processes for immaterial labor into eBay's technology, Omidyar and his team helped create a new economic sector ready for colonization by consumer culture, a virtual setting to engage in the neoliberal work and play of advanced consumption. In the network society, labor must be as flexible as information. Companies that seek to be flexible, modular, and scalable (again, like digital information) increasingly seek nonpermanent contract employees for as-needed skilled labor. The internet has also created a new economic sector that politicians and business pundits have envisioned as a financial panacea or niche for the "self-employed." It is not surprising that the eBay entrepreneur has become a popular job title in the press and, to a lesser extent, in the real world. United Press International, for example, recently heralded the rise of the eBay entrepreneur with a copious dose of upbeat nostalgia.

> The technology that powers the online auctions at eBay.com—and other online sites—actually is creating a new way of life for many. Online entrepreneurs are springing up once again, as if it were the boom era of the 1990s, this time selling goods nationally with the same relaxed air of an old fashioned flea market.[29]

The issue of whether a significant number of Americans are actually making it as self-employed online entrepreneurs became a hot topic when high monthly unemployment numbers from the U.S. Bureau of Labor Statistics (BLS) were released in September and October 2004. The high numbers were challenged by such heavy hitters as Vice President Dick Cheney, who asserted that the statistics failed to account for the 400,000 Americans who earn a living through eBay. The *Wall Street Journal* and other business pundits also criticized BLS numbers. "When a higher ratio of people make their livelihood as independent consultants to their old company, or as power sellers on eBay," the *Journal* claimed in an op-ed piece, "they don't show up in the establishment survey that provides the most widely used employment figures."[30] The *Journal*, however, was itself blasted for its editorial, which critics found to be apologetic and misleading.[31] I suggest that like the online community, the online entrepreneur is best understood not as an individual, a group, or a job category as much as a contemporary technology narrative, part and parcel of neoliberal ideologies, a discursive formation of the network society.

I have argued in this chapter that eBay's community discourse supports and extends the practices of advanced capitalism and consumer society. Are there ways, however, that the affective labor of this community might challenge the dominant paradigm of material production and consumption? eBay may have, as Lisa Bloom suggests (see chapter 15), a democratizing effect on some communities by eliminating middlemen and connecting directly small-scale producers with small-scale consumers. The development of affective labor and online collective knowledge communities such as Wikipedia can serve to promote positive social development in contrast to the proliferation of the machinic-type immaterial labor increasingly required of consumers. The sundry user interfaces that netizens deal with each day are designed for habituations. Yet each click and scroll can have important social, cultural, economic, and political implications. Affective labor communities may offer the potential to question naturalized assumptions about the efficiency of machinic labor.

Hardt suggests that affective labor might strengthen social bonds and solidarity across social hierarchies, thereby producing communities of shared experience with the will to challenge and possibly change oppressive social practices or institutions. In the case of the eBay community, for example, we might consider whether the production of collective knowledge encourages critical "consumption literacy." The community produces a large amount of knowledge about how material value is created, as well as product manufacturing, pricing, retailing, and so forth. But how many members achieve a critical awareness of such issues? And what is the likelihood that critical dialogue would go anywhere within forums where people mostly come to talk about the business and technology of online auctions? Although the cultural productions of the eBay community are varied and nuanced, from a critical and political economic perspective, eBay remains the perfect network society store because it so effectively applies ICTs to harness human labor within the consumption cycle, allowing citizens, who let their fingers do the walking, to perform multiple facets of their neoliberal postmodern consumer identities and techno-libertarian subjectivities.

eBay Director of Marketing Kevin McSpadden explains that the firm's 2004 American TV advertising campaign "is really a celebration of the trust that happens every day on eBay. eBay is more than the trading of stuff. It's about a sense of community experienced one-to-one."[32] McSpadden comes close to acknowledging that while eBay deploys the language of community, it is really a network of P2P goods and services. Conforming to Castells's vision of the network society, eBay is a network of individual people, bits of information, social and financial transactions, and representations of material objects. eBay's version of the network society imagines an efficient network, a technological assemblage facilitating neoliberal identity maintenance necessary for citizen-consumers to support the smooth flow of commerce. Just as the network society is a worldview that understands contemporary society through the metaphors, narratives, and infrastructures of ICTs, eBay uses its discourse of community to elevate the labor output of its members above the mundane, yet vital, work they perform at no charge to the company.

NOTES

1. Manuel Castells, *The Rise of the Network Society* (Oxford: Blackwell, 2000).
2. Consumption always entails labor. Advertising, widely held as a key development fueling the rise of industrialized consumer societies, requires consumers to work to distinguish among similar products. Shopping at retailers such as grocery, clothing, or hardware stores involves work too.
3. Adam Cohen, *The Perfect Store: Inside eBay* (London: Piatkus Books, 2002), 28.
4. The other three values are as follows: "We believe that an honest, open environment can bring out the best in people. We recognize and respect everyone

as a unique individual. We encourage you to treat others the way you want to be treated." eBay, "eBay's community Values," http://pages.ebay.com/help/newtoebay/values.html?ssPageName=comm:f:f (accessed May 13, 2005).

5. Jan Fernback, "Using Community to Sell: The Commodification of Community in Retail Web Sites," paper presented at the Third Annual Conference of the Association of Internet Researchers, October 13–16, 2002, Maastricht, the Netherlands, para. 24.
6. On communities as a collective imaginary, see Benedict Anderson, *Imagined Communities* (London: Verso, 1983). Anderson shows that American revolutionary period newspapers proselytized the idea of American nationhood and hence national identity—the nation as a community. The project of the American national community continues, propelled by the mainstream press, educational and civic institutions, and governmental bodies that create sundry narratives of community.
7. J. Siegel et al., "Group Processes in Computer-Mediated Communication," *Organizational Behavior and Human Decision Processes* 37 (1986): 157–87. Hierarchical forms of communication also occur in online settings. See R. Spears and M. Lea, "Panacea of Panopticon: The Hidden Power in Computer-Mediated Communication," *Communication Research* 21, no. 4 (1994): 427–59.
8. See Cohen, 28–29, 31–37.
9. Members face possible suspension when their rating reaches –4 points. Suspension also occurs after copyright violations, supplying false contact information, habitual nonpayment after winning auctions, and receiving a valid fraud complaint.
10. Howard Rheingold, *The Virtual Community: Homesteading on the Electronic Frontier* (Reading, MA: Addison-Wesley, 1993); and John Perry Barlow, "A Cyberspace Independence Declaration," *Electronic Frontier Foundation*, February 9, 1996, www.eff.org/Misc/Publications/John_Perry_Barlow/barlow_0296.declaration.txt (accessed June 21, 2005).
11. Cohen, 50.
12. Susan Leigh Star, "From Hestia to Home Page: Feminism and the Concept of Home in Cyberspace," in *The Cybercultures Reader*, ed. David Bell and Barbara M. Kennedy (London: Routledge, 2000), 639.
13. David Bell, "Scaling Cyberspaces: Introduction," in Bell and Kennedy, 629.
14. Datamonitor, *eBay Inc. Company Profile* (Williamstown, MA: MindBranch, 2004), 20.
15. Castells, 180.
16. Ibid. Although Castells has been criticized for promoting a decidedly postindustrial worldview, many social theorists and sociologists recognize similar practices across a range of new economy businesses. Michael Hardt argues "All of the forms of production exist within the networks of the world market and under the domination of the informational production of services."

Michael Hardt, "Affective Labor," paper presented at NEURO, Networking Europe, February 26–29, 2004, Munich, Germany, 5.

17. Hardt, "Affective Labor," 7.
18. Robert Reich, *The World of Nations: Preparing Ourselves for 21st-Century Capitalism* (New York: Knopf, 1991) 177. Cited in Hardt, "Affective Labor," 8.
19. Antonio Negri and Michael Hardt, *Empire* (Cambridge, MA: Harvard University Press, 2000).
20. Hardt, "Affective Labor," 9.
21. Ibid. Feminist scholars have studied women's emotional and caregiving work as examples of affective labor.
22. Many eBayers never interact directly with eBay community forums and neither offer nor utilize the affective labor that forums make possible; however, even these individuals must labor to use the auction technology that makes eBay e-commerce possible.
23. Kevin Robins, "Cyberspace and the World We Live In," in Bell and Kennedy, 90.
24. Kevin Robins and Frank Webster, *Times of the Technoculture: From the Information Society to the Virtual Life* (London: Routledge, 1999), 223.
25. Cited in Cohen, 7.
26. See Patricia O'Connell, "The Constant Challenge at eBay," *Business Week*, June 30, 2004; Tony Kontzer, "eBay Hit with Complaints," *InformationWeek*, June 21, 2004; and Bob Sullivan, "Man Arrested in Huge eBay Fraud," MSNBC.com, June 12, 2003, http://msnbc.msn.com/id/3078461 (accessed January 15, 2005).
27. pkagel, "eBay Suckers," *F150 Online Forums*, January 2, 2003, www.f150online.com/forums/archive/topic/71528-1.html (accessed December 20, 2004).
28. Jonathan Lillie, "A Critical Analysis of EU Mobile Narratives and the Ideal Citizen of the Mobile World," paper presented at the International Communication Association, May 26–30, 2005.
29. United Press International, "The Web: New Wave of Online Entrepreneurs," November 10, 2004, http://washingtontimes.com/upi-breaking/20041110-090817-3841r.htm (accessed May 12, 2005).
30. "Missing Jobs Found," *Wall Street Journal*, October 11, 2004, A18.
31. See, for example, "Wall Street Journal Editorial Misled Readers about State of the Economy," *Media Matters*, October 13, 2004, http://mediamatters.org/items/200410130004 (accessed May 12, 2005).
32. Theresa Howard, "Ads Pump up eBay Community with Good Feelings," USA Today.com, October 17, 2004, www.usatoday.com/tech/webguide/internetlife/2004-10-17-ebay-community-ads_x.htm (accessed May 5, 2005).

7

The Perfect Community

Disciplining the eBay User

KYLIE JARRETT

"Community" is a key term in the eBay universe. The company overview of eBay Australia boldly proclaims it as "the world's largest personal online trading *community*,"[1] and the theme of community is central within the history of the company as described by Adam Cohen.[2] Within developer Pierre Omidyar's conceptualization of the auction site was a pragmatic notion of using community members to take over the support work generally done by a company's employees and thus reduce his efforts and costs. But underlying its development was also an ideal typical of early internet culture in both commercial and nonprofit arenas: the ideal of a perfect community, based on a social contract, where people made real connections with each other.[3]

Community on eBay also has a vital economic function. It is elemental in establishing the consumer trust that enables the site to function.[4] eBay's success has depended upon the construction of community and community norms that effectively police the activities and transactions on the eBay site, providing the "private ordering" as described in David Baron's account of eBay traders.[5] Community also provides the site with a range of commercial advantages specific to the e-commerce environment. It increases the site's "stickiness"—a key factor in repeat consumer investment—by creating compelling content. The affective environment also increases consumer "switching costs"—the financial, temporal, or emotional costs involved in connecting to and becoming engaged with another product or site—and promotes consumer lock-in. This in turn produces "network effects," which simply means that the greater the number of buyers, the more appeal the site has to sellers, and the greater the number of sellers, the more attractive eBay is to buyers.[6] Coupled with its first-mover advantage, this mobilization of community in terms of commercial advantage has been fundamental in making eBay the premier auction site globally.

Yet community on eBay is neither merely a convenient economic driver nor a simple reflection of Omidyar's libertarian ideals. It is also a disciplining tool within a framework of neoliberal governance wherein direct government (or corporate) intervention is rolled back in favor of a form of diffused control that highlights individual agency and empowerment. The particular representation and construction of individual action and community on the site serve to discipline users, in the sense deployed by Michel Foucault,[7] into a regime of practice in which collective surveillance of individual agency produces "safe" trading and thereby ensures the company's success.

Using insights provided by critical or sociolinguistics,[8] this chapter explores the particular discursive mobilization of community on eBay as an example of the disciplining power typical of contemporary neoliberal political economy. In doing so, this analysis does not accord any *a priori* existence to the community referred to on the site; neither does it imply that community relations experienced by members are false or misleading. Rather, it investigates the *representation* of community in the site's structures and how that particular discursive formation works as a unique articulation of power relations. An exploration of the linguistic (grammatical and semantic) elements as well as key structural features of the site (hypertext and feedback mechanisms) reveals a powerful, seductive disciplining machinery, reflecting principles of liberal self-governance. It is my underlying contention that eBay functions as a prime example of a new, more liberalized form of disciplining, involving a reliance on a vision of neo-Panoptic surveillance in which the work of the elite guards, encased in the central tower in Jeremy Bentham's original vision, is now diffused and taken up by those who are surveyed. My argument is that in the discursive representation of community relations on eBay, the watchers and the watched become indistinguishable in an (almost) perfect articulation of self-directed governance. By exploring the language of the site and how eBay encourages compliance with its policies, it is possible to see a reflection of the broad neoliberal political economy and, in doing so, open up criticism of the exercise of power in that domain. To make this claim, however, it is first necessary to define the contours of ideal neoliberal governance.

AUTONOMY, COMMUNITY, AND NEOLIBERALISM

In his analysis of contemporary practices of governmentality, Nikolas Rose contends that liberalism, as a rationality of governance, problematizes the very idea of government itself.[9] Liberalism's emphasis on the active freedom and autonomy of its subjects renders direct forms of state intervention invalid. Liberalism is thus, from the outset, intrinsically concerned with the problem of how political sovereignty can be legitimately exercised without contravening the rights and interests it attributes to subjects. But most important, for this principle of government to be effective, it "requires of the governed that they freely conduct themselves in a certain rational way."[10] This demands intervention on a micropolitical level, often at the level of the individual, but one mediated through impersonal, objective—and therefore ideally politically neutral—institutions. In order to fulfill these competing criteria, a liberal government works "at a distance," utilizing an array of technologies of the self—technologies that produce subjects already geared to the dictates of liberal rule—rather than forcible imposition of its will. This hegemonizing impetus places a premium on seemingly noncoercive mechanisms of internal discipline, sites of normative judgment and expertise through which "correct" practice is inculcated and normalized within the psychology of the individual citizen. Liberal government is achieved through managing the "conduct of conduct": "through educating citizens, in their professional roles and in their personal lives—in the languages in which they interpret their experiences, the norms by which they should evaluate them, the techniques by which they should seek to improve them."[11]

In what Rose describes as advanced liberal democracies, this expertise has become increasingly specific and inverted. Rather than existing as norms, or moral injunctions, to be instilled in citizens by an exterior dictate, expertise regarding conduct has become increasingly self-directed and self-determined. The reconfiguring of the citizen that occurred in the transition from the welfare state to advanced or neoliberal capitalism allowed government to "conceive of these actors in new ways as subjects of responsibility, autonomy and choice, and seek to act upon them through shaping and utilizing their freedom."[12] This reconfiguring involves duties and obligations on behalf of rational subjects. Individual citizens are asked to become active and involved in the management of their own lives and its risks, to accept greater responsibility for their own actions. This internalization of the conduct of conduct produces a subject that Rose describes as a self-steering self, obliged by the dictates of liberal government to "be free": "to construe all aspects of life as the outcome of choices made among a number of options. Each attribute of the person is to be realized through decision, and justified in terms of motives, needs, and aspirations of the self."[13] Effectively, the self-steering self must take responsibility for its own way of being in the world, to control its own destiny through a series of rational-critical choices intended to optimize, wherever possible, individual goals and opportunities.

Thus, in Rose's interpretation there is a two-pronged quality of liberal governance. One is the minimization of direct government intervention and instead its diffusion through institutional regimes of discipline. This ensures the (relative) autonomy of individual citizens. The other is what Rose terms the "responsibilization" of individuals for their own practice. Neoliberal freedom, then, is necessarily companioned with responsibility.

As Rose argues, a key site for the "responsibilization" of the autonomous self within advanced liberal governments is "community." The ethic of liberal governance demands that government govern without governing society, leading to a problematization of government intervention at the level of mass society. But more important, the specification of active and responsible subjects of government associated with neoliberal democracies changes the relationship between individuals and the social. Under neoliberalism, society—the broad, overarching formation organizing political strategies—is dethroned from its dominant position in the conceptual and moral framework of individual citizenship "regulated through the mediating party of the State"[14] to be replaced with the amorphous idea of community "as a new territory for the administration of individual and collective existence, a new plane or surface upon which micro-moral relations among persons are conceptualized and administered."[15] Community—smaller and multiple social formations—becomes a key institution for the delineation and policing of ethical values that serve to sustain liberal societies and markets.

Cohen's account of eBay's history clearly indicates the role of community as such an organizing principle. He cites Omidyar's observation that the brand experience on what was then AuctionWeb (eBay's precursor) was centered on how customers treated each other, noting Omidyar's conviction that for his customers to have a positive experience of the site, he had to find a way to make them treat each other well. It was at this time that Omidyar developed the Feedback Forum, the central plank of community on eBay, in order to "enforce good behaviour."[16] In this articulation, community is explicitly identified as the "territory for the administration of the individual and collective existence" of the eBay market, constructed to ensure compliance with a (loose) regulatory environment. How this is achieved, though, is not clear in Cohen's account. By delving further into the representation of community on the eBay site today, it is possible to see the particular mechanisms by which community serves this function and how it disciplines its users into "good behavior."

COMMUNITY VALUES AND AUTONOMY

The key site for the articulation of community on eBay is the declaration of community values. These five principles establish the ethical framework that (ideally) structures the interactions of community members and, consequently, what establishes a sense of a secure trading environment. The declaration reads as follows:

> eBay is a community that encourages open and honest communication among all its members. Our community is guided by five fundamental values:
>
> [1.] We believe people are basically good.
> [2.] We believe everyone has something to contribute.
> [3.] We believe that an honest, open environment can bring out the best in people.
> [4.] We recognise and respect everyone as a unique individual.
> [5.] We encourage you to treat others the way you want to be treated.
>
> eBay is firmly committed to these principles. And we believe that community members should also honour them—whether buying, selling, or chatting with eBay friends.[17]

The "we" in these statements is ambiguous. At times it appears to refer to eBay as a corporate entity, and at other instances to the community of users. However, a closer reading of the text indicates that the firm imposes these values on its users. In the anthropomorphizing statement following the fifth principle, eBay-the-firm moves to separate itself from community members and, particularly in the use of the moral imperative "should," to declare its position as authorizing agent of the site's particular set of community values.

This question of authority becomes blurred, however, when the tone of the declaration is taken into account. Although referred to as fundamental, the weak modality by which eBay expresses its five principles converts these utterances into guidelines or suggestions. The firm's limited use of direct imperatives, and its reliance instead on declarative statements of belief, deny these utterances the status of commands. Further, the use of conditional, modulated expressions such as "We believe people are basically good" as opposed to the strong modality of "People are basically good" works to mitigate the company's expression of corporate power. The one notable use of an imperative in the list is also a weakened verb form. Community members are *encouraged* to treat others the way they would like to be treated, rather than directed to do so—"You *will* treat others ..." This style of representation further mitigates the exercise of power in eBay's declaration.

In neoliberal fashion, eBay discursively aligns its stated *values* (as opposed to rules) with morality, affect, and emotion rather than, for instance, a legislative or punitive discourse. The declaration of the Christian ethos of "Do unto others" and the construction of these guidelines primarily as "beliefs" locate them in an immaterial, internalized field of action—the field of self-fashioning.[18] In John Searle's analysis of the performative qualities of speech acts, the mental process verb "to believe" is associated with assertion and, as such, the verb is not essentially or typically about convincing another individual.[19] The beliefs in eBay's community values therefore read less as commands to action than as expressions of the inner sensibility of some putative ideal community member, be that eBay-the-firm or any one individual seller or buyer. Although eBay may be declaring the principles and the rules that users must (or "should") follow when using the site, the weakness of the modality with which they are expressed allows them to be read instead as a vague, strangely affective, and already existent sensibility. eBay represents, and thereby defines, the determining values of its community less as an effect of its own direct injunctions and more as an emergent property of vaguely defined yet "warm and fuzzy" affective entities.

Throughout the entire site, eBay's representation of itself minimizes its own authority, either through a weak modality or by offering its injunctions against behavior in the form of advice to sellers and buyers. This self-definition continues in its promotion of the brand outside of the confines of the online community. Despite its significant economic power, eBay actively sustains a "little guy" folksy image in its public relations and advertising campaigns, from the persistent characterization of CEO Meg Whitman as a self-effacing "den mother" to the perpetuation of the acknowledged marketing ploy of the PEZ legend on the Australian website's overview of the company.[20] This is not to argue, however, that this representational style necessarily equates an actual concession of power to consumers. eBay's ability to make unilateral decisions, such as releasing consumer information to law enforcement officials, remains intact.[21] Nevertheless, the company chooses to *represent* itself in a manner that appears to deny its own power.

THE AUTONOMOUS USER

eBay's mitigation of its own authorizing power establishes it in a relationship with its users marked by a degree of equity. It positions itself as within the community rather than dictating terms from above. If power is relational in conversational discourse, as argued by sociolinguists,[22] then in this appearance of withdrawal from an authorizing role, eBay extends more authority to its traders. Thus, the company not only adopts a minimal governmental model typical of contemporary neoliberal state governments, but in doing so also foregrounds the activity of users.

eBay's position as a commercial site within a hypertextual medium further positions buyers and sellers as agents. The status of any utterance as hypertext opens it up to consumer agency. All anchor text is actional and dependent on consumer choice for activation. Direct imperatives, commonly used within e-commerce sites and marketing generally, are thus typically read by users as offers; the imperatives are transformed from commands into polite interrogatives by the effects of hypertext. This further mitigates any use of direct imperatives on the site. It would be a naïve Web user or shopper who understood the grammatical imperative, enhanced by its hypertextual underscoring,

> Learn more about buying.[23]

as an actual command to do so. Instead, the imperative has the inverse effect of hyperactivating and extending power (and responsibility and therefore greater consequence) to the user's own choices—"If I wish to learn more about buying, I can decide to click here." In such a way, the *interactive* site positions the individual as the central figure in determining actions taken at the site.

This is further evidenced in eBay's constant reminders that "safe" trading involves users taking the initiative to research their own sellers, goods, or buyers.[24] eBay will not tell a user what to buy or whom to trust. Instead each individual entirely determines these choices. Coupled with the mitigation of the company's authority at the grammatical level, this hypertextual and conceptual framework of action extends a sense of autonomous agency to the individuated eBay user.

This representation of the relationship between eBay and its users can be understood in relation to the liability concerns of the company, as described by Baron.[25] eBay takes little to no responsibility for the vast majority of items sold on its sites and instead situates itself as a mediator only. Instead the onus is on sellers and buyers to ensure the authenticity or legality of sale objects, with eBay acting merely as a venue rather than driver of content. In linguistically denying its own agency within the site, and by offering apparent deference to that of the user, eBay discursively works to circumvent as much as possible corporate responsibility for fraud and misrepresentation by buyers and sellers, and insinuates itself as no more responsible than any other "community" member for what transpires on its site. In this legal environment, it is imperative that eBay represent its users as relatively autonomous and therefore relatively powerful, even as this representation has the effect of interpellating eBayers as individuals with a sense of autonomy, choice, and self-direction. Although users are capable of rejecting any given interpellation, this particular formation is central within the discourse of safe trading on the site. On eBay, buyers are clearly expected to be self-choosing, self-directed, and self-steering individuals.

THE RESPONSIBLE USER

In a "free" marketplace such as eBay, where almost anything and everything are exchanged, the construction of users as entirely self-choosing is fraught. Individually empowered consumers can potentially seek to maximize their own profit at the expense of others, and without interventionist external controls there is potential for fraud and mistrust (see chapter 8). Yet for most users, eBay is a "safe" trading environment. Consequently, there must be some policing that delimits the absolute autonomy of the liberal consumer otherwise represented on the site. In part this occurs through eBay exerting itself as an arbitrary authority involved in direct policing (see chapter 17). But there is also a more diffused exercise of authority that has enabled the multitude of "safe" trades to occur. It is my argument that this policing is effected through a "responsibilization" of consumers in terms of community standards and community-directed surveillance.

The first responsibilization occurs, ironically, through the autonomy extended to the user. By linguistically and structurally withdrawing from a position of authority, eBay also withdraws from responsibility for ensuring "safe" trading. If all actions and the eBay experience are seemingly an effect of users' choices, it is users who become solely responsible for ensuring effective trades. Simultaneously, the user becomes the agent responsible for any negative trading experience. Such an outcome is reflected in the preponderance of active verb forms attributed to user action as opposed to that of eBay: "To be protected by eBay's safety measures including the Buyer Protection Program, it is essential you always complete your transaction on the site,"[26] for example, could be rephrased as "eBay will provide safety measures providing the transaction is completed on the site." Such a rephrasing would highlight eBay's activity and responsibility over that of its site's users. Instead, as currently organized by eBay's discursive practices, negative experiences are represented as an effect of an individual's failure to research buyer, seller, or goods properly, or to have utilized secure financial exchange systems such as the company's escrow facilities. It becomes the user's failure to apply "common sense," rather than a systemic failing of the company or its website, that results in a bad trade.[27] Representing and structurally locating eBay users as autonomous agents in this way renders them as the sole or principal agents of their own trading success or failure. In this individuating discourse, individual users take on responsibility for the nature of the eBay experience.

It would appear, then, that eBay's discourse is primarily concerned with the individuation of users and their personal responsibility in producing the eBay experience. However, as represented on the site, each individual's success is also bound to community activity. "Since the early days of eBay, members have helped other members be successful on eBay."[28] Successful trading is consistently linked to reviewing a trader's reputation, which is an effect of community judgment. This is explicitly stated on the site's "About Feedback" page, where leaving feedback is positioned as important, for it "helps everyone in the community know what it's like to deal with that member and impacts the success and behaviour of other eBay members."[29] Buyers and sellers are here made aware that it is the social contract among members that is fundamental to any one individual's trading, binding the individuated user back into community relations as an organizing principle.

Community is also underscored in the four guidelines that form the first point of eBay's "Safe Trading Overview."[30] The first refers to individual responsibility, but the second suggests learning from other users on a community chat board. The third warns against trading with members outside the community as defined by the borders of eBay's website. And the fourth explicitly ties safe trading to the "Do unto others" ethos outlined in the community values: "eBay is a friendly and open community so it is important you treat everyone with the same integrity you expect to receive from others."[31] As vague as this golden rule may be, on eBay it is identified as commensurate with safe trading. Individuals must be *responsible for* their own actions but also *responsible to* the community in order to achieve success on the site.

NEOLIBERAL, NEOPANOPTIC

eBay's Feedback Forum technology formalizes the kinds of ethical framing I have just discussed. The forum provides a clear example of a mechanism intended to discipline the eBay user. By offering to all users a record of any other user ID's trading history, it serves as a Panoptic surveillance tool, albeit in an updated, perhaps more subtle form. Bentham's Panopticon, as described by Foucault, employs guards occupying a central tower who can observe the activity of the prisoners in the cells arrayed around the tower. The prisoners, however, cannot see the guards and so are unaware of when they are under direct surveillance. Foucault's argument is that the prisoners, always potentially exposed to the guard's gaze and judgment of their behavior, internalize that gaze and take on the guards' judgment as their own. They come to police their own activity. As Foucault says, the major effect of the Panopticon is "to induce in the inmate a state of conscious and permanent visibility that assures the automatic functioning of power."[32]

On eBay, the Feedback Forum serves as such a device. Whether a buyer or a seller, the individual user, conscious of the *possibility* of censure for conduct inconsistent with community values, *polices her or his own conduct*. On eBay, this occurs not only out of fear of reprisals but also, and I would suggest primarily, for the success the site associates with adherence. Each individual's benefit from a trade, in the form of positive feedback and possible subsequent trade, is maximized by adopting the fair trading principles that govern the site and define the community. Consequently, the user does not need to be constantly and punitively policed by external forces. Instead, buyers and sellers internalize and accept the disciplinary logic undergirding the rules of the site, inculcating them into their own practices in order to maximize their own trading benefits. The normative judgment of the eBay community is thus also normalizing.

eBay's use of surveillance, though, renovates that of Bentham's Panopticon. In Bentham's original prison, surveillant power was associated with a powerful elite, located in the central control tower of the prison, watching each prisoner. However, in the model utilized by eBay, all buyers and sellers have the opportunity to view and see the consequences of any other's actions. Rather than surveillance being effected by a centralized elite guard, the forum distributes the power of surveillance to *all* buyers and sellers within the eBay community. In this neo-Panopticon, the watcher and the watched are no longer differentiated. The power to police and the power to discipline are, thereby, decentralized and diffused. This is in keeping with eBay's discursive withdrawal from a position of absolute authority and its emphasis on individual responsibility. It is not eBay as an elite authority that disciplines, but "the community," with each individual taking on responsibility for ensuring adherence to community norms by other members and her or himself.

This is clearly a more liberalized Panopticon than Bentham's model, but not only in that it denies the centralization of power in an appointed elite. It is also more liberal in that it effects its disciplining, not in the form of coercion by an external force, but disguised as an exercise of free will and autonomous, responsibilized activity.[33] Buyers and sellers on eBay are not *forced* to publicly display their profiles and thereby submit to collective scrutiny. Rather, they are led to compliance through the alignment of successful trading, either as buyer or seller, with submission to surveillance. The site makes clear the potential penalty that may be exacted on those who resist the community's gaze: "Keep your member profile public—buyers may be wary of trading with someone with a private member profile."[34] This spells out that success is possible *only* for those who willingly accept community surveillance rather than those who seek to avoid it. Nonetheless, this subjection is represented as each trader's free choice.

The site also encourages users to submit to neo-Panoptic scrutiny. "Openness" is valorized repeatedly: feedback is given in "the spirit of providing openly-available information,"[35] the opening statement of eBay's community values equates openness with honesty, and the *Australian e-Commerce Safety Guide 2005*, accessible from eBay's Security and Resolution Centre, states, "Empowering individuals to make sensible decisions and an open and transparent community are the foundations of any crime-fighting strategy."[36] To be open to surveillance, then, becomes the cornerstone of safe trading on eBay. Surveillance is represented as good, even desirable, for the community and the individual (whose interests are discursively aligned), but by making it ostensibly optional, eBay ensures that compliance seems to remain a matter of individual free choice.

eBay's combination of a discursive style that autonomizes, and thereby responsibilizes, individual users with its surveillant community feedback technology amounts to the perfect neoliberal disciplining assemblage. The Feedback Forum is primarily a form of instrumental control, a key goal of which, in Foucault's terms, is to restore "the obedient subject, the individual subjected to habits, rules, orders, an authority that is exercised continually around him and upon him, and which he must allow to function automatically in him."[37] In this instance, the obedient subject is one who accepts community values as defined by eBay and who, therefore, engages in fair trading.

In Foucault's reckoning, such a form of enforcement must be accompanied by a system of signification that involves the methodical and objective cataloging of crime and the establishment of an irreversible relationship between that crime and its punishment. Without evidence of what is deemed appropriate, the immanent punitive power of surveillance does not function. It is in "the representations of his interests, the representation of his advantages and disadvantages, pleasure and displeasure," that a penalty can "gain control of the individual."[38] Thus, what I will call the "technique of representation" and the "technique of surveillance" work together synergistically, like a network effect, to constitute a disciplined individual. The former codifies behavior, and the latter effects the control, the coercion that ensures the inscription of that behavior into the soul or self of that individual.

On eBay, the discourse that appears to minimize eBay's direct intervention and that highlights the individual responsibility of users to the community is a technique of representation, signifying the interests, practices, and values of the ideal user to buyers, sellers, and browsers alike. Such discourse represents the value of autonomy and self-direction by associating trading success with the practice of individual research. But the site also signifies the importance of community norms, "open and honest" communication for instance, in achieving that goal. This representational system is enforced and made into a coercive schema by the surveillance and encoding of individual practice provided by the feedback mechanisms.

Through these techniques, and therefore through the notion of community upon which they rely, the form of corporate governance that eBay effects acts "at a distance." It is this that aligns eBay's disciplining with that of neoliberal governance. Like contemporary state governments, eBay effects the dual movement of minimizing direct intervention and diffusing power through institutionalized disciplining practices articulated around a vaguely defined concept of community. But also like neoliberal state governments, in doing so eBay reduces the visibility of its power, making it more elusive, more amorphous, and therefore more difficult to directly oppose. This is the particular technique of power in operation in what Zygmunt Bauman refers to as "liquid modernity." He argues that in neoliberal capitalist societies, the solid fixity of Bentham's Panopticon has ceded to a more fluid, dynamic, mobile regime of power that is increasingly invisible and that defeats traditional forms of resistance.[39] Diffused power such as that exerted by eBay denies a clear and externalized target of opposition. The success of eBay then is not merely as an online auction site. Perhaps its greatest success is also as a model of neoliberal governance that, through its use of the seductive appeal of free choice organized by individual responsibility to community norms, is almost impossible to resist.

PERFECT COMMUNITY, PERFECT DISCIPLINE

What my analysis reveals, then, is the *a priori* addressing of the eBay user as an autonomous, self-directed individual but one for whom benefits accrue by aligning her or himself with the values of the broader community. The site creates a subject position for its users embodying the key characteristics of an ideal neoliberal subject—autonomous and responsibile. The user can reject this interpellation, but the disciplining feedback mechanism of the site and the "punishment" of bad or unsafe trading that follows from resistance serve to ensure a general acceptance of this position. In its disciplining role, eBay is not only a *product of* liberal ideals of autonomous, self-directed, but restrained individuals, but also *productive of* subjectivities aligned with these ideals.

This productive capacity is important, as Omidyar's dream of a perfect market can only be actualized in relation to an equally "perfect" community of self-directed, self-maximizing liberal subjects. It is vital, then, that the site encourages disciplined and ethically bound consumers. Yet producing such self-disciplining, productive capacities is more broadly important still, as eBay also serves as one site, among many, in which the currently hegemonic ideal of liberal citizenship is perpetuated and reinforced (see chapter 6). The disciplining power of the site makes eBay the perfect community[40] not only for the company's affectively connected users, but also for the contemporary political economy.

It is perhaps this final point that is most important, for it indicates the broader significance of eBay and this analysis of its mobilization of community. The site clearly and persuasively articulates a normative model of governance commensurate with the contemporary neoliberal political economy and offers an ideal model of such government. Activating individual autonomy, but at the same time responsibility to a set of norms located in a "community," certainly "liberalizes" power but without reducing any of its potency. But my analysis does not merely reveal eBay as an example of the effectiveness of neoliberal governance models. It also reveals methods for identifying and understanding the subtle, potentially invisible techniques of power associated with that form. By investigating how eBay articulates its power relations, it is possible to understand more about the techniques of power now utilized in broader political arenas. Further exploration of the mobilization of similar discourses of community self-policing within politically charged environments, such as, for instance, community-based care for the elderly, can offer useful insights into the workings of power within the contemporary state. But even more significant, identifying these techniques can open the way to new interventions into the exercise of power in neoliberal economies. In its clear and transparent articulation of community as a disciplining tool, eBay is a guide to understanding and engaging with the political economy of this age.

NOTES

1. eBay, "Company Overview," http://pages.ebay.com.au/community/aboutebay/overview/index.html (emphasis added; accessed December 3, 2004).
2. Adam Cohen, *The Perfect Store: Inside eBay* (London: Piatkus, 2002).
3. Ibid., 8.
4. Josh Boyd, "In Community We Trust: Online Security Communication at eBay," *Journal of Computer-Mediated Communication* 7, no. 3 (April 2002): www.ascusc.org/jcmc/vol7/issue3/boyd.html (accessed October 17, 2002).
5. David P. Baron, "Private Ordering on the Internet: The eBay Community of Traders," *Business and Politics* 4, no. 3 (2002): 245–74.
6. Ibid., 253.
7. Michel Foucault, *Discipline and Punish: The Birth of the Prison*, trans. Alan Sheridan (1977; London: Penguin, 1991).
8. Critical or sociolinguistics is the study of the relationship between language and culture and/or the use of language in society, specifically in terms of power and ideology. It focuses on language use *in situ* rather than the essential physiological or grammatical principles behind utterances, and is based on a belief that language is a central vehicle in the construction of individual identities and therefore that analysis of texts can expose the workings of ideology in society.
9. Nikolas Rose, *Powers of Freedom: Reframing Political Thought*, (Cambridge: Cambridge University Press, 1999); also Nikolas Rose, *Inventing Our Selves: Psychology, Power and Personhood* (New York: Cambridge University Press, 1998); Nikolas Rose, "The Death of the Social? Re-figuring the Territory of Government," *Economy and Society* 25, no. 3 (1996): 327–56; and Nikolas Rose, "Governing 'Advanced Liberal' Democracies," in *Foucault and Political Reason: Liberalism, Neo-liberalism and Rationalities of Government*, ed. Andrew Barry, Thomas Osborne, and Nikolas Rose (London: UCL Press, 1996), 37–64.
10. Graham Burchell, "Liberal Government and Techniques of the Self," in Barry, Osborne, and Rose, 24.
11. Rose, *Inventing Ourselves*, 76.
12. Rose "Governing 'Advanced Liberal' Democracies," 53–54.
13. Rose, *Inventing Ourselves*, 100.
14. Ibid., 330–31.
15. Ibid., 331.
16. Cohen, 27.
17. eBay, "eBay Community Values," http://pages.ebay.com.au/help/confidence/community-values.html (accessed December 3, 2004).
18. Rose, *Powers of Freedom*, 41–43.
19. John Searle, *Speech Acts: An Essay in the Philosophy of Language* (New York: Cambridge University Press, 1969).

20. eBay, "About eBay Overview," http://pages.ebay.com.au/community/aboutebay/overview/index.html (accessed December 3, 2004). Cohen notes that eBay has successfully leveraged this image to combat competitors such as Onsale, 96–98. See also Patricia Sellers, "eBay's Secret," *Fortune* 150, no. 7 (October 18, 2004): 50–81.
21. See Jonah Engle "Buyer Beware: eBay Security Chief Turns Website into Arm of the Law," *Nation*, June 20, 2003, www.thenation.com/doc.mhtml?i=20030707&c=1&s=engle (accessed December 2, 2004).
22. See Roger Fowler and Gunther Kress, "Rules and Regulations," in *Language and Control*, ed. Roger Fowler et al. (London: Routledge and Kegan Paul, 1979), 26–45.
23. eBay Australia home page, www.ebay.com.au (accessed January 11, 2005).
24. eBay, "Safe Trading Overview," http://pages.ebay.com.au/help/confidence/overview.html#G1 (accessed January 11, 2005).
25. Baron, 250–52.
26. eBay, "Safe Trading Overview."
27. Ibid.
28. eBay, "Community," http://pages.ebay.com.au/aboutebay/community.html (accessed January 11, 2005).
29. eBay, "About Feedback," http://pages.ebay.com.au/help/feedback/feedback.html (accessed December 3, 2004).
30. eBay, "Safe Trading Overview."
31. Ibid.
32. Foucault, 201.
33. Zygmunt Bauman, *Liquid Modernity* (Cambridge: Polity Press, 2000).
34. eBay, "What Is Feedback?" http://pages.ebay.com.au/help/feedback/questions/feedback.html (accessed January 11, 2005).
35. eBay, "Safe Trading Overview."
36. "Avoiding Fraud," in *Australian e-Commerce Safety Guide 2005*, http://pages.ebay.com.au/securitycentre/EcommGuide_2005.pdf (accessed March 4, 2005), 8.
37. Foucault, 128–29.
38. Ibid., 127.
39. Bauman, 9–11.
40. This does not mean that eBay's community is any less "real" or full of affective importance for its members. It is, however, to identify eBay's community as, at the same time, a seductive tool of normalization within neoliberal societies.

8

"Black Friday" and Feedback Bombing

An Examination of Trust and Online Community in eBay's Early History

LAURA ROBINSON

In August 1999, eBay announced new reserve auction policies that sparked a community-wide crisis known as "Black Friday." Although the policy changes were economic in nature, committed eBay members interpreted them as an attack on the eBay community. When eBay's administration attempted to restore an economic frame as the basis of discussion, members swarmed eBay's message boards to mobilize protest and organize an online boycott.

Within this context, I administered an online questionnaire composed of open-ended queries to members openly critical of the new policies; members were asked to describe their own experiences and trust in the eBay system. I emailed fifty-nine members who had posted to eBay's Discuss New Features Board during a two-hour period on August 23, 1999. Within the hour, I received two emails from eBay members I had not contacted; both asked to participate in the study. One informed me that my original email had been posted on other boards serving the eBay community. In the subsequent forty-eight hours, unsolicited members continued to notify me of their interest in taking part in the study, even expressing indignation at not being invited. I then posted an open call for members on the Discuss New Features, eBay Café, and AOL Café boards. On their own initiative, eBay members on several boards repeatedly posted this "invitation" during the subsequent three days. This recruitment procedure generated an emergency sample of thirty-one individual members. Given the time frame constraints created by the Black Friday crisis, an emergency sample was the only sampling method available. As such, this data cannot be generalized to the eBay user population as a whole; rather, the data reveal how these committed eBay members, feeling aggrieved and invested in the crisis, made sense of their participation in eBay.

More specifically, the data shed light on how self-selecting committed members approached their own relationship with the eBay community and the eBay administration. Through it, we understand their perceptions of the events preceding this crisis and the steps that they believed eBay could have taken to avert it. Members reported that Black Friday acted as a catalyst that brought other long-standing problems to a head. From this perspective, outcry over the new policies may be interpreted as a second-order trust problem. Respondents voiced deep concern regarding larger issues of broken community, most notably their collective and individual disillusionment with the Feedback Forum. Ongoing issues of broken trust and the feedback system created a malaise ripe for Black Friday to explode as a full-blown crisis. Black Friday was the tipping point that caused members to critically evaluate their vision of eBay, marking a brutal shift in their perception of eBay as an idealized community to eBay as a community betrayed by its own administration.

Black Friday is a crucial juncture in eBay's history that underscores the commercialization of the internet during the late 1990s. The crisis occurred midway between eBay's initial public offering (IPO) on September 24, 1998, when eBay was capitalized at more than 2 billion USD, and the dot.com collapse that began on April 14, 2000. Adam Cohen notes that after the IPO, during online commerce's unprecedented growth in the late 1990s, economic mandates undermined Pierre Omidyar's original vision of eBay and its community.[1] Thus, this early chapter in eBay history provides important insight into issues of trust and community during a pivotal moment when market dictates collided with community expectations.

BLACK FRIDAY, AUGUST 20, 1999: OUTAGES AND RESERVE AUCTIONS

In the summer of 1999, eBay was plagued by a series of devastating "outages" or site crashes during which buyers could neither access nor bid on auctions.[2] eBay ends auctions at a specific "hard" time that cannot be altered or extended by any party to the transaction. Under normal circumstances, buyers can bid until the last second. Since many bidders wait to "snipe" or outbid other buyers in an auction's final seconds, the highest bids are often made literally at the last second. The 1999 outages prematurely arrested bidding—buyers could not access auctions, bids were diminished, and auctions closed with artificially low bids. Sellers were forced to honor these bids and, in some cases, practically give away expensive wares at a fraction of their worth.

In response to the outages, sellers claimed that eBay encouraged the use of "reserve auctions." In reserve auctions, sellers set a minimum price that bidders are obligated to meet to win the auction. While the reserve price is not disclosed in a listing, the current bid on a reserve auction is accompanied by a statement indicating whether or not the seller's reserve price has been met. If bidders do not meet or exceed the reserve price, the auction concludes without a winner. Reserve auctions protect sellers against unprofitable sales because sellers are not forced to accept inferior bids.[3]

By placing the onus on sellers, members felt that eBay forced them to use reserve auctions as a risk-management strategy. Sarah[4] explained, "The recurring outages on eBay are one major reason why sellers need the protection of reserves, especially in view of eBay's reluctance to confront the fact that 'intermittent availability' (a cowardly euphemism if I ever heard one, and another example of refusing to accept responsibility) poses an unacceptable risk to sellers who do not use reserves." Kelly reported sending eBay the following message: "Be sure to explain about the outages that happen so frequently on eBay and also explain that it is actually true that you [eBay] advised the sellers to be sure to put reserves on their items so that their items would be protected from selling way below their values in case of an outage."[5]

In response to complaints about outages, members reported that eBay promised sellers free listings as compensation for fees already paid for compromised auctions.[6] However, members claimed that eBay never honored this promise. Even worse, members said that fast on the heels of a series of devastating outages, eBay announced new policies governing the reserve auctions that the site had promoted to sellers concerned by outages. Under the new policies, eBay required sellers to begin reserve auctions at no less than 25 percent of the reserve price, and a charge of 1 USD would be added to the listing fee. Sellers described this as a double blow. First, the new policies required extra fees from sellers to use the very feature eBay had encouraged despite the company's failure to ensure site stability. Second, sellers would no longer be able to choose their own starting price for reserve auctions.

Members reported that eBay's announcement of these changes late on Friday, August 20 unleashed the Black Friday crisis. Stewart elucidated the overwhelmingly negative reaction to the policies: "The changes were poorly thought through... . They didn't take their bread and butter users into consideration when they made them and finally they announced and implemented them in about the very worst way possible ... right on the heels of several days of disastrous system outage and performance problems which infuriated many, many users." Martha delineated, "eBay has become famous for their service outages. Early complaints resulted in their recommendation to use reserve auctions to protect merchandise that was in an auction affected by outage. Now they have recently decided to extort an additional fee for using reserve auctions." Mae sent the following message to eBay that expresses the infuriation members reported feeling:

> Your [eBay's] first email to me about the important changes to eBay reserve auction rules I found to be a total insult to all of us sellers >: ... I wonder why you [eBay] didn't mention the other very important reason for why we use reserve auctions which is ... WARNING WARNING!!!!! OUTAGES EBAY IS DOWN ... OUTAGES EBAY IS DOWN ... OUTAGES EBAY IS DOWN ... AND NO ONE CAN BID ON YOUR VALUABLE ITEMS ... AND IT ISN'T PROTECTED BY A RESERVE YOU WILL BE GIVING IT AWAY ... remember it was your [eBay's] kindly advice that we should simply put reserves on our items so that we would then be protected...

Members accused eBay of betraying its community by creating an unreliable venue, placing the burden of protection on sellers, and then penalizing them with additional fees.

"IT'S ONLY A DOLLAR"

In response to the community's negative reaction, eBay's founder Pierre Omidyar (known as "Pierre" to the eBay community)[7] delivered his now infamous "It's only a dollar" message. According to members, Omidyar explained the rationale for the policies: "Reserve price auctions had two fundamental problems, from our point of view: one, buyers don't like them; and two, they cost more for us to support," adding, "It's only a dollar."[8] Members interpreted the tone and content of Omidyar's message as hypocritical because he claimed that reserve auctions were costly for the site, yet failed to acknowledge that in practice, sellers often listed items multiple times before receiving an acceptable bid. Kelly argued, "While I use reserves on 90% of my auctions you must also remember that I pay a listing fee when I list the reserved item. If the item doesn't sell ... I relist the item with a reserve again. Now I've had a number of items that I've relisted for four or more times... . Each time I do this I pay the listing fee."

Members reported their willingness to pay relisting fees to ensure a fair selling price as long as they remained in control of the starting price. However, sellers explained that while the eBay administration argued that opening reserve auctions at 25 percent of reserve prices would encourage bidders, this rationale ran counter to the "basic psychology of bidding." According to Katherine, the new policies would have resulted in decreased revenue for both eBay and sellers: "No! no! no! ... in my thirty years as a dealer ... if the auctioneer tries to get the bidding started at a too high figure we all sit on our hands ... it works the same way on eBay, if that starting bid is too high no one bids... . I just recently sold an item that I had a reserve price on for $2500 ... my starting bid was $50. I wouldn't have dared to have put in a much bigger starting bid because I wouldn't have got any action." Sarah affirmed, "Anyone conversant with the basic psychology of bidding (and I would hope that includes someone at eBay administration) must realize that a low opening bid hooks people's interest and permits them to commit themselves gradually to an item." Sellers believed that by charging an extra dollar per reserve auction, perhaps eBay would have made more money, but contended that by forcing reserve auctions to begin at 25 percent of reserve price, both sellers and eBay would have lost revenue.

ONLINE PROTEST: THE COMMUNITY'S RESPONSE TO BROKEN TRUST

In addition to economically damaging aspects of the crisis, members saw the policies as a violation of their community. Sarah explained,

> One reason we are all so angry is that so many of us bought into the eBay rhetoric about this being a community. In a community, decisions are made after discussion, when some consensus is reached. eBay is not a community, friends—the fact that eBay blamed this reserve policy on the whining of bidders ... is a good example of how they exploit their own rhetoric. We may have been chumps to believe that this is a community ... eBay's just betrayed the trust of all eBay users and showed its contempt for bidders as well as sellers! ... eBay has not been forthright ... and hurt a lot of us in the process.

Katherine confirmed,

> I am very UNHAPPY with the fact that Pierre made his sellers sound like they were morons. I am very UNHAPPY with the fact that Pierre gave the UK a free five weeks of listings and kept delaying our one day of free listings, which were to PAY for the June outage... . I am very UNHAPPY with the fact that Pierre does not respect his COMMUNITY enough to apologize for offending them... . I am very UNHAPPY with the fact that Pierre has NOT

> addressed STABILITY… . Yes … I am unhappy about the changes BUT mostly because of the way they were presented and the attitude behind it.

Many respondents reported being dependent on eBay for their livelihoods; for them, insult was added to injury. Mike explained, "I do object to the rude and insulting manner that was used to inform and justify them [the new policies]." Not surprisingly, the multibillionaire Omidyar later referred to his "one dollar" message as "those famous words I wish I could retract."[9]

Feeling estranged from the administration, members framed eBay as two opposing camps: community versus the administration. Elizabeth lamented the loss of community: "I really believed that we were a COMMUNITY and that is the feeling I had being there. Like going to the park and meeting up with friends … but now I learned that the friends are the buyers and sellers and the landlord who keeps telling us that it is a VENUE but forces HIS ideas down our throats has changed my mind about eBay." Danielle redefined the site from community-based to hierarchical: "[T]he whole attitude of eBay has shifted from a partnership based [on] mutual benefits to an us (the sellers) and them (the management) mentality." These members' new visions of eBay separated the site administration from its community of users.

Members responded to the new policies with a boycott. Lisa explained, "I'm boycotting. I hate them. The complete lack of concern or civility eBay has shown over the past few weeks has completely turned me off from ever using eBay again." Nancy reported, "I'm not selling on eBay right now. I'm boycotting them because of the price increase to those of us who have a reserve price, because we have quality merchandise and need to protect our investment." Danielle felt that it was unethical to list on eBay during the crisis: "I cannot list right now on eBay with the atmosphere the way it is and the way we are being treated by the founder … and the UNDERHANDED things he has done by giving the UK five weeks of free listings but not mentioning it to the US who have been waiting for our ONE day of free promised for us in June for July but moved yet again." Members felt driven to boycott because of what they framed as eBay's disreputable behavior. Aurora explained, "[I] believe it is unconscionable. Their excuses for instituting the changes were bogus and unsupported by fact. Their manner of dealing with this has been inept, rude and insulting to any intelligent person. [I] believe they are just greedy." Members began to call eBay "Greede-Bay" because they believed that its administration was willing to sacrifice community to corporate profit.

LARGER ISSUES OF BROKEN TRUST: RETALIATORY FEEDBACK

Black Friday brought other issues of broken trust to a head. Members explained that further cleavages existed between the official site rhetoric and the reality experienced by committed members. They asserted that the feedback system was systematically undermined and devalued.[10] While eBay rhetoric asserted that the percentage of negative feedback was very low, members reported that this was not necessarily an accurate reflection of members' experiences. Further, they claimed that the eBay administration was well aware of the problems plaguing the feedback system but did nothing to protect its community.

Members explained that feedback was not transparent. Bob elucidated, "Positives are left on non transactional basis by friends, etc. Ten plus or 100 plus really makes no difference."[11] Kate asserted, "It is still too easy to give false registration information on eBay. Many have multiple ID's and bid on their items to run up the bid price. Some have [a] 'bidding ring' they belong to and they act together to influence the prices of their items." For Kate, when eBay failed to protect members against unethical behavior, eBay broke promises implicit in its rhetoric regarding the Feedback Forum's integrity.

Even if feedback was from a genuine transaction, positive comments were frequently "padded," as Stewart explained: "The feedback system on eBay has become a joke, it is so ineffective. People actually solicit feedback from others during transactions … not in ways that violate eBay's rule but still in ways which compromise how genuine the comments really are." When positive feedback was left by a user who would not have left it without solicitation, its value was diminished. Moreover, feedback ratings alone were inadequate guides to sellers' trustworthiness because feedback ratings generated by numerous transactions of low-cost goods could produce higher levels of positive feedback than a feedback rating from fewer transactions featuring expensive items. Barbara revealed, "Feedback is easy to get if you are selling trading cards and posting 200 auctions at a time … the seller who sells high end items but limited to how many … may deserve the same attention as a person with high numbers." In order to interpret positive feedback, competent members were forced to decipher the mechanisms behind it. Often, the only way to do this was to read the text comments in the Feedback Forum in addition to the composite score to ascertain whether or not positive feedback was what it appeared to be.

By reading these comments, competent members ascertained the feedback's real value. Michael reported, "eBay has monkeyed with it [feedback] to the point that I read positive and neutral comments also because neg comments have been devalued." Once negative comments were "devalued," positive and neutral comments became mediums by which members recorded negative transactions. Elizabeth explained how a positive or neutral comment could really indicate a negative: "Sellers seem to have a fear of retaliation in regards to giving negative feedback. I am not sure that all are honest. 'Transaction completed' means almost negative. I don't care if positive is checked." For these members, the numerical value assigned to a comment had significantly less value than the comment itself.

Even more damaging, members reported that sellers were so zealous in guarding their reputations that they acted in an individually rational manner that was collectively irrational. That is, they protected themselves against negative feedback at the cost of undermining the entire Feedback Forum because they felt that eBay did not regulate feedback. Although eBay finally allowed space for rebuttal to negative feedback, eBay would not remove or change any user's comments. Unless the user nullified his or her registration, unjustified negative feedback remained on the system in perpetuity. Competent members knew they must protect their feedback because dishonest users employed negative feedback unscrupulously, often in revenge.

"Retaliatory feedback" was the members' term for unjustified or unwarranted negative comments. Stewart explained, "Users can easily leave 'grudge' negative comments about others to deflect the fact that the poster of the negative comments is the real culprit in a given problem rather than the receiver of the comment. Also many users do not post negative feedback at all at times when it is genuinely appropriate because of fear of retaliation from the person that caused the problems in the first place." According to these members, deadbeat bidders were unethical users who placed bids they later did not honor. Sellers gave negative feedback to these bidders and were stung when the "culprits" themselves gave the defrauded sellers negative comments. Buyers also reported being victimized by retaliatory feedback. Mae related her experience: "[The] seller did not send me the items. I left negative feedback. They then retaliated with negative feedback on my feedback rating and wrote me many nasty, hysterical emails." In this cycle, honest members explained how they were punished by losing money, either as a defrauded buyer or as a seller in listing fees. When they attempted to warn others about a user's unprincipled behavior, their own reputations were unjustly maligned. One member described the double victimization by an unscrupulous user and the administration that did not police the Feedback Forum: "If someone feedback bombs you, eBay will do nothing."

Members shared that users who prized their reputations and sought to protect them were unable to give negative feedback when it was due. Bob explained why he no longer left negative feedback, although he knew this ultimately devalued the system: "I don't leave negative feedback anymore. The only two negative comments I received were from deadbeat bidders who never paid. I left them negative feedback so they responded in kind. I vowed never to leave negative feedback again. I told eBay they should modify their system ... if sellers like me don't use it, then it has little value." Aurora reported that one corrupt user targeted multiple members to inflict a heavy toll of damage. She recounted asking eBay to address this problem: "I have had fellow eBay users recently get horrid feedback from a pest who has NO feedback. We have tried for two weeks to get eBay to address this problem and have had NO response other than a form letter email stating that they are concerned." A user with no feedback history gave Aurora retaliatory feedback. The feedback, therefore, was nontransactional. Although members informed eBay that the cycle of retaliatory feedback threatened the feedback system's reliability, they received no response. Thus, retaliatory feedback degraded trust in the Feedback Forum in two ways: members trusted neither the veracity of the feedback system nor eBay's willingness to right attacks on it. Ultimately, this forced members to further subvert the system to protect their profiles. Members believed that eBay was no longer a trusted guarantor of reputational information; trust in the institution was eroded, and the basis for interpersonal trust was compromised.

REPUTATIONAL LITERACY

In an effort to remedy this dilemma, sophisticated members developed expertise to interpret feedback. Aware of the cycle of retaliatory feedback, members said they often went to great lengths to evaluate negative comments. Steve reported: "I DO read all pages ... even if it's 40 pages if someone I want to buy from has some negatives I want to know WHY and WHAT they have done to correct it. And if I feel they have addressed the problem ... I WILL bid from them... . I have only had a few problems and there were other sellers who were also having problems with the same people I was, I found this out by checking feedback." Not only did Steve read every page of feedback, but he also used the item number on negative comments to find the member's own feedback page to evaluate that user's behavior. Sophisticated members know how to follow the "trail" of comments given by any user. Marsha explained that she always performed this procedure:

"I check feedback on anyone that I deal with, both remarks left for them and by them."

Competent members gathered information to make informed decisions about a user's reputation. Sarah reported, "I would look at the comments, when they were given, by whom, and then check the negative commenters' feedbacks—if sellers had a lot of feedback and only one or two negatives and those seemed to be from people I describe as cranky I ignored it." By checking on the commenter's own feedback, members could decide to ignore unwarranted "negs." Michael stated "In cases where several negatives occur, one always looks for a trend in behavior patterns." By discovering such trends, competent members decoded feedback subverted by unscrupulous users.

DEADBEATS AND TOURIST BIDDERS

Members attributed the dramatic climb in retaliatory feedback and subversion of the feedback system to an influx of new bidders attracted by eBay's aggressive advertising campaign. Bob stated his belief that "the amount of new users lured in by eBay's ad campaigns aren't coming to the site unprompted. This means that the general level of authentic desire is lower than what you'd find in the new user who seeks out the site or stumbles on it naturally." Pat explained, "THE SITE HAS GROWN SO MUCH AND THERE ARE SO MANY USERS THAT CONSIDER EBAY A PLAYGROUND INSTEAD OF THE WONDERFUL GATHERING PLACE IT IS DESIGNED TO BE. THE ADS LISTING 'BILLY'S VIRGINITY' AND 'MY SISTER'S PANTIES,' ONLY HURT THE REPUTATION." Because they lacked "authentic desire" to join the eBay community, such newbies were viewed as treating the site and feedback as a "playground."

Committed members linked waves of deadbeat bidders to eBay's advertising strategies. Marsha claimed, "We've had more deadbeat bidders in the last two months than in the previous year." George confirmed, "The influx of new artificially enticed bidders has created a glut of deadbeats lately. One in seven fails either to make contact or to pay." Mike named them "this ridiculous influx of 'tourist' bidders." His word choice is important; tourists visit a place without intending to stay. "Tourist bidders" indulged in retaliatory feedback because they were not invested in the eBay community. When they flouted the eBay site's protocol and feedback, invested members were forced to protect their reputations from retaliatory feedback. In this cycle, both invested and tourist bidders acted in individually rational manners that resulted in the collective, irrational subversion of the eBay feedback system.

EMPTY RHETORIC, ABANDONED COMMUNITY

At the time of data collection, eBay asserted that four controls made trading on the site "safe." The first was the Feedback Forum. Second, eBay offered free fraud insurance for up to $200 worth of goods per transaction with a $25 deductible. Third, eBay's Safe Harbor staff "protected" the site from abuse. Fourth, users could choose to use the escrow service, i-Escrow, for especially valuable items.[12] Members bitterly condemned eBay's free fraud insurance. Steve expanded, "This is just f***ing insulting! Up to $200.00 what a laugh." Elizabeth delineated, "The whole insurance deal is a sham as bad as insured mail. Collection, turn around, and the $25.00 deductible still have you at a loss; no, it is another attempt to extract user fees because it is a revenue-enhancing feature that plays on fear." Moreover, Steve claimed that while eBay presented this insurance as a free benefit, this was not the case: "We treat this as a joke. This offer was to be only until Sept. … then we would start having to pay. This was not covering the first $25, which leaves out most transactions on eBay. AND they state that people must NOT have ANY negative feedback … and this eliminates many who have been given a negative by someone as retaliation. eBay covered their a&& on this… . This is a joke… . If eBay CARED about the COMMUNITY they would help out the person who loses a $12.00 amount to fraud as they would $200.00."

Manipulation of the feedback system generated distrust in the entire eBay institution. Members believed that just as eBay refused to intervene in cases of retaliatory feedback, it did not police itself on other fronts. For example, according to Steve, eBay refused to honor its insurance agreement even if retaliatory bidding had already victimized a member. Marsha encapsulated this distrust: "I'd be willing to bet they've never paid a claim … everyone says it's impossible to get anything out of eBay. Attila the Hun must be their public relations officer." These members reported they had little or no confidence in the administration's willingness to protect its community. Sarah reported, "I have [apprehensions] now to a greater degree after I have been burned by a seller who cashed my check and then skipped…. eBay's contact information is generally worthless; and it takes them far too long to close down auctions of dishonest sellers or dealers offering illegal goods." Like Sarah, Bob believed that eBay's rhetoric of safety was hollow: "I have yet to receive credits promised to me, I was ripped off by another seller and eBay told me they couldn't do anything about it. It didn't make me feel safe." Betsy related her experience: "[A]fter having been sent a bootlegged CD ROM, I spent many an hour informing eBay … but now they want me to PAY to inform them of something eBay should be monitoring… . [T]hey've sent me this form for months … and yet … they are selling a pirate VHS episode 1 The Phantom Menace. But will they respond to my report? … I have over thirty that have had no response." According to Betsy, trust was violated not only by fraudulent users but also ultimately by the eBay administration itself. These members felt that by employing a rhetoric of safety promising multiple avenues of institutional recourse, eBay gave them a false sense of security; however, once another user broke their trust, they unsuccessfully attempted to hold the institution accountable. In this way, members reported that their original trust in the Feedback Forum was predicated on the claims made by the eBay institution so that once the company did not make good on its word, they felt betrayed twice over.

REPUTATION, BLACK FRIDAY, AND SHATTERED COMMUNITY

Analyzing the socioeconomic frames that my respondents employed in this moment of crisis affords a unique vantage point from which to examine the networked dynamics of collective and interpersonal trust on eBay during a critical period in the site's history. Black Friday sheds light on the interplay between the administration's economic agenda and the idealistic visions of eBay's purpose and character embraced by committed members. Despite what they saw as numerous proofs of administrative neglect, members desperately wanted to believe in their community. Black Friday forced them to face the slippages between reality and the administration's community rhetoric. Prior to the crisis and ongoing issues of broken trust in the feedback system, members viewed eBay as a vibrant community governed by mutual respect between members and the site administration. The vision of community embraced by many members had as much to do with norms of democratic governance as with the regulation of a marketplace.

Invested eBay members framed both Black Friday and the damaged feedback system as the administration's betrayal of its own rhetoric of communitarian values. They felt that more than an economic injustice had been perpetrated against them. They felt disempowered by what they perceived as a suddenly distant, tyrannical, and insulting authority. Especially during the crisis, these eBay members framed the administration's policy change in terms of damaged community despite what they saw as attempts by eBay's administration to confine the terms of the debate to the new policies' economic effects.

For respondents, eBay's introduction of exploitative policies without notice or consultation was a deeply offensive violation of the implicit contract between members and a humanized eBay administration, represented by "Pierre" and "Meg." The same is clear for what members framed as the administration's passive acceptance of retaliatory feedback, tourist bidders, and feedback bombing in the face of the community's cries for help. Members saw the "GreedeBay" administration as increasingly profit driven, spurred by a mercenary agenda with little place for social ties. In contrast, members clung to the original communitarian vision; they saw their relationship with the site and its community as a social compact with economic benefits. Black Friday shook members' emotional investment in this ideal. One lamented, "I had all my eggs in the eBay basket, but they threw them on the ground and broke them. I feel like they will be happy to see me go, I just haven't figured out exactly why."

Members' boycott of eBay became a protest against perceived unethical gambits by the administration that violated the social contract between members and administration. The boycott was effective. eBay repealed the most offensive elements of its new policies, including the dollar charge and the forced opening bid equaling 25 percent of the reserve price.

Despite the trauma of Black Friday, several months afterwards, all respondents remained registered with eBay. Yet one must ask if they truly had a choice. Although the majority of respondents expressed interest in diversifying to other auction sites, there was really nowhere else to go. Moreover, in moving to other auction sites, members would have lost the very community they sought to preserve. In economic terms, it is likely that after Black Friday, previously loyal members stayed with eBay primarily because less developed alternative sites lacked member populations of comparable size and thus afforded fewer opportunities for profitable transactions. If this was indeed the case, then the administration's attempt to frame the site as an economic venue rather than a community was successful, much to the detriment of the members' cherished community ideals.

NOTES

1. Adam Cohen, *The Perfect Store: Inside eBay* (Boston: Little, Brown, 2002), 304–5.
2. If a potential buyer had already found and bookmarked an item before an outage, that buyer could still access its listing during the outage.
3. Although reserve auctions protect sellers, Steven Andersen found that they might attract fewer total bids. See Steven Andersen et al., "Seller Strategies on eBay," UCSC Working Paper (April 2004), http://repositories.cdlib.org/uscsecon/564.
4. All members' names are pseudonyms. Excerpts preserve members' use of ellipses and capital letters, as well as all errors in grammar, usage, and punctuation. All citations are limited to members' self-reported perceptions of eBay.

5. In response to my online questionnaire, respondents included copies of their messages to eBay.
6. Sellers pay eBay a listing fee for each auction whether or not the object sells. Additionally, sellers pay eBay a sliding percentage of any winning bid.
7. Members repeatedly called eBay's founder and CEO by their first names, Pierre and Meg, which indicates members' desire for close community as well as the administration's early efforts to encourage it.
8. Quoted verbatim from respondents' self-reported answers.
9. Cited in Cohen, 206.
10. Users gave feedback by leaving scores of 1/positive, 0/neutral, or –1/negative. As the numeric values indicate, positive and negative ratings raised or lowered a user's score, creating a composite rating. When users conducted multiple transactions with each other, only the first feedback score was counted numerically. This restriction prevented attempts to undermine another user's reputation, but could distort scores because users with thousands of successful transactions could theoretically have a feedback aggregate of only several hundred. eBay did not remove negative comments from the system, although users were eventually given the opportunity to respond to "negs" and to mutually withdraw feedback. Officially, users who accumulated a net negative score of –4 were prohibited from further using the site. For further analysis of the reputation system, see chapters 7 and 9.
11. It was not until March 2000 that all feedback became transaction based. At the time of data collection, therefore, nontransactional feedback was a serious concern.
12. i-Escrow received both the payment and the item for a fee of five percent of the selling price. The seller did not receive payment until the buyer inspected the item and deemed it acceptable; the seller had the same opportunity to inspect and approve returned items before the buyer received a refund.

9

Return of the Town Square

Reputational Gossip and Trust on eBay

LYN M. VAN SWOL

Building trust online between strangers is difficult. In this chapter I examine how eBay has handled the problem of building trust for auction transactions through its Feedback Forum system. I discuss the relationships among vulnerability, uncertainty, trust, and concern for reputation, and I also provide readers a summary of social science research on eBay relating to trust and reputation. Although the majority of eBay participants interact with strangers, the reputation system serves to communicate trust through a person's eBay user ID and online profile. Because of the ease of switching trading partners on eBay and the transparency of someone's reputational rating, one can quickly establish a calculated form of trust and choose among sellers based on their reputations. People cannot trust one another unless they share some form of community or network of relationships, and eBay's technology makes it easy to develop such a network because one has instant access to how other people within the network rate their participation with a certain user. This trust drives commerce on eBay, as sellers' reputations affect their selling prices as well as the willingness of potential bidders to participate in their auctions. This online dynamic, I argue, is in contrast to those trends in modern society that obscure trust in favor of mechanisms such as insurance or regulation. Through the use of technology, eBay auctions rely, ironically, on a decidedly old-fashioned method of reputational gossip to develop trust: the return of the town square.

Although the online auction industry is only a decade old, participation has risen exponentially and annual sales among many millions of people run in the several billions of dollars. The National Consumers League in Washington, D.C., however, reported that auction fraud is a top online complaint.[1] One of the challenges facing consumer-to-consumer online auctions is establishing trust between buyers and sellers. Donna Hoffman, Thomas Novak, and Marcos Peralta explain that lack of trust is an obstacle that stops many consumers from engaging in internet commercial transactions.[2] While an attractive price on an item may be necessary for someone to bid, price alone may not be a sufficient inducement. As Patricia Doney and Joseph Cannon and others have found, trusting a seller is an important prerequisite for bidding.[3] Therefore, scholarship is needed to examine people's perception of trust for internet auctions and to examine mechanisms that can increase this trust.

TRUST, UNCERTAINTY, AND THE PROBLEM OF ANONYMITY

Roger Mayer, James Davis, and David Schoorman define trust as "the willingness to be vulnerable to the actions of another party based on the expectation that the other will perform a particular action important to the trustor, irrespective of the ability to monitor or control that other party," and Russell Hardin further explains that "trust involves giving discretion to another to affect one's interest."[4] Although we trust certain people everyday and approach others with a certain amount of default trust or generalized trust, we usually form a more specific type of interpersonal trust for people with whom we interact on a regular basis. Interpersonal trust is an expectation accumulated over a history of interaction that a person is competent and has one's best interests in mind. As a considerable body of social science research argues, this expectation constitutes a person's positive reputation.[5]

Trusting another person makes one vulnerable to and dependent on that person's actions, a vulnerability that stems from uncertainty about another's motives, inability to monitor the other person, and risk that the person one is trusting may hurt one's own interests. Uncertainty, risk, and trust are interrelated in that if the risk to self that attends another person's actions is low, then uncertainty remains low and the need to trust is irrelevant.[6] Research undertaken by myself and by others indicates that the greater the uncertainty and risk in a relationship, the more important the need to establish trust.[7] For example, I found that when participants interacted in an unregulated market in which sellers were able to deceive buyers, trust was much more important to buyers than when they interacted in a market in which sellers' behavior was regulated and there was little uncertainty. Further, buyers established higher trust in sellers in the unregulated market. Arun Vishwanath, moreover, found that in high uncertainty-avoidance cultures such as Japan, in which people tend to approach interactions with greater perceptions of risk, potential participants in online auctions were less likely to bid when sellers provided insufficient information about the product than were participants from low uncertainty-avoidance cultures such as the United States. Presumably, auction participants in Japan need more information than Americans, especially visual information about merchandise in the form of pictures, to help reduce uncertainty and increase trust.[8]

Establishing trust is especially important in online auctions because of the increased perception of risk and uncertainty that people have of internet auctions. Earlier research conducted by Janet Sniezek and myself found that in face-to-face interactions, a certain amount of trust is the default for most people, and this trust is greater than is the case with non-face-to-face interactions.[9] However, people approach internet transactions with more distrust and uncertainty for several reasons: there is more anonymity for internet transactions than face-to-face transactions because people often use screen names or user IDs, and online communication is more impersonal and has less richness due to lack of nonverbal cues and other reductions in social information. Also, media stories about internet fraud fuel people's anxiety, and one cannot physically inspect the merchandise in an online auction. An internet auction site such as eBay makes it quite easy to become an online seller. However, buyers therefore may be much more wary of transient sellers or sellers switching user IDs.[10] As Sulin Ba and Paul Pavlou note, "[I]t is very easy for a dishonest seller to masquerade as an honest one, luring an unsuspecting buyer into a fraudulent transaction."[11] Finally, the absence of strong regulation in most internet auctions increases uncertainty and raises trust concerns. As Peter Kollock and I have shown separately, trust becomes more important in situations lacking regulation because individuals experience more risk and uncertainty.[12]

Because people approach internet auctions with less default trust, building interpersonal trust becomes all the more important. Ethan Katsh, Janet Rifkin, and Alan Gaitenby explain that "the less of a … human persona that is automatically available … the more necessary it is for the marketplace that wants to build trust to put in place mechanisms that do create persona."[13] eBay has put in place several such mechanisms in an effort to solve the problem of low trust in internet auctions. Some solutions, such as the company's escrow service that protects buyers and sellers by acting as a trusted third party during the transaction and overseeing the payment process, help reduce participants' vulnerability to fraud through the use of enforcement mechanisms. However, other eBay policies try to reduce participants' uncertainty about their trading partner by providing information about the trading partner. The most popular and effective of these latter solutions is eBay's Feedback Forum system.

EBAY FEEDBACK

eBay's philosophy is to "make as few rules as possible and get out of the way,"[14] a philosophy reflected in the company's Feedback Forum rating system and its low level of regulation for almost all its auctions. Early on, eBay's founder, Pierre Omidyar, realized that a system was needed so that people did not contact eBay with every complaint.[15] He set up a public rating system in which people could post their complaints and compliments for all other users to view. After each transaction, the highest bidder and the seller have up to ninety days to leave one another feedback as positive, negative, or neutral and to leave an accompanying message of up to eighty characters. While initially feedback could be left by any interested viewer whether she or he had been involved in the transaction or not, as Laura Robinson discusses (see chapter 8), in March 2000 eBay amended its feedback mechanism so that today only the winning bidder of any one auction as well as that auction's seller can leave feedback. eBay referred to this change as instituting a system of "transactional feedback."[16]

All eBay users have a number next to their user ID that represents their aggregate feedback profile, the number of positive comments received from different individual users. For each positive comment received from a different user, the system adds one point; and for each negative comment, the system deducts one point. Once a user reaches a feedback profile of ten, the system places a gold star next to his or her user ID, and the color of the star changes as he or she amasses more positive comments from more people. A user can check the full feedback profile of another user by double-clicking on his or her feedback profile number.

The feedback rating system helps foster trust between buyers and sellers by reducing the uncertainty of interacting with an anonymous stranger over the internet. It provides a transparent public reputation and works to discourage fraud by allowing people to spread the word about fraudulent buyers and sellers.

EBAY REPUTATION

Game theorists have outlined many ways to reduce deception and increase cooperation in exchange situations involving uncertainty about another party's actions.[17] For example, one might monitor all transactions and sanction cheaters.[18] This would be similar to using an escrow service for every transaction. However, doing this would entail higher transaction costs for monitoring every trade and reduce possibilities for buying low-priced items on eBay. Another solution is to engage in repeated transactions with the same person and establish a relationship in which the short-term costs of cheating outweigh the relationship's long-term benefits.[19] However, given the high number of users on eBay and their geographic dispersion, this solution is not feasible. A third solution is to allow participants to communicate, because communication tends to increase cooperation. While many eBay buyers and sellers get to know one another through eBay's discussion boards or email, this is time consuming and not feasible for eBay's "Power Sellers" who often maintain several hundred concurrent auctions. Further, communication does not always lead to cooperation and can lead to lying.[20] Therefore, while not "perfect," eBay's system of feedback profiles may be the most practical solution to building interpersonal trust and discouraging deception for short-term gain.

Trusting another person is risky, but reputation systems provide a popular and effective way to attenuate that risk.[21] Research on online stores has found that reputation is the most important factor in building trust in a store,[22] and information about past behavior of other actors in a social dilemma is important to sustaining cooperation.[23] Information about past behavior, that is to say someone's reputation, is also important in developing interpersonal trust.[24] For example, in surveying eBay buyers and sellers, I found that perceptions of importance of trust and reputation were highly related: the more importance buyers and sellers placed on trust, the more importance they also placed on a good reputation.[25]

Interpersonal trust typically is accumulated either over a history of interaction with a person[26] or through discussion with third parties. In the nonvirtual world, these can be time-consuming processes. On eBay, however, the Feedback Forum makes a person's reputation publicly available, and one can learn instantly how many people (sometimes hundreds) have rated their interaction with a certain person. Because of the instant availability of public reputations, even in the anonymous environment of online auctions, people are able to develop enough interpersonal trust to cooperate in monetary transactions under conditions of low regulation.

eBay's reputation system seems to work for several reasons. As Carol Heimer notes, "Trustworthiness of members is produced jointly by members' dependence on the group and the group's capacity to monitor and sanction."[27] eBay meets both these conditions. Because eBay is the largest internet auction site, members are highly dependent on it, as few viable alternatives exist. Also, the feedback system grants members strong power to monitor and sanction one another. eBay members can develop trust because eBay constitutes a dense network in which the possibility of recourse is convincing, and members derive rewards from interacting with others in a network that makes violations of trust costly.[28] Also, the feedback system makes user reputations transparent and available to anyone, and most often it is easy to find alternate trading partners if one person proves untrustworthy.

Writing in 1995, just before online auctions started to achieve popularity, Bernd Lahno stated that "individuals may have selfish reasons to cooperate in elementary trust games if they live in a world characterized by ongoing social interaction, reputation effects, and the possibility to substitute interaction partners. The value of a trustworthy reputation may be so high that it becomes rational to resist temptations to seize short-term advantages."[29] eBay meets all the conditions Lahno identifies: buyers and sellers hope to keep trading on eBay, it is generally easy to find another seller or buyer because there are millions of users, and reputations are very transparent in feedback profiles. This transparency and ease in switching partners encourage cooperation and trust by making the long-term benefits of reputation more important than the short-term benefits of fraud. Due to eBay's size, one can often find several sellers auctioning even the most unusual merchandise. However, although one can learn quite a bit about a person's trading history through researching his or her feedback profile, one probably does not actually know that person. Therefore, because of this anonymity, one does not feel obligated to maintain a relationship or interact with that person, and one would have few qualms about being promiscuous among sellers to capitalize on a seller with the best reputation. I propose that this promiscuousness drives the need to maintain a good reputation to prevent other eBay users from moving onto greener pastures. Hence, maintaining a good reputation is crucial. For example, Charles Wood and Robert Kauffman found that coin sellers with highly rated eBay reputations sold coins for 6.8 percent more than low-rated sellers, and Thomas Ottaway, Carol Bruneau, and Gerald Evans provide evidence that a seller's positive reputation increases the final bid amount.[30] As a popular self-help guidebook about eBay states, "On EBay, all you have is your reputation."[31] A good reputation signals "forbearance from opportunism," and the better the reputation, the larger the costs of deception and endangering that reputation.[32]

When faced with a risky situation in which one's outcome is linked to another's behavior, in other words a trust situation, one can try to decrease vulnerability to the other person or decrease uncertainty about the other person. From surveying eBay buyers, I found that only one buyer out of eighty-four reported using an escrow service for any trade.[33] Overwhelmingly, buyers on eBay use the route of decreasing uncertainty by putting stock in a good reputation, rather than decreasing vulnerability by using an escrow service. This strategy of decreasing uncertainty has generally been a strategy used in traditional societies in which people know one another.[34] In modern societies, however, people try to decrease their vulnerability through such means as insurance or regulation. A key example of new information technology application, eBay nevertheless operates by using the very old-fashioned, traditional method of reputational gossip to develop trust. Because of our increased interactions with strangers in modern society, relying on reputation often is not an effective strategy for dealing with other people, but eBay uses technology to make it possible to know the reputations of millions of people. In other words, eBay institutes something like a virtual town square, or at least a virtual public sphere, where an adequate level of trust gets bartered through the ease of switching trading partners. By making a person's trading history available to anyone, eBay may have hit on a method to replicate virtually an aspect of the face-to-face trust-building mechanisms "of old."

Interestingly, however, eBay's reputation feedback system uses this traditional method of reputational gossip without the social ties that normally accompany it. Building trust and a reputation with someone through repeated interactions usually also builds up a relationship between the two parties and a sense of mutual obligation to continue the interaction. However, no such ties or obligations exist with eBay's method of reputational feedback because participants are often anonymous. In a traditional framework, the time spent building the relationship and the ties felt to the other person may deter parties from engaging in deception. Trust may have a basis in familiarity, benevolence, and goodwill. On eBay, however, it may be precisely the lack of relationship coupled to the potential for promiscuousness on the part of participants that deters deception. Individuals may refrain from fraud and maintain their sterling reputations to prevent other participants from moving onto something better given their relative ease of finding alternate trading partners within such a large market. Therefore, within an online auction, the decision to trust may be more calculated and less based on familiarity and goodwill.[35] However, the decision to trust, either within a relationship or with a stranger in an online auction, requires some form of community. Again, and as Heimer finds, people cannot trust one another unless they share some form of community or a network of relationships, and eBay's technology facilitates developing a network of relationships as one can easily view how others in the network rate any one individual in question[36] (see chapter 7).

Generally, research categorizes reputation systems in two ways: as small systems based on gossip with reputation information gathered face-to-face through interactions with the person or from people who know the person, or as large systems in which determination of reputation is done bureaucratically according to a set of rules or regulations. eBay's reputation system acts as a small system, even though it is a large system available to a very large set of people. The Feedback Forum, therefore, does not fit into previous categorizations, but research and theoretical understanding of systems that confer reputations remain scant.[37] Therefore, research on eBay such as I present here may call into question this traditional categorization given that eBay uses a very different method for dealing with uncertainty than generally used in either modern or traditional societies. Interestingly, while eBay is able to recuperate aspects of the "town square" through its use of reputational gossip, the exchange of reputations itself is done within a technological structure that is highly controlled by eBay as a corporation—eBay set up the Feedback Forum and can change it to suit its corporate goals.

RESEARCH WITH EBAY AND REPUTATION

In 2001, I conducted research into eBay's Feedback Forum and hypothesized that buyers surveyed would view trust and reputation as more important than sellers due to the greater amount of uncertainty faced by buyers.[38] I found that as uncertainty about a transaction increases, reputation becomes more important as a mechanism for reducing uncertainty, and buyers experience greater uncertainty.[39] While sellers may be more vulnerable in the online world than in bricks-and-mortar retail situations, it is, in fact, buyers who make the first gesture of trust by submitting payment to sellers before receiving merchandise. I found that although many sellers said that nonpaying bidders were "disappointing" and "frustrating" and made them angry, the consequences of a nonpaying bidder are less for the seller than those facing a buyer who fails to receive merchandise or receives substandard merchandise after having already paid. One seller commented that "you get paid before delivery so trust really isn't an issue." Utpal Dholakia's research confirms this comment and finds that sellers are less interested in buyers' feedback profiles than buyers are interested in those of sellers.[40] Others indicated that nonpaying bidders are a cost of doing business and seemed to understand that some people get auction fever and bid above their budget. Therefore, eBay sellers have less risk and uncertainty than buyers. Further, buyers have more risks in the online world because they cannot physically inspect the merchandise; a larger information asymmetry exists between buyer and seller on eBay than in bricks-and-mortar retail settings. Thus, eBay mechanisms may be biased toward sellers and create more uncertainty for buyers. Ba and Pavlou state, "Trust is especially critical when two situational factors are present in a transaction: uncertainty (risk) and incomplete product information."[41] The more risk and uncertainty in an interaction, the more important trust becomes. Katsh, Rifkin, and Gaitenby found that 75 percent of complaints to a mediation service offered on eBay were from buyers,[42] and my own research confirms that buyers did rate trust and reputation as more important than did sellers, and they were more concerned about situations that would diminish the amount of information they could learn about trading partners. I further discovered that the buyers' greater perception of risk was reflected in comments they made at the end of the survey I asked them to complete. Buyers said, "You are taking a chance because you really don't know who you are dealing with," and, "Caveat Emptor."[43] Therefore, I find that (even with the Feedback Forum) buyers on eBay are more vulnerable than are sellers and more sensitive to uncertainty.

Vishwanath also found a strong link between concern for trust and concern for reputation on eBay. He compared seller reputation and participation for three countries that differ in their general level of interpersonal trust: people in Canada tend to have a high amount of default interpersonal trust in other people, people in France tend to have lower default interpersonal trust, and Germany falls between the two. Vishwanath reasoned that "cultures with high levels of interpersonal trust would require lesser [*sic*] information about senders than cultures which exhibit lower levels of trust" because people in cultures with higher levels of trust would approach an online auction transaction with less uncertainty than people in cultures with lower levels of trust.[44] Indeed, he found that people in Canada were more willing to participate in eBay auctions if the seller had low feedback ratings than were people in France. Therefore, in France people approach transactions on eBay with less trust and more uncertainty than people in Canada, and because of their greater uncertainty, participants in France were more concerned with reputation as a means to help reduce their uncertainty and supplement their lower levels of trust than participants in Canada.[45] Vishwanath's research on eBay Canada is limited by the fact that it relies on eBay's English-only Canadian site, which therefore may limit participation by the 75 percent of French-speaking Canadians who do not communicate well in English, if at all. Hence, eBay Canada at present cannot offer the more unified linguistic sample that is the case on the German and French sites.

Ba and Pavlou simulated an online auction and had eBay participants take part in the simulation and rate the trustworthiness of sellers. They found that buyers trusted sellers more and were willing to pay more to sellers with better reputations. Further, the importance of trust in increasing the price of an item was greater for more expensive items in which the buyer took more of a risk in trusting the seller because the seller had a higher incentive to cheat. Ba and Pavlou also examined data from actual eBay auctions and found that negative feedback had a more detrimental effect on the price a seller could command for more expensive items than for lower-priced items. As buyers bid on more expensive items, they take higher risks, become more concerned with the effects of reputation, and reward a good reputation with a price premium in their bidding.[46]

The survey I undertook also examined differences in trust for high-risk and low-risk items. I define "high-risk auctions" as auctions in which condition and authenticity of the item are extremely important and could be faked fairly easily. I found a significant positive relationship between the amount that participants who were surveyed traded in high-risk auctions and the amount of deception they had incurred. I also discovered that the amount that participants traded in high-risk auctions did not significantly correlate with the importance they placed on trust or concern for trading partners' reputations, but the amount participants traded in low-risk auctions did correlate with these two factors. There was, however, a correlation between the amount that participants traded in high-risk auctions and the extent to which they had formed ongoing relationships with their trading partners. Possibly because of higher risk, participants in high-risk auctions use other means of attenuating risk than only the feedback system. For example, they form trading relationships in which the prospect of future business reduces the likelihood of fraud.

I also conducted a post hoc examination of some high-risk eBay auctions and found that Power Sellers are especially prominent in these auctions. Large Power Sellers dominate the sale of precious and expensive gemstones and expensive art on eBay. This indicates that buyers may be unwilling to deal with small sellers when purchasing especially risky items, and small sellers may be unable to profitably sell this type of merchandise because of greater uncertainty. I conducted a separate post hoc examination of eBay coin auctions; third parties authenticate many of the rare coins sold in these auctions, thus reducing for buyers' uncertainty and risk, and rendering trust less important.[47] Recognizing the risks of high-risk auctions, buyers and sellers have turned to other means to reduce risk such as forming an ongoing relationship with a certain seller, purchasing from large Power Sellers, and selling authenticated merchandise. The value of a good reputation, therefore, may only go so far toward reducing uncertainty about a seller. For especially risky auctions, buyers use other mechanisms to reduce uncertainty and vulnerability (see chapter 15).

USES OF REPUTATIONAL FEEDBACK SYSTEMS BEYOND EBAY

I have highlighted the importance of trust and reputation for eBay users, especially for buyers, and indicated that eBay's Feedback Forum is instrumental in fostering consumer-to-consumer transactions in a high-uncertainty environment. Under this system, people willingly send money to complete strangers who are not even using their real names and often live a long distance away. This says volumes about the power of reputation, and the Feedback Forum could be a template applicable to other online situations. I further contended that previous classification of reputation systems does not apply to eBay. The company uses a form of reputation system traditionally associated with small-group, face-to-face interactions in more traditional societies, but eBay is also able to use technology to create a dense network among its millions of users. Further, the ease of finding an alternate partner on eBay—what I have identified as a promiscuous dynamic—makes maintaining a good reputation important as a means of standing out in the crowd. As more businesses aim to conduct forms of commerce on the internet, they must ensure that customers feel safe conducting business within its many virtual environments. Establishing trust, therefore, is a necessary condition for both online individual-to-individual transactions and business-to-consumer transactions. As the example of eBay suggests, decreasing feelings of uncertainty and vulnerability is essential to this end.

NOTES

1. Stephanie Gallagher, "Got Internet Auction Fever?" *Kiplinger's Personal Finance Magazine*, July 1999, 43; and Stephanie Gallagher, "Where, Oh Where, Did That Beanie Go?" *U.S. News and World Report*, March 15, 1999, 71.
2. Donna L. Hoffman, Thomas P. Novak, and Marcos Peralta, "Building Consumer Trust Online," *Communications of the ACM* 42, no. 4 (April 1999): 80–85.
3. Patricia M. Doney and Joseph P. Cannon, "An Examination of the Nature of Trust in Buyer-Seller Relationships," *Journal of Marketing* 61 (1997): 35–51; and Sirkka L. Jarvenpaa et al., "Consumer Trust in an Internet Store: A Cross-Cultural Validation," *Journal of Computer Mediated Communication* 5, no. 2 (1999): http://209.130.1.169/jcmc/vol5/issue2/jarvenpaa.html.

4. Roger C. Mayer, James H. Davis, and F. David Schoorman, "An Integrative Model of Organizational Trust," *Academy of Management Review* 20 (1995): 709–34; and Russell Hardin, "The Street-Level Epistemology of Trust," *Politics and Society* 21 (1993): 505–29.
5. Roderick M. Kramer, "Trust and Distrust in Organizations: Emerging Perspectives, Enduring Questions," *Annual Review of Psychology* 50 (1999): 569–98; Julian B. Rotter, "Generalized Expectancies for Interpersonal Trust," *American Psychologist* 26 (1971): 443–52; Bernard Barber, *The Logic and Limits of Trust* (New Brunswick, NJ: Rutgers University Press, 1983); Cynthia Johnson-George and Walter C. Swap, "Measurement of Specific Interpersonal Trust: Construction and Validation of a Scale to Assess Trust in a Specific Other," *Journal of Personality and Social Psychology* 43 (1982): 1306–17; and Joseph M. Whitmeyer, "Effects of Positive Reputation Systems," *Social Science Research* 29 (2000): 188–207.
6. Debra Meyerson, Karl E. Weick, and Roderick M. Kramer, "Swift Trust and Temporary Groups," in *Trust in Organizations*, ed. R. M. Kramer and T. R. Tyler (Thousand Oaks, CA: Sage, 1996); Christine Moorman, Gerald Zaltman, and Rohit Deshpande, "Relationships between Providers and Users of Market Research: The Dynamics of Trust within and between Organizations," *Journal of Marketing Research* 29 (1992): 314–28; Kramer, 569–98; Partha Dasgupta, "Trust as a Commodity," in *Trust*, ed. D. Gambetta (New York: Basil Blackwell, 1988), 49–72; and Janet A. Sniezek and Lyn M. Van Swol, "Trust and Expertise in a Judge Advisor System," *Organizational Behavior and Human Decision Processes* 84, no. 2 (2001): 288–307.
7. Jarvenpaa et al.; Peter Kollock, "The Emergence of Exchange Structures: An Experimental Study of Uncertainty, Commitment, and Trust," *American Journal of Sociology* 100 (1994): 313–45; and Lyn M. Van Swol, "The Effects of Regulation on Trust," *Basic and Applied Social Psychology* 25 (2003): 221–33.
8. Arun Vishwanath, "Comparing Online Information Effects: A Cross-Cultural Comparison of Online Information and Uncertainty Avoidance," *Communication Research* 30 (2003): 579–98.
9. Amitai Etzioni, "Making the Personal Connection," *Chicago Tribune*, March 13, 2000, sec. 4, 1, 4; and Sniezek and Van Swol, 288–307.
10. Arun Vishwanath, "Manifestations of Interpersonal Trust in Online Interaction," *New Media and Society* 6 (2004): 219–34; Malcolm R. Parks and Kory Floyd, "Making Friends in Cyberspace," *Journal of Computer Mediated Communication* 1, no. 4 (1996): http://209.130.1.169/jcmc/vol1/issue4/parks.html; and Jarvenpaa et al.
11. Sulin Ba and Paul A. Pavlou, "Evidence of the Effect of Trust Building Technology in Electronic Markets: Price Premiums and Buyer Behavior," *MIS Quarterly* 26 (2002): 243–68.

12. Kollock, 313–45; Robert D. Putnam, *Making Democracy Work* (Princeton, NJ: Princeton University Press, 1993); and Van Swol, 221–33.
13. Ethan Katsh, Janet Rifkin, and Alan Gaitenby, "E-commerce, E-disputes, and E-dispute Resolution: In the shadow of 'EBay law,'" *Ohio State Journal on Dispute Resolution* 15 (2000): 705–34.
14. "EBay, Cyburbia's New Subdivision Stokes a Boom," *Washington Post*, January 31, 1999, A1.
15. Adam Cohen, "The Attic of E," *Time*, December 27, 1999, 74–81.
16. Adam Cohen, *The Perfect Store: Inside eBay* (Boston: Little, Brown, 2002), 238.
17. Anatol Rapoport, Andreas Diekmann, and Axel Franzen, "Experiments with Social Traps: Reputation Effects in the Evolution of Cooperation," *Rationality and Society* 7 (1995): 431–41; and Rick K. Wilson and Jane Sell, "'Liar, Liar …' Cheap Talk and Reputation in Repeated Public Good Settings," *Journal of Conflict Resolution* 41, no. 5 (1997): 695–717.
18. Elinor Ostrom, Roy Gardner, and James M. Walker, *Rules, Games, and Common-Pool Resources* (Ann Arbor: University of Michigan Press, 1994).
19. Robert M. Axelrod, *The Evolution of Cooperation* (New York: Basic Books, 1984).
20. Robin M. Dawes, Jeanne McTavish, and Harriet Shaklee, "Behavior, Communication, and Assumptions about Other People's Behavior in a Commons Dilemma Situation," *Journal of Personality and Social Psychology* 50 (1977): 543–49; David Sally, "Conversation and Cooperation in Social Dilemmas: A Meta-Analysis of Experiments from 1958–1992," *Rationality and Society* 7 (1995): 58–92; and Wilson and Sell, 695–717.
21. Whitmeyer, 188–207.
22. Jarvenpaa et al.
23. Wilson and Sell, 695–717.
24. Dasgupta, 49–72; and Kramer, 569–58.
25. Lyn M. Van Swol, "EBay and the Return of the Town Square: How eBay Uses Reputational Gossip to Build Trust," paper presented at Digital Communities: Cities in the Information Society, November 2001, Chicago.
26. Johnson-George and Swap, 1306–17.
27. Carol A. Heimer, "Solving the Problem of Trust," in *Trust in Society*, ed. K. S. Cook (New York: Russell Sage Foundation, 2000), 18.
28. Heimer.
29. Bernd Lahno, "Trust, Reputation, and Exit in Exchange Relationships," *Journal of Conflict Resolution* 3, no. 3 (1995): 509.
30. Charles A. Wood and Robert J. Kauffman, "What Factors Drive Final Price in Internet Auctions? An Empirical Assessment of Coin Transactions on eBay," paper presented at the meeting of Institute for Operations Research and the Management Sciences, November 2001, Miami, FL; and Thomas A. Ottaway, Carol L. Bruneau, and Gerald E. Evans, "The Impact of Auction Item Image

and Buyer/Seller Feedback Rating on Electronic Auctions," *Journal of Computer Information Systems* 43, no. 3 (Spring 2003): 56–60.

31. Marsha Collier, *EBay for Dummies* (Foster City, CA: IDG Books Worldwide, 1999), 326.
32. Jarvenpaa et al.
33. Van Swol, 2001.
34. Heimer.
35. Ba and Pavlou, 243–68.
36. Heimer.
37. Whitmeyer, 188–207.
38. Van Swol, 2001.
39. Kollock, 313–45.
40. Van Swol, 2001; and Utpal M. Dholakia, "The Usefulness of Bidders' Reputation Ratings to Sellers in Online Auctions," *Journal of Interactive Marketing* 19, no. 1 (Winter 2005): 31–40.
41. Ba and Pavlou, 244.
42. Katsh, Rifkin, and Gaitenby, 705–34.
43. Van Swol, 2001.
44. Vishwanath, 2004, 223.
45. Ibid.
46. Ba and Pavlou, 243–68.
47. Van Swol, 2001.

10

Of PEZ and Perfect Price

Sniping, Collecting Cultures, and Democracy on eBay

NATHAN SCOTT EPLEY

Adam Cohen's enthusiastic history of eBay, *The Perfect Store*, provides two intertwined stories of eBay's genesis—the "official" story and the "real" story. The official story, as recounted by Cohen, is that Pierre Omidyar

> believed in market capitalism, but he was troubled by the gap between theory and practice. Financial markets were supposed to be free and open, but everywhere he looked he saw well-connected insiders profiting from information and access that were denied to ordinary people. It occurred to him that the internet could solve this problem by creating something that had never existed outside of the realm of economics textbooks: the perfect market… . [T]he playing field would be level. Buyers would all have the same information about the products and prices, and sellers would all have the same opportunity to market their wares. The auction format would, as classic economic theory taught, yield the perfect price, because items would sell at the exact point where supply met demand.[1]

Unfortunately for the fledgling company that sought to expand its market, the media were not particularly interested in covering a story about the internet and perfect price. "Nobody wants to hear about a thirty-year-old genius who wanted to create a perfect market," realized Mary Song, eBay marketing director and employee number three (83). In crafting a more humanized pitch for press releases and potential investors, Song developed a false "real" story, invoking both romance and collecting culture: Omidyar began eBay, she announced, to help his fiancée find and trade PEZ dispensers. The PEZ legend mirrors the official story's ideal of eBay as a gigantic, rational market where individuals buy and sell freely and fairly. At the same time, it grounds the abstractions of Omidyar's market ideology in the everyday. Plastic PEZ dispensers are quintessentially banal and disposable pieces of popular culture, but Song's legend understands how they are made memorable and precious through the practices of collecting subcultures. The official story of eBay's founding positioned the company to become "the World's Online Marketplace" that "makes inefficient markets efficient for millions of users,"[2] yet Song's mythic real story, resonating with communities of collectors trading everything from high culture objets d'art to mass-produced bric-a-brac, may convey even more about the auction site. If the official story is about a democratic marketplace, the PEZ legend is about democratizing culture.

Auctions, as Cohen notes, are only efficient as a way to determine price in markets where items' values are indeterminate and hard to know in advance (45). Value in such a situation depends on the cultural capital[3] of the item, whether a museum-quality antique auctioned at Sotheby's or a purportedly "museum quality" Franklin Mint "Howl of the Wind" collector plate more likely to be found on eBay. However, as several other chapters in this book attest, eBay auctions affect price in other trading contexts, and the discourse of perfect market and perfect price has increasing influence in the offline world.

In December 2003 the company announced it had begun selling raw price data collected from its auctions. One eBay senior vice president told the *Wall Street Journal*, "It is an incredibly intriguing asset to have eBay better known as the definitive source for prices… . [I]t is the best pure market reflection of the meeting of supply and demand."[4] The three companies that signed up as of the initial announcement apparently agreed that eBay, with 235 million auctions in the third quarter of 2003, comprised a large enough sample to provide representative market prices. For upward of 10,000 USD a year, they would receive continually updated raw data from completed auctions, which they would then mine and scrub for prices. The three companies fashion very different products. The Professional Golfer's Association (PGA) uses the data to offer a free online price guide through PGA.com for used golf clubs. Claiming its service will help expand the secondary market for golf equipment and thus grow the sport, PGA.com repeatedly compares itself to *Kelly's Blue Book*, the definitive U.S. price guide for used automobiles.[5] The software developer, Intuit, uses the data to provide a database of fair market value for almost 10,000 household items for ItsDeductible, software that helps U.S. taxpayers calculate deductions for charitable donations.[6] Ándale, the auction management firm, draws on the data to market a research tool targeted at eBay high-volume Power Sellers that provides "the average sale price, conversion rate, number of listings, and other selling information along with eBay-specific selling recommendations."[7]

eBay, then, enjoys increasing authority as an arbiter of price, and it is reasonable to assume (if not conclude) that price on eBay generally approximates whatever "fair market value" is in these days of increasingly ubiquitous online consumption. For many buyers and sellers, the eBay price is now the "real" price. Yet what is troubling here is the assumption by eBay, Ándale, the PGA, and some eBay users that price on eBay is more neutral than other mechanisms for determining value. The official discourse of perfect market/perfect price occludes recognizing that value on eBay is rendered though the myriad practices of millions of actual users, all of whom nonetheless act within a highly disciplined, technologically enforced structure. Negotiations of value take place in a multiplicity of contexts, and eBay value is no more perfect or free than earlier regimes of retail value such as that developed by bricks-and-mortar retailers. I am interested, therefore, in untangling eBay's perfect market/perfect price discourse from its "real story" of collecting cultures, and to do so I first examine ways in which eBay's auction format and the practices it encourages work to destabilize simple understandings of how eBay achieves price equilibrium. Because collecting cultures can never be fully separated from the "official story" of perfect market, I enrich my analysis with observations of members of collecting subcultures who regularly buy and sell on eBay and who possess a specialized knowledge of their collectible categories, Depressionware glass, Fiestaware, and My Little Pony dolls. In the second part of the chapter, I make links between price on eBay and expertise within collecting subcultures that indicate the fiction of a universal "set-in-stone" perfect price.

EBAY'S AUCTION FORMAT, OR WHY WE SNIPE AND WHY IT MATTERS

A number of factors affect price valuation on eBay—including the length of an auction, a seller's reputation rating, and the use of minimum bids and reserves. "Flipping"—buying from bricks-and-mortar stores to resell on eBay—and "Buy It Now"—an option often available for purchases of new goods at prices just below retail—are factors in price, and they point out that conventional distinctions between primary and secondary markets, and between bricks-and-mortar and virtual markets, are less and less relevant.[8] eBay's standard auction format[9] also destabilizes simple understandings of price equilibrium by promoting "sniping"—waiting until the very last seconds of an auction to submit a bid. Sniping is no secret. *Wall Street Journal* editorials rhapsodize its joys, guidebooks describe how to do it better (research your competition's bidding patterns in earlier auctions), and programmers offer software agents to snipe automatically in case a buyer doesn't feel like sitting at the computer waiting for each auction to end. Even though many users disdain sniping as unfair, eBay's help pages admit "sniping is part of the eBay experience."[10]

eBay's standard auction format is a hybrid, modeled in part on "English-style" auctions in which bids start low and increase by increments until they reach a maximum and only one bidder remains. A pure English auction isn't over until all bidders have bowed out at least once, twice, three times, and the item is officially declared sold to the highest bidder as the auctioneer's gavel strikes the auction block. On eBay, however, this format is modified and auctions end after a preselected period of time chosen by the seller—three, five, seven, or nine days. In this way, eBay also resembles a "second-price sealed-bid auction." In this auction format, interested parties submit a sealed bid with their maximum price up front, without knowing what others have bid. At the auction's close, the item goes to the highest bidder at a price established by adding a predetermined incremental amount to the second highest bid. In both English style and second-price sealed-bid auctions, bidders have no incentive to bid early or late, just as long as they bid in time.[11]

eBay's interface reflects the hybrid nature of its standard auction format. Consistent with the logic of a second-price sealed-bid auction, the site's help pages advise buyers to bid up front the maximum they are willing to pay for an item. Taking this bid as proxy, eBay's automated bidding function will continue to bid automatically, raising each bid by a minimum increment set by the seller, up to each bidder's maximum. Users can follow any item's Bid History, which shows successively higher incremental bids, even though most individual bids have been placed by the proxy software agent. The interface record of the auction, thus, invokes the logic of an English-style auction. Moreover, eBay directly undermines its advice that bidders should set their maximum at the outset by considerately notifying those outbid with an email containing the text "Don't let this get away" and providing a helpful link to raise their bids by setting a new maximum. Despite the official advice, eBay presumes consumers' "private value"—what the individual is willing to pay—will change. As one study finds, many people bid more than once (the average number of bids for each bidder is 1.89).[12] Continuing to raise bids incrementally through the duration of an auction represents an escalating level of commitment characteristic of eBay novices.

Such users may be considering the effort already expended in bidding and seek to justify their initial bid by bidding again.[13] Research suggests a "herd behavior bias" may be at work as auctions with existing bids attract more bids over comparable, or even better, auctions without bids.[14] Yet another explanation for incremental bidding is that some bidders misunderstand eBay as a pure English auction in which they must continually raise their bid to stay on top.[15] Even experienced buyers get caught up in incremental bidding. "My private price will sometimes change because of the incremental part," comments Jessica, an economics graduate student and avid collector of My Little Ponies, "because it's incremental, you're not thinking 'I'm paying forty dollars for this, you're thinking 'I'm paying a dollar more.'"[16]

eBay's hybrid auction structure, therefore, helps produce diverse bidding strategies that often depend on the user's level of experience. Jessica explains,

> If I see something I really want, I will actually watch it until it's about a day or two out. And, if I see something I sort of want, I'll stick it on the watch list. And, it's kind of funny … if I don't want it that much—it's a, 'eehhhh, it's nice to have'—I'll put in, like, a ten dollar bid, I mean, it's like, if I could get that thing for "x," I would pay it, and I'll put a bid on it … just whenever, just as soon as I see it, and the reason for that is that watching an auction takes time and I don't have time to be at my computer unless it is something I really want, so really for me, it's the time more than the money, and I think that's true for a lot of people.

Most buyers discover that eBay's advice runs counter to rational, strategic bidding behavior. The format's hybridity encourages sniping: bid-early-bid-again effectively drives up price, while sniping during the last seconds can lower prices in an implicit collusion among buyers against the seller.[17] In the case of Jessica's "eehhhh" item, her 10 USD bid stakes a claim if the item generates no additional interest, and unless incremental bidders intervene to drive up the price, the bid will remain at 10 USD until (or unless) snipers attempt to snag it at the last moment.

Experienced eBayers snipe as close as possible to the end of an auction to preempt further bids—in general, the more experienced one is on eBay, the more likely one is to bid late and only once.[18] A survey by Alvin Roth and Axel Ockenfels further suggests that users believe sniping keeps prices low and avoids competitive bidding wars.[19] Sniping also amplifies, however, the competitive pleasures of the auction. Conventional wisdom emphasizes how participating in an eBay auction can be "an exciting kind of sport."[20]

One guide to collecting insists that "nothing can match the heart-pounding excitement as a sale winds down to its final seconds and you wait to see if your high bid will be outdone."[21] Another gushes about the joy of clicking the Web browser's Reload button during the auction's final minute as each new bidder momentarily takes the lead.[22] Caught up in last-minute bidding wars, desiring all the more that item so desired by someone else, novice bidders in particular may find it all too easy to bid considerably more than their predetermined "maximums."

Holding the winning bid on a coveted item, only to see it sniped at the last second, works to encourage more competition and more sniping. Sniping may be part of the pleasure and excitement of eBay, but as Pam, one enthusiastic eBayer I interviewed, explains, "When you get sniped, someone stole it from you, right? … I literally will look at that person's name who won it from me at the last minute and I will really think evil thoughts toward coolblue22 or whoever it is." eBay's interface, and a potential confusion about how the site works, exacerbate this sort of competitive reaction. When the second-highest bidder looks back at a completed auction, the winning bid shown is only greater by the nominal amount of the minimum increment. It's easy for eBay novices to conclude that they always just barely lose by a dollar or so, when in fact, because the winning bidder's maximum bid is never shown, the interface obscures potentially substantial differences in the estimation of value between the two bidders.

Sniping may be rational, but it is by no means a universal strategy. If everybody sniped, eBay auctions would actually become second-price sealed-bid auctions. Research shows that sniping is not equally effective for all items and product categories. Sniping is more common for antiques, with their more indeterminate values, than for computers, for example, and snipers do no better than anyone else on standardized electronic gear attracting many different bidders.[23] These findings suggest that sniping articulates to the buyer's knowledge: the more one knows—about an item and about eBay in general—the better sniping works. In other words, sniping is more effective if combined with expertise, and specifically the sort of expertise that members of subcultural collecting communities acquire by carefully monitoring the sale of items on eBay (and in other contexts). Within a collecting subculture, a well-known trader can raise the potential price of an item merely by showing interest. Savvy eBayers hunt for merchandise by "bid stalking": searching by user name to find items on which frequent competitors are currently bidding. As one antique dealer explains,

> The most difficult part is ascertaining the genuineness of a particular piece. If it is fake then I lost the game and my knowledge

> was inadequate. This is where it is important not to bid early on an item. If you are well known as an expert and you bid, then you have authenticated the item for free and invite bidding by others.[24]

Sniping is strategic, even assuming that each item has only private value, but items on auction also develop "common value" produced, as this dealer points out, through the exchange of information during the bidding process. The greater one's expertise, therefore, the more imperative sniping becomes. A high early bid might intimidate potential competitors from participating and keep the price low, but it might just as well inspire their competitive spirit. In either case, information exchanged through studying an item's bidding history creates an incentive to bid late in order to gather as much information as possible. Sniping, as Roth and Ockenfels state, "responds to the strategic incentives created by the possession of information in a way that interacts with the rules of the auction."[25]

The information asymmetry among buyers that contributes to sniping complicates simple understandings of perfect price, as does information asymmetry among buyers and sellers. Omidyar designed eBay's Feedback Forum reputation system with the understanding that an online auction required a considerable measure of trust, particularly a buyer's trust of a seller, as in most cases payment must be received before merchandise is shipped. A growing volume of social science research on eBay generally suggests that buyers will pay a premium price to sellers with impeccable reputations; however, precisely how a seller's reputation affects price depends on the type of goods sold.[26] Research also suggests that a bidder's reputation, in contrast, is not considered useful by sellers, although it does significantly correlate with the successful completion of eBay auctions.[27] While the reputation system may generate a measure of trust (see chapter 9), it only partially mitigates information asymmetries. In general, the eBay buyer simply doesn't know the true quality of the item. Information asymmetry classically leads to "adverse selection costs." For instance, if eBay buyers don't know if the digital camera they are looking at is of good quality and condition or not, they will assign it a value that splits the difference between best- and worse-case scenarios. Sellers of high-quality merchandise, therefore, on average earn less than their wares are worth and ultimately tend to withdraw from the market. Sellers of low-quality goods, however, can make more than the goods are worth and are perfectly happy. Overall, the eBay market ends up with mostly low-quality sellers—they have the most incentive to stay—but since buyers are regularly getting less than they bargained for, the value they are willing to pay also goes down. Adverse selection costs created by information asymmetry on eBay thus keep eBay prices lower than in a market where buyers feel they are taking less risk.[28]

EXPERTISE: COLLECTING COMMUNITIES' SUBCULTURAL CAPITAL

Frequently dubbed "the heart and soul of eBay," collectors have long used the site to determine market prices for products, particularly for "retired" items no longer actively marketed or produced by the original manufacturer. Such items constitute "eighty to ninety percent of [eBay's] collectibles market."[29] This market is far more fickle than annually published collectible price guides are able to reflect. eBay listings produce "rareness" and then take it away in almost real time. For instance, in 2002, when "rare" Scarlett O'Hara Barbies flooded the site, savvy collectors knew immediately the now not-so-rare dolls, recently worth over 75 USD, would quickly plummet in value to around half the original price.[30] As eBay's category manager insisted that same year, "eBay is a pretty immediate reflection of buying and selling habits."[31]

While prices may achieve equilibrium where supply meets demand, in accordance with economic theory, demand on eBay is filtered through performed histories that, as they engage memory, are more than simply marketing. Pam, for example, recounted her early experiences with the site as she attempted to recreate Christmases from a remembered childhood. Her first eBay purchase was bubble lights like the ones her grandmother had owned:

> It's not the same going to somewhere like Restoration Hardware and looking at their bubble lights, they're not the same, and I don't know if it is because they don't come in a beat-up box … it doesn't produce the same feeling at all. And I guess part of it, it has to be—it has to have somebody's memories in there with it, and that's another part of it, I think, that's important to me… . They've specifically been loved by other people and I feel that that comes with it when you buy it, I really do.

Pam believes a kind of "energy" passes on with objects that others have used and loved for decades. After her grandmother died, she spent hundreds of dollars on eBay, and while she admits she probably paid more than some of the ornaments and decorations were worth, she doesn't regret any purchase: "What wouldn't I pay for that memory … I never set an amount." Pam pays a premium for memories. In contrast, when she collects Fiestaware she has a clear sense of what each piece is worth. "That little house [ornament] that reminded me exactly of the house that I used to take to bed with me at Christmastime, I would take it off the tree and take it to bed with me, I may never see another one of those in my whole life, so what will I pay for that, versus I have five websites that I could get Fiestaware on." Although not all items on eBay are valued though participatory experiences that engage memory, sufficient numbers of eBay sales rely on articulations of history through narratives so that the discourse of perfect price equilibrium seems naïve.

Bidders engaging in incremental bidding during the course of an auction also engage in a possession ritual though which they imaginatively lay claim to the item. Pam followed this pattern precisely, and when asked if she would bid the same way today, three years after her purchase of the bubble lights, she replied,

> I'd do the same thing probably. I'd probably have to have an idea of what I would pay in mind, but I think I would still lord over it and hold on … knowing full well that I'm probably driving up the price of the item as I do that. I think as I used eBay more I found out that that's what I was doing, I was driving my own price up by doing that, so maybe even for the precious items I might not bid so early … so I guess I should amend that, because I was brand new on it—Fiestaware gave me practice on it.

Pam's answer illustrates the important relationship between developing expertise and paying lower prices. As online trade in a collecting subculture matures, prices stabilize for more common items because communally produced values are widely available, archived on community forums and sites such as eBay.[32]

The production of distinctions among items (and among collectors and their relative expertise) comprises much of the work of collecting subcultures. Much of the intercourse in these communities, in other words, involves knowledge about collections, or "subcultural capital."[33] eBay's structure facilitates the development of subcultural capital. It allows for easy monitoring of listings and the prices paid for items, and collectors can converse on discussion boards and forums. The content of online collector discussions, as Jessica points out, is often about price:

> Pricing is always a question, because it's a collector's market … if you have a custom pony how much is it worth, and then there's well, how much work goes into it and how much time, you know. "How much would you pay for a 'blah'?" "Well I'd paid this." "Well I remember back when we could get her for that" (laughs).

> So, there's an outside way to share information and talk about it, so there's almost an agreed upon price for some of the rare ponies that are common, and even the common ponies.

Again and again, active collectors insist that "you have to do your homework." Works such as Greg Holden's *Collector's Guide to eBay* focus on how to amass information on collectibles. The advice of one collector, quoted in *Civil War Times Illustrated*, is typical:

> Once in a while, I find a little nugget on eBay… . Recently, I bought the dog tag of a soldier who served in the Irish Brigade for $1,300 [USD]. A dealer would have charged 1,700 to 1,800… . You have to know what you are doing. You really have to watch for the fake stuff… . Sometimes the item is misdescribed (this is where doing your homework is important). Or the picture isn't good.[34]

As also discussed by Rebecca Ellis and Anna Haywood (see chapter 3), savvy eBayers troll for items with misspelled crucial terms. Picking up misidentified items cheaply, they may return them to auction with correct spelling and appropriate marketing.[35] Perhaps more commonly, collectors' expertise allows them to acquire items cheaply from nonexperts. For example, a trivet collector, attending eBay's 2004 "eBay Live" convention in New Orleans, made the New Orleans *Times-Picayune* with her tale of finding on eBay a 1905 trivet for 5 USD, only to clean off layers of paint and discover it was worth over 100 USD.[36] As Jessica points out, on collectors' forums, "There is really no incentive to be honest, and it's happened more than once that somebody's had a really rare collector's item and someone's managed to nick it from them by saying 'Oh, well, you know those aren't worth much, but I'll take them off your hands for … ten bucks.' And it turns out it's a fifty dollar pony." In its many manifestations, then, information asymmetry among collectors will continue to complicate price valuation on eBay.

Even without the availability of price data reprocessed by Ándale or PGA.com, the vast quantity of information available in eBay categories and discussion forums (on and off eBay) is changing the knowledge practices of collectors. Traditional intermediaries—dealers and experts whose cultural capital helps determine value—are increasingly marginalized as eBay users do their own research and trade directly with each other. eBay has also opened up many collecting communities to less traditional collectors, particularly those more invested in the objects themselves rather than the subcultural community based in expertise and trade. Works such as Holden's *Collector's Guide to eBay* assume that collectors both buy and sell. A 2004 A. C. Nielson survey commissioned by *Gifts and Decorative*

Accessories trade magazine, however, discovered that approximately 37 percent of eBayers are collectors, but that of those, most are "unintentional" collectors, who may, among other things, be less likely to resell part of their collection.[37] Pam insists she wouldn't consider selling part of her collection (though she might give it away). Refusing to reconvert subcultural capital to economic capital by trading in collectible items, unintentional collectors may imagine their collecting practices and notions of value in ways quite incompatible with the discourse of perfect market/perfect price.

EBAY DEMOCRACY

> The whole point of My Little Pony is to acquire the My Little Ponies. Once you have them, there isn't much to do with them.
>
> **Jessica, a collector**

Fundamental to the perfect market/perfect price discourse are claims about eBay's democratizing effects. With eBay as "the great leveler" (Cohen 68), all sellers are created equal, all buyers have equal chances to bid, and, most important, old offline hierarchies no longer apply. This is the democratic—and libertarian—promise of eBay's "official" origin story. eBay epitomizes an increasingly ubiquitous, approving belief that perfect markets function perfectly when good people are free to trade without interference. The complicated interactions of knowledge, desire, and memory in the everyday practices of collectors, however, demonstrate that price cannot be so easily generalized, much less perfected. It is in this sense that the PEZ myth is much more the "real" story of eBay's genesis than the ostensibly true and "official" story. Collectors' stories, in other words, undermine the fantasy of perfect market/perfect price.

Imagined in this way, eBay's "real" and official origin stories are in tension, but they also work in concert, collapsing everyday life into free markets and rendering democracy a figure only for neoliberal ideologies about work and self. eBay's technologies permit easy navigation of extensive categories, rapid searches for objects and people, aggregating lists of objects and users that facilitate comparison of price and quality, individualized interfaces to manage consumer relationships, and virtual performance spaces such as forums and message boards for subcultural communities. Such structures can potentially reduce information asymmetry between buyers and sellers, increasing buyers' power such that they "may come to think of price as something they direct and control, rather than something given to them."[38] The availability of price data, both through the labor of watching auctions and through a site such as PGA.com, empowers users and undermines hierarchies of taste and cultural capital. Of course, this individual empowerment within everyday life articulates only weakly to political empowerment in the public sphere. The flipside of eBay's democratizing of commerce and culture is the neoliberal "ownership society," under which the principal responsibility is "personal responsibility" (see also chapter 7). Under this vision of democracy, labor is more and more autonomous, flexible, and "affective,"[39] while "free" mostly applies to markets and to trade.

NOTES

1. Adam Cohen, *The Perfect Store: Inside eBay* (Boston: Little, Brown), 6–7. Additional page numbers of this reference are cited parenthetically.
2. eBay, "Company Overview," May 2005, http://investor.ebay.com/downloads/CorporatePresentation.pdf (accessed September 14, 2004).
3. See Pierre Bourdieu, *Distinction: A Social Critique of the Judgment of Taste* (Cambridge, MA: Harvard University Press, 1984).
4. Nick Wingfield, "At eBay, Even Sales Prices Are for Sale," *Wall Street Journal*, December 8, 2003.
5. PGA, "FAQ," http://valueguide.pga.com/faq.php (accessed September 17, 2004).
6. Intuit even guarantees the accuracy of valuations should the U.S. Internal Revenue Service dispute deductions (that is, as long as one uses the current year's version of the software). Intuit, "Press Release," www.intuit.com/about_intuit/press_release/2003/12-02b.html (accessed September 17, 2004).
7. Andale, "Press Release," http://corp.andale.com/x-press_researchpro_unveils.html (accessed September 18, 2004).
8. For an economic analysis of "Buy It Now," see Timothy Matthews, "The Impact of Discounting on an Auction with a Buyout Auction: A Theoretical Analysis Motivated by eBay's Buy It Now Feature," *Journal of Economics* 81, no. 1 (2004): 15–52.
9. The majority of auctions on eBay take the standard form discussed in this chapter. eBay also offers "best offer auctions," live online auctions, and "multiple item auctions," also known as "Dutch auctions." See eBay, "Formats Overview," http://pages.ebay.com/help/buy/formats-ov.html. On Dutch auctions, see Elena Katok and Alvin E. Roth, "Auctions of Homogeneous Goods with Increasing Returns: Experimental Comparison of Alternative 'Dutch' Auctions," in *Management Science* (INFORMS: Institute for Operations Research, 2004), 1044–63.
10. eBay, "Outbid," http://pages.ebay.com/help/buy/outbid-ov.html (accessed August 4, 2005).
11. Axel Okenfels and Alvin E. Roth, "The Timing of Bids in Internet Auctions: Market Design, Bidder Behavior, and Artificial Agents," *AI Magazine* 23, no. 3 (2002): 79–88.

12. Ibid.
13. James H. Gilkeson and Kristy Reynolds, "Determinants of Internet Auction Success and Closing Price: An Exploratory Study," *Psychology and Marketing* 20, no. 6 (2003): 547.
14. U. M. Dholakia and K. Soltysinski, "Coveted or Overlooked? The Psychology of Bidding for Comparable Listings in Digital Auctions," in *Marketing Letters* 12, no. 3 (2001): 225–237, cited in Gilkeson and Reynolds, 540.
15. Axel Okenfels and Alvin E. Roth, "Last-Minute Bidding and the Rules for Ending Second-Price Auctions: Evidence from eBay and Amazon Auctions on the Internet," *American Economic Review* 92, no. 4 (2002): 1094.
16. Interview, 2005. I identify informants with pseudonyms.
17. Okenfels and Roth, "Last-Minute Bidding," 1095.
18. Okenfels and Roth, "The Timing of Bids," 86. Research on coin auctions showed that "the median winning bid was placed after 98.3% of the auction duration had elapsed, while a quarter of the winning bids were placed after 99.8% of the duration had elapsed (i.e., the last 8 minutes of a 3-day auction)." P. Bajari and A. Hortacsu, "The Winner's Curse, Reserve Prices and Endogenous Entry: Empirical Insights from Ebay Auctions," *RAND Journal of Economics* 34, no. 2 (2003): 329–355, cited in Sanjeev Dewan and Vernon Hsu, "Adverse Selection in Electronic Markets: Evidence from Online Stamp Auctions," *Journal of Industrial Economics* 52, no. 4 (2004): 505.
19. Okenfels and Roth, "Last-Minute Bidding," 1100.
20. "My True Love Sniped for Me," *Wall Street Journal*, November 26, 2004, W11.
21. Greg Holden, *The Collector's Guide to Ebay: The Ultimate Resource for Buying, Selling, and Valuing Collectibles* (New York: McGraw-Hill/Osborne, 2005), 13.
22. Linda Lindroth and Deborah Newell Tornello, *Virtual Vintage: The Insider's Guide to Buying and Selling Fashion Online* (New York: Random House, 2002), 23.
23. Assertion by economist David Lucking-Riley, cited in Lee Gomes, "E-Commerce Sites Make Great Laboratory for Today's Economists," *Wall Street Journal*, October 11, 2004, B1.
24. Okenfels and Roth, "Last-Minute Bidding," 1100 n. 23.
25. Ibid., 1099.
26. Research on eBay auctions of silverware, for instance, suggests a seller's reputation has little impact on closing price (Gilkeson and Reynolds, 559), and research on stamp sales suggests reputation's effect on price is modest (Sanjeev Dewan and Vernon Hsu, "Adverse Selection in Electronic Markets: Evidence from Online Stamp Auctions," *Journal of Industrial Economics* 52, no. 4 [2004]: 500). A study on auctions of proof coins, in contrast, suggests seller reputations have "significant impact" on final bid amount (Thomas A. Ottaway et al., "The Impact of Auction Item Image and Buyer/Seller

Feedback Rating on Electronic Auctions," *Journal of Computer Information Systems* 43, no. 3 [2003]: 60), as does another study on a wider range of items (Sulin Ba and Paul A. Pavlou, "Evidence of the Effect of Trust Building Technology in Electronic Markets: Price Premiums and Buyer Behavior," *MIS Quarterly* 26, no. 3 [2002]). Some research suggests buyer participation increases when sellers have high feedback ratings (Arun Viswanath, "Manifestations of Interpersonal Trust in Online Interaction," *New Media and Society* 6, no. 2 [2004]), and common sense, along with some data (James H. Gilkeson and Kristy Reynolds, "Determinants of Internet Auction Success and Closing Price: An Exploratory Study," *Psychology and Marketing* 20, no. 6 [2003]), indicates that greater participation leads to higher prices.

27. Utpal M. Dholakia, "The Usefulness of Reputation Ratings to Sellers in Online Auctions," *Journal of Interactive Marketing* 19, no. 1 (2004): 31–40.
28. In their research on stamp sales, Dewan and Hsu find that adverse selection costs on eBay average a 10–15 percent reduction in price versus an online auction providing multiple mechanisms for verification of merchandise such as estimated appraisals and refund guarantees. See also chapter 15 in this book, for a discussion of the extra labor required by online sellers of fine art and antiques in producing documentation adequate to counter the perception of risk in online purchasing of such items.
29. Kevin Pursglove, eBay's senior director of communications, cited in Meridith Schwartz, "Where Have All the Collectors Gone?" *Gifts and Decorative Accessories*, June 1, 2002, 66. Presumably, Pursglove means dollar value rather than number of listings.
30. Alexandra Peers, "Art Journal: Goodbye, Dolly!—Old Barbies Join Beanie Babies in Collectibles Market Bust: Half Off on 'Pink Splendor,'" *Wall Street Journal*, January 4, 2002, W1.
31. Cited in Schwartz, 66.
32. My informant Jessica made this clear about the My Little Pony market.
33. Sarah Thornton employs the term "subculture capital" in her work on music subcultures, *Club Cultures: Music, Media, and Subcultural Capital* (Hanover, NH: University Press of New England, 1996). Subcultural capital is not always easily reconverted into cultural capital, although subcultural knowledge of, for instance, certain antiques more directly articulates to the "legitimate" cultural capital that most concerns Bourdieu (see note 3, above).
34. Don Troiani, "Finding Nuggets," *Civil War Times Illustrated* 41, no. 2 (2002): 73.
35. Dana Schemo, "In Online Auctions, Misspelling in Ads Often Spells Cash," *New York Times*, January 28, 2004, A1. Despite the *New York Times*' discovery, searching for misspellings is common knowledge among experienced eBayers and is frequently mentioned in eBay guidebooks. My informant Jessica also commonly searches for misspellings of My Little Pony, as well as

French spellings, since some rare variants of the toys were originally released only in Europe.

36. Chris Bynum, "Another Man's Treasure," *(New Orleans) Times-Picayune*, June 11, 2004.
37. Meridith Schwartz, "The Accidental Collector," *Gifts and Decorative Accessories*, June 1, 2004, 100.
38. Mui Kung, Kent B. Monroe, and Jennifer L. Cox, "Pricing on the Internet," *Journal of Product and Brand Management* 11, no. 5 (2002): 274.
39. See chapter 6 for a discussion of affective labor and eBay.

11

Auctioning the Authentic

eBay, Narrative Effect, and the Superfluity of Memory

KEN HILLIS

In late 2004, eBay launched a multimedia ad campaign titled "The Power of All of Us." The campaign's American TV component included four commercials. One, titled "Toy Boat," opens with a boy playing with his toy boat at the beach. A textual overlay tells viewers the time is 1972, the place Cape Cod. As the scene dissolves, we see the tide take the toy far out to sea. It sinks to the bottom only to be retrieved decades later as part of the catch of an industrial fishing boat of unspecified Asian origin. A fisherman picks the toy boat from a net full of fish; the next scene shows the boy, now a thirty-something fellow, gazing with wonder at the image of the boat in an eBay listing on-screen. Viewers also see a framed painting of the boat on the wall behind the monitor. A voice-over asks the audience the following questions about memory, its maintenance, and its retrieval: "What if nothing was ever forgotten? What if nothing was ever lost?" Before eBay, all that remained of the boat was its framed representation on a wall. Now, however, via the magical power of eBay-the-virtual-archive, a treasured childhood object is returned to the competent neoliberal subject and, along with it, even more treasured memories and associations from his past. "Toy Boat" asks viewers to associate memory with objects and their retrieval, and to think about the past as essentially a material object that can be reappropriated into the present through the medium of eBay. Because eBay is about exchanging objects, the ad implies that memories not associated with fetishized objects are less valuable than those that are. Value is implicit here, both the psychic needs that the boat's use value might help fulfill, and the boat's exchange value within a capitalized flow of goods and memories.

Marc Andreessen, co-creator of the prototype Web browser Mosaic, when asked to comment on the success of the eBay phenomenon, remarked that he never thought people had so much junk in their garages. Andreessen's work was pivotal in designing the browser interface upon which Web ventures such as eBay operate. His pithy remark, however, disregards the culture of serial consumption, the fetishization of commodities upon which this culture depends, and the resulting superfluity of still useful goods that accumulate in the garages he mentions. As Andreessen understands, many of these goods now end up on eBay, and this chapter examines the performative and indexical qualities many eBay sellers embed in their listings of objects for sale. These qualities are intended to be memorable. I argue that they also fuel the exchange of superfluous objects and help infuse into them new forms of use and exchange values, ones where exchange itself can seem a form of use.

I am not referring here to objects purchased online chiefly on the basis of price and convenience, in other words, for their practical use value. I focus instead on what might be considered exceptional auctions, often of collectibles though not exclusively so, where the experiential claims of authenticity, memory, and truth that sellers fabricate through the images and textual narratives they upload to the site together produce narrative effects crucial to profitable sales outcomes. Such auctions can also be thought of as "media friendly," and while they constitute only a small fraction of overall eBay listings and sales volume they are, nevertheless, crucial in advancing the site's ongoing success. The role of such collectibles and media-friendly auctions, such as the 2004 sale of a grilled cheese sandwich purportedly embedded with the face of the Virgin Mary and which sold to an internet casino for 28,000 USD (see chapter 13), promotes or hypes interest in the broader site. While the monetary value for vehicles and related goods exchanged on eBay Motors far exceeds that of all eBay's categories for collectibles combined, eBay management continues to refer to collectors and collectibles as "the heart and soul of eBay." Unlike the sale of a used 2000 Mazda Protege, collectibles and media-friendly listings with strong "human interest" and appeal to fetishized Western desire to acquire, under the rubric of collecting, what previously was missing or lost operate as a kind of advance brigade of publicity that attracts a volume of site visitors far in excess of any proportional relationship to these listings' commercial value. Media friendly eBay auctions, therefore, while constituting a minority of listings, increase overall site activity in no small part because their promotion and consumption as visible entertainments render the eBay brand vivid and memorable.

In thinking through narrative effect on eBay, I first note that business writers and analysts have assessed the increasing centrality within consumer culture of what they have variously identified as an "entertainment economy" or "the experience economy."[1] An economy reliant on entertaining experiences requires articulating the complex and seemingly endlessly compelling social dynamics of entertainment to the exchange of commodities themselves. The eBay auctions I discuss—auctions, for example, that allow bidders to participate vicariously in the punishment of a seller's supposedly naughty children—exemplify one feature of this economy of fun at work. Linking shopping to fun has long been promoted by advertising. A key factor of eBay's financial and cultural success, however, lies in the pervasive shift in emphasis from shopping as an activity organized around buying and selling to shopping *for* experience as a valuable activity or end in and of itself. This shift is part of a related and ongoing naturalization of the link between experience and the commodity form. Consuming experience online links directly to the organization of eBay's site as a series of virtual "stages" upon which individual sellers design, construct, and perform memorable or enjoyable experiences for which purchasers are willing to pay. The narrative effect of these performances exceeds the transactional logic that comprises the commonsense understanding of eBay as a giant garage sale, swap meet, or the old-fashioned auction house writ virtual.

In thinking through narrative effect on eBay, I also note that digital technologies increasingly intersect with human desires and social needs. As Hubert Dreyfus and Gilles Deleuze have differently argued, the West builds its philosophies, internal and logical contradictions included, as an array of complex technologies.[2] In the case of eBay, we see the strong influence of AuctionWeb's founder, libertarian computer programmer Pierre Omidyar, who wrote a series of software programs for the website in the belief he was creating the platform for a "friction-free" marketplace. People, however, often use technologies in complex ways unanticipated by their designers. As Karl Marx noted, we each make history, but we do so under circumstances never completely of our choosing. eBay, then, as an information machine and an array of user and corporate practices, exemplifies the power of technological assemblages to influence social relations. As a set of social practices, moreover, the eBay experience is a living part of culture, and its members are witnesses to the worlds that they are actively making, for better or for worse.

Sharon Zukin notes that when one buys on eBay, one also buys the seller's story about the object;[3] in the examples from the site I discuss, eBay allows for a coupling of the commodification or branding of authenticity on the part of the seller to a bidder or prospective buyer's experiences. For bidders, these experiences can be constituted either through participating vicariously in aspects of the seller's emotional or psychic reality through consuming the personal narratives that sellers include to induce a sale, or through the successful buyer's retrieval of memorable aspects of his or her past through purchase of a meaningful object. If purchased, such an object may then be held in the purchaser's personal archive or collection, where it shifts status from a memory trigger or mnemonic device exteriorized on eBay to something that concords with Walter Benjamin's comment that interiority is the spatial hallmark of collecting. The West fetishizes the exteriorization of memory onto objects, and the kind of culture of collection that eBay supports also depends upon the importance of objects to memory processes, of objects as traces of the past or the material real that help buttress a claim to personal authenticity and a sense of self that endures over time. This occurs at the very moment that many media and other corporate strategies promote accepting that those aspects of memory recall that do not rely on objects such as photographs or toy boats are unimportant because they cannot be turned into commodities.

THE COMMODIFICATION OF AUTHENTICITY

As Marx argued, the fetishization of commodities requires removing evidence of the history and material conditions under which they are produced. This process abets purchasers' forgetting about the labor value inherent in an object for sale and instead promotes purchasers' abilities to project onto commodities meanings encouraged through advertising, such as that owning a Prada jacket or wearing a Tom Ford fragrance, for example, might temporarily substitute for, or perhaps augment, meaningful interpersonal relationships. I should note, however, that competing theories of the fetish have too often focused on making the other strange and on emphasizing a presumed sense of personal lack that supposedly drives the transfer of desires onto visible material objects. As Peter Stallybrass has noted, what these European anthropological and psychoanalytic theories of the fetish actually demonized "was the possibility that history, memory, and desire might be materialized in objects that are touched and loved and worn."[4] eBay inverts any such demonization to celebrate the articulation of history, memory, and desire to acquiring objects such as toy boats; I suggest, then, that projecting desires onto a fetish is a way of producing affective value.[5] Regis Debray argues that "we would never understand that things can speak to us about human beings if inanimate objects were not endowed with a kind of social soul,"[6] and in the case of an object purchased on eBay, as enacted in the "Toy Boat" commercial, a purchaser might seek to experience a re-membering of some aspects of his or her past and thereby a quality of re-enchantment of the present through the object's acquisition. I also want to point out that some media-friendly eBay listings become sensational though transient commodities in themselves, receiving millions of hits from temporarily fascinated viewers and corresponding mass media attention.

I have noted eBay's centrality within the new economy predicated on staging entertaining experiences, and I will discuss four listings for the differing ways they raise questions about how eBay sellers produce authenticity. I consider the first two listings in tandem. The first, from June 2004, is by eBay ID tribleheart and titled "Selling Son's Beloved Play Station 2 For Punishment!" This auction ended with a winning bid of 122.50 USD—a typical price one might pay for a Play Station. The listing's narrative component informs readers that the seller's thirteen-year-old son, home alone with teenage friends, broke a bugle the seller also had listed on eBay, then proceeded with friends to drink a case of beer and finally a bottle of Dom Perignon 1995 his parents had been saving for over a year for that "special" occasion. Much of the narrative is clichéd. It also takes the form of a rant against disobedient children. A strikingly similar but far more successful marketing appeal is at work in a December 2004 listing by a set of California parents first using eBay ID magumbo_2000, and then, after the first sale fell through due to hoax bidding, eBay ID mandirpro. Both listings feature the headline "Bad Children get no Nintendo DS: Santa will skip our house this year." The parents seek to punish their boys by selling the Christmas present they had intended to give them. Additional text in mandirpro's second listing includes the wording "Relisted for the THIRD TIME. WE WILL NOT GIVE UP. No kidding. Three undeserving boys have crossed the line. Tonight we sat down and showed them what they WILL NOT get for Christmas this year. I'll be taking down the tree tomorrow. (December the 23rd)." Unlike the first example, this more mean-spirited narrative remains silent as to why the boys need punishment. What could they have done? The unknown has the potential to raise the stakes, to increase viewers' interest in this listing because it implicitly invites them to imagine what the boys might have done and in so doing draws them more deeply into its narrative by asking them to complete the story. Bidders, therefore, compete to purchase the vicarious experience of punishing the boys at a distance—the auction's successful bid of 5,300 USD suggests more is up for bids than consumer electronics alone. All bidders, in effect, contribute to the story line and its narrative effect. Arguably, the winner completes the story, yet all bidders, in raising the object's final price incrementally, influence the story's final outcome and accrue to themselves a quality of authenticity; story collapses into sale. A review of mandirpro's earlier eBay transactions, moreover, reveals that the parents had purchased on eBay an identical model Nintendo DS in early December 2004 for the reasonable price of 192 USD. While it is also reasonable to conclude that this earlier purchase may well have been intended as a Christmas gift, the rationale underlying the striking increase of more than 5,000 USD in resale, I suggest, lies in the listing's exceptional entertainment value (the successful bidder is the same online casino that purchased the aforementioned and by now infamous Virgin Mary Grilled Cheese sandwich) coupled with the related possibility, available to any viewer, to imagine, and reimagine (if so desired), the story's outcome. In so doing, such imaginative and entertained viewers also create their own forms of affective or use value and, if they bid, help increase the object's eventual exchange value. To do so through the bidding experience is not insignificant, for bidding is a serious game constituting a form of consumption and production in itself.

I've raised the issue of commodity fetishism, and before introducing my next example of narrative effect I need to acknowledge something else that is critical to our relationships with objects, and this is their importance in rooting our sanity. The phenomenological psychologist Robert Romanyshyn notes that we count on objects to keep their place—in their fidelity to us and in the way they keep to the places we assign them and thereby help root our sanity is constituted one of the most elemental relationships between us and the world around us.[7] Given that not all the objects for sale on eBay are recycled from the dim recesses of the garages Andreessen identifies, it follows that some of the stories that sellers post on eBay may also be understood as apologies to these objects, as respectful attempts to help resettle something that was once more valued but is about to be let go (see chapter 2). The issue of what constitutes a "true" story on eBay, and how it retains a trace of the authentic, is key to my argument, and the narrative effect of the divestment ritual forming part of the next listing I discuss seems intended to help resettle a valued object.

In February 2004, eBay ID vassho listed his grandfather's vintage handmade shirt for sale with a starting bid of 49.99 USD. In part his narrative read,

> This shirt I understand was made by his mother in 1920s in Chezkoslovakia to protect them during some conflicts with other countrys as they invaded Chezkoslovakia, As they where in hiding to protect themselfs this shirt was a sign of portection a piece of clothing that kept him alive so to look past them and to move on as he was a young boy… . I am only selling this because me and my son have run into some hard times as I am a single father, farmer

> disabled vet, and due to the circumstances I am sure my Father would of wanted it this way.

The story of the shirt, an object that, in Stallybrass's terms, was "touched and loved and worn,"[8] makes a strong claim to authenticity, and the careful focus on detail provided by the listing's images supports the claim. Numerous syntax and spelling errors also lend the listing's narrative a quality of guilelessness—an increasingly valuable trait on eBay for establishing claims of authenticity in the many listings of collectibles appealing to memory and identity. The seller includes six images that successively reveal detailed features of embroidery and other aspects of the shirt's tailoring. The seller is willing to divest himself of an object imbued with important memories and magical properties. Perhaps this is why the shirt didn't sell—the listing's narrative effect worked against a sale, suggesting that the shirt's use value to the seller remained too high, the trace of its very personal origins too evident to allow prospective purchasers to imagine how it might be "friction free" or even ethical to wrench the shirt from the seller's lived world in a way that would allow them to truly possess the garment—to imbue it with their own unique meanings, and historical or fantastical allusions.

Another exceptional eBay listing, "Size 12 Wedding Dress/Gown No Reserve: Sure is a Beauty! Cheap! Used Only Once!" was listed in April 2004 by eBay ID horseplaypublishing. The seller fabricates an elaborate narrative. It begins, "I found my ex-wife's wedding dress in the attic when I moved. She took the $4000 engagement ring but left the dress. I was actually going to have a dress burning party when the divorce became final, but my sister talked me out of it. She said, 'That's such a gorgeous dress. Some lucky girl would be glad to have it. You should sell it on eBay.'" The initial narrative continues for several hundred words. As Figure 11.1 indicates, the seller, too large to fit into the dress, nevertheless models it himself (blanking out his face) as he claims he could not persuade any woman to model it for him. The misogynist account belittles the ex-wife but as the quirky listing became a Web phenomenon, clocking 8.6 million hits in a week, the seller twice updated his narrative. Readers came to learn that due to the listing he received several marriage proposals, sundry comments on cross-dressing, stern lectures on marital fidelity, and valued peer support from other sympathetic ex-husbands. At one point the bidding exceeded 10,000 USD. When it became clear to eBay, however, that some bids were bogus and others from members swept up in a bidding frenzy, the company interceded to help cull nonlegitimate bidders. The winning bid for the dress was 3,850 USD, but this bid, too, was a hoax and the sale fell through. The seller became an overnight celebrity, appearing on *The Today Show* and

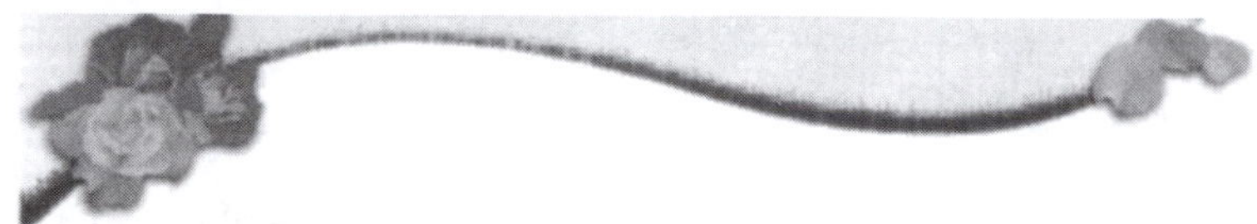

For Sale: One Slightly Used Size 12 Wedding Gown. Only worn twice: Once at the wedding and once for these pictures.

Make: Victoria

Style: 611

Size: 12

Divorce forces sale

I found my ex-wife's wedding dress in the attic when I moved. She took the $4000 engagement ring but left the dress. I was actually going to have a dress burning party when the divorce became final, but my sister talked me out of it. She said, "That's such a gorgeous dress. Some lucky girl would be glad to have it. You should sell it on EBay. At least get something back for it." So, this is what I'm doing. I'm selling it hoping to get enough money for maybe a couple of Mariners tickets and some beer. This dress cost me $1200 that my drunken sot of an ex-father-in-law swore up and down he would pay for but didn't so I got stuck with the bill. Luckily I only got stuck with his daughter for 5 years. Thank the Lord we didn't have kids. If they would have turned out like her or her family I would have slit my wrists. Anyway, it's a really nice dress as you can see

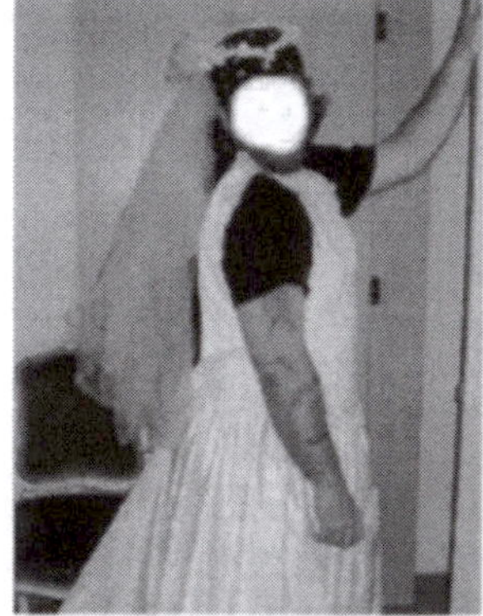

Figure 11.1 "Size 12 Wedding Dress/Gown No Reserve."

accepting an option for film rights. However, a follow-up article in the *Houston Chronicle* exposed key claims of the seller's narrative as untrue. When asked by a reporter if the dress really was his ex-wife's, the seller sidestepped the question, "I got the wedding dress, I wanted to get rid of it. I was going to burn it and had the idea of selling it on eBay. I needed to sell it on eBay … and I needed to make it stand out."[9] What is interesting here is the way a partial lie achieves a quality of authenticity, and not only by virtue of the outrageous and immediate quality of the media-friendly listing's diarist, weblogish style, though this is a factor in the confessional culture that presses increasingly hard on everyday American life organized, in the words of James Kunstler, according to the interpenetrating trilogy of the "dark raptures of nonstop infotainment, recreational shopping and compulsive monitoring."[10] Of at least equal importance is what undergirds the seller's comprehension that the narrative accompanying the listing's images needed to make the dress stand out. To achieve this, the seller participates in the commodification of his own authenticity, a participation driven by the cynical logic of advertising informing the claim that "the truth is that which sells." Though the first aborted auction required that the seller relist the dress for sale, within a system of exchange that positions money as the principal value, then, "If it sells, it's true, it's authentic" even as, at the same time, key goals of the seller for publicity (he revealed in interviews a desire to resume his musical career) have been realized whether the dress sold or not. How might this be so? I propose that although the dress did not sell at this particular auction, what did successfully "sell" or exchange millions of times was a trace of the seller himself in the form of a self-commodifying emblem—the image-text combination itself as an archived form of virtual collectible. A quality or a trace of authenticity imbues in his staged narrative account, as confirmed by the listing's 8.6 million hits. Benjamin observed that "the presence of the original is the prerequisite to the concept of authenticity,"[11] and in all of the above examples, whether the narrative is "true" or not, the original is not only the object offered for exchange. The original, in a fashion similar to the logic of reality TV, is also the seller-as-protagonist selling himself and his history as affective entertainment.

The issue of telepresence is critical in assessing the kinds of online narratives I've described. Telepresence (the sense, supported by networked digital information technologies, of going somewhere else while remaining "here," and therefore an experience of being neither fully here nor fully there yet also both at once) allows eBay browsers, bidders, and purchasers alike to experience a trace of the original—in this case, that of the psychic states of the supposedly angry parents, grieving grandsons, and finding-it-hard-to-let-go ex-husbands. But something more is at stake. As Debray observes, a

> monotonous reliance on video-documented realia ... produces in modern consciousness a priority on the immediate, the factually positive, the reportable, and the graphic. Paradoxically, however, because of its equation with the real itself, we as viewers accede to such representation being basically all there is *for the moment*... . [At this moment, viewers go] *beyond* the critical margin of skepticism or minimal disbelief that Lionel Trilling seemed to have in

mind when he wrote, "It is characteristic of the intellectual life of our culture that it fosters a form of *assent* which does not involve actual *credence*." (138)

I understand Trilling's observation as a description of hegemony—of the production of consent—and, with respect to viewers who go beyond merely "buying into" the vendor's story about the wedding gown, suggest that while they are confirming that the truth is that which sells, their mass viewing and reviewing of this listing also point to the rise of the partially perceived, partially manufactured need to believe that the image online transmits a trace of the original, a potent desire the existence of which the millions of hits during one week tend to confirm. Debray further supports my contention here in finding that "representations have become so pervasively mediate that they seem *im*mediate to everyone who can 'experience' them at once and yet so immediate (in the indexical directness of the trace's relation to its … source) that experience itself becomes indirect, placing greater emphasis on superficial and abstract consciousness of positive contexts mediating it than on the raw datum itself" (n.9, 137).

In the case of eBay, mediated indirect experience and superficial and abstract consciousness of positive contexts exploit the bourgeois fetishization of trivia noted by Henry Krips even as they also go beyond it.[12] Taken together, indirect experience, fascination with trivia, yearning for easy or "objective" access to memory retrieval, and an aura of intense experience fueled by mass media fascination with "oddball" eBay listings allow eBay users to accord equal if not greater credence to the online representations and simulations of sellers' lived worlds and objects than these users accord to actual objects such as wedding gowns or consumer electronics that remain off-screen. In remaining off-screen—in remaining, therefore, in a zone of potentiality actualized by a bidder only if she succeeds in winning the auction—material objects remain experientially virtual on eBay, and it is only their representations online that are experientially accessible for all viewers save one. In this, I suggest, technologies such as eBay facilitate an inversion of naturalized thinking about the relationship between the virtual and the actual. With the listings I have discussed, we see a coming to be of a situation in which it is the virtual that becomes experientially actual. This is, moreover, for all browsers and unsuccessful bidders a situation in which actual objects remain experientially virtual. Enter the trace as a means to allow desire for an object to be experienced as more than just "lack." Experiencing a trace of an object can render desire more pleasurable, can move desire experientially from a state of anticipation to one approaching the pleasure of possession. This move is crucial to online auctions of collectibles and other unique items where all but the successful bidder might otherwise suffer "lack."

THE SPACE OF THE TRACE

I've raised the issue of the index and the trace, and I'll now discuss it in greater detail. While the vendor of the wedding dress doubtless would have preferred it to sell, his underlying strategy was to use eBay to produce for viewers a certain kind of affective value (possibly useful in refashioning his career). For the millions of individuals who looked at his listing, I am reminded of Benjamin's observation—one that anticipates Debray's suggestion about the effects of indexicality—that "everyday the urge grows stronger to get hold of an object at very close range by way of its likeness, its reproduction."[13] Benjamin is writing about acquiring an iconic material object—a photographic reproduction of an original artwork, for example—but the listing's millions of hits suggest individuals took away something of use value from it too. What is the nature of this affect, "thing," or value? In attempting to answer this question, I find it productive to consider Charles Peirce's concept of the index. Peirce argued that the index is a representation whose relation to its object consists in a correspondence in fact. As understood by Debray, "[L]ater refinements of Peirce's original insights led to understanding the index as some remaining fragment of the object or contiguity with it causally, such … as in the case of [a] relic for a saint" (137). Debray further notes that reading indices "relies on recognizing the essential relation of immediate *causation* between the object and the referent that is videotic, photographic, televisual … or pixellated based on photography or some kind of camera technology that digitizes the *trace of the real object* imagined" (138). An index, then, is a representation that individuals perceive as having a trace of its referent in itself. And, if it is so perceived, it is also a phenomenological and mnemonic mechanism for bringing the past into the present and transforming the lost into found. In the example of the wedding dress, I suggest that in an age of digital simulation, an index or trace of the historical uniqueness that inheres in both the dress and its seller becomes momentarily available to each of the millions of site visitors. Repeat viewings mean repeat experiences of this immediate and insubstantial essence. Modifying Benjamin's terms, the object these browsers had the urge to get hold of "up close and personal" was a trace of the author and experiential access to the meaning or essence of the dress. The listing itself, with its ability to be downloaded, printed, and forwarded to others, is as much an exteriorized (and therefore archivable) experiential trace of the lived world of the author as it is of the dress. Moreover, the Peircian understanding expressed in such phrases as "a correspondence in fact" and "some remaining fragment of the object" to identify the quality of the trace here points to an additional related factor crucial to the sale of commodified authenticity on eBay. This is the increasingly naturalized belief that the Web constitutes a space.

As E. H. Bassett and Kate O'Riordan and I have argued,[14] spatial metaphors promoting the belief that the Web is a space allow individuals to conceive of the technology as locating human actors in social space. But I will go further and suggest that conceiving the Web as a kind of space flows not only from corporate hype or spatializing metaphors but also from Web interfaces' increasing facility in allowing virtual space to be experienced phenomenologically as a trace of (and therefore arguably approaching an equivalence of) material space itself, as if seeming therefore to retain and transmit "some remaining fragment of the object." Rob Shields observes that "virtual spaces are indexical, in Peirce's sense, in that they are interstitial moments,"[15] and I link his observation to the ability of eBay as a virtual space to suggest to users that the objects on view float at the limit of potentiality—purchase us, the narrative effects produced by an emblematic combination of text and images seem to say, and we will arrive at your doorstep in all our materiality and purported historicity, an elsewhere with a past that will rematerialize just for you. Yet, to return to an earlier observation, for most viewers, the countless millions of window shoppers and failed bidders alike, these objects remain virtual in their sense of always remaining elsewhere—their potential to fully actualize on the successful bidder's doorstop courtesy of PayPal and the postal service also points back equally if not more forcefully to their having been entered into the virtual realm in the first place. Here, rather than the virtual always tending toward its actualization, it is equally possible to discern that materiality, courtesy of information machines such as eBay, can tend toward a state of ongoing and repeat virtualization, one where the virtual object also takes on fetish qualities and where pleasure taken in an object reverts to desire. The issue of potential and potentialization, then, points not only to how the virtual may actualize but also to the reverse dynamic. In both situations, potentiality and indexicality occupy Janus-like positions along the virtual-actual continuum, although for browsers and failed eBay bidders alike the actual objects remain illusory and distant; a desirable and aesthetically engaging experience of the virtual is as close as these individuals may get. Experience gained through exchange of images comes to constitute the affective or use value for many viewers even as this exchange also contributes to the eventual exchange value of the object.

Geographers theorize space as the matrix for relations—space organizes through distance and propinquity the objects located within it, humans included. It follows that, as interfaces become more intelligent, users might also experience traces of objects for sale in the spatialized, image-reliant online representations of these objects as well. To buttress part of my argument here I will make a brief detour to counter objections that individuals are savvy and know that digital images are only simulations (and therefore freed from such concerns as whether a representation is truthful to its original) at times subject to falsification,[16] for as philosopher Catherine Wilson, discussing the epistemology of computer-mediated experience and presence, notes, "[T]he human ability to distinguish simulacra from real things and simulations from real events, has been made to carry too much psychological weight."[17] Among other outcomes, Wilson's cautionary speaks to the flood of Neoplatonic Web practices, eBay included, that implicitly and explicitly invest online emblems, avatars, and other software "agents" with real powers and corresponding attributes of being. The image of the wedding dress coupled to its experience by viewers becomes the actual real, whereas for all but the successful bidder the dress remains in Plato's Cave.

1997

The eBay listings I have discussed are all from 2004, and each relies on an emblematic combination of text and image to establish the claim of authenticity and thereby a simulation of truth so important to the sale of certain kinds of fetishizable collectibles and memorabilia listed on the site. As in the use of emblems more generally, on eBay a listing's textual component "polices" or promotes (not always successfully) a preferred meaning or interpretation for the accompanying images. While eBay's Picture Services feature makes it easy to include JPEG images on an eBay listing, as late as 1997 this was not the case. It was also widely assumed then that strangers would never trade with other strangers online sight unseen. Yet during this same transitional period, at the advent of the Web and the popularization of Netscape and Internet Explorer as the next generation of Andreessen's browser technology, sellers on AuctionWeb already understood that "at the very least, [purchasers] wanted to get a look at what they were bidding on."[18] Therefore, a high-quality image of an object for sale already was seen as crucial in obtaining a good price. Few sellers, however, had the technology and bandwidth to upload digital images. And for those who did, AuctionWeb, unlike eBay today, did not provide an image-hosting service. Sellers had to contract with separate image-hosting services and link these sites to their AuctionWeb listing, making it difficult for most to mount any images at all.

I want to draw attention to three simultaneous processes taking place in 1997: (1) eBay sellers realized that a high-quality digital image was essential in securing a good price for the objects they were selling; (2) few, however, could upload such images to image-hosting services or the early eBay site; and (3) users of text-based Internet Relay Chat (IRC) also understood the value of an image in providing more information about the person with whom they were chatting. However, they faced the same technical difficulties as sellers on AuctionWeb. Indeed, one individual with whom I chatted in 1997 told me he had concluded there were no more than a few dozen JPEGs circulating among the thousands of folks using certain IRC channels worldwide. He supported his contention by noting that he had been emailed back his own picture by a man with whom he had been chatting on IRC and who, as the sender, insisted to my informant that the picture was indeed of him. While we also see here a quirky example of the economics of scarcity at work, I wish to connect these three points to suggest that 1997 marks a cultural and technological pivot—the advent of the Web and cheaper access to scanning devices and easier-to-use image-uploading and -downloading software allowed the beginning of greater exchange of images online. Yet this development remained coupled to a lingering sense, confirmed by an older understanding of the internet as text based, that online images were more subject to falsification, misuse, and misrepresentation than the photography of old. The online image, then, had not yet been fully imagined as a site of *potential*—of retaining a trace, potentially actual, of the real object, even though some eBay sellers already had an implicit grasp of the power of the online image to articulate to the power of the trace.

In *On Photography*, Susan Sontag argues that photography is more than a rendered image, "it is also a trace, something directly stenciled off the real, like a footprint," and Anne McClintock also points to photography's long-standing relationship to "the romantic metaphysics of inner, individual truth."[19] If eBay's founders hoped to enable a "perfect marketplace," the metaphysics and reality of the trace today find a "perfect home" on the Web with its telepresent ability to suggest that what is lost, elsewhere, or in the past is also potentially at hand yet at the same time lodged at the intersection of the technology itself and the desire for actual presence on the part of viewers (again, all of whom except for the winning bidder will never possess or hold the object evoked by the image). At the same time, we live in a period when more and more people accept the meaning of photography as a process that includes producing the vivid digital imagery they encounter online through settings such as eBay. Further, because of the close association between space and sight, an implicit understanding of the Web as a series of (illuminated) spaces for human agency helps the image online accrue seemingly material and even forensic qualities.

Much, therefore, has changed since 1997. Despite a general awareness that "anyone" can easily manipulate a digital image with programs such as Photoshop or PaintShopPro, images produced with digital cameras may now be considered admissible in American courts,[20] and eBay's success reveals how the digital image is increasingly accepted as part of making a truth claim, as retaining a trace of the original, even as individuals willingly concede its ability to be faked or made the central part of a hoax. Here we see again how such practices may invert Lionel Trilling's definition of hegemony to suggest that a widespread belief in the digital image now outweighs the importance of lingering doubts it may be a fake. Further, as participants within a visual culture, eBay members also have learned, in concert with acquiring easier-to-use information machines, that the digital image makes more of a claim (like a footprint) when it contains a trace of the truth than when it is so manipulated it appears to contain none at all (see chapter 12). If, as either a buyer or a seller on eBay, one buys into the belief that the image carries a trace of the original, then the image can serve as a bridge between the "there" of the seller and the "here" of the buyer and also of the past of the object and the future it may acquire if and when it reaches the hands of a buyer and the appreciating status of a private collectible it may then come to enjoy. Within the experience economy eBay helps stage, experiencing the digital trace increasingly takes center screen whether this is when we are selling an idea of ourselves as promotional entertainment, looking to meet others for conversation or perhaps hooking up through online chatrooms, or selling an object with which we purport to have intimate or long-standing associations. The following are two examples. One is an extract from a chatroom profile posted in early 2005 in which the profile owner writes that "no pic means no chat. No reason today not to have a pic. If you figured out how to get to this site then you should figure a way to download a pic." I draw the second from the May 2005 funeral rites for Pope John Paul II, during which countless individuals used cell phones to record images of his corpse during the twenty seconds they were allotted to file past the bier. Gianluca Nicolette, media commentator for *La Stampa*, observed that "in the past, pilgrims would take away with them a relic, like a piece of cloth on the saint's body. Here there's been the transposition to a level of unreality. They're bringing home a digital relic."[21]

Capitalism's commodification of all aspects of experience, however, is also at work here. The dynamic whereby individuals confer credence on the possibility that a trace of the real inheres in an online image runs parallel to an accelerating process of self-commodification whereby one can only become a "truly" successful commodity after one is fully willing to see oneself as an image. Therefore, as eBay's surveillant and self-policing Feedback Forum already suggests (see chapter 7), the production of trust between online strangers seeking the "perfect" or "friction-free" exchange value of an object increasingly demands the commodification of personal authenticity too, of affect itself, before a transaction is likely to take place. How "friction free" can that be? In any event, an earlier "obvious" belief that strangers would never trade on the Web failed to account for the full hegemonizing power of "the eBay experience," which articulates human sensation both to "the affective enjoyment of the present" (for anthropologist Victor Turner, a definition of experience itself)[22] and to the self-commodification of members who infer the trace of the real not only in the objects displayed but also across the entertaining virtual stages of eBay's countless listings.

MEMORY TRACES

As experienced on eBay, commodified authenticity lodges within an understanding that if there is a winner, there may be more losers still. Such a competitive setting helps to reposition memory and authenticity discursively so that they better concord with the competitive logic of social Darwinism that increasingly stalks the neoliberal subject, at least in settings such as eBay where "the market" has achieved fully naturalized status. The potential for authenticity, partly lodged in the visible fetish virtual object, partly in the success of a listing's overall narrative effect, is a latent exchange value available for transfer and thereby actualization to the highest bidder. Therefore, the Western fetish for memory in its external, material forms supports thinking we can fully access memory and the past through objects purchased in which we also believe inhere forms of affective value. Access to memory understood to operate in this way, then, would seem to be on its way to becoming a competitive process. While, for example, the many Pillsbury DoughBoys and DoughGirls listed on eBay suggest there is plenty of memory related to certain mass-produced items to go round, in the case of more unique objects such as the toy boat, the winner has access to the whole nine yards and everyone else who might be interested is left with a trace and the nostalgia this might induce. If, within the experience economy that eBay organizes, authenticity is available to the highest bidder, then the kinds of dynamics raised in this discussion of eBay constitute a new form of sensational micropolitics at work on updating the ways that history is written by the winners. For if advertising has convinced many that the truth is that which sells, on eBay—an interstitial site of material and immaterial cultures—history, as it were, becomes a series of vivid exteriorized impressions "written" and published by the winners, and the contemporary winners on eBay and the wider Web are composed not only of purchasers acquiring objects collected for their auratic and memory-resonant qualities, but also of sellers who manage to transmit, and hopefully leave, a trace. Hardly a trivial pursuit. And hardly friction free. For how could it be in a setting that promotes the pernicious but disposable belief that nothing need ever be lost or forgotten?

NOTES

I would like to thank Terry Rollins, eBayer extraordinaire, for his generous insights into the eBay process and for drawing my attention to several of the kinds of listings discussed in this chapter. Thanks also to Philip Hartwick and Doug Coon, and to David Pinkerton for bringing Lemonhead into our lives; she brings great charm to the cover of this book. This chapter is adapted from Ken Hillis, "A Space for the Trace: Memorable eBay and Narrative Effect," *Space and Culture* 9, no. 2 (2006).

1. Joseph Pine and James Gilmore, *The Experience Economy* (Cambridge, MA: Harvard Business School, 1999); and Michael J. Wolf, *The Entertainment Economy* (New York: Times Books. 1999).
2. Hubert L. Dreyfus, *What Computers Still Can't Do: A Critique of Artificial Reason* (Cambridge, MA: MIT Press, 1992); and Gilles Deleuze, *Cinema 1: The Movement-Image*, trans. Hugh Tomlinson and Barbara Habberjam (Minneapolis: University of Minnesota Press, 1986).
3. Sharon Zukin, *Point of Purchase: How Shopping Changed American Culture* (New York: Routledge, 2004).
4. Peter Stallybrass, "Marx's Coat," in *Border Fetishisms: Material Objects in Unstable Spaces*, ed. Patricia Spyer (New York: Routledge, 1998), 183–207.
5. For a superb discussion of the relationship between fetishism and affective value, see Amy Villarejo, *Lesbian Rule: Cultural Criticism and the Value of Desire* (Durham, NC: Duke University Press, 2003).
6. Regis Debray, *Transmitting Culture*, trans. Eric Rauth (New York: Columbia University Press, 2000), 49. Additional page numbers of this reference are cited parenthetically.
7. Robert Romanyshyn, *Technology as Symptom and Dream* (New York: Routledge, 1989).
8. Stallybrass, 186.

9. Louis Parks, "On eBay, Wedding Dress for Success," *Houston Chronicle*, April 30, 2004, www.chron.com/cs/CDA/ssistory.mpl/front/2540131 (accessed June 10, 2004).
10. James Howard Kunstler, "The Long Emergency," RollingStone.com, 2005, www.rollingstone.com/news/story/_/id/7203633?pageid=rs.N (accessed April 6, 2005).
11. Walter Benjamin, "The Work of Art in the Age of Mechanical Reproduction," in *Illuminations*, trans. Harry Zohn, ed. Hannah Arendt (New York: Schocken, 1969), 220.
12. Henry Krips, *Fetishism: An Erotics of Culture* (Ithaca, NY: Cornell University Press), 137.
13. Benjamin, 223.
14. E. H. Bassett and Kathleen O'Riordan, "Mediated Identities and the Ethics of Internet Research: Contesting the Human Subjects Research Model," paper presented at Crossroads in Cultural Studies Conference 2, 2002, Tampere, Finland; and Ken Hillis, *Digital Sensations: Space, Identity, and Embodiment in Virtual Reality* (Minneapolis: University of Minnesota Press, 1999).
15. Rob Shields, "Hypertext Links: The Ethic of the Index and Its Space-Time Effects," in *The World Wide Web and Contemporary Social Theory*, ed. Andrew Herman and Thomas Swiss (Routledge: New York, 2000), 145–60.
16. In terms of embodied sensation, a simulation and a representation may not, after all, be so far apart experientially.
17. Catherine Wilson, "Vicariousness and Authenticity," in *The Robot in the Garden*, ed. Ken Goldberg (Cambridge, MA: MIT Press, 1999), 76.
18. Adam Cohen, *The Perfect Store: Inside eBay* (Boston: Little, Brown, 2002) 66.
19. Susan Sontag, *On Photography* (New York: Penguin Books, 1977), 154; and Ann McClintock, *Imperial Leather: Race, Gender, and Sexuality in the Colonial Contest* (New York: Routledge, 1995), 124.
20. In May 2004, Hany Farid, professor of computer science at Dartmouth College, introduced software to detect manipulation of digital imagery. Farid's program analyzes the array of pixel clusters constituting digital photos and generates a diagram indicating altered areas. Ryan Bigge, "Debunking Photoshop Fakery," *New York Times Magazine*, December 12, 2004, 62–63.
21. Cited in Elisabeth Rosenthal, "The Cellphone as Church Chronicle, Creating Digital Relics," *New York Times*, April 8, 2005, A10.
22. Victor Turner, *From Ritual to Theatre: The Seriousness of Human Play* (New York: PAJ Productions, 1982), 14.

12

Between the Archive and the Image-Repertoire

Amateur Commercial Still Life Photography on eBay

JAMES LEO CAHILL

Consider the individual images in Figure 12.1. Each is an example of amateur commercial still life photography (ACSL) on eBay and indicative of what I suggest is an emergent genre of photography (to the extent that term still applies in the age of pixels). ACSL photographs are seller-submitted images taken by amateur photographers of items listed for auction. Millions of eBay sellers have developed their own practice of photo-imaging (a term that encompasses analog and digital means of production) that is a major component of the site's visual economy. The status of these photographs as positivist recordings of the items for sale does not exhaust or contain the images. Rather, a quality of latent semiotic unruliness offers something in excess of their evidentiary status, and I am interested in theorizing this excess.

I first consider the aesthetic and technical conventions of ACSL photography, then discuss theoretical arguments about the truth claims accorded to amateur photographs due to their supposed naïveté. I do so to argue that the ACSL aesthetic trains individuals to identify with commodities. I then theorize eBay's status as a collection in itself—as a not-quite archive of amateur images. Drawing on concepts of the archive and the image-repertoire developed by Jacques Derrida and Roland Barthes, I chart a relationship between collections and re-collections. I argue that eBay is an ephemeral, porous archive, or rather a *mal*functioning mnemonic machine, which is to say a machine perfectly attuned to the demands of capital. eBay sets in motion and sustains desires for accumulation and expenditure while also indexing a compulsion to forget. The force of this compulsion, energized by the "going, going, gone" temporal experience of auctions and their erasure from computer memory after sixty days, helps drive consumption and eBay's profits. The questions I raise and the issues I discuss,

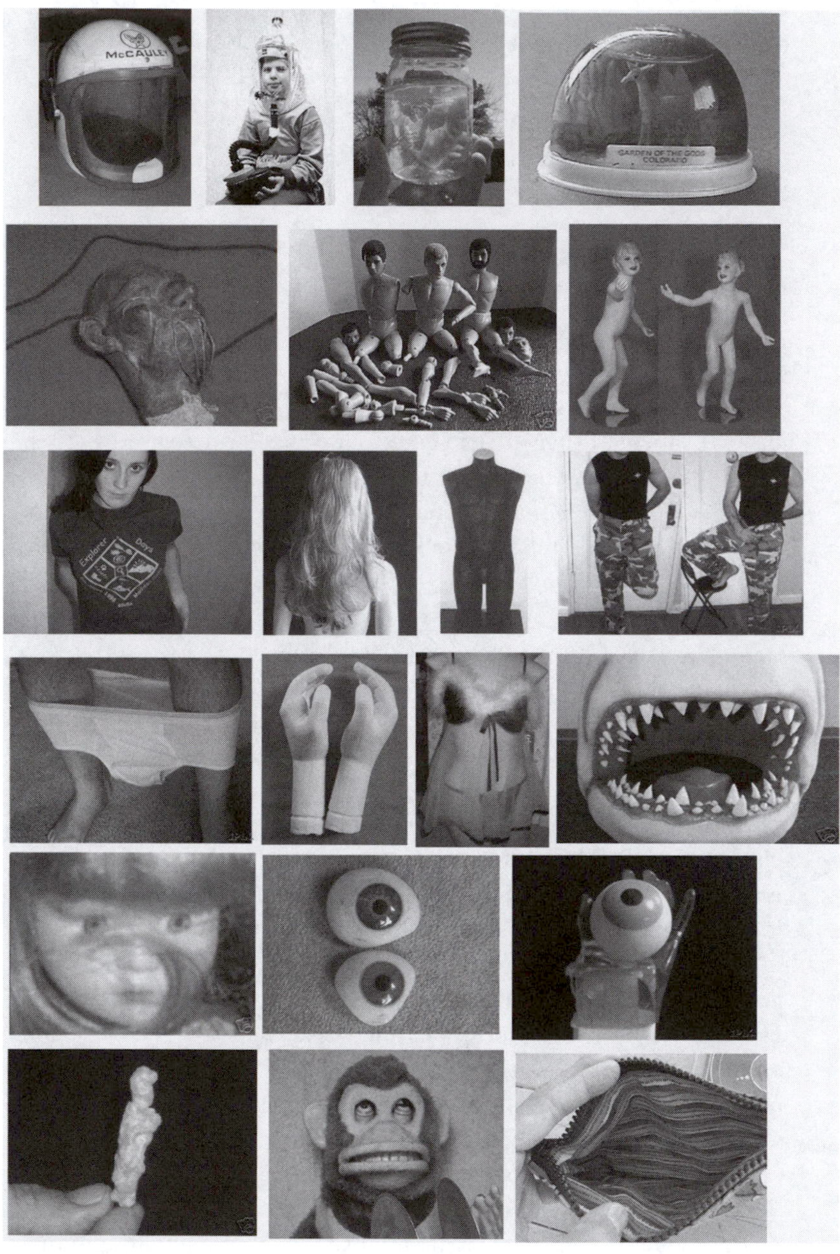

Figure 12.1 Examples of amateur commercial still life photography.

while focused on eBay practices, are applicable across broader contexts not only because we are living through an era of proliferating mnemonic technologies such as networked computing, but also because they touch on the enormous privatization pressures that often aim at defunding institutions of public memory such as museums, libraries, and art galleries in the name of the commodity and its mechanisms of circulation such as eBay.

THE AESTHETIC AND TECHNICAL CONVENTIONS OF ACSL

The amateur commercial still life is not the only photographic practice associated with eBay; many mail order and wholesale businesses operating on the site use professionally produced stock images. However, self-produced images of secondhand items constitute the site's dominant set of photographic conventions. Despite the many sellers and wide variety of goods photographed, the look of these images has remained remarkably consistent over eBay's first decade. The factors shaping these conventions index a convergence of practices instituted and guided by eBay, practices and discourses of amateur photography in relation to everyday life, and the logics of commercial photography and display.

The characteristics of amateur photography such as poor focus, eccentric framing, indifferent lighting, and unruly shadows are considerably minimized in ACSL.[1] But they have by no means vanished (thankfully), as evidenced in Figure 12.1 by the extraneous glare of a distant window on a snow globe, the blurry close-up of a doll's face, and the shadows obscuring the faces of dismembered GI Joe dolls.[2] Unlike the traditional subjects of amateur photographs that document family members and events such as birthdays, holidays, vacations, graduations, and weddings,[3] ACSL images focus primarily on objects for sale. To the extent that they are documents, they appropriate the clinical aesthetic of forensic photography to present clear, functional images of the objects' surface qualities and other important attributes. Sellers typically submit a frontal view of the listed object, a second view from another angle, and a separate close-up of defects or key details—the sutured lips of a shrunken head, the view into the mouth of a taxidermied shark (Figure 12.1). Typically shot in isolated close-ups against neutral backgrounds, ACSL photographs appear initially as denarrativized and rely on accompanying textual descriptions to narrativize the life of the item up for auction (see chapter 11). The textual elements of eBay listings act as elaborate captions, illustrating the image while also anchoring its significance in the sales pitch: "Buy Me." Sellers often remark on their limitations as photographers: "Photos do not do it justice," "Has to be seen to be believed," "The luster looks dulled in the photograph, but I can assure you it is highly polished in person," and so on. At the same time, these portraits of everyday objects are enactments in their own right, small single-click dramas staged for the camera. In this sense, they reference the uncanny objects in depopulated Dutch still life painting and its descendants in advertising.[4]

ACSL images re-present the material presence of objects in an attempt to appeal to sensual and tactile apprehension. This attribute, combined with the frequent isolation of objects in these images from a legible mise-en-scène, invites their importation into viewers' fantasy. Both the image of the underwear around a man's ankles and the shifting pose of the headless man in camouflage pants invite the eye to the imagined space outside the frame and invite the viewer to complete the picture. The frequent use of close-up also offers objects as up for inspection and attempts to compensate for the inability to touch them—a tactile knowledge often crucial to the purchase of goods.[5] This is literalized in the images of the hand holding a jar containing false teeth and the puffed cheese snack in the shape of the Virgin and Child; appearing as if in hand, these images hail us into the position of beholder as potential buyer. They blur naturalized distinctions between categories, wavering between the aesthetics and aims of amateur and commercial photography, and between the functional attributes of the document at its most banal and the still life as an enchanting, sensual invitation to fantasy.

Sellers who submit images to eBay do not come to the site without some familiarity with basic conventions of photography, advertising design, and product display acquired from living in image-saturated consumer societies that provide near-universal apprenticeship in the visual logics of consumerism. Yet, as Henri Lefebvre notes, "[T]he familiar is not necessarily the known,"[6] and an immersion in the society of the spectacle does not guarantee full competence in successfully reproducing this logic. eBay, however, reinforces these latent understandings with tips and training in photography offered on its tutorial page, "Selling Basics"; in seminars held at periodic "eBay University" conventions around the United States; and on partner pages such as the Hewlett-Packard (HP) Digital Photography Zone.[7] "No matter how well you describe your item," eBay advises, "most buyers want to see a picture before they purchase. So before you sit down at the computer to list your item, the first step should be to take great photos."[8] A. B. Russell, author of an ongoing "Photography for eBay" column in eBay's monthly Web newsletter, *Chatter*, begins each column with a reminder of the stakes of good photography: "A picture is worth a thousand words, especially on eBay. A good photograph can often mean the difference between selling an item or not."[9] Russell offers step-by-step tutorials on acquiring or improvising basic equipment, lighting setups and techniques, controlling composition and mise-en-scène, using portrait techniques for objects (particularly the use of backlighting), and photographing with human models. Mixing insider knowledge with scrappy, improvisational methods for rigging equipment on the cheap, Russell's column comes close to being a style guide for ACSL photography. His aim is clearly stated: "I'm going to show you what I have done to save money and still make (at worst) better than average photos." Russell helps sellers produce images that rise above the presumed naïveté of most amateur photographs by appropriating techniques from commercial photography.

"Photography for eBay," to the extent that Russell's column reads as an aesthetic statement of the corporation's photographic ideal, mobilizes and transforms the rhetoric of the amateur so important to the mythos of eBay. The apocryphal story that Pierre Omidyar built the site to help his fiancée track Pez dispensers, the site's invocation of the face-to-face interactions of flea markets, and its early motto, "Your Personal Trading Post," are in keeping with the 1990s discourse of the Web as a democratic space of empowered amateurs. Although the massive expansion of the site and its public offering of stock have altered the terrain and raised the stakes for the company, an aura of the amateur still holds currency in eBay's corporate identity, and more important, in the sales pitches offered by individual sellers' photographs on the site. Russell plays upon this tension quite effectively. He writes, "Photos—good photos—will help you sell your items and get more for them. That's why major companies pay a lot of money for professionals to photograph the things they make and sell." Russell's repeated references to the supposedly unlimited budgets of design professionals and major companies (other than eBay, of course) have the effect of positioning professional photography as both an object of admiration and a point of differentiation, something to strive for yet also keep at bay. To be sure, Russell reminds readers not to expect *Martha Stewart Living*-quality images on a microbudget: "As I have [said] before, I'll keep these ideas as simple and inexpensive as possible. Remember, though, that the photographers who make images for large companies spare no expense when it comes to their equipment." The column strongly advocates for the amateur approach, offers clear and genuinely useful lessons, and sets in motion an empowering narrative of the little person against the giant corporation: "Remember the amount of money these companies have spent to produce these images. Also remember that in a lot of cases, these companies are in direct competition with you as an eBay seller."

In addition to helping produce the ACSL genre through its training tips, eBay exerts a more direct—if oblique—influence through how it handles images uploaded to the site. eBay recommends relatively low-resolution rates of 400x300 pixels and 72 dots per inch to economize image-uploading time and server space. It allows users to post one free image per auction (though this cannot be said to be truly free, as one pays to list items on eBay); each additional image, including the 64x64 pixel thumbnail images appearing alongside many listings in search results, costs a fee administrated through the site's Picture Services program.[10] Although each fee is nominal, they add up, resulting in a more judicious choice of images used in listings so as to keep the number at a minimum. Picture Services automatically formats images uploaded onto the site; adjusts them to a uniform resolution, pixel size, and contrast; and imprints them with a watermark of a small camera icon in their lower right corners (visible in some individual images in Figure 12.1).[11] These applications initiate a feedback loop. People create their photographs to meet the demands of the site (taking photos that will easily transpose into a thumbnail, and so forth), and the site then standardizes these images as both low-resolution and legible through its automated image-editing programs that add a varnish of professional legibility yet also maintain the images' amateur charm (even adding to it through enforced low resolution). At the interface of the amateur and the professional, the individual and the corporation, a screen-based aesthetic has developed that itself may be understood as offering a "snapshot" of a visual convention in process. One might, then, consider eBay a mode of rephotography, a photograph of photography itself.

IN THE IMAGE OF THE AMATEUR

Although the distinctions between amateur and professional-commercial categories of photography blur in ACSL (if they were ever firm to begin with), the implicitly assumed naïveté of the amateur photograph—the image of the amateur—remains a determining force in any truth claims the images mount. The notion that amateur photographs cannot but speak direct truth (about the medium and its social contexts) is a repeated theme in the critical literature on photography.[12] Roland Barthes argues that amateur photographs express nothing less than the essence of photography, its intractable nature, its indexical relationship to reality, its deictic language of a pointing finger: look at this.[13] This transparency ironically results in the experience of a mournful encounter with the *absence* of the object, what Barthes terms a *punctum*, a small puncture, prick, or wounding, that marks photography's primary phenomenological experience. The *punctum* is a subjective response that strikes one with the melancholic absence of the object pictured. Contrary to the pejorative sense of "unprofessional, a hobbyist" often applied to amateur status, Barthes inverts this valuation of the amateur by drawing on its other sense of "one who loves or is fond of," from the Latin *amare*, to love. For Barthes, the camera in the hands of the amateur—the lover as opposed to the professional technician—intensifies the truth claims and the *truth* of the photograph. He imagines that "in the field of photographic practice, it is the amateur ... who is the assumption of the professional: for it is he who stands closer to the *noeme* of Photography"—that is, its defining ontological property, its indexicality.[14] Barthes suggests that *all* amateur photographs are at root documentary photographs, unwavering in their recording and expression of this essential kernel of truth: that the camera stood before the object and recorded its presence in time and space.

Like Barthes, Susan Sontag ascribes the power of the truth claims of amateur photographs to their lack: the artless naïveté or paucity of intentionality that opens up the images to greater social truths. Sontag's writings critically examine the widely held belief that "photographs furnish evidence." Vacillating between a Platonic critique of images and a deep fascination with them, she notes the irresistible pull of photographs: "Whatever the limitations (through amateurism) or pretensions (through artistry) of the individual photographer, a photograph—any photograph—seems to have a more innocent, and therefore more accurate, relation to visible reality than do other mimetic objects."[15] This understanding of amateur photography as "truer" also implies a suspicion of professional photography as somehow "artificial," manipulative, or deceptive, further removed from raw indexicality (a questionable dichotomy that does not hold for very long in most contexts).

While Barthes and Sontag offer models for simultaneously considering the universal and particular characteristics of amateur photographs, they depend upon a static and now somewhat dated understanding of amateur photography that meets its limits when considering digital-imaging practices within eBay's networked commercial contexts. ACSL images on eBay deploy "amateur" as an aesthetic strategy that calls into question the existence of an unreflective naïveté as the defining property of amateur photography. eBay sellers are hardly unreflective and naïve about the images they produce. They draw upon the visual rhetoric of a knowing sense of amateurism to confer veracity to the digital images presented. On eBay, the lack ascribed to amateur photography is converted into a surplus—it helps produce desire in the viewer to bid on the "truthful" object.

Despite any ontological shifts in the nature of photography brought about by digital imagery and its separation from a direct physical correspondence to the subjects it records, ACSL images on eBay still function primarily as documentary evidence. In fact, the value of the amateur aesthetic might actually increase in the age of digitization because of its associations with authenticity and "innocent" modes of production. eBay images articulate the burden of proof (this is what you'll get) with seduction (this is what you want). This is not in itself so different from other forms of commercial photography. However, in combination with sales pitches for secondhand goods exchanged at a distance between strangers (albeit branded and supported by the "neutral" corporate intermediary, eBay), the lack-as-potential-surplus takes on a pivotal role in establishing credibility to suspicious but desiring consumers who hope for pleasure in possessing the object. This lack may even become a selling point in its own right, as demonstrated by "reflectoporn," images on eBay that feature the nude figure of the photographer reflected in the shiny surfaces of items for sale such as tea kettles, television screens, guitars, and an On-Star Navigation System.[16]

In addition to helping produce exchange value, the lack-as-potential surplus at the heart of the eBay amateur aesthetic supports a specific mode of consumption that marketing scholar Douglas B. Holt describes as "decommodified authenticity," a pattern of consumption whereby certain consumers "locate subjectivity in what they perceive to be authentic goods, artisan rather than mass produced, and auratic experiences that are perceived as removed from, and so minimally contaminated by, the commodity form."[17] Such individuals avoid mass-market consumption because they believe it translates into a contrived subjectivity; economically and psychically, they invest deeply in their consumption habits, seeming all the more interpellated as consumers through their supposedly nonconsumptive consumer behaviors. eBay flatters such anticonsumption fantasies with the promise of a decommodified experience, exemplified by the amateur aesthetic of the images and the often "folksy" narratives that accompany objects and help personalize the anonymous transactions. Sequentially, then, the ACSL "look" helps decommodify objects and by doing so recommodifies them, particularly in the case of secondhand goods. The amateur production of what traditional high-culture modernist aesthetics judges as a "failure" can be profitable in vetting the capacity of the photograph to document the truth and to help render the item for sale more authentic and unique, "a real find" so to speak.

The photographic habits developed through eBay offer sellers a potential gain, both in profits and in empowerment acquired from learning new photographic techniques. Sellers acquire a more critical eye and therefore an increased ability to see or deconstruct the processes of an image's construction. This knowledge denaturalizes yet also reinforces fundamental techniques of commercial photography. Whereas the traditional subjects of amateur photography have been critiqued as ideologically complicit in buttressing the family as a conservative structure, ACSL trains producers and consumers in the visual logics of consumerism, ever focused on the transaction. The accumulation of techniques is reproductive of consumer subjectivities and a deeper identification with the photo object as a will-to-commodify.

ARCHIVAL IMPULSES AND THE IMAGE-REPERTOIRE

The millions of user-produced ACSL images circulating on eBay constitute one of the largest collections of amateur photography, online or otherwise, and the diversity of desires catered to has called into being a rather broad assemblage of images. eBay's archival possibilities drive the impulse to see eBay's impromptu gallery of amateur images of everyday objects as the image of an archive (see chapter 5 for a separate discussion of eBay-as-archive). Its combination of two mnemonic technologies, the photograph (as visual record) and the database (as structure and storage mechanism), allows eBay to host an enormous rotating collection of ACSL images, organized taxonomically by bidding categories, yet the accretion, permanence, and promise of futurity that the traditional meaning of "archive" implies do not describe eBay. With respect to the transient nature of its listings and the images they contain, eBay can be seen to operate according to the logic of the traveling exhibition installed for a set period of time in the exhibit halls of galleries and museums. Sixty days after an auction ends, eBay deletes the listing, a clearing of (computer) memory that leaves few visible traces. Sellers can purchase server space with eBay and potentially repost images, but generally the images are no longer available for public consumption. Moreover, unlike objects in the traditional archive, items on eBay are for sale. Yet the site arguably mobilizes something of an archival impulse in the sense theorized by Jacques Derrida, who situates the archive in relation to memory "at the place of originary and structural breakdown of the said memory"—in other words, the foundations of the archive are forgetting and amnesia.[18] Since there is no archive desire without forgetting, eBay's archival impulse is a monument to a partial victory over forgetting.

To more precisely account for eBay's ephemeral archive in the context of its commercial purposes, I turn to the concept of the "image-repertoire" as developed in Barthes's later writings. Image-repertoire offers a compelling descriptive of eBay as a photo database, and the appellation also helps theorize the productivity or labor ACSL photographs effect as an assemblage. A repertoire is a reservoir of shared knowledge, committed to memory, and easily recollected. A repertoire of images, then, works as an image "bank," a term useful for its English-language associations with money. A temporary re-collection of images, a site of transient storage, accumulation, circulation, and investment, repertoire also implies performativity, invoking a capacity for repetition in a manner that does not preclude variation. The development of ACSL images into a stable set of aesthetic conventions exemplifies the performative aspects of repertoire—they are produced and then displayed. "Repertoire" also refers to a set of tactics and possibilities possessed by the images posted on eBay as mechanisms for interpellating the viewer into a specific point of view such as positioning the beholder as desiring buyer.

For Barthes, the image-repertoire is the reservoir of illusions and visual phenomena (self-perceptions, fantasies, photographs, video, film, and so forth) through which the subject is both constituted and constitutes him or herself. In extending his argument, I am interested in thinking through convergences and differences between the image-repertoire and the archive in relation to eBay in order to clarify how eBay constitutes a subject of knowledge and desire specific to the website. eBay as image-repertoire, I suggest, is an exteriorized supplement to the Lacanian Imaginary.[19] A brief consideration of image-repertoire in its original context helps elaborate the stakes of the concept and its usefulness for the project at hand.

Barthes's translator, Richard Howard, offers "image-repertoire" as his interpretation of the original French, *l'imaginaire d'images* (the imaginary of images).[20] He also uses it to translate *l'Imaginaire* (Imaginary), excluding instances when Barthes directly invokes Jacques Lacan or when the term appears in quotation marks. In the original French, the relationship between the idea of the image-repertoire and Lacan exists on the surface, articulated through the word *l'Imaginaire*; Howard's translation places Lacan at a slight remove, allowing the term additional resonances.[21] Regardless of translation, Barthes's phrase remains ambiguous, its meaning slightly altered each time it appears. In *Roland Barthes by Roland Barthes*, the image-repertoire/*l'imaginaire d'images* is something to which one is "condemned," a devouring "total assumption of the image," "a trap," and a "grimace."[22] In *A Lover's Discourse*, the meaning of image-repertoire mutates and holds some of the ambiguity (in the Freudian sense) of archive fever. It is still something inescapable from which one must flee—"I try to wrest myself away from the amorous Image-repertoire: but the Image-repertoire burns underneath ... it catches again"—yet it is also mourned when one is exiled from it, as a loss of "that raving energy known as the Image-repertoire."[23] In *Camera Lucida* Barthes returns to the vexing adherence of the subject to the image, noting that this "stickiness" of the image, concretized in the taking of a photographic image, is petrifying and alienating. Barthes underscores the point with a slippage from first to third person:

> In terms of image-repertoire, the Photograph (the one I *intend*) represents that very subtle moment when, to tell the truth, I am neither subject nor object but a subject who feels he is becoming an object: I then experience a micro-version of death (or parenthesis): I am truly becoming a specter.[24]

For Barthes, the image-repertoire shifts from a drama of misidentification with the image-object as the source of alienation to a potential metamorphosis, a becoming-object. This final move—emphasizing the subject of the image-repertoire as becoming-object—is central to my use of the term.

As a collection of amateur photographs, the eBay image-repertoire (in relation to the Lacanian Imaginary) stages its own lover's discourse. It works to promote and uphold notions of the amateur as lover of the image/object *and* as a lack. This lack can be understood in two ways: as the "failed" amateur image lacking a professional veneer, and as the "failed" unity of signifier and signified, image and object that produces the tantalizing gap or lack that mobilizes desire[25] (in the case of ACSL on eBay, to possess through purchase the fetish object). eBay reinforces and trains the desires of subjects toward specific ends consonant with the goals of the corporate entity that hosts this amateur image-repertoire, molding the amateur *as lover of objects/objets*. This is less a love for any particular object than it is a generalized love for the photographic object as—to coin a term—an *objet petit amateur*: the amateur image-object and its symbolic lack as a proxy and pathway for desire.[26] The image indicates the lack of the physical object's presence, igniting the desire to possess it, and as such holds the promise of its possible presence through purchase. To love the *objet petit amateur* is to love the lack that fuels desire—the lust for the fetish aspect of the commodity. The image-repertoire eBay organizes catalogs numerous potential *objets petit amateur* to ignite the desire for consumption of the previously consumed: a process of reconsumption. The repertoire implies repeatability yet it is also fraught with "forgetfulness," operating as an impeccably *mal*functioning mnemonic machine, the image-repertoire as a porous or *a-mnemonic* archive. To wit, the traditional archive supposes a stable collection that one may return to again and again at one's own pace and to engage with objects that are not for sale. Like the traditional museum, it emphasizes a clear distinction between the interior collection and the exterior realm of the everyday, and articulates the stable collection and control of memory with power. The image-repertoire, as developed here in relation to eBay and the logic of commodity fetishism, promises a plenitude of unique objects (for unique prices) situated on the receding temporal horizon of "going, going, gone," thereby connecting the control of forgetting with power.

A number of this volume's contributors comment on eBay's recent U.S. ad campaign in which a TV spot ends with the question, "What if nothing was ever forgotten?" While the phrase speaks to the ability to use eBay's image-repertoire as a kind of lost-and-found service, forgetfulness itself is a primary function of eBay's image-repertoire to the extent that it is so often the condition of possibility for further accretion. Forgetfulness sets into motion and maintains a velocity of desire that passes through accumulation, abreaction, and amnesia. And this, perhaps, is the core work performed by eBay's evocative, succinct, and mediated question—it asks us to never forget, to always remember the centrality of forgetting, and to infer that lack itself drives the core meaning of eBay. The millions of entries in eBay's database form a dynamic collection of images of objects, still life images that index the petrification and reanimation of everything by capital, including its reaches into the most intimate of spheres. The images also point to the fantasy of a profitable clearing out—of the attic, the basement, the garage, the closet—of returning the forgotten items crowding the dark spaces of our homes to memory written in light, photographed and illuminated on the computer monitor. Finally, the listings of which the images form a crucial part—as ephemeral placeholders—perpetually disappear, clearing the site of a history or evidence of objects that sold or failed to sell; this is the necessary clearing (akin to masking the object's origins of production) that reignites and perpetuates the fetishistic desires to consume more. This forgetting—a "creative destruction"—is the very condition of possibility of consumption fueling contemporary capitalism.

AFTERIMAGE: FROM COLLECTIONS TO RECOLLECTIONS

Although eBay's archival function indexes forgetting, the structural breakdown of memory, as Derrida suggests, is the archive's condition of possibility. Something remains recoupable despite this threat of liquidation. Figure 12.1 offers one possible recombinant remnant that bridges the forgetting of the image-repertoire and the highly selective memory of the archive, and perhaps offers a point of articulation between the two. The figure is composed of files cut and pasted from my own collection of ACSL eBay images, downloaded souvenirs of a sustained engagement with the website over the past five years as a lover of amateur images (one way of using eBay for free). The montage of individual images is part of a larger picture that offers in congealed form the serendipitous connections and encounters I have had while cruising eBay (though admittedly the montage is the product of an aesthetic intervention beyond mere categorical homologies, and is composed solely of images that were sufficiently sticky to "catch my eye"). In preparing to write this chapter, I first compiled a rough version of the figure as a referent for the aesthetic and technical conventions of ACSL photography. As I looked through eBay's countless images of banal objects, I had in the back of my mind Christian Boltanski's strikingly depersonalized 1973 photographic inventory of the banal personal effects of a young man who had committed suicide.[27] I realized as I completed the figure that I had rather unwittingly produced my own image-repertoire as shaped by eBay, eBay's Imaginary filtered through my own imaginary, and as such the figure remains somewhat uncanny and inscrutable to me. Yet as an image-repertoire of images encountered in eBay's image-repertoire, it anchors these fleeting pictures together as an archive of sorts—a collection of snapshots of my experience available to me and others for later reflection and critical thought. In producing the figure and writing about amateur imaging practices associated with eBay, I hope readers look carefully at the images and come to their own conclusions. For although the ACSL genre's clear patterns of standardization and uniformity exist across the collection of images on eBay and strongly direct their meanings toward the sale, the individual images comprising the figure, and the many, many more that continually come and go across the site, demonstrate a range of creativity, complexity, and wit that is a testament to the resourcefulness, drive, and excess of the amateur.

NOTES

I am grateful to Peter Krapp for his critical insights during the writing of this essay. I also thank my sister Mary Cahill for assistance with Figure 12.1.

1. Graham King offers a humorous taxonomy of amateur photography's graphic and formal tropes, including the distortions, lack of clarity, and supposedly illogical choices made in many images, in *Say "Cheese"! Looking at Snapshots in a New Way* (New York: Dodd, Mead, 1984), 48–60.
2. The effect of the shadowed image of dismembered GI Joe dolls, remnants from the Vietnam era, is particularly uncanny at a moment when images of

wounded and disfigured soldiers injured in Iraq have been suppressed from circulation in U.S. media. Within this context, the child mannequin suggests a perverse recasting of Nick Ut's 1972 photograph of the young napalm victim, Kim Phuc.

3. For a discussion of how art practices can remediate amateur photography rendered in slide formats, see chapter 14.
4. Although this connection does not follow to the letter Hal Foster's careful art historical argument, the connection between contemporary commercialized imagery of commodities and Dutch still life paintings is indebted to his fascinating examination of the convergence of the three forms of fetish—anthropological, Marxist, and Freudian—in this mode of painting. Foster notes that all three forms of fetishism endow objects with special powers and a register of autonomy that emerges in the special luminous qualities of Dutch still life paintings: "[I]nert appears animate, the familiar becomes estranged, and the insignificant seems humanly." Hal Foster, "The Art of Fetishism: Notes on Dutch Still Life," in *Fetishism as Cultural Discourse*, ed. Emily Apter and William Pietz (Ithaca, NY: Cornell University Press, 1993), 253.
5. On how consumers "pet" objects for sale, see Malcolm Gladwell, "The Science of Shopping," *New Yorker*, 1996, www.gladwell.com/1996/1996_11_04_a_shopping.htm (accessed May 17, 2005).
6. Henri Lefebvre, *Critique of Everyday Life*, vol. 1 (1958; reprint, London: Verso, 1991), 15.
7. HP Digital Photography Zone (in Association with eBay), Hewlett Packard, 2005, http://one165.fairmarket.net (accessed May 17, 2005).
8. eBay, "Selling Basics," http://pages.ebay.com/educational/sellingbasics/photos.html (accessed May 17, 2005).
9. A. B. Russell, "Photography for eBay" (eBay, 2002–2005), http://pages/ebay.com/community/chatter/archive (accessed May 17, 2005). Citations are drawn from December 2002 and February and March 2003 issues.
10. In May 2005, each additional image cost 0.15 USD; slide shows cost 0.25, supersized pictures 0.75, and various combinations of services ranged from 1.00 to 2.00 USD. For 9.99 USD, 50 MB worth of images can be stored on eBay's server indefinitely. eBay's Picture Services also offer access to image-editing software, an "auto-fix" feature, and options to "supersize" pictures and automate image slide shows.
11. Sellers are not required to host additional images on eBay. Subscription-based image storage and rendering services such as ActionPix, Flickr, HostPix, iPix, MyPhotoSpace, and PhotoBucket have emerged as a peripheral service industry in eBay's billion-dollar economy.
12. For an articulate challenge to received notions of the amateur, see Heidi Rae Cooley, "'Identify'-ing a New Way of Seeing," *Spectator* 24, no. 1 (2004).
13. Roland Barthes, *Camera Lucida: Reflections on Photography*, trans. Richard Howard (New York: Hill and Wang, 1981), 5.

14. Ibid., 98–99.
15. Susan Sontag, *On Photography* (New York: Penguin, 1977), 5–6.
16. Questions of self-portraiture and performative photographs on eBay merit further attention. Examples of reflectoporn as covert exhibitionism can be found at "Indecent Exposure," *Snopes*, 2003, www.snopes.com/photos/kettle.asp (accessed May 17, 2005).
17. Douglas B. Holt, "Does Cultural Capital Structure American Consumption?" *Journal of Consumer Research* 25, no. 1 (1998): 14.
18. Jacques Derrida, *Archive Fever: A Freudian Impression*, trans. Eric Prenowitz (Chicago: University of Chicago Press, 1996), 11.
19. Jacques Lacan, *Ecrits: A Selection*, trans. Bruce Fink (New York: Norton, 2002), 1–7. The Imaginary is the register of images, typically in reference to the structure of misidentification that exists between an image or semblable (similar other) and one's body. The Mirror Stage is the genesis of the fiction of a unified self in the neonate (6–18 months old), conferred through a specular counterpart, typically other bodies (especially that of the mother), and the child's own reflection in the mirror. The image, which becomes internalized, is the fantasy of a unified self with which the child—still in a state of immobile prematurity—identifies. From the outset, then, this fantastic image supposes an alienation or fundamental gap or lack between the image and the self, which only intensifies when the child enters language and the realm of the Symbolic.
20. For the original French, see Roland Barthes, *Oeuvres Complètes*, ed. Èric Marty (Paris: Seuil, 2002).
21. Barthes's l'Imaginaire also invokes Sartre's essay of the same title. For Sartre's influence on Barthes, see Jean-Michel Rabaté, "Introduction," in *Writing the Image after Roland Barthes*, ed. Jean-Michel Rabaté (Philadelphia: University of Pennsylvania Press, 1997), 1–8.
22. Barthes's discussion of the image-repertoire as a "total assumption of the image" and "trap" paraphrases Lacan's March 11, 1964 lecture, "What Is a Picture?" Jacques Lacan, *The Four Fundamental Concepts of Psychoanalysis*, vol. 11 of *The Seminar of Jacques Lacan*, ed. Jacques-Alain Miller, trans. Alan Sheridan (New York: Norton, 1998), 107.
23. Roland Barthes, *A Lover's Discourse: Fragments*, trans. Richard Howard (New York: Hill and Wang, 1978), 106–9.
24. Barthes, *Camera Lucida*, 13–14.
25. Barthes claims in an interview that the amateur is without image-repertoire or narcissism because the amateur is separated from agendas of mastery or markets. I am suspicious of this claim for its romanticized, ahistorical definition of the amateur, particularly in relation to the specific contexts considered in this essay. Barthes, "Twenty Key Words for Roland Barthes," in *The Grain of the Voice: Interviews 1962–1980*, ed. Linda Coverdale (Berkeley: University of California Press, 1991) 216–17.

26. My coinage draws on Lacan's use of *objet petit a*. For Lacan, the *object petit a* is not an object per se, but an image of an object that serves as a cipher for an absence or lack and drives the desire to fulfill it. Lacan emphasizes the symbolic and implicitly visual dimension of the *objet petit a* as "something from which the subject, in order to constitute itself, has separated itself off as organ. This serves as a symbol of the lack, that is to say, of the phallus, not as such, but insofar as it is lacking. It must, therefore, be an object that is, firstly, separable and, secondly, that has some relation to the lack" (Lacan, 103).
27. Christian Boltanski, *Inventaire des Objects ayan Appartenu à un Habitant d'Oxford* (Munster: Wesfalisher Kunstverein, 1973).

13

"Virgin Mary In Grilled Cheese NOT A HOAX! LOOK & SEE!"

Sublime Kitsch on eBay

SUSANNA PAASONEN

On November 22, 2004, bidding closed on eBay item #5535890757, "Virgin Mary In Grilled Cheese NOT A HOAX! LOOK & SEE!" The winning bid was 28,000 USD. The listing's narrative indicated that the seller, Mrs. Diana Duyser of Florida, had made the grilled cheese sandwich in 1994. When she took a bite, she saw grilled in the bread's surface the apparent face of the Virgin Mary. Duyser packaged the sandwich in cotton balls, placed it in a plastic box, and kept it by her bed for the next decade. According to Duyser, it never molded or crumbled, and she came to see it as invested with miraculous powers—or "blessings"—that over the years helped her win a total of 70,000 USD at a nearby casino. Duyser had to list the sandwich for auction a second time, as eBay removed the first listing, believing it to be a hoax. During the first auction, bidding reached 22,000 USD. On the second listing, after attracting considerable publicity, the sandwich received close to 2 million hits and was purchased by the internet casino GoldenPalace.com, a company known for its flashy promotional stunts and history of eBay purchases.[1]

Almost immediately, the sandwich (Figure 13.1) inspired hundreds of spin-off listings ranging from Virgin Mary in Grilled Cheese (VMGC) domain names and email addresses to display cases and rotating holy shrines. There were offers for specialty sandwiches and foods, including Hello Kitty cheese melts, toast in which one could see both Mary and Elvis (buyer's picture optional), and a burned fish stick with the apparition of Jesus. Sellers offered VMGC T-shirts—"I Ate the Virgin Mary Grilled Cheese … It was Sacrilicious!" "Got Mary?" "Is Heaven's Kitchen Out of Cheese and Bread?" "The Father, The Son, and The Holy Toast"—along with the image of the sandwich printed on coffee mugs, bumper stickers, lunch boxes, tote bags, Christmas ornaments, and thong underwear. The VMGC inspired

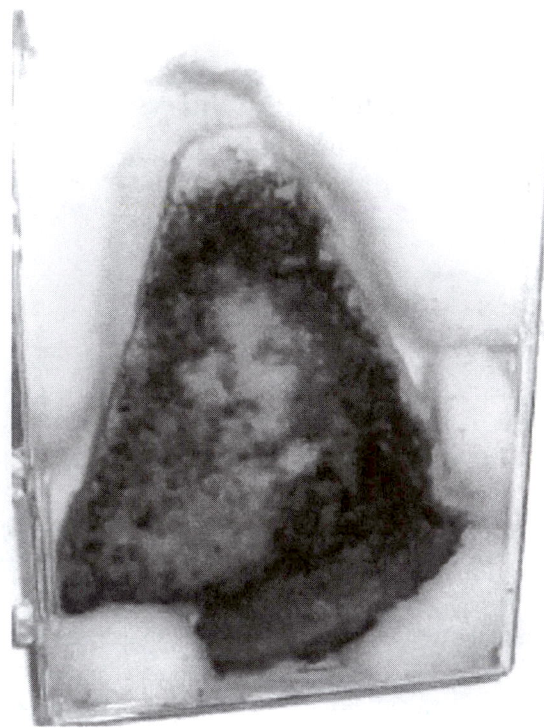

Figure 13.1 Virgin Mary grilled cheese sandwich in plastic display case.

Figure 13.2 "Virgin Eating Grilled Cheese" and "Virgin Mary Grilled Cheese Rotating Holy Shrine."

numerous arts and crafts items—watercolors, paintings, digital prints, statues, and drawings—and to attract notice and turn up on site searches, a number of sellers listed non-VMGC items with the disclaimer "Not Virgin Mary Grilled Cheese Sandwich." The VMGC auction was reported internationally as a peculiar internet incident and an oddity characteristic of U.S. popular culture.[2] In other words, the sandwich was an instant case of both eBay folklore and Americana. As was the case with earlier attempts to sell souls on eBay, the item quickly became famous: peculiar eBay listings can attract intense interest during their period of sale, but they also tend to be quickly forgotten. The VMGC, however, has enjoyed a more long-standing fame—in this sense, it has transcended the temporal limitations of eBay auctions.

The incident exemplifies a fusion of several categories that may appear incompatible at first glance: the sacred and the commercial, the sublime and the banal, the reverential and the parodic. In order to understand this fusion—or melting, given the material properties of the item—this chapter explores the mutability of commodity value from four intertwining perspectives: commodified Christian iconography, the relationship between the sublime and the banal, eBay as a peer-to-peer value system, and how acts of interpretation allow a mundane snack to be read as a divine sign.

MIRACLES FOR SALE

Objects believed invested with sacred qualities have historically also been market items, and relics of saints—pieces of bone or wood, a fragment from a rosary or garment—have formed a complex market of their own.[3] While relics are associated with miraculous powers, theirs is a tumultuous history of looting expeditions, duplications, fabrications, and claims for authenticity. The line between pilgrimage and tourism has tended to be blurry, as has the one between religious keepsakes and tourist souvenirs.[4] Apparition sites such as Lourdes have spurred the manufacture of keepsakes sold to pilgrims and other tourists for a multitude of reasons. For believers, religious statues and images are not mere souvenirs but metonymically contain some trace of their site of purchase or the miracle they signify.[5] They are therefore somehow "contagious" in that they are invested with some power of that site.

Apparitions of Mary have been reported in greater numbers since the 1980s than in the preceding one-hundred-year period, and television, radio, and the internet globally transmit these latter-day events.[6] People claim to have recognized Madonna-like shapes on windows, chimneys, underpass walls, reflections, and fences and often interpret them as divine critiques of secular consumerist values. Apparitions and the people arriving to witness them sacralize mundane places, but the religious experiences that the apparitions and witnesses together assemble are also open to commodification in the form of keepsakes from T-shirts to key chains.[7] Such keepsakes are exemplary of serial production, while relics sealed in display cases and contemplated at a distance are exemplary of what Walter Benjamin discussed as "cult value" (descriptive of objects invested with aura, sacred value, and uniqueness).[8] The VMGC sandwich stored in its plastic box is a hybrid; it remains firmly rooted in the mundane equally as its promotion on eBay advances claims for its cult status. Made of Publix brand white bread and Land O'Lakes American cheese, it both transcends these material properties and remains grounded in, confined by, them. These basic materials were transformed into a sandwich itself, then transformed into an otherworldly sign.

Apparitional foodstuffs (a mournful Jesus in a fried tortilla or a boiled egg, Mother Teresa in a cinnamon bun) have been reported since the 1970s. While some have been put on display, others have been consumed.[9] The eBay items discussed here (the original VMGC sandwich missing a bite and the numerous spin-off listings relying on parody, imitation, and ready-made art practices) indicate a recent turn where an object interpreted as a miraculous apparition and a personal blessing is packaged, transformed into a commodity, and listed on eBay as a kind of good-luck charm available to the highest bidder. A reading of the sandwich as a critique of consumerism, therefore, would clearly be beside the point, given that these items and their histories indicate how individual religious experience and consumerism easily conflate without apparent contradiction. Monetary value becomes an objective measure of the item's value: Duyser connects the sandwich to high wins at a casino, and the high winning bid is seen as evidence of the item's exceptionality.

According to a *Miami Herald* story, Diana Duyser is neither a Catholic nor particularly religious. It is useful, therefore, to regard the sandwich less in terms of personal faith and its manifestations than as emblematic of a wider American cultural landscape. While religious movements and churches elsewhere are hardly alien to the power of money, the interpenetration of religion, market economy, and commerce in the United States is a case apart. In his studies of the history of American religious culture, R. Laurence Moore charts a development where churches and preachers increasingly harmonize their teachings with the dictates of a market economy. As American religion and commercial popular culture interpenetrate each other, religion itself becomes a marketable cultural commodity.[10] With the proliferation of Christian consumer culture (spanning the relatively novel branches of Christian music and video productions, T-shirts, fish medallions, and "What Would Jesus Do?" bumper stickers to more traditional books, prayer cards, candles, postcards, posters, and statuettes), "the consumption of mass-produced goods can now be justified as serving a holy purpose," thus largely effacing the contradictions between capitalism and Christianity.[11]

A special feature rising from this cultural landscape is an emphasis on the value of personal experience over that of religious authority, one encapsulated in the born-again belief in Jesus as a personal savior. At the same time, individual experience is not directly accessible to others' perception or analysis, which leads to some fluidity in terms of what religion signifies as a collective system of values and ideas.[12] The VMGC listing conveyed some of Duyser's personal experience in order to help produce and promote the item's value and meaning. eBay provided the platform for this mediation of personal emotion, and Duyser functioned as both the item's chronicler and curator. Visitors and other sellers participated in this meaning making by contemplating the narrative and accompanying photographs of the sandwich, commenting on them, and creating items of their own, whereas traditional media such as television and newspapers tended to pin down the meanings of the VMGC and dismiss it as simply "too much" to be taken seriously. Perhaps this sense of excess, of not quite fitting in the categories of the sacred and the commercial, the extraordinary and the mundane, explains some of the item's attraction—its meanings refuse to be fixed as it leaks through familiar, naturalized categorizations. The incident has also made visible how eBay, as a marketplace and as a site of interaction and display, enables a negotiation and perhaps even a reworking of the art-culture system in which objects are categorized as high art, craft-based folk objects, or mass culture products, and are valued and priced accordingly.[13]

Not all VMGC spin-off items were meant to sell inasmuch as to be displayed in a themed exhibition of affiliated items: "Virgin Mary Grilled Cheese Rotating Holy Shrine" (150,000 USD), "Virgin Mary in Grilled Cheese Picture Drawing Sketch" (300 USD), "Blessed Grilled Cheese Virgin Mary Creation Kit" (399.99 USD or 6,000 USD "Buy It Now"), "Virgin Mary Kate and Ashley Olsen in Grilled Cheese! (THIS IS A HOAX)" (533.79 USD), "Bush enjoys Virgin Mary Grilled Cheese for Christmas!" (98.50 USD), "Virgin Mary's Used Gum in Grilled Cheese!! LOOK & SEE" (99,999,999 USD), and "TOP SECRET Virgin Mary Grilled Cheese Conspiracy report" (4.99 USD, fifty available) only make sense as parts of a network of items, commentary, and interaction.[14] This online gallery (Figure 13.2) had no single curator or censor (outside the general rules of eBay auctions, including prohibiting sales of unpackaged foodstuffs), and anyone could freely join the exhibition as a seller. As a technological assemblage, eBay brings together curious visitors, sellers, purchasers, browsers, and the technical capacities of the auction site itself. Consumers become producers, sellers, and artists, and visitors engage in commentary as well as purchase, and become sellers themselves. Modern categories of "high," "craft," and "mass" appear to be in flux in the process.

A SUBLIME SANDWICH?

If, in everyday uses of language, the opposite of the sublime is the banal—the mundane and trivial—in aesthetics, the idea of the sublime has been countered by the beautiful (as connected to notions of harmony, completeness, and ability to please). In a romantic and not too subtly gendered division, the sublime is something astonishing, upsetting, and even painful that shakes rather than soothes the individual.[15] Sublimity is an encounter with otherness that is awe-inspiring, overwhelming, inexplicable, terrifying, as well as elevating—an experience that somehow escapes the limits of experience and presentation alike and refuses to conform to the flow of everyday life.[16] In its strongest sense, sublimity evokes affective reactions and shakes one's understanding of being in the world. In his discussion of sublime and religious experience, Richard White places the two in parallel with one another because both connect the individual to a greater force beyond herself, to a transcendent otherness beyond appropriation.[17] This would seem to apply especially to those experiences of the sacred that do not follow routine practices of worship—such as apparitions.[18]

Diana Duyser has described her initial encounter with the VMGC as an experience of total shock. The apparition frightened her in the act of enjoying her daily bread and made her call out for her husband. Duyser's shocking experience can be understood as a sublime encounter with something astonishing, a power beyond herself. Yet her listing's narrative quickly turned to the banal in focusing on how the sandwich helped her win money. Of all VMGC spin-off items, only the burned fish stick with an imprint of Jesus laid claim to status as an apparition, and its impression of Jesus had a "stunning" effect on the man frying it for dinner, who then established causal links between seeing the apparition, winning money at bingo, getting a new job, and finding a good deal on a car. These lucrative instances express a highly material understanding of "blessing" as sudden monetary profit that may not be entirely in line with the teachings of Christian theology.

The VMGC made its way, via eBay, to the status of an exalted commodity without evoking general dismay or outrage over its claims to the sacred. The case was decidedly different, however, for two consciously high-artistic productions also drawing from religious iconography and its cultural associations, namely Andres Serrano's *Piss Christ* (1989) and Chris Ofili's *The Holy Virgin Mary* (1996). These works famously combine excrement and Christian imagery—Jesus and urine, and the Virgin Mary and elephant dung, respectively—and have been celebrated as cutting-edge examples of visual art. In the dominant art-culture system, these works stand for high art, whereas the VMGC is located in the realms of crafts and mass culture (the kitchen, bedroom, online auction, and casino). Comparing the reception of these items makes evident some of the workings of the art-culture system, as well as possible departures from it.

Conceptualizing the sublime in relation to the visual arts and avant-garde, Jean-François Lyotard identifies it as a shock effect bordering on the ugly and strange—it forces the addressee to feel.[19] Both *Piss Christ* and *Holy Virgin Mary* can be seen as giving rise to the sublime as discomfort rather than pleasure. They transgress conventions of good taste and, in Lyotard's words, "appear to the public of taste to be 'monsters,' 'formless' objects, purely 'negative' entities."[20] Publicity surrounding the pieces fanned moral outrage and censorship, and led to acrimonious debate over freedom of expression, blasphemy, and the intactness of religious iconography.[21] In the visual arts, such acts of transgression are associated with critical agendas, the questioning of norms that can invite intervention by self-appointed guardians of the status quo (including religiously motivated moral censors and public figures such as former New York City Mayor Rudolph Giuliani). In the discourses and practices of the dominant art-culture system, professional artworks exhibited in galleries are assumed to contain and are accorded a density of meaning seldom attributed to objects not aligned with the system's definition of art.

Contrary to the offerings of high culture, the VMGC is sister to the field of folk crafts, vernacular curio displays, and knick-knacks mostly made by women.[22] Produced in the feminized realm of the kitchen by Duyser, a work-from-home jewelry designer selling her products on eBay since 2002, the sandwich is easy to identify as craft based. The element of craft is certainly explicit in the customized sandwiches and other copycat items it inspired—from the sandwich carved with a smiley face, to toasts with images of the Olsen twins and Joan Collins, to a handcrafted statue of a VMGC

Sandwich Fairy. If one steps outside a naturalized understanding of "art" as relying on the romantic and singularly inspired notions of the artist as a conveyor of complex meanings, and the linked assumption that high art is separate from crafts and mass culture, then spin-off items—like the original sandwich—may well be considered art. Independent of her intentions, Duyser, via eBay, introduced an item that became internationally known and gained considerable density of meaning worthy of some contemplation.

Rethinking the relations of art, craft, and mass culture on eBay necessitates a departure from the naturalized aesthetic dictates of the cultural elite and the consequent effacement of "lower" pleasures from the field of art.[23] Critiquing modernist understandings of art, philosopher Giorgio Agamben argues the need to include an understanding of poetics, *poiesis*, as productive human action in coming to terms with the distinction between the artist who produces the work of art and the critics and other viewers who consume it. For Agamben, products of *poiesis* have a double status as either reproducible or original: whereas the former characterizes the *products* of technics, the latter characterizes *works* of art.[24] Agamben indicates how, under the dominant art-culture system, products may not inhabit both categories—"that which is reproducible cannot become original, and that which is irreproducible cannot be reproduced."[25] This is the tension or paradox first brought to play during the 1910s in the form of readymades produced by artists such as Marcel Duchamp. The readymade challenged the naturalized, modernist aesthetic categories that Agamben identifies and critiques, and disavowed an ontological definition of art.[26] As with these "disquieting" readymades, the VMGC is both a product and a work, reproducible and original, teetering between categories.[27]

Furthermore, as with readymades, the VMGC is a "found object," yet, unlike them, it has not been displayed in galleries or museums. Neither has Duyser laid claim to any artistic agenda—quite the contrary. Ultimately, the sandwich has a troubled relationship to intentional authorship since it stands for both *poiesis* and *auto-poiesis* (self-creation). While Duyser prepared the sandwich, she denies manufacturing the pattern on its top: the pattern is an apparition not crafted by human hand. GoldenPalace.com refers to Duyser as the sandwich's "inventor," rather than creator, who has merely uncovered its "actual nature." This sense of the automatic and autonomous echoes, inadvertently perhaps, Karl Marx's discussion of commodity fetishism, of seeing products as "endowed with life, and entering into relation both with one another and the human race." According to Marx, commodity fetishism erases signs of production in ways that are analogous with the "mist-enveloped regions of the religious world."[28] The VMGC conflates these misty regions and commodity culture quite literally as a simultaneously consumable, religious apparition-as-fetish and fetish-as-apparition.

Sublimity is indicative of an otherness that overwhelms by virtue of size, whereas the sandwich is rather diminutive and hardly intimidating in scale. Yet the sheer size of the phenomenon also constitutes a level of the sublime: while the sandwich is tiny, public and private interest in it has been monumental. This sense of size constitutes a form of social sublimity—a collective creation equally characterized by astonishment, bewilderment, amusement, and dismay. In any case, it incites the addressee to feel.

The VMGC sandwich lays claims to the ability to convey—as well as to enable—sublime experience, but it is hardly terrifying. Rather it is unthreatening, domestic—safe. As an example of *mirabilia*, natural *or* artificial marvels,[29] the sandwich might easily find a "natural habitat" on the pages of tabloid magazines among news of alien encounters, celebrity sex scandals, and bodily disfigurations. Numerous newspaper articles, eBay spin-off items, and other commentaries have marked the sandwich as literally "cheesy"— banal and in bad taste. These commentaries draw from normative criteria of taste and practices of exclusion that support the symbolic status of art as separate from crafts and mass-produced objects.[30] Even if the VMGC can be read as blurring these categories in the multiple readings it enables, these categories also define it as an emblem of the banal that fails to reach the criteria of good taste. As Agamben points out, good taste necessitates its opposite, bad taste: good taste has "inexplicable inclination" toward its opposite, and art needs this other to be understood as art.[31] Following this dynamic, the sandwich has come to represent a category generally titled "kitsch."

Influential American art critic Clement Greenberg defined kitsch as bad taste appealing to the masses, or—in Greenberg's regressive term—"peasants."[32] Effortless kitsch is the other against which Greenberg and other aesthetic theorists of modernity define good taste and modernist high art, and this division is irreversibly tied to distinctions of class. In contrast to sublime experiences of shock, kitsch is devoted to the pursuit of beauty, of that which pleases. As "lamentable taste,"[33] kitsch has been seen as characteristic of popular religious iconography appealing to the aesthetic sense of the wider public. Defined against normative criteria of good taste, kitsch is frozen as something flat and obvious, a problem in itself rather than an issue worth exploring. In her cultural history of kitsch, however, Celeste Olalquiaga departs from this elitist set of understandings, reading kitsch as the tangible, familiar, and accessible products of consumer culture. Kitsch involves "an attempt to repossess the experience of intensity and immediacy through an object," but (like the sixty-day history of an eBay listing) these experiences are transitory and accompanied by a sense of loss.[34]

With the mass production of commodities, authenticity has, according to Olalquiaga, become the ultimate fetish because commodities are not singular but are copies and variations on a theme. The commodity can be "rescued from its apparent banality" by investing it with personal meaning and value and, consequently, with a sense of uniqueness.[35] In this framework, kitsch is not about any purported "bad taste of the lower classes," but about a personal relationship to objects that, although banal and ordinary, are also extraordinary. As argued by Ken Hillis in chapter 11, producing this extraordinariness through narratives that also commodify is pivotal to the success of certain eBay listings. Sellers narrate their memories and create "object biographies" that mark the items as special and detach them from their (possible) mass-produced origins. Visitors engage with these narratives and—as is the case with the VMGC—are inspired to craft new ones. This engagement points not only to the affective value of the fetish, but also to *collective*, rather than simply individual, engagement with it. Spin-off items are markedly social, are intended to be shared with others, and are not confined within any one category of good or bad taste, or of art or kitsch. If anything, they tend to be irreverent.

Yet as copies and commentaries, spin-off items further endowed the VMGC with an aura of authenticity as the original to which they all referred. The sandwich became, through narration and affective investment, "elevated" from a processed foodstuff, to a personal sign of divine encounter, to an internationally known object of popular culture. For this trajectory of meaning—and the consequential transformation of the object's properties—to occur, the sandwich's uniqueness had first to be established in a credible manner. Duyser's role as witness has been crucial for the VMGC's elevation to an icon of popular culture: the sandwich's exceptionality is, after all, a product of her portrayal of an extraordinary personal encounter with the pattern of the sandwich's golden grease speckles.

HOW TO READ AN OBJECT

As is also the case with fetishism, sublimity involves a *relationship* between the object and the individual who interprets it as part of making sense of her experience. The object is experienced as overwhelming only "insofar as it is taken to represent something beyond itself."[36] Consequently, religious experience necessitates an act of interpretation by which the interpreter attaches the signifier (a pattern on bread) to a signified (Mother of God).

Interpreting the pattern as the Virgin Mary—rather than, say, Shirley Temple or Marlene Dietrich—is a product of a specific horizon of expectation.[37] But if religious apparitions are understood as personal experiences of the sublime, as encounters with an otherness impossible to present (let alone represent), how is this other possibly *recognized* in the realm of the visual in order that the apparition be auctioned off?

Historian David Morgan points out that for centuries, the production and circulation of religious representations have formed a *doxa*—a theory or a form of knowledge based on things seen before—of likeness against which novel images can be recognized. Applied to an everyday object, this literacy of "visual piety" can transform an object into a "spiritual Rorschach blot," incidental marks on which are interpreted "as images of a particular discourse."[38] In an exercise of visual piety, Duyser immediately recognized the figure of the Virgin on the sandwich she was eating, and hence her interpretation was beyond question: "I would like all people to know that I do believe that this is the Virgin Mary Mother Of God. That is my solemn belief."

Since faith-based belief is notoriously difficult to argue against, the truth claim lodged within Duyser's interpretation has to be accorded some value—at least in the sense that it has helped legitimize her as earnest and guileless and has positioned the VMGC as lacking a secondary layer of meaning, such as cultural commentary, satire, or irony. The appearance of guilelessness is an important component of eBay selling, and Duyser's commentaries and persona invest the sandwich with a uniqueness that elevated it to an iconic status independent of anyone's belief in its divine dimensions. When David Kerr, representative of GoldenPalace.com, was asked if the casino would be disappointed to discover the sandwich was less than a decade old, he flatly stated, "If it is, it's still a magical sandwich."

Duyser has unswervingly declared her faith in the sandwich's supernatural origins and powers. Her eBay item description was liberal in its use of English grammar and heavy with exclamation marks, aiming to convey some of the affective relation she felt toward the sandwich. Her listing contained numerous misspellings, which, along with the general phrasing, were subject to ironic commentary in various spin-off listings. The sandwich's second eBay listing advertised a sense of immediacy, as if its narrative had been written on the spur of the moment. In this sense, the narrative's grammatical legibility was less significant than the legibility of the item's apparitional, "bigger-than-words" status. Unpolished, emotional, and apparently spontaneous, the description was firmly lodged in a realm of textual innocence void of not only sacrilegious intent but also the kinds of critical agendas read into similar enterprises within high art, as well as the intentional fabrication characteristic of tabloid news items. Establishing a claim to authenticity is central; as a peer-to-peer value system, eBay relies on establishing trust through item descriptions and feedback options (see chapters 8 and 9). Since potential bidders had no unmediated possibility to assess the credibility of the alleged miracles—to *witness* them—Duyser listed television, radio, and newspaper coverage as additional evidence to support her personal testimony. This also guarded the sandwich against eBay's policy of banishing hoaxes. Having been banished once, the sandwich returned, bolstered by additional claims of sincerity.[39]

Sincerity implies innocence and directness, a position void of vested interests, yet a sincere position is also one defined by a certain lack of analytical perspective. Whereas artists such as Serrano and Ofili inhabit the discursive space of high art where irony functions as a form of cultural superiority,[40] Duyser has no access to a similar position of distance. In her mixed role as witness and chronicler, Duyser remains personally attached to the sandwich. If her reading of it lacks a secondary layer of meaning, then the reading is also an "other" against which critical commentators can mark their distance, their acts of questioning and alternative interpretations. This dynamic of distance and proximity is explicitly connected to class and hierarchies of taste where distance is also a form of looking down upon something. Posing self-consciously at a news conference in a GoldenPalace.com trucker hat and a baggy "Virgin Mary In Grilled Cheese" T-shirt, the figure of Duyser fits the picture almost too impeccably.

To the degree that the VMGC sandwich has become an icon of popular culture (as representatives of GoldenPalace.com have asserted), Duyser has become a figure emblematic of the contemporary American intertwining of capitalist logic and religious sentiment. The religious experience in question is decidedly individual, and interpreting the sandwich is less a question of theology than personal feeling. In Sara Ahmed's terms, the sandwich is a "sticky" object, one saturated with affect apparent in Duyser's statements and discussions concerning it.[41] Affect does not reside in an object, and Ahmed relies on Marx's theory of capital to argue that affect is "an effect of the circulation between objects and signs (= the accumulation of affective value)."[42] The more the signs circulate, the stickier the object becomes. Through her numerous media appearances, Duyser has become a sign herself, both enhancing the stickiness of the sandwich and anchoring its possible referents. If affect indeed accumulates through the circulation of signs and objects, then the wide interest in the VMGC gave it affective value that translated into exchange value. In a virtuous circle, the listing's viewers uploaded a sign of their interest, as displayed by the hit counter, and the high number of visits again inspired new visitors and media attention, with more ensuing stickiness.

The VMGC is a particularly sticky and successful eBay item: its exchange value underwent a radical increase compared to that of its original materials of composition; the seller and the buyer alike declared their satisfaction with the exchange; and commentators worldwide have been inspired by the case's peculiar mixture of the trashy and the sublime. The item's stickiness owes also to its dynamic location in between opposing, and perhaps even incommensurable, categories. Marked as a sign of divine encounter, it is also a mundane consumable, a sales item, and the butt of jokes and parodies. Debates concerning the sandwich rendered visible divisions of class, criteria of taste, and affective relation to objects that all "stuck" to the sandwich and elevated it into something exceptional. Stickiness coincided with sublimity and scale, yet also with banality.

Publicity further increased the sandwich's value—both as an attention value measurable by the listing's number of hits, and as monetary value—but simultaneously shaped it into a commodity with a limited life span in the public eye: in March 2005, the sandwich was already overshadowed on the GoldenPalace.com site by news of the casino's purchase of a Nacho Cheese Doritos chip resembling the pope's mitre for 1,209 USD on eBay, and a McDonald's Lincoln Fry for 75,100 USD on Yahoo! auctions.[43] The sandwich may already be old news, but eBay items that fail to sell—such as the Jesus fish stick and numerous other spin-offs—suffer even faster oblivion. In these instances, affective investments are short-lived. As circulation between signs and objects comes to a halt, affective and exchange values collapse. The VMGC sandwich has lost some of its stickiness but retains its aura; the spin-off items were considerably less sticky from the start.

If the VMGC is an icon, it is one representative of a cultural landscape in which religious sentiment and consumer capitalism, kitsch and spirituality have become interpenetrable. The incident illustrates the brief trajectory from the sublime to the banal, but it has also provided an outlet for working through and debating the meaning of these ambiguities and interpenetrations. Furthermore, the hundreds of spin-off items exemplify how eBay is a peer-to-peer system for estimating the meaning and value of objects—as well as taking pleasure in them—in ways that do not simply reproduce the values of the dominant art-culture system. The "Virgin Mary In Grilled Cheese" has been a catalyst for peer-to-peer exchanges and displays, media narratives, and debates. In the process, it also has become suspended across hierarchies of class, cultural capital, and taste in ways that have made it into a considerably sticky fetish.

NOTES

1. For example, GoldenPalace.com purchased the soccer ball used by David Beckham in his 2002 World Cup failed penalty kick. It has also purchased time machines and, in March 2005, won the right, with a bid of 15,199 USD, to officially rename an eBay seller—a woman formerly known as Terri Ilagan—to GoldenPalace.com. Other promotional stunts include naming new simian species and sponsoring the casino's name on the bellies of pregnant women, cleavage, and the bodies of newborn babies and streakers. The stunts, or "GoldenPalace.com Events," are listed on the company's home page. In early 2005, visitors were invited to create customized "virgin grilled cheese" with their own photos.
2. This was clear in the BBC online news coverage on November 17 and 24, 2004 ("Woman blessed by 'the holy toast'" and "'Virgin Mary' toast fetches $28,000"). In the United States, journalist Jim DeFede drove across the country to deliver the sandwich to its new owners in Las Vegas and wrote a blog, "Follow the Cheese," depicting his encounters and reflections on religion and the Unites States en route. For details of the VMGC incident, I have drawn from BBC, *Miami Herald*, and ABC online news coverage, and GoldenPalace.com and eBay auction records.
3. For several centuries, the market for relics was almost nonexistent but has revived online, to the degree that an International Crusade for Holy Relics has been formed to battle their sale on forums such as eBay.
4. Jean-François Mayer, "La 'Révélation d'Arès': Naissance d'un Pèlerinage dans la France Contemporaine," *Social Compass* 48, no. 1 (2001): 71.
5. Jean Rémy, "Editorial: Pilgrimage and Modernity," *Social Compass* 36, no. 2 (1989): 142.
6. Manuel A. Vásquez and Marie F. Marguardt, "Globalizing the Rainbow Madonna: Old Time Religion in the Present Age," *Theory, Culture and Society* 17, no. 4 (2000): 120, 128.
7. Ibid., 122–23, 138.
8. Celeste Olalquiaga, *The Artificial Kingdom: A Treasury of the Kitsch Experience* (New York: Pantheon Books, 1989), 88–89; and Walter Benjamin, *Messiaanisen sirpaleita*, trans. Raija Sironen, ed. Markku Koski et al. (Jyväskylä, Finland: KSL and Tutkijaliitto, 1989), 146–47.
9. This is a case of a homemade tortilla with a vision of Christ, consumed by a Mexican woman in 2003—not to be confused with the healing flour tortilla with a vision of Christ from 1977, still displayed in New Mexico, or similar incidents reported in 1977 and 1983.
10. R. Laurence Moore, *Selling God: American Religion in the Marketplace for Culture* (New York: Oxford University Press, 1994), 243, 256, 271.
11. Heather Hendershot, *Shaking the World for Jesus: Media and Conservative Evangelical Culture* (Chicago: University of Chicago Press, 2004), 4.
12. R. Laurence Moore, *Touchdown Jesus: The Mixing of Sacred and Secular in American History* (Louisville, KY: Westminster John Knox Press, 2003), 2.

13. Lynn Spigel, *Welcome to the Dreamhouse: Popular Media and Postwar Suburbs* (Durham, NC: Duke University Press, 2001), 313, 319.
14. It should be noted, however, that several such items were listed as a means to support children, students, or affording health care. In these instances, spin-off sandwiches became tools for dispensing and acquiring charity.
15. Edmund Burke, *A Philosophical Inquiry into the Origin of Our Ideas of the Sublime and the Beautiful* (1757; reprint, Oxford: Oxford University Press, 1990).
16. Rachel Zuckert, "Awe and Envy: Herder contra Kant on the Sublime," *Journal of Aesthetics and Art Criticism* 61, no. 3 (2003): 217–32.
17. Richard White, "The Sublime and the Other," *Heythrop Journal* 38, no. 2 (1997): 128–30.
18. Vásquez and Marquardt, 125.
19. Jean-François Lyotard, *The Inhuman: Reflections on Time*, trans. Geoffrey Bennington and Rachel Bowlby (Stanford, CA: Stanford University Press, 1991), 97, 100.
20. Ibid., 125.
21. Anthony Fisher and Hayden Ramsay, "On Art and Blasphemy," *Ethical Theory and Moral Practice* 3, no. 2 (2000): 137–67; and Jane Caputi, "On the Lap of Necessity: A Mythic Reading of Teresa Brennan's Energetic Philosophy," *Hypatia* 16, no. 2 (2001): 18–19.
22. Spigel, 319.
23. Pierre Bourdieu, *The Field of Cultural Production: Essays on Art and Literature*, ed. Randal Johnson (New York: Columbia University Press, 1993), 25, 236; also Armstrong, 155–60.
24. Giorgio Agamben, *The Man without Content*, trans. Georgia Albert (Stanford, CA: Stanford University Press, 1999), 59–61.
25. Ibid., 63–64.
26. Helen Molesworth, "Work Avoidance: The Everyday Life of Marcel Duchamp's Readymades," *Art Journal* 57, no. 4 (1998): 51.
27. Agamben, 64.
28. Karl Marx, *Selected Writings*, ed. David McLellan (Oxford: Oxford University Press, 1977), 436.
29. Olalquiaga, 211–12.
30. Isobel Armstrong, *The Radical Aesthetic* (Oxford: Blackwell, 2000), 155.
31. Agamben, 13–20.
32. Clement Greenberg, "The Avant-Garde and Kitsch" (1939), in *Kitsch: An Anthology of Bad Taste*, ed. Gillo Dorfles (London: Studio Vista, 1969), 121.
33. Dorfles, 142.
34. Olalquiaga, 291.
35. Ibid., 16–17.
36. White, 127.
37. The spin-off item "The Virgin Mary Grilled Cheese Could be Greta Garbo!" promised "possible evidence" of the sandwich's true referent.

38. David Morgan, *Visual Piety: A History and Theory of Popular Religious Images* (Berkeley: University of California Press, 1998), 125, 143.
39. The impression of sincerity—or lack thereof—may also explain why the fish stick with an imprint of Jesus failed to sell. First, it was put on auction only after the VMGC sandwich had sold and was easily identifiable as a copycat listing. Second, when publicizing his reasons for auctioning the item, the seller provided a far less certain reading of the fish stick than had Duyser of her sandwich. According to an interview, he initially identified a resemblance to a rock star, whereas his young son suggested Jesus. If an apparitional experience is one of shock and unease, a familial guessing game does not quite fit in and raises questions concerning sincerity.
40. Agamben, 55.
41. Sara Ahmed, *The Cultural Politics of Emotion* (Edinburgh: Edinburgh University Press, 2004), 194–95.
42. Ibid., 45.
43. The Lincoln Fry is a four-inch French fry displaying a partial likeness of U.S. President Abraham Lincoln. Crafted from polyurethane, it was used in McDonald's TV ads parodying the "Virgin Mary In Grilled Cheese" phenomena. Purchasing the item, GoldenPalace.com appropriated McDonald's parody as a form of homage while also adding to its collection of pop cultural curiosa.

14

eBay and the Traveling Museum

Elvis Richardson's *Slide Show Land*

DANIEL MUDIE CUNNINGHAM

> For inside [the collector] there are spirits, or at least a little genii, which have seen to it that for a collector—and I mean a real collector, a collector as he ought to be—ownership is the most intimate relationship that one can have to objects. Not that they come alive in him; it is he who lives in them.
>
> **Walter Benjamin, "Unpacking My Library"[1]**

In his essay, "Unpacking My Library," Walter Benjamin invites us to join him in his private library to reflect on what it means to be a book collector. Sitting amidst "the disorder of crates that have been wrenched open, the air saturated with the dust of wood, and the floor covered with torn paper" (61), Benjamin explains how a collector forms a special relationship with the thing collected. Passionate in his description of beloved volumes, Benjamin reveals that "one of the finest memories of a collector is the moment when he rescued a book to which he might never have given a thought, much less a wishful look, because he found it lonely and abandoned on the market place and bought it to give it its freedom" (65–66).

A sense of responsibility informs Benjamin's understanding of what it means to be a collector, because he or she will invariably act with "the attitude of an heir" (68). Secondhand books—captive, collecting dust, and unread for the longest time in thrift stores and book exchanges—instill such an attitude because they are acquired or inherited with the knowledge that they once formed part of another's prized collection. According to Benjamin, secondhand books are granted new life when collected, and a "process of renewal" occurs: "I am not exaggerating when I say that to a true collector the acquisition of an old book is its rebirth" (63). As the book is renewed, it "comes alive in him" in much the same way that the collector comes alive by inhabiting them. In becoming part of a greater collection, the secondhand book is reborn bearing its collector's face and signifying meanings specific to the collector's cognitive library of memories, emotions, and histories. Benjamin articulates a poetics of memory in collecting: "Every passion borders on the chaotic, but the collector's passion borders on the chaos of memories" (61–62). Memory is chaotic because, in addition to being embodied, it lives inside the objects we collect. Changes in meaning occur when those collections (in their entirety or not) appear in the secondhand marketplace, and are eventually adopted into a new set of circumstances. Whether public or private, a collection acts as a repository of memory—an exterior mnemonic device—because both the collector and viewer interpret a collection based on their subjective ties to the objects in question.

For Benjamin, the collector is a romantic figure, and justifiably so, considering the care and passion with which he describes a collector's relationship to the thing collected. The romance of collecting is owed in large part to the roles that nostalgia and memory play in the shaping of a collection. The urge to collect things from the past often stems from their ties to uniqueness, innocence, and authenticity. Mining the past of its rare treasures allows us to relive a time when life was sweet and unfettered by the soullessness of contemporary capitalism. The phenomenon of eBay reverberates with the sentiments Benjamin expresses in his essay in that eBay acts as a memory machine, where even the most personal items are returned to the secondhand market, ready for potential rebirth through new ownership. eBay participates in and actively encourages the chaos of passion and memory, because while preloved items will always bear some trace of their previous owner's identity, the former owner is largely forgotten. All that remains are objects awaiting a "process of renewal." But, as I will argue, what makes eBay unique as a secondary marketplace is the way it *remediates* past technologies and secures them in the digital archives of the present.

eBay fosters Benjamin's poetics of memory through the resale of personal items such as family photographs, especially those reliant on obsolete or fading media formats such as the 35mm slide transparency. In addition to preserving the representational histories and memory imprints embedded in photographic images, a collector of slide photographs safeguards a medium fast becoming redundant. Photographic slide shows, like Benjamin's unpacked library, are archives of memory supported by their owners' urge to tell the stories of their lives to others. But what happens when a slide collection's owner discards these personal histories in eBay's secondhand marketplace? In 2001 Australian artist Elvis Richardson began *Slide Show Land*, an ongoing art project composed of slides bought through eBay. These private, amateur snapshots of travel, family life, landscapes, and architecture reveal family dynamics now severed from the referent of their originating source. A window revealing past customs, conventions, and ideologies, the slides are "renewed" by Richardson, their adoptive collector. Imprinting her own subjectivity and history on these found objects of "human ephemera,"[2] Richardson explains that her desire to buy the slides from eBay stemmed from being adopted and having "an empathetic attraction to personal items I find in thrift stores and in the rubbish, objects that are not wanted or loved anymore." Richardson also notes that in buying the slides, "I felt I was rescuing them, preserving their history, which was otherwise destined for oblivion. Collecting these slides and keeping the collections together is a way to keep the families themselves together."[3] Like Benjamin, Richardson is a lifeguard rescuing objects invested with the trace of others' memories so that they might be renewed and brought back to life as art objects.

By performing a close reading of *Slide Show Land*, and the way eBay users discard evidence of personal histories at auction, I will investigate eBay to articulate the ways in which it raises questions about the value (or non-value) of personal history in relation to slide photography. Are such histories too difficult to preserve, comprehend, and maintain, once formats such as the slide are rendered redundant? How is history, as a representation of memory and perception, discarded or reformatted once a media format becomes an outmoded technology?

Having amassed a collection of more than 30,000 slides, Richardson has exhibited her traveling slide museum in New York, Alabama, Sydney, and Christchurch galleries.[4] Multiple slide carousels are positioned "on long tables, flea market style,"[5] and are projected simultaneously onto second-hand screens at automatically timed intervals (Figure 14.1). Richardson encourages viewers to interact with the work by selecting any carousel they desire. This strategy counters a dominant convention of art being off-limits to viewers in terms of touch and viewing conditions. Moreover, a viewer can resist seeing the collections in sequence and instead choose random configurations of slides from one or more of the collections. Since 2004, Richardson has altered the viewing experience by transferring the collections onto DVD, a development I discuss below.

Situated on each carousel is a tag indicating the geographic source of the collection and its eBay purchase value. Richardson has paid as little as 2 USD for such slides and, in one instance, purchased a collection of 2,500 slides from an amateur photographer in California for 67 USD. Dealers from secondary markets rather than the photographers themselves list many of the slides on eBay because they often derive from deceased estates.

Figure 14.1 *Slide Show Land* by Elvis Richardson, 2002. Courtesy of the artist.

This fuels Richardson's adoptive desire to rescue these abandoned collections of "vernacular" photography from the dustbin of history and honor their origins by sequencing them in the order in which they were taken.[6] In sequence, the slides contrast the unshelved chaos of Benjamin's unpacked books, "not yet touched by the mild boredom of order" (62).

I first encountered *Slide Show Land* in 2002, when it was installed at Room 35, Gitte Weise Gallery, Sydney, and was struck by the wonder it instilled, a wonder in keeping with Stephen Greenblatt's definition: "the power of the displayed object to stop the viewer in his or her tracks, to convey an arresting sense of uniqueness, to evoke an exalted exaltation."[7] The "uniqueness" of the work relates to the way the slides are derived from the photographic closets of strangers' personal history and memory banks, but paradoxically there is a familiarity about these images in that they recall family dynamics, travel customs, and even (amateur) photographic conventions (see chapter 14) that are recognizable despite the anonymity of the subjects depicted. This familiarity and recognizability, due in large part to the nostalgia in which the slides are soaked, evoke for many the homespun slide show and memories of having staged such a slide show or, at worst, sat with barely concealed boredom as a family member or friend screened slide after slide of a recent travel adventure.[8]

The slides are also unique because, unlike the infinitely reproducible nature of photographs printed from negatives, or the images on eBay produced with digital technology, slide transparencies are part of an original positive strip of film cut apart and placed in cardboard or plastic mounts. They are irreplaceable once damaged or lost. Although transparencies can be duplicated or used to print conventional photographs, they are touched by their owners' hands and retain an aura of authenticity. Benjamin notes that daguerreotypes require "proper light," are "one of a kind," and are "kept in a case like jewellery."[9] This same uniqueness applies to slides as historically specific and "one of a kind," and contributes to their marketability on eBay.[10]

The uniqueness of the slides Richardson collects makes them apt art objects because one of the prevailing myths about art (especially "masterpieces") is that their visual power derives from their uniqueness and authenticity. Greenblatt argues that when displayed in museums, masterpieces possess "the power to arouse wonder, and that power, in the dominant aesthetic ideology of the West, has been infused into it by the creative genius of the artist."[11] By adopting other people's original images and inserting the individual collections into a larger body of work, Richardson evokes wonder while simultaneously resisting a myth of "creative genius" because she was not originally involved in their production. In a sense, the wonder of *Slide Show Land* derives not from any dated notion of artistic genius or originality, but rather from the way its authenticity has been borrowed or bought through eBay (see chapter 11).

Ironically, masterpieces from an official history of art are often viewed through the slide format in the pedagogical contexts of museum studies and art history.[12] History is told through images, projections, a telling in keeping with the stories told during the slide show. Often taken in domestic, private space, Richardson's once-orphaned amateur slides destabilize art history hierarchies, and question what kind of images constitute art because, as abandoned images, they are suddenly invested with the cultural capital of high (or at least higher) art. Since analog slide technology endures in art history departments, *Slide Show Land* takes on a self-reflexive and ironic character because it counters an official art history by inserting private, forgotten narratives into the institutional contexts of the museum, gallery, and academy. Anthropological museums privilege the kind of familial domestic customs and conventions represented in Richardson's slides, while art institutions only do so when ironic postmodern artists (for example, Mike Kelley and Cindy Sherman) resignify the private as public or the raw material of everyday life as art (see chapter 13).

Richardson's work also reveals how personal histories become difficult to preserve, comprehend, and maintain once the slide format becomes redundant. By performing a rescue mission on anonymous private histories that might have never again seen the light of day, Richardson demonstrates how it is not only certain media formats that face extinction, but also personal history itself. When a house is burning, family photographs are the first thing rescued after people and pets. But the growing market for slides on eBay and other secondhand markets illustrates how some media formats do not take kindly to posterity. Photographs may be passed down through generations of families, but slides seem to be treated as easily discarded anomalies.

Earlier I noted that many of the slides available on eBay derive from deceased estates auctioned by secondary dealer markets. Slides, it seems, die along with their owners. Perhaps they become too onerous to view when the appropriate technology of the projector becomes scarce. Like LPs rendered unplayable when a turntable is discarded or breaks, a slide is often severed from the nostalgic gravity of private history because it relies so heavily on specific viewing conditions. While daguerreotypes may also be "one of a kind" or subject to viewing in "proper light," their historical, cultural, and aesthetic value is assured by their close ties to early photography. Less glamorous in this respect, slides cannot be displayed permanently without a projector, yet to keep a projector switched on for an indefinite time period risks damaging the transparency. A format deemed unviable for long-term preservation, the slide passes away, redundant as a technology, deleted from cultural memory.[13]

A deceased technology once popular with generations of families also now deceased, the slide says much about the way the photograph is inextricably linked to death. In *Camera Lucida*, Roland Barthes explores the relationship of photography to death and refers to the *punctum* of a photo—a minor detail in the image, "that accident which pricks me"—as capable of transforming the reading of a photographic image.[14] Barthes refers to the formless "intensity" of time as a *punctum* because when looking at photographs, we are looking at moments frozen in representation, potentially dead in reality. Barthes writes, "The *punctum*, more or less blurred beneath the abundance and the disparity of contemporary photographs, is vividly legible in historical photographs: there is always a defeat of Time in them: *that* is dead and *that* is going to die."[15]

The images in *Slide Show Land* enact the notion of "time as *punctum*" not only because they refer to representations of people who are dead or going to die, but equally because the format of the slide is itself subject to a similar process of erasure.[16] Personal history, as a representation of memory and perception, is discarded once the media format used to depict that history is obsolete. But, as with so many collectors who use eBay to build their collections of cultural minutiae, Richardson counters the process of redundancy written into the design of media formats by foregrounding the rich archives of personal history and memory embedded in these objects. *Slide Show Land* is, as Richardson claims, "for the nostalgic and lost"[17] because of the way it preserves both personal histories and the media technologies once used to capture them. Under the tutelage of their new owner, Richardson's anonymous slides resist a fixed, singular, or "unique" interpretation. In a renewed environment they become subject to a viewer's understandings of the cultural ritual of the "familiar" and familial slide show.

While Barthes uses historical photographs to illustrate "time as *punctum*," there are resonances of this notion with the way eBay listings work. An eBay auction differs from "real-world" auction formats largely because the seller decides how long an item will be listed and because bidding stops once time has run out.[18] The thrill of eBay derives largely from the urgency of the auction's looming *dead*line. In his memoir on eBay obsession reprinted in this volume (see chapter 1), William Gibson informs readers that "with less than an hour to go before the auction closed, I was robotically punching the Netscape Reload button like a bandit-cranking Vegas granny, in case somebody outbid me." An awareness of time and its rapid passing informs users' responses to eBay, as we see in Gibson's use of the site to boost his collection of (appropriately enough) rare watches. But what happens to a particular eBay listing? After sixty days, it disappears from eBay's publicly available but temporary archive of recent auctions to make room for new listings. As with much of the rhetoric around the temporal nature of the Web, the eBay listing is never meant to be permanent; when browsing through listings, users are aware that the listing (and the page containing it) will soon die. The same "defeat of time" is an imperative driving the activities of selling and purchasing on eBay, and is made all the more resonant when the images used to illustrate the listing are either collectible historic photographs or photographs reconstructed from dying media formats such as the slide. Two points of finality, then, emerge here: one is the moment the auction ends, and the other is when its listing disappears. If a bidder "wins" the item, that commodity stands in as a record of the auction process—that past event and event passed.

In 2004 Richardson began experimenting with transferring the slide collections onto DVD to expand their potential to travel beyond the gallery and back into the domestic realm they so insistently represent. Richardson scans the slides individually, including their cardboard mounts, on a flatbed scanner, thereby emphasizing the material and physical authenticity of the slide format. Ironically, the artist's original intention to preserve the nostalgic storytelling performance of the slide show is lost or perhaps *remediated*. In their book *Remediation*, Jay David Bolter and Richard Grusin argue that the ideologies of "newness" that underpin new media are based on modernist rhetoric that insists new technologies cannot make significant contributions to culture unless they dispense with the past. Digital media never really break with the formal considerations that structure past technologies; instead, they become subject to a process of remediation. Defined as "the formal logic by which new media refashion prior media forms,"[19] remediation relies on the contrasting strategies of "transparent immediacy" (where representations efface the "presence" of the medium) and "hypermediacy" (where representations foreground the "presence" of the medium). According to Bolter and Grusin, the "double logic of remediation" is set into action by these dual strategies, whereby "[o]ur culture wants both to multiply its media and to erase all traces of mediation: ideally, it wants to erase its media in the very act of multiplying them."[20] Photography stresses immediacy in the way its ties to the "automatic" efface its mechanical and chemical processes as well as its relationship to the photographer. Conversely, the presence of photography, its hypermediacy, is highlighted by technologies like the slide projector and its significant spectral ancestor, the late Renaissance magic lantern, because a viewer is always aware of the projector's cumbersome presence.[21] While the slide projector remediates to a large extent the operations of the magic lantern, eBay also plays a large role in remediating the dying technology of the slide.

By being digitally reformatted and presented on DVD, Richardson's slides undergo a process of remediation that shows how new digital media cannot entirely be divorced from the formal language of past media. When viewed on a television screen, Richardson's slides are no longer projected onto a white screen where particles of light and dust unite with the whirring, hypnotic rhythm of the clunky slide projector. With the slides reformatted onto DVD, the artist, rather than a viewer who might feel compelled to linger over some images longer than others, now determines the timing of the sequence. More important, the slide image becomes documented twofold. As scanned "documents" of discarded family "documentation," the slides become museum-like specimens to be contemplated in the frame of their seemingly peripheral mounts. In its tactile state, the mount originally was a functional means of framing the slide, making it compatible with the slide tray, including Kodak's carousel. Once scanned, however, the mount is "photographed" like the image contained therein and becomes an active part of the overall digital image presented on screen. A viewer is made aware that once digitally reformatted, the analog slide format faces extinction only in the sense that it has become remediated, swallowed whole by digital screen-based technologies in a paradigm shift.

In a similar manner, eBay itself is a site that, through its strategies of display, remediates slide technology. eBay provides several optional means of including an image in a listing. A seller may mount a thumbnail photograph on a listing's page, elect to include a thumbnail as part of her or his listing's hyperlink that will be included in the results of a search of eBay listings (Figure 14.2), or include in the listing a "Picture Gallery" composed of a number of images of the object for sale. These ways of including an image in a listing heighten an item's visibility when searching, and also demonstrate how digital contexts remediate the slide image. That the formal constraints of the slide endure on eBay is ironic considering the way eBay positions the slide as a "collectible" category due to its status as a dying media format. eBay listings that do not contain a thumbnail in the hyperlink may instead include a camera icon that links to an image of the eBay item. The icon of the camera makes explicit the ties that photography has to consumer culture, and the way eBay relies on the photographic as much as Richardson depends on eBay for her photographic practice. eBay's depiction of the thumbnail (as slide) and camera icon (as link to a photograph) ultimately highlights the way older technologies are remediated through the foregrounding of eBay's hypermediacy.

eBay sellers' ability to mount an image "gallery" of a listed object (resonating with a "galleria" of retail outlets) implies that the listed object has an art object's aura. Of course, art is a commodity like any other, but art galleries often deliberately efface art's relationship to the commodity and enforce an aura of unattainability even when a price list is available upon request (see chapter 15). Greenblatt argues that objects in museums especially function in this respect because, unlike eBay, "the treasured object exists not principally to be owned but to be viewed."[22] That a museum probably purchased the object for its collection is secondary to its power as an official historical object. Economic "value" is glossed over by historical and cultural value.

The framing device of the slide mount is a space that encloses representations of histories, memories, customs, and commodities. According to Greenblatt, "[T]he frames that enclose pictures are only the ultimate formal confirmation of the closing of the borders that marks the finishing of a work of art."[23] When presented on DVD, *Slide Show Land* resists

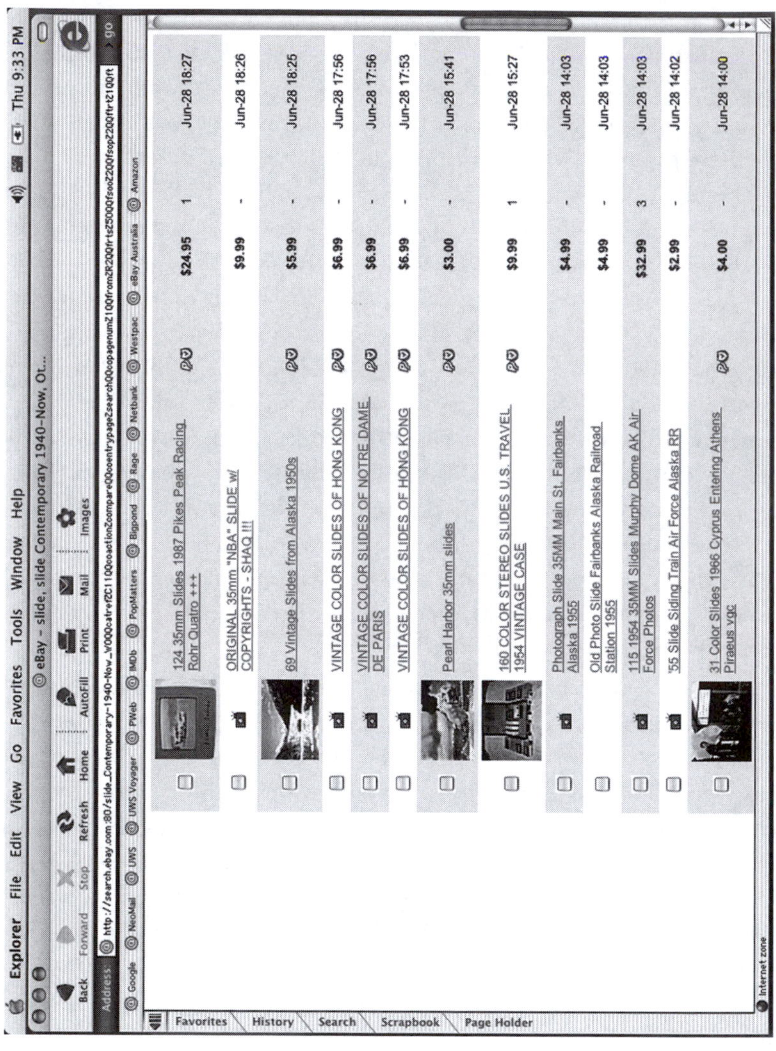

Figure 14.2 eBay remediates the slide.

this notion in that the frame of the mount becomes an essential part of the overall image. The work of art is not "finished" within the "border" of the slide mount, just as Richardson stresses the overall unfinished nature of the project. Surely the work cannot be completed as long as there are more slide collections to collect from eBay, for each slide exists only in its connections to a greater whole. In a sense, the strong community focus found on eBay (despite the users' relative anonymity) resonates in the slides because they speak to community and connectedness, however unknown the depicted subjects remain. If suggestive of a digital thumbnail, the slides cannot be "contained" or "finished" because by implication viewers would be directed to "go to a larger picture." And the larger picture here is the open-ended meanings and interpretations encouraged by images that are at once familiar and anonymous.

As Benjamin claims, "[O]wnership is the most intimate relationship" a collector has with his or her collections. This intimacy is forged by the amorphous mnemonic characteristics imposed on objects by collectors. But no matter how "anonymous" a collected object such as the slide transparency might be, its familiarity is owed in large part to the way analog media formats are subject not only to Benjamin's "renewal" but also to the ongoing process of digital remediation performed by eBay. Memory, then, is fashioned not only through the accumulation of objects but also through the refashioning of technologies by which those objects are imaged.

NOTES

The author extends grateful thanks to Marise Williams and Drew Bickford, who provided invaluable feedback on several drafts of this essay. Thanks also to Elvis Richardson, who was generous with her time and *Slide Show Land* resources.

1. Walter Benjamin, "Unpacking My Library: A Talk about Book Collecting" (1931), in *Illuminations*, trans. Harry Zohn (London: Fontana, 1992), 69. Additional references cited parenthetically.
2. I borrow this phrase from Australian photographer Edwina Richards, whose book *People I Don't Know in Photographs I Took of Something Else* reframes her private archive of snapshots by emphasizing "human ephemera: people I didn't know or hadn't consciously noticed before, passing through the backgrounds of the hundred of photographs I'd taken over the years" (Sydney: Peninsula Paper, 2002), 2.
3. "Alumni Spotlight: An Interview with Australian Artist Elvis Richardson," Columbia University, School of the Arts, Visual Arts, http://63.151.45.66/index.cfm?fuseaction=news.viewNewsDetails&newsID=11.

4. The collecting of anonymous slides for the purposes of art also informs the work of the Trachtenburg Family Slideshow Players, www.slideshowplayers.com. The self-professed "indie-vaudeville conceptual art-rock pop band" takes slides bought from garage sales and thrift stores and "turn[s] the lives of strangers into pop-rock musical exposés based on the contents of these slide collections." Cited in CD liner notes, Trachtenburg Family Slideshow Players, *Vintage Slide Collections from Seattle*, vol. 1 (Hoboken, NJ: Bar None Records, 2003).
5. "Alumni Spotlight."
6. Val Williams defines "vernacular photography" as found photography that through its use by a new owner has the potential to resist traditional notions of authorship. "Vernacular photography is important," writes Williams, "because it is open to any kind of interpretation. It can be refashioned, re-imagined, resequenced, made into a multitude of different stories." Val Williams, "Lost Worlds," *Eye* 55 (Spring 2005), 22.
7. Stephen Greenblatt, "Resonance and Wonder," in *Exhibiting Cultures: The Poetics and Politics of Museum Display*, ed. Ivan Karp and Steven D. Lavine (Washington, D.C.: Smithsonian Institution Press, 1991), 42.
8. Super 8 film shares an affinity with slide photography because of the way both signify memory. Australian filmmaker Emma Crimmings writes, "For many people, Super 8 film has become synonymous with what they understand to be 'memory.' Saturated colours seep into one another, the film's graininess quivering and accumulating like dust on every frame… . At a slender 8mm in width, this tiny memory strip stutters through a camera burning everyday life onto emulsion at 24 frames per second." Emma Crimmings, "Traces: Naomi Bishops & Richard Raber," in *Remembrance + the Moving Image*, ed. Ross Gibson (Melbourne: Australian Centre for the Moving Image, 2003), 37.
9. Walter Benjamin, "A Small History of Photography," in *One-Way Street and Other Writings*, trans. Edmund Jephcott and Kingsley Shorter (London: New Left Books, 1979), 242.
10. To date, a specific category for slide photography does not exist on eBay. In an eBay search I conducted on March 17, 2005, most of the posted auctions for slide collections were found in the "Collectibles" category, and subcategorized under "Photography: Contemporary (1940–Present)." How eBay defines "contemporary" remains elusive, as a majority of the photographic items listed were dubbed "vintage" in their sellers' descriptions.
11. Greenblatt, 52.
12. Artists also use the slide format to document their work and promote it to galleries. Increasingly, however, digital photographic technologies are eclipsing this practice, contributing to the obsolescence of the slide format.
13. A related reason for the decline of slides lies in the proprietary nature of slide technology. While Kodak had competitors, none of them had the highly

successful and patented carousel. And Kodak charged a small fortune for a slide projector (and replacement light bulbs), which is, technologically, a very straightforward device—thus severely limiting its market to the upper-middle-class domestic sphere and the larger institutional market. Unlike the camera, the slide projector never was fully a part of the consumer marketplace for earlier image-rendering technologies.

14. Roland Barthes, *Camera Lucida: Reflections on Photography*, trans. Richard Howard (1980; London: Vintage, 1993), 27.
15. Ibid., 96.
16. While the slide show is becoming obsolete in analog contexts, it is also reformatted in the digital realm by PowerPoint, a program using the vocabulary of the slide show and allowing for incorporating text, sound, animation, and hyperlinks.
17. Elvis Richardson, artist website, www.elvisrichardson.com.
18. For a discussion of the peculiarities of eBay's standard auction format, see chapter 10 of this book.
19. Jay David Bolter and Richard Grusin, *Remediation: Understanding New Media* (Cambridge, MA: MIT Press, 1999), 273.
20. Ibid., 5.
21. For a history and discussion of the magic lantern, see Joscelyn Godwin, *Athanasius Kircher: A Renaissance Man and the Quest for Lost Knowledge* (London: Thames and Hudson, 1979).
22. Greenblatt, 52.
23. Ibid., 43.

15

❑ The Contradictory Circulation of Fine Art and Antiques on eBay

❑ LISA BLOOM

The fine art and antiques sector of the economy has long been dominated by nineteenth-century patriarchal business practices and high-end auction houses such as Sotheby's and Christie's. In this chapter I argue that eBay has helped effect a set of democratizing shifts in this sector. As a technological assemblage, eBay provides for a new form of commerce that opens up certain social possibilities even as it forecloses others, and I point to contradictions between democratic notions of "community" and how eBay's language of "community" operates discursively within what is essentially a site for commercial transactions based on free-market libertarian "ethics." eBay's Feedback Forum system instills a form of seemingly transparent community self-governance that obviates the need for eBay the corporation to regulate and monitor transactions closely (see chapter 7). Transparency and its implied qualities of trust and social bond underwrite eBay, a setting where business transactions take place as an open expression of supply, demand, and evaluation. eBay thus exemplifies a new economic efficiency at work, one where flows of goods between buyers and sellers bypass costly intermediaries who once monopolized access, stock, and expertise.

As I detail below, eBay has enabled a move away from corporate intermediaries such as Sotheby's and Christie's and their traditional social filters based on elite assumptions about gender-, race- and class-based forms of social relations. Email as a direct yet impersonal form of communication and the anonymity afforded by eBay user IDs play an important role in the erosion of gender and class barriers in the fine art and antiques market. eBay also offers an almost immediate market access previously unavailable in the bricks-and-mortar international art market of old, and it has aided the flourishing of the fine art and antiques sector outside of older metropolitan centers. eBay's democratizing influences are complex, and I examine eBay in relation to the rise and fall of other internet auction houses such as the former Sothebys.com and the role of internet research sites such as Artnet.com and Artfact.com. This account highlights the culture of traditional auction houses and shows how eBay has influenced bricks-and mortar businesses. I also assess how eBay's democratizing influences work differently for buyers and sellers. I bring to this study my academic training in visual cultural and gender studies and my insider's knowledge as a seller on eBay of fine art and antiques.

To examine the complex changes that working for an online auction house brings to the embodied experience of these workers, I draw from my ethnographic research conducted with a small group of individuals working for a woman-owned American company selling fine art and antiques on eBay. The company started business on eBay in May 2000 and was a Sothebys.com associate from May 2001 until Sothebys.com's demise in February 2003. Through its association with Sothebys.com and eBay, the company quadrupled sales between 2000 and 2005.

SOCIAL CLASS, EBAY, AND BRICKS-AND-MORTAR AUCTION HOUSES

Given eBay's populist founding myth that it was built on trading Beanie Babies and Pez dispensers and on message board chatter, it seemed unlikely there would ever have developed much of a connection between the world of fine art and antiques and the online auction site. But the record shows that the eBay community bought and sold both popular culture *and* fine art and antiques since eBay's inception. Indeed, collecting communities and art and antique dealers were among the earliest and most enthusiastic posters to the discussion boards on eBay's predecessor site, AuctionWeb. As Pongo, one of AuctionWeb's more famous characters, explained, "[A] lot of the early users were retired antiques dealers who could barely turn on their computers."[1] It was in part because of the strong presence of these individuals on eBay that in April 1999, at the peak of the U.S. dot.com boom, eBay bought Butterfield & Butterfield, a well-known West Coast auction house, for 260 million USD. eBay then launched "Great Collections," the firm's Web portal entry for selling high-end art and antiques consigned to Butterfield & Butterfield. In January of the same year, Sotheby's, the international auction house, announced it would spend 25 million USD to start Sothebys.com, and a few months later it unveiled the joint venture SothebysAmazon.com. In June 2002 Sothebys.com also initiated a collaboration with eBay, and while this alliance lasted only one year it had more lasting influence on the art and antiques business than is commonly acknowledged: the alliance demonstrated the viability of sites such as eBay for buyers and sellers of fine art and antiques, particularly in the low- to mid-level price range.[2]

Though these early online ventures were influential in many ways, a significant reason for their failure—including that of eBay's Great Collections, unsuccessfully rebranded as "eBay Premiere" in January 2001—to secure a niche within the high-end fine art and antiques market lies in the fact that the economic efficiency that online auctions offer is less valued in this market than in others. In the words of Sotheby's chronicler, Robert Lacey:

> When people buy at Sotheby's, they are seeking to satisfy a variety of needs. They may explain their motives in terms of taste, or history or sentiment, but they are laying out their money fundamentally in hopes of acquiring something that can bring a new dimension to their lives. They are bidding for class. The ostentatious and insecure are seeking to validate themselves in the eyes of others. The passionate collector is driven by the quasi-spiritual impulse to possess beauty. But all are making their purchase in pursuit of some extra validation for themselves.[3]

The experience of bidding in a high-end auction house cannot be duplicated online. The interpersonal dynamics peculiar to the kind of internet commerce championed by eBay make it harder to engage in the personalized face-to-face chit-chat through which personalities and social attributes become manifest in live auctions. Sotheby's management had difficulty distinguishing between and providing for the differing needs of the face-to-face side of its traditional business and the new cultural demands faced by the dot.com venture. Management applied Sotheby's long-standing practices of expensive banquets, lavish pampering of clients, and heavy spending on marketing to its far less lucrative dot.com business. The abundance of spending on the internet department itself was evident through the uncharacteristically high salaries for its tech and marketing employees and large sums spent on print ads in venues such as the *New York Times* and *The New Yorker*. This aggressive spending on marketing, particularly in the beginning, was seen as a way to lure high profile art and antique dealers to become participants in the Sothebys.com online venture through the inclusion of dealer property in expensive dot.com advertisements. Another rational for its aggressive investment in marketing was to set itself ahead of the competition, particularly against the rival auction house Christie's, who initially considered starting its own online venture but eventually changed course and decided against it.

On eBay, clients as well as businesses are not so easily coded through appearance, age, education, class, or gender as they are in traditional auction settings. In general, online interactions tend to be less hierarchical and in theory promote diversity in an online organization's culture. One of the most commented upon advantages of the internet is the depersonalization of interlocutors through their assumption of online screen names. On eBay the ability of buyers and sellers to use anonymous user IDs can allow for a less inhibited presentation of self; however, sellers must adhere more strictly to traditional codes of ethics premised on a unitary, professional self. Nevertheless, email introduces compensatory advantages—sellers read correspondence and respond to it when ready. This can reduce the pressures of aggressive or manipulative telephone and face-to-face conversations, particularly those dealing with issues of price.

eBay's more democratic example inspired the organization of Sothebys.com. According to one woman interviewed for this project, Sothebys.com was more innovative than Sotheby's bricks-and-mortar operation in limiting hierarchical differences and reducing formalities among employees. Sothebys.com practiced more open hiring practices and promoted and rewarded younger employees, including women, who were not from the same high-elite social class from which the traditional firm recruited many of its employees. Sotheby.com's Content and IT employees were all under thirty, largely middle class, and paid at least double the salary of staff members whose positions did not require specialized skills or experience.[4] The company also took the (then) unusual step of training international dealers in how to sell their inventory on its site. This less centralized model of shared expertise and initiative comes closer to an eBay business model than what one would usually associate with an elite auction house.

The pressures of ongoing lawsuits at Sotheby's[5] and overspending on customer relations at its online division (already 100 million USD in debt) forced the firm to terminate its joint venture with eBay in February 2003.[6] Sotheby's minimized its internet presence and refocused on live auctions of valuable fine art and antiques. In the wake of this collapse, smaller internet-based fine art and antiques businesses and U.S.-based regional auction houses that had been important to eBay from the beginning acquired greater market shares of internet-based fine art and antiques sales. Yet this period was short-lived, as many of the medium- to large-sized established auction houses such as Doyle's and Swann's resumed their internet presence through eBay live auctions—a hybrid format combining live auction and internet-based sales.

THE ROLE OF ONLINE ART RESEARCH SITES

Art-related sites such as Artnet.com, Askart.com, Artprice.com, and Artfact.com that survived the dot.com crash repositioned themselves as research and advertising sites. They remain significant online presences and exert enormous influence on the way fine art and antiques are bought, sold, and valued. While subscribing to these services can be costly (especially to Artfact.com and Artnet.com), they have been a great leveler in providing access to expertise, standardized information and pricing, images, and auction records for listed artists and decorative arts that were previously available only through very expensive reference books. In certain ways, these sites actually provide more information since online auction records often feature digitized color images of the object, a feature less economically feasible in book-based auction records. Websites such as Artnet.com have become important mechanisms internationally for determining prices in a more detailed and direct way, and they enable individuals located outside of metropolitan centers with the best public art libraries to access the same information as experts working for major auction houses or museums. These sites, combined with the eBay search engine of completed auction listings and search engines such as Google, have made the internet essential for researching the history of fine art and antiques.

Sites such as Artnet.com and Artfact.com have also given workers in online fine art and antiques businesses an edge over clients. In some cases, this is because employees are more adept at Web-based research than clients, who often are less comfortable with computers and lack the skills to use sites such as Artnet.com properly and on a regular basis. Thus, knowledge and confidence gained through using these sites have opened up commercial and social possibilities for women and a younger generation of eBay sellers of fine art and antiques. Another advantage for these sellers is eBay's provision of access to an international fine art and antiques virtual marketplace that bypasses costly antique fairs and auction houses and that gives customers who are located anywhere and have Web access the means to buy and sell across spatially dispersed markets. This is significant since following the decline in value of the U.S. dollar relative to other major currencies, U.S.-based objects have become cheaper to acquire for foreign buyers and eBay businesses located anywhere in the United States now benefit from access to national and international clienteles. Indeed, many regionally based American auction houses that simultaneously conduct live and eBay-based auctions now claim that their sales are international as well. An examination of networked art auctions therefore reveals that the work involved links people globally in a virtual space of international commerce. eBay and the internet have facilitated the rise of smaller firms selling fine art and antiques. Because such firms are more horizontal in their organizational structure than older firms such as Sotheby's they can be seen as maintaining aspects of the myth of eBay as the quintessential American small town writ virtual, built on word of mouth, and sustained by people's feelings of belonging.

SELLERS, INVISIBLE LABOR, AND COSTS OF EBAY

Despite the desirable democratic possibilities for which eBay has allowed, many of the above-noted technological and social changes in the way commerce is conducted on eBay have taken place at considerable cost to sellers. While the internet's technological structure helps foster the illusion of costless reproductions and instantaneous sales, the labor entailed in listing an object on eBay in a highly professional way and completing an internet transaction is enormous. To compensate for buyers' inability to personally examine an object before purchase, many serious online sellers provide very detailed cataloging information including extensive condition reports and photographs. Requisite skills range from expertise in photography to fine art cataloging, research, writing condition reports, expertise with computers, and shipping and packing, among others. These practices of cataloging and photography follow those of older art catalogs produced by bricks-and-mortar auction houses, but often include greater detail, including biographies of artists, four to six photographs per item, and extensive condition reports. While the form of these descriptions may not be innovative, a crucial difference is the amount of labor involved, part of it in producing the seemingly effortless transparency required in online selling and achieved in part through the labor required to provide more detailed cataloging information.

Just as issues of labor get erased from eBay's discourse of friction-free ease, myths about eBay's "community" and democratic structure tend to occlude issues of costs, particularly those incurred by sellers who must pay listing fees whether or not their item sells.[7] Conflict lying just beneath the surface of this myth is seen in message board discussions of eBay's fee structures. eBay's transaction fees are considerable if one consistently sells hundreds or thousands of items at one time. For high-volume or high-value sellers, transaction fees can equal the cost of retail space rental in major metropolitan areas, and any fee change has a fairly large impact. It should be noted, however, that since fine art and antiques dealers typically use eBay to supplement their bricks-and-mortar businesses, eBay fee increases frequently are not considered high relative to, for example, fees for participating in live art and antiques fairs. Nevertheless, since eBay remains understood as a site for bargains (versus art and antiques fairs, where objects sell at full retail price), fee-related costs, advertising included, remain contentious for many eBay sellers, particularly those with relatively low profit margins. A central concern related to fee increases is that there is little competition from any comparable auction site. This exposes all smaller sellers, such as those employing a small number of individuals working in basements, garages, or spare rooms in a house, to arbitrary fee changes. eBay's democratizing influence, then, should be understood in relation to the size of a seller's business and her or his ability to survive changes in market conditions, fee increases included.

GENDER AND CLASS IN INTERNET-BASED FINE ART AND ANTIQUES SALES

The size or scale of a business is an issue of particular importance to women in the field. Female employees at a woman-owned fine art and antiques eBay-linked business pointed out the difference between eBay small businesses with ample staffs and those with one or two employees. These women indicated that the larger the staff, the less isolated they felt when dealing with aggressive or harassing clients, most of whom were older men. One way these employees dealt with harassment was to post egregious client email in a public place such as the bathroom door and have other staff comment on them publicly. Such correspondence would range from the mildly flirtatious to outright condescension and hostility. These oftentimes gendered forms of aggression would manifest themselves when a buyer objected to an object's sale price, when he was buying fine art somewhat erotic in nature, or if the object arrived damaged or was lost. In certain ways, this continued the patriarchal social relations of the male-dominated fine art and antiques business. Regardless of an individual's sexual orientation or gender makeup, the structure of the communication situation remains presumptively heteronormative and heterosexual, and those with less power are feminized and discursively positioned as passive (even in those situations where aggressive email originates from women buyers). Further complicating these exchanges is the fact that, of the employees I interviewed, most have more formal education than their clients. Clients often hail from rather complex class positions; though they may operate within a very elite world of collectors, museums, connoisseurs, and high art, they are not always of that world and were not born into it.

For the women and men working for this eBay-linked art and antiques business, questions of expertise and knowledge also were commonly areas of contention, for clients often presume their expertise is superior to that of employees, especially if the buyer is male and the employee female. In the estimation of some well-heeled clients, many of whom are collectors or dealers, their expertise is always superior, even when they deal with highly educated individuals in online situations that allow for more democratized access to fine art and antiques research sites such as Artnet.com and Artfact.com.

Working for a smaller online seller did have some advantages over working for firms such as Sothebys.com, according to one of the women I interviewed for this project. She claimed to enjoy more power and control over clients in being allowed to block the bidding of more difficult clients. Wealthy clients, therefore, had to be polite to staff if they wanted to purchase a particular object only available through this business. Clients also had to accept they would not be pampered merely because they wanted to do business. As at Sotheby's and Christie's, this firm's employees still had to contend with a power imbalance in social class, age, and wealth between themselves and clients. However, online performances of class, gender, and social privilege were not as charged as in face-to-face encounters.

The explanation for this lies, in part, in the ability of an online business to dispense with the gendered expectations placed on women's self-presentation in businesses such as Sotheby's and Christie's, with their tradition of *bon chic, bon genre*—well-dressed, attractive individuals with prep-school demeanors and vocal and verbal abilities indicating high cultural capital. Women working for these firms are also expected to appear more docile as befitting a "feminized" support role for the men in charge. I have already noted, however, that the move by women to use the internet and eBay to break out of this mold is less unproblematic than one might expect. The internet does work to women's advantage in that differences in age and social class, expressed through money, appearance, and class versus education, may not be as apparent through email exchanges as in face-to face encounters. However, these women must also work with dealers and collectors who routinely maintain more than one username and who prefer anonymity, even as these women are expected to reveal their own personal identities. For example, buyers are often dealers working as middlemen; they use different screen names to conceal from their own clients the fact that they originally acquired an object on eBay that they hope to sell to a client at a higher price. Thus, it is difficult for employees to readily know whether they are dealing with a buyer looking to purchase an object for his or her own collection or one operating as a middleman for an unknown third party. This introduces an unfavorable imbalance for the men and women working at the internet company I studied. As a result, a split has developed between online sellers and buyers in terms of ethical behavior, and is reflected in the imbalance of communication behavior noted above.

It is in building client relations that contradictions between democratic notions of "community" and commercial-based transactions become most evident. On the one hand, eBayers often share expertise as members of a civic-minded community, but on the other, expertise can be used as a weapon in business transactions to set the terms of an unequal power relationship. Significantly, no one I interviewed believes eBay propagates entirely new and nonsexist modes of interaction, since much of the correspondence between sellers and buyers reflects the culture at large, including still-intact stereotypical cultural narratives and underlying patriarchal assumptions. In the same way, the performance of social class is recirculated online. A shipping coordinator for a small fine art and antiques business explains,

> I often notice how some customers really try to force an impression of their social status on me by going out of their way to claim that "expense doesn't matter" for shipping methods while, on the other end of the socio-economic spectrum, there are those who complain about paying $100 [USD] for shipping a $1000 painting to another country. Plus, a lot of buyers overseas will ask me to mark items as having a lower value than they actually possess on customs forms so they don't have to pay extra fees that their countries impose for expensive items, as if every penny matters. There have even been a few occasions when people will call my line and ask about an item still up for auction about which they are very enthusiastic. When I explain to them that I'm "just the shipping coordinator," and that I rarely see any items that are not already sold, their tone becomes condescending, as if I'm out of my league in speaking with them because I don't have the appreciation for the piece that they do.

This class narrative extended even to the form of payment itself. The shipping coordinator continued,

> I was also reminded of what X was just telling me the other day. He said that it seemed to him that people who buy paintings tend to pay by money order or wire transfer while antique/decorative arts buyers use PayPal, as if the former are older elitists who don't even know what PayPal is.[8]

Since even different forms of payment can connote cultural and social distinctions, one needs to understand eBay's democratization of markets as still inflected by the cultural practices of older, more sanctioned art and antiques businesses.

FEEDBACK AND COMMUNITY

Social relations limited to exchanging payment and address information during the transaction and buying period play out differently through the feedback mechanism on eBay than in traditional venues such as Sotheby's. eBay's feedback mechanism is crucial since it makes the site appear more transparent and therefore more egalitarian for online trading, and it is where the ethics of a "self-regulating community" are most visibly manifest. Feedback has a double-edged nature: a substitute for adequate corporate regulation of the site, yet also a tool for unscrupulous buyers to intimidate legitimate sellers in a marketplace with little to no oversight. Feedback offers the appearance of transparency and helps sustain the myth of community constantly invoked by eBay, but as Laura Robinson (see chapter 8) argues, it is also a widely contradictory mechanism that functions poorly when self-interests clash and competition is intense. Feedback remains a permanent, public record of buyer-seller communication and sets up a permanent consumer rating for eBay sellers who often risk their reputations if they receive poor feedback. This is less the case with buyers, unless their feedback is consistently negative.

The feedback mechanism has been used by eBay management to transfer the work of site regulation onto community members (see chapters 6 and 7). However, forms of online fraud have become too complex for the feedback mechanism to adequately police, and eBay plans to introduce a "report this item" button on each listing. Fraud is a growing problem on eBay in terms of both the electronic takeovers of sellers' accounts by hackers and the increase of fraudulent messages purporting to be about fraud to eBay sellers and buyers. Because hackers mimic official eBay emails in style and graphics, their activities have created an enormous communication problem: eBay buyers and sellers can no longer readily differentiate from a real or a fake message from eBay. Moreover, counterfeit goods and cheap knock-offs plague the online marketplace in a number of categories, including artwork, jewelry, designer accessories, and autographed sports memorabilia. Tiffany & Company launched a lawsuit against eBay in late 2004, accusing the company of trademark infringement by facilitating and promoting the sale of thousands of pieces of counterfeit Tiffany jewelry. Analysts predict the outcome of the case, expected to go on trial in 2006, will have a major impact on e-commerce no matter how it is decided and may adversely affect eBay's successful business model as solely a facilitator of sales among buyers and sellers.[9]

THE PARADOX OF DEPERSONALIZATION AND COMMUNITY IN EBAY FINE ART AND ANTIQUES TRANSACTIONS

Utopian ideals structured eBay's founding moment, and it is not surprising that some of the myths of the internet and eBay persist, such as the idea that eBay is a "a great leveler giving people with social disadvantages a place to excel."[10] Such an assertion trades in the same utopian logic parodied in the famous *New Yorker* cartoon depicting two dogs seated at a computer, one saying to the other, "On the Internet, nobody knows you're a dog."[11] eBay might fulfill these kinds of utopian desires more for buyers, but sellers cannot hide behind their screen names in the same way that buyers can, and eBay regulations enforce this "ethical" imbalance.

Buyers and sellers in the fine art and antiques sector do not share the sense of fervor and community on eBay equally. Clearly, there has been more enthusiasm on the buying side as evidenced by the superlatives often used in feedback to describe successful transactions. eBay has been so successful with buyers in this regard because it offers the kind of immediate consumer satisfaction traditionally enjoyed by the wealthy who are able to pay to have their exact desires translated into a satisfying object combined with the pleasurable experience of having made the winning bid. In certain ways, eBay has been able to offer an extreme form of niche marketing at bargain rates for people of average means, or for those with means who want items traditionally available through high-end retail customer service but who do not want to pay full price. It is in this respect that an eBay commercial transaction can nourish a sense of "community" in the self-interested competitive environment of the marketplace. This is where the small-town metaphor makes the most sense since it establishes a deep, reiterated reciprocity between objects of consumption and consumers' desires as well as between buyers and sellers.

Opposite the cheerleaders, who are mostly buyers, stand the detractors, who are often the sellers. For the most part they are more worried that eBay, as a putatively alternative online community, has evolved into a virtual monopoly. Rosalinda Baldwin, an eBay message board regular, claims that eBay at the beginning was "a great leveler—one of the most powerful democratizing forces [I] had ever encountered," but "Meg changed us from a community into a commodity. And you know, like sheep, if she had to slaughter a few million of us for profit, it was for our own good, she will say."[12] For Baldwin, eBay has evolved into a near monopoly that controls access to a unique marketplace and increasingly displays the classic indifference of monopolies toward the needs of small businesses and communities.

The discourses of eBay commerce certainly promise greater efficiency for all by cutting out intermediaries and increasing direct trade across regions and national borders. These shifts have helped erode traditional hierarchies of class, gender, and geography—hierarchies long associated with bricks-and-mortar fine art and antiques business models. Yet these shifts have also given rise to a newly minted sense of community linked to forms of consumer satisfaction in which buyers purchase what they want from their office or home. eBay has given birth to an intriguing, at times contradictory form of social space in which the relative impersonality of the internet, combined with more personal customer service, enables new forms of businesses in which sellers and buyers nourish a sense of "community" not directly based on social class, appearance, or personal relations. Direct yet impersonal emails between buyers and sellers partially hidden behind user IDs make the site work, paradoxically, as a community that also allows younger sellers, women, and minorities to enter a field previously organized by the assumptions prevalent within elite older male social networks. Given eBay's contradictory directions, it is not surprising that many business writers as well as community board posters have written about the company with extreme idealism and enthusiasm, and later with disappointment. It is, therefore, only through more sober and nuanced assessments of eBay from the perspective of both buyers and sellers that we can begin to understand the contradictions of eBay's market-based democratic populism and its influence on digital markets and digital capitalism in the area of fine art and antiques.

NOTES

1. Adam Cohen, *The Perfect Store* (Boston: Little, Brown, 2002), 68.
2. The online auction site Igavel.com, started by Lark Mason, a former employee of Sothebys.com, is an important example of an alternative site to eBay that has been successful in selling low- to mid-range fine art and antiques.
3. Robert Lacey, *Sotheby's Bidding for Class* (Boston: Little, Brown, 1998), 15.
4. Thanks to Amy Huntington, former senior producer of Sothebys.com, for allowing me to interview her on this topic.
5. Samuel Pennington, "Sotheby's CEO and Chairman Resign, Dividend Suspended," *Maine Antique Digest*, April 2000.

6. Brooks Barnes and Nick Wingfield, "Sotheby's Ends EBay Venture, Citing Losses," February 5, 2003, http://sg.biz.yahoo.com/030205/72/372pr.html.
7. See "Ebay's Joy Ride: Going Once … A Sellers' Rebellion May Be the Least of Its Worries," *New York Times*, March 6, 2005, sec. 3, 1.
8. Thanks to Dustin McWherter for his helpful comments.
9. See Katie Hafner, "Seeing Fakes, Angry Traders Confront eBay," *New York Times*, January 29, 2006, http://www.nytimes.com/2006/01/29/technology/29ebay.html?_r=1&emc=eta1 (accessed January 29, 2006).
10. Cohen, 68.
11. On the intersection between communication technology and the prosthetic community, see Sandy Stone, "Split Subjects, Not Atoms; or, How I Fell in Love with My Prosthesis," in *The Cyborg Handbook*, ed. Chris Gray (New York: Routledge, 1995), 393–406.
12. Cohen, 220–1.

16

My Queer eBay

"Gay Interest" Photographs and the Visual Culture of Buying

MICHELE WHITE

Most large-scale capitalist enterprises promote stereotyped gender positions and heteronormative relationships. eBay is no exception, and it does so through its site design and business strategies, but some sellers resist eBay's limited representations and address. By using the term "gay interest" in their listings, sellers render alternative positions and garner better prices. Gay interest listings appear in such varied categories as "DVDs & Movies," "Books," "Men's Clothing" (mostly thongs and briefs), "Women's Clothing" (leather and PVC pants and Winnie the Pooh T-shirts), "Home & Garden" (bookends depicting attractive men), "Sporting Goods" (mostly socks and briefs), "Toys & Hobbies" (*Teletubbies*' Tinky Winky and Bat Girl), "Coins" (medals with images of men), and "eBay Motors" (chaps and other leather items).[1] These gay interest listings, and the ways that they address the company and consumer, are a reminder of the ongoing conflicts among eBay, buyers, and sellers over desires to articulate traditional gender roles, to imagine different sorts of identity formations, to represent marriages and nuclear families at the expense of other social and cultural experiences, to describe gay and queer desire in detail, and to make a profit from eBay activities.

All gay interest sellers present a different position than eBay's standard address, but gay interest photography sellers engage in a more radical process by remaking and rewriting the past that images are believed to convey. Vintage photography sellers use the term to designate a commodity they believe gay individuals would want and thereby acknowledge the diverse sexualities of collectors; indicate that gay, lesbian, queer, transgendered, and bisexual individuals and relationships have been photographically portrayed; and queer the past by describing same-sex duos and groups as gay. These gay interest photography sellers integrate gay politics and desires into eBay not only by making their listings a visible part of the site but also by suggesting that vernacular photography—such as the images in many individuals' family albums—have gay content and depict gay people. This chapter considers how these oppositional and "queer"[2] vintage photography buying and selling strategies confuse stable categories, desires, and subject positions and thereby undermine eBay's normalizing discourses. Tensions between eBay's procedures and the contrary work of gay interest vintage photography sellers on the site merit close attention because eBay tries to elide its inscription of stereotyped gender positions and heteronormative relationships by claiming to provide an unbiased setting for individuals to buy and sell objects and attain the best price.

GENDER, SEXUALITY, AND EBAY

eBay's apocryphal and often repeated origin story, which indicates that Pierre Omidyar started the site so that his then-fiancée could trade Pez dispensers, makes heterosexual unions an implicit part of the site.[3] NetLingo dictionary and a variety of newspapers support the purported connection between eBay and wedding engagements when indicating that "10 diamond rings" are sold on the site every hour.[4] eBay's pink "banner" advertisements for engagement rings, which address women through the use of a gender-specific color, also link the site and auctions to future marriages. The ads indicate that eBay can resolve women's fears that they will "be single forever" by enabling couples to reasonably acquire the accoutrements of heteronormative relationships.[5] Through these narratives, eBay forcefully associates its site and auctions with heterosexual marriages, although some of these representations could individually evoke other forms of commitment. eBay also takes part in conventional conceptions of identity and desire by indicating that women's fulfillment can only be achieved through heterosexual relationships.

eBay also renders its site as a series of gender-specific settings by indicating that some objects are only appropriate for men or women. Site advertisements for "guy stuff," for instance, offer electronics and computer games and make it seem as though only men are the appropriately gendered consumers for technologies.[6] This articulation of gender-specific forms of shopping and engaging with objects is antithetical to reaching the widest number of consumers for eBay's auctions. Omidyar and other eBay employees depict the site as the perfect market—where all subject positions and types of consumers are addressed in an open marketplace—yet limit the possible purchasers for items through site advertising and representations. This indicates that the site produces social norms as well as having an economic function.[7]

The Power of All of Us website, which eBay uses as an advertisement, also emphasizes heteronormative positions and depicts the family as a nuclear structure. It represents the "future of eBay" as a light-skinned mother, father, and two children about to travel toward a "community" of architecturally similar houses and desires.[8] The site's flash sequences depict a series of shapes that are "filled in" with images of gendered individuals, inviting buyers and sellers to slip easily into these roles and narratives. eBay's television spots "Clocks" and "Maze," also available on the site, further render the relationship between buyers and sellers as a form of heterosexual union. In "Maze," a woman's confused search through an incomprehensible labyrinth of goods is resolved when she finds "the one thing" she wants "from the one person who has it" and is united with a man through a bundled rug. eBay uses these advertisements to relate buyers' and sellers' engagement with objects to heteronormative romances between people. The site's promotional discourse suggests a direct connection between the "thousands of people who love what you love" and "the one" partner right for "*you*"—provided this individual subscribes to heterosexual norms. eBay promises it can then enable the individual to "find them."

Individuals with varied identities and desires engage in eBay trading and internet viewing. A less familiar narrative about eBay's Jim Griffith, or "Uncle Griff," is more aligned with and acknowledges lesbian, gay, queer, bisexual, and transgendered positions. "Griffith, an early eBay employee, posted popular messages about 'wearing a lovely flower print dress,' donning women's attire while 'milking the cows,' and other instances of textually narrated drag where he incorporated participants into his imagined forms of cross-dressing."[9] Management continued this company history of drag and the temporary queering of gender positions when it put on a fashion show for employees that included cross-dressed participants.[10] Uncle Griff's cross-dressing stories offer wonderful representations of men temporarily occupying alternative gender positions. They can nevertheless also demean women by indicating that it is funny, grotesque, and humiliating when men adopt aspects of women's performances, and they can elide gay desires and practices by replacing them with temporary instances of drag.[11]

STRUCTURING EBAY'S INTERFACE AND VISUAL CULTURE

Using the eBay site may be described as "viewing," and buyers and sellers are trained to read, look, and perform in specific ways. eBay's viewing process is structured by varied lists and categories that create a set of objects and relationships between objects, and articulate what is recognizable and purchasable. They also suggest how things are to be understood, help to articulate collecting, and produce gender, race, and sexuality differences. In eBay, categorizing, representing, and viewing images are complicated practices that have social, political, and economic significance extending beyond the interface. eBay's category system often enforces the binary gender system. Women, for instance, become the default consumer in the "Jewelry & Watches" category and are mentioned in item descriptions, but not in the categories. A "Men's Jewelry" subcategory prevents individuals from easily buying such items as chains, collar buttons, cuff links, necklaces, pins, and watches without engaging in gendered contexts and mandates.

Buyers find listings for items by using eBay's menu-driven category system, the search function, or previously saved searches. In each case, buyers' terms are filtered through and related to eBay's categories. For instance, when buyers search using a particular term, the results specify how many items are in each category and there is the option of continuing to view through these eBay-specific categories. eBay buyers, and especially sellers, must accept eBay categories, think like the structure, and view in particular ways in order to successfully engage eBay's visual interface (see chapter 4 for a succinct account of skills needed to search both items within and across categories). eBay suggests that "feedback received from the eBay Community and from experts in the affected fields" determines the category system.[12] However, some sellers indicate on a regular basis that eBay's categories make their listings difficult to find, and categories are not accepted by all sellers and buyers.[13] The system also marginalizes some forms of collecting and sexual desires. eBay forces many erotic materials into its "Mature Audiences" category that requires special registration and cannot be searched from the main part of the site,[14] and, as Michael Petit argues (see chapter 17), eBay ends auctions that make certain erotic desires and collecting too visible. eBay has resisted critical and art interventions into the politics of its category system. Mendi and Keith Obadike's "Blackness for Sale" (see Figure 1.1), which offered an ironic commentary on black masculinity and its contemporary valuation in varied social situations, was ended without explanation.[15]

eBay's categories also make it more difficult to think and view from gay, lesbian, and queer positions. Such lifestyle events as weddings are articulated through the "Wedding Apparel" category and varied eBay advertisements, but gay and lesbian identities are not articulated or acknowledged by eBay's category system. "Wedding," "baby," and a variety of other category descriptors, along with sellers' accompanying listings and images, tend to support a heterosexual system of relationships and desires even though such concepts are not specific to any sexuality position. eBay's categories suggest a whole system of knowledge because they have links to subcategories and a set of "unique" titles and accompanying listings written by sellers. The category system affects the final price of auctioned items and contributes to larger cultural conceptions about what kinds of people and identities should be visible and identifiable.

"GAY INTEREST" AND "LESBIAN INTEREST" VINTAGE PHOTOGRAPHY

Vintage photography sellers use "gay interest" as a search term to provide another viewing structure within eBay's category system. Their listings materialize the attributes and sexuality of a body they indicate once was in front of the camera, and a contemporary gay cultural body that has desires, including desire for a particular past and to acquire things. In using the term, gay interest photography sellers render gay pasts and longings, even though some eBay viewers would not identify the portrayed individuals as gay. Descriptions such as "Materials from the estate of a Professor of Romance Languages," which were "purchased in 1996 from his gay nephew," render gay families and collecting practices.[16] Such "gay photographs" allow sellers to render, in the words of one seller, a "record of gay culture … that remain[s] a historic part and contemporary component of gay culture." [17] These comments suggest that readings of gay sexuality suffuse varied aspects of images. A sexual past and desiring present are produced when sellers read images and indicate that it "looks like the top right corner guy is cruising the guy with his tongue out."[18] These sellers use the terms "gay" and "gay interest" to represent relationships that would have been and are described in a variety of ways in the nineteenth, twentieth, and twenty-first centuries.

The "gay interest" search term requires more consideration in a culture where, as Alexandra Chasin suggests, the "way that gay men and lesbians in the United States come to understand themselves as 'gay,' and as 'American,' has everything to do with understandings of the relationship between citizenship and consumption."[19] eBay's "Community" link, which according to Cohen made eBay distinctive and profitable, offers buyers and sellers a message system designed to facilitate a form of citizenship along with better buying and selling strategies.[20] Gay interest items, and the sellers who describe them, visualize bodies and desires left out of the eBay category system while supporting eBay's indication that citizenship and community are achieved by buying and selling. Gay interest sellers overturn part of eBay's heteronormative structure by making gay interest into a kind of category even though they still must work within eBay's category and representational systems.

Gay interest auctions in the "Antique (Pre-1940)" photographic images category usually designate images as being of interest to men. They include studio as well as vernacular images of men together (more specifically, sailors, soldiers, sports teams, and fraternity boys); men with their shirts off, from the back, or "from behind"; nudity, genital bulges, and partially or wholly visible penises; images of men touching, almost touching, or even close together; muscled and good-looking men, and effeminate gestures or "dapper" dressing.[21] The "gay interest" search term has many facets. It makes gay desire visible to individuals who buy photographic images; suggests the particular practices of some gay, lesbian, queer, transgendered, and bisexual photo collectors; recontextualizes images in ways that queer the past when vintage images of swimmers or men with their arms around each other are described as "gay"; works to provide evidence of gay histories and collecting practices; acts as a marketing strategy; and tells wonderful and fantastical stories about images.

The series of listings of vintage photographs from eBay ID pelicancan's "late gay uncle's photo albums," for instance, suggests a history of gay collecting and documenting by providing descriptions that relate a history told to the seller by his uncle (Figure 16.1). The photographs depict men in same-sex arrangements, though the descriptions propose details of gay relationships and histories that the images do not convey.[22] pelicancan describes society's acceptance of the sexuality of the "Bridges brothers": "Uncle said the brothers were gay, but it wasn't called that back then in 1916. He said the brothers preferred the company of men and no one made a big deal about it."[23] Through pelicancan, the uncle also describes intolerance toward "a college group called The Greeks, that gathered in their rundown clubhouse … to discuss the ways of the ancient greeks. Uncle said it was a flimsy pretext to talk about homosexual love and all of its glories," and someone burned the clubhouse down when their sexuality became "common knowledge."[24] pelicancan uses these descriptions to connect camera and photograph to the historical narrative, since the images usually do not represent the chronicled events. He also guarantees the veracity of descriptions and that the photograph is a mechanical record of a particular scene by indicating that the device was recognized by sitters who "look surprised at having their picture taken" and "smile shyly for the camera."[25]

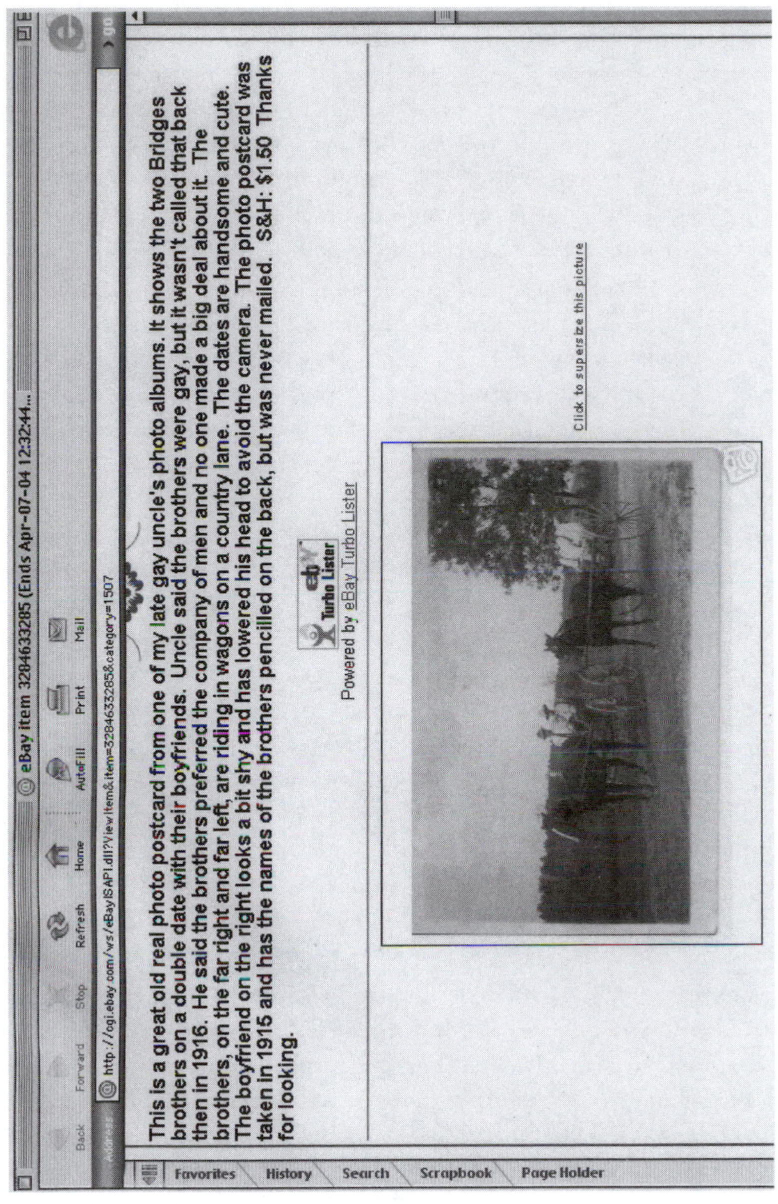

Figure 16.1 "Vintage Photo Gay Brothers Double Date In Wagons 1916."

pelicancan's narratives about named individuals and particular times appear along with his listings of representations with erotic content that are, as suggested by a variety of sellers, of gay interest. For instance, pelicancan presents images of "two handsome, young men sitting closely together under a tree"; men "pressing their knees together"; and "smooth, tanned bodies clad in tight swim trunks."[26] Such gay interest listings refuse the idea of a seamless history or homogeneous photographic viewing practice, and sellers' accounts of earlier times and relationships become intermeshed with contemporary queer readings of images. The multiform narratives of pelicancan and other sellers make the complicated distinctions between photographic documentation and imaginative reading difficult to identify.

As the number of images sold from the uncle's albums grows, and pelicancan renders an ever more elaborate history of gay lives and homosocial erotic relationships, I sometimes wonder if other images are added into this urtext, or even if the whole narrative is constructed and the uncle stands in for the many desiring subjects who view these images and the many men who have had intimate, erotic, and committed relationships with men. Such doubts can be troubling because resistances to gay interest listings on eBay, as I discuss in more detail below, also usually reject gay and lesbian pasts and the processes of reading images differently and queerly. Nevertheless, there must be ways of considering the narratives about particular images while supporting sellers' gay interest practices, queer readings, and gay and lesbian histories. The process of queering images, by attributing them to a gay uncle, is also related to gay interest practices and could have a productive effect. Diverse readings, and even misrepresentations, are a possibility with any eBay item. Buyers engage in varied evaluation practices that speak to such issues. In pelicancan's case, buyers provide verification of his readings through enthusiastic evaluations that note, "item, as described"; "Nice photograph with a great history"; and "As always, imaginative photos illustrating little-known corners of history."[27] Their expressive comments indicate a desire to retrieve, read, and enjoy gay history through photographs.

Sellers sometimes use the "gay interest" term for vintage photographs considered of interest to women, but the term "lesbian interest" is more often employed by sellers who address an erotically charged male viewer through mass media images of "lesbian" relationships and the imaginary viewing body of a lesbian buyer. "Lesbian interest" images portray groups of women nude, topless, in bondage, spanking each other, and wearing lingerie; "bush sisters" with visible pubic hair; women hugging, touching, almost touching, or even close together; and women in suits, coveralls, and other "masculine" attire. As this list suggests, many sellers use the terms "lesbian" and "lesbian interest" to indicate erotic images of women together that men might enjoy. Such sellers, however, are unable to imagine these photographs as part of a lesbian past or continuum in which women had and continue to have erotic relationships with women without needing to address a male viewer. For instance, eBay ID fouraker describes a "collection of 1950s era nude images that were found in an elderly lady's attic," uses the term "lesbian interest," and then indicates that they "evidently belonged to her late husband."[28] eBay ID vuky14 uses the term "lesbian interest" and notes that the "photo was found in Grandpa's estate and no one in the family had an explanation"; it might be an image from "one of the largest 'red light' districts in America," and "definitely wasn't Grandma."[29] Imagining that such material is only capable of erotically addressing men is politically troubling because it enables heterosexual male eBay buyers to colonize lesbian identity, histories, and desires. Equally troubling, item listings almost never overtly acknowledge crossed desires and identifications. For instance, women are not addressed as potential buyers of gay interest listings that offer images of men together, and most eBay sellers do not imagine the kinds of queer women, for example, who sleep with men *and* produce and enjoy homoerotic male slash fiction and yaoi comics.[30] Gay and lesbian interest listings nevertheless change eBay's assumed narratives and address of images by making gay, lesbian, and queer desires visible, even though this visibility is at times denied.

THE PRICE OF GAY INTEREST VINTAGE PHOTOGRAPHY

pelicancan describes his uncle's photographs, but most gay and lesbian interest listings do not identify the photographer or depicted people because the production histories of these images are no longer known. This makes the meaning of these photographs more open to interpretation; at the same time, they are usually presumed to be a direct and unmediated depiction of a particular time. Roland Barthes writes that the "photograph is always invisible: it is not it that we see," and Susan Sontag suggests photography is more than a rendered image or interpretation: "[I]t is also a trace, something directly stenciled off the real, like a footprint."[31] In the case of gay interest images, these attributes render a situation where the images remain associated with the photographic trace of the real and, yet, the "real" is changeable; eBay sellers produce gay identities when they queer photographs by "finding" and reading gay pasts. Judith Butler and Biddy Martin note that one "of the prime strategies of lesbian and gay studies has been to 'queer' what had otherwise seemed to be 'straight': mainstream cinema, pop music, novels, indeed, the 'nation' itself."[32] While some vernacular photography sellers do make queering part of their practices, not all eBay viewers are familiar with these political strategies, nor do they find them acceptable.

John Ibson, an academic and collector, purchases photographs that represent intimate relationships between men. He argues, however, that the term "gay" has a historic specificity and therefore does not describe early photographic representations of men. He indicates that with eBay, "'Gay' or 'Gay Interest' is often given to any photograph of two or more men doing no more than standing close to each other."[33] In describing a photograph where two men "share a single chair" and "one man sits on the other's lap," Ibson notes, "I purchased this photograph on eBay; it was offered as a portrait of a gay couple, and the high price I had to pay for it suggests that many bidders accepted that designation and wanted it for that reason."[34] By suggesting he has the knowledge and authority to read images correctly, Ibson resists the pleasures of queering images on eBay—where reading images raises larger questions about the ways that society and desire are normatively conceived.

The numbers vary, but each week on eBay there are usually more than three hundred photographic images listed as "gay" and a lower but still significant number listed as "lesbian" and "gay interest." Gay interest vintage photographic images garner higher prices than related material.[35] For instance, a listing that notes in its title that the photograph is of two men holding hands will usually sell for a much higher price, occasionally reaching 400 USD, while an image of a man and a woman holding hands usually sells for less than 15 USD. Images of Asian, black, and Latino/a subjects, especially those from the nineteenth century, also garner higher prices than images of whites. Such prices indicate that images of people who are gay, men in intimate contact with men, and people of color are valuable. However, the prices of gay interest images may incorrectly suggest that such representations, and their related identity positions, are also rare.

The prices of gay interest photographs and the practices of gay interest sellers do not lead all buyers and sellers to value such images, accept the people that are represented, or tolerate the ways that photographic materials are described. Disagreements arise over gay interest listings, and some eBay buyers and sellers express homophobic opinions about these practices. eBay ID gargantua added a "Disclaimer" to his listings because of the numerous homophobic emails he received from irate viewers. He attempts to protect himself and the ways that the term "gay interest" reflects on his selling and sexuality by indicating that "'GAY is a Search Word … Not a LABEL or SOCIAL COMMENTARY about the VIEWER or the SUBJECT of the photo."[36] gargantua's announcement that viewers should not send "caustic email" indicates that gay interest provides social commentary resisted by some eBay viewers. The negative reactions to such terms further indicate that selling in this category can be difficult, as well as indicate the ongoing cultural unease with the possibility of gay pasts and presents and the ways that this possibility can affect the viewer's cultural and sexual identity. Gay interest listings suggest that vernacular photographs, including the viewer's own family albums and images, can also be read and desired differently and may contain unnoticed indications of gay, lesbian, and queer family histories.

Some sellers more overtly express their unease when using the "gay interest" search term and more directly resist being connected to gay sexualities. eBay ID speakswithmusic states, "I am not thinking of anything sexual … not referring to the people in the images, but the culture that some of the eBay shoppers identify themselves with," and adds that buyers "comment that the people in my images can't be proven to be gay or lesbian. Some call me names."[37] Sellers' disclaimers and indications that they are not "thinking of anything sexual" suggest their ambivalence in thinking about and making fully visible considerations of gay sexualities. eBay listings that comment negatively on the use of the "gay interest" term also appear in search results and try to undermine the politics of gay interest listings by questioning gay and lesbian desires and buying practices.

An eBay seller of movie ephemera, who includes negative comments about the "gay interest" search term in his listings, has encouraged a discussion about the term on his listserv. Bruce Hershenson notes that listings for Sal Mineo "invariably include the phrase 'Gay interest'" and that "this greatly diminishes Sal Mineo and is also downright offensive."[38] Readers support Hershenson's arguments and indicate, "What does it matter one way or the other" if he was gay, that the term is a "marketing ploy," that in using it sellers "stoop to any means to get a few extra dollars," and that it suggests a "narrow-minded, probably bigoted" seller. Each listing on eBay is, of course, a form of marketing, so such assertions only make sense given the larger social context where displacing alternative sexualities supports beliefs that heterosexuality is the only acceptable form of identity and desire.

The ambivalent ways that some sellers use the "gay interest" search term allow them to attract gay buyers while placating other eBay viewers. eBay ID hansonenterprises describes an image as "two gay military men" but then notes, "I do not know for sure that they are homosexual, but they certainly appear to be very 'friendly.'"[39] Some sellers explain their use of the "gay interest" search term, which trains buyers in the ways that images can be read, and defend their motivation to buyers who might otherwise angrily respond. For instance, eBay ID babs-loves-b-bay notes, "They are sitting closely as if they might be a couple, which is why I marked it gay interest."[40] Sellers reduce their responsibility and include potential buyers in the reading and identification by posing questions such as "Might we say a bit of gay intent?"[41] eBay ID lexo206 lists an item as "1940's Gay Sailors @ California Night Club" but then indicates that "I don't think there [*sic*] gay … in fact I think there [*sic*] talking about the girl in the background."[42] These ambivalent narratives continue the advertising strategies that Danae Clark describes in which fears of alienating consumers have resulted in "gay window ads" only recognizable to some consumers—instances where homosexuality is both referenced and denied.[43] This is a common strategy among eBay gay interest sellers.

Some sellers employ such strategies because gay interest listings can articulate identity in ways they do not desire. Heteronormative assumptions tend to associate individuals who positively describe gay themes and have an interest in gay, lesbian, and queer sexualities with these positions rather than acknowledging the variety of political and ethical reasons for accepting and articulating gay, lesbian, and queer desires. A gay identity, wanted or not, can be produced across the eBay site. Buyers often look at sellers' auctions in order to determine their reliability, their knowledge of objects, and if there is anything else of interest to purchase in order to lower shipping costs. Individuals also sometimes look at the listings of what another buyer has purchased in the last sixty days to try to determine the buyer's motivation and highest bidding price for a particular item they also want. These kinds of viewing strategies occur because sellers often encourage buyers to look at their other auctions, and the site design provides varied ways to investigate buyers and sellers. Thus, buying and selling "histories," including engagements with gay interest listings, render an identity for eBay viewers.

Of course, it is not always men who sell gay interest images of men, but gay interest vintage photography sellers rarely present information in their listings about their gender.[44] Some photo sellers further complicate their gender by using vintage photographic images of individuals to stand in for their business and user identities. These images rarely correlate to the seller's gender as it is articulated by first name and email comments. The connection between gay interest listings and sellers' shifting gender representations suggests queer subject positions and desires. These flexible gender representations offer a more overt version of the crossed desires that are rendered when sellers envision heterosexual men's visual enjoyment of women's erotic encounters with women through the imagined body of a lesbian viewing subject.

COLLECTING AND PERFORMING GAY HISTORIES AND DESIRES

While some sellers deny the political significance of gay interest, others foreground gay desires and viewing pleasures with comments such as "this is how i like them. very round bodies," "dreamy wrestler. ya gotta like the body profile," and "BE STILL MY HEART. THIS MAN IS ABSOLUTELY GORGEOUS."[45] Still other sellers weave current politics into the sale of images. endymian offers a nineteenth-century image of a man in drag and wants "to say to george bush" that "if your amendment goes through you and dick cheney will never be a legal couple."[46] He calls his eBay store, where other items are available for purchase, "the stonewall endymian gay photo shop" in order "to honor the men whose defiance of new york city police brutality against gay men in 1969 triggered the modern gay liberation movement"; and he views the "sale of gay merchandise on ebay as a celebration of gay identity and one tied inexorably to the gay liberation movement."[47] In such cases, selling practices allow individuals to support their current political positions with gay, lesbian, transgendered, and queer pasts.

Despite such positive political work, "gay interest" sales can articulate essentialist notions of what gay looks like. eBay sellers indicate that a studio photograph of a Tarzan character "is gayer than gay" and that a man in another photograph "is gay indeed! He wears a lighter suit but sports polka dot socks!"[48] Some amount of essentialism may be unavoidable because, as John Elsner and Roger Cardinal suggest, "Collecting is classification lived."[49] Objects become understandable because of the ways they are described and related to other things. Collecting, in part the desire to acquire and group items, requires articulating a set of essential attributes. Broadly, sellers render essentialist ideas about sexuality and desire when queering images and suggesting that being a sailor or dressing in a dapper manner indicates someone is gay.

The limiting effect that queering can have on an array of possible gay identities, which suggests a rupture between gay and queering, can be at least partially resolved by employing such tactics as irony and parody when finding gay elements in images. eBay ID gargantua uses varied images and texts to self-represent as the "500 pound go-rilla." He articulates his difference by referring to buyers' opposable thumbs, creates fanciful tales, and reuses familiar phrases to connect his images to aspects of contemporary gay culture.[50] In depicting a 1920s image of shirtless young male rabbit hunters, he notes, "Kill the wabbit! Kill the wabbit! And you might as well have a few poppers & take your shirts off while you do."[51] The phrase "Make LOVE not WAR" accompanies a group of male sailors touching each other.[52] gargantua playfully combines narratives about clubs and other familiar conventions in order to encourage his viewers to continually read culture differently. His use of word play, cartoon "self-portraits" depicting himself as a purple gorilla, and other distinctive visual aspects of his site indicate that sellers also construct themselves. However, few eBay sellers use these kinds of elaborate performative strategies to represent themselves, to queer images, and to render objects.

THE POLITICS OF EBAY PHOTOGRAPHY

Gay interest sellers such as gargantua and endymian tell imaginative stories about photographs. For instance, endymian describes a representation of men, arranged in pairs and behind one another, as a complicated set of erotic relationships (Figure 16.2):

> james at top left can never keep his hands off tom at top right; bob at middle left carries a big stick which larry at middle right covets—well its a very good lookin stick don't you agree—now teddy in front row left always reads the personals so you see why he has a paper rolled beneath his arm and pete who sits front right next to him hopes he will finally read his personal.[53]

Figure 16.2 "gay int tintype 6 affectionate men overthetop."

According to endymian, this practice is a "str8 forward reading of photographic material" by "your egay photo speacialist [*sic*]." His description suggests that photography is incredibly difficult to read and understand while at the same time presumed to be a direct record of a particular time and objects. endymian and other eBay sellers employ photographs and photo-like images to render a past for gay, lesbian, queer, transgendered, and bisexual individuals even as critical debates continue about the ways that photography supports dominant conceptions of individuals and society and functions as truth. For instance, Shawn Michelle Smith indicates that photographic conventions produce very rigid conceptions of family.[54] This resonates with eBay's "model" family depicted on its The Power of All of Us website. Photography, photographers, and the individuals photographically portrayed tend to render highly constructed images of the family and its roles while eliding the ways such representations are produced. The "gay interest" search term extends and transforms such culturally and photographically produced classifications and views.

eBay and its narratives about gay interest have an effect that exceeds the site. This is because collecting is a key part, as Elsner and Cardinal argue, of how people "accommodate," "appropriate," and "extend the taxonomies and systems of knowledge that they have inherited."[55] Collecting gay interest photography and seeing gay interest listings on eBay also indicate the sorts of reconfigurations of identity and desire occurring in other social settings. Gay interest collections help complicate and queer dominant conceptions of society and highlight the value of gay, lesbian, and queer histories because the "categories into which" people and things "are assigned confirm the precious knowledge of culture handed down through the generations."[56] At the same time, the multiform desires that circulate in gay and lesbian interest collecting and the boundlessness of collectors' desires, as Michael Camille argues, "strain the limits of the heterosexual matrix" and "problematize the logic of oppositions structuring it."[57] Sellers of gay interest narratives and desires try to render a different form of culture and knowledge than what eBay management produces.

I have argued that eBay gay interest listings reconceptualize photography and make gay desires visible. Nevertheless, there may also be ways that gay interest listings support normative conceptions of identity and desire. As Eve Kosofsky Sedgwick argues, the category of the homosexual is instrumental in articulating heterosexuality and consolidating normative power. The "positing" of a gay interest "other" is, according to Craig Owens, "a necessary moment in the consolidation" of the straight couple and accompanying "cultural body."[58] Gay interest vintage photography listings often center the unspoken but visualized "straight interest" of eBay buyers. It is my hope, therefore, that this chapter contributes to a wider understanding of the ways that queering and queer readings can prevent binary oppositions and the insistent centering of heterosexuality.

It is also important to consider further reconfigurations of eBay and the politics of gay interest listings. eBay's "My eBay" link, which stores information about an individual's searches and transactions, claims that buyers and sellers can maintain a version of the self and a form of the personal through the interface. This customization promises to support the individual's identity and desires even as eBay participates in heteronormativity. Sellers' gay interest listings can begin to constitute "My Queer eBay" and encourage multiform readings and desires. These actions may seem aligned with eBay's ever-proliferating "What if nothing was ever forgotten? What if nothing were ever lost?" discourse so My Queer eBay should also be organized through political and critical strategies. My (and Our) Queer eBay strategies might include refusing to be the consolidated "other" used to articulate heterosexuality, rewriting our own photographic and narrative "pasts," considering what happens to heterosexuality when men occupy the position of a conceptualized lesbian viewer, indicating that straight is gay (one of the things that happens with gay interest listings), and reading images in queer ways for everybody's messy desires.

NOTES

1. eBay, "eBay–gay interest, DVD, Men's Clothing, and VHS items at low prices," http://search.ebay.com/gay_interest_ (accessed November 24, 2004). Buyers can engage with gay interest listings by putting the term into eBay's search engine; categories and items listed change on an ongoing basis.
2. "Queer" is employed in a variety of ways. Recuperated from its status as an insulting term by the gay community, it has come to indicate someone who is lesbian, gay, bisexual, transgendered, or intersexed; conceptualizes sexuality and eroticism outside the straight/gay binary; and offers a political challenge to normative politics and sexuality. At points these positions overlap and diverge. For instance, queer can be part of an identity politics and refer to the specificity of a particular gay man's desire or challenge identity politics by suggesting a more mutable understanding of self and desire. The term was popularized by Queer Nation and their actions in public spaces. Queer theory is often linked to the work of Eve Kosofsky Sedgwick, who identifies as sexually queer and is married to a man. See Eve Kosofsky Sedgwick, *Epistemology of the Closet* (Berkeley: University of California Press, 1990). For a brief history of queer, see Wikipedia, "Queer," http://en.wikipedia.org/wiki/Queer.

3. Adam Cohen, *The Perfect Store* (Boston: Little, Brown, 2002), 11, 83. The Pez myth was created by Mary Lou Song as part of a marketing campaign.
4. NetLingo, "eBay," www.netlingo.com/lookup.cfm?term=eBay. This statistic is also mentioned in "Antifraud Measures to Protect eBay Users," *Detroit News*, October 15, 2003, www.detnews.com/2003/business/0310/15/b04-298127.htm; and Miguel Helft, "What Makes eBay Unstoppable," *Industry Standard*, August 6, 2001, www.findarticles.com/p/articles/mi_m0HWW/is_30_4/ai_77826049 (accessed February 21, 2005).
5. eBay, "eBay—Costume, Antique, Vintage Jewelry," http://jewelry.listings.ebay.com:80/Vintage_Antique_Costume_ (accessed October 24, 2004).
6. eBay, "eBay—Collectibles, Advertising, Animals," http://collectibles.ebay.com (accessed November 10, 2004).
7. This is similar to the ways that toy manufacturers and stores use pink and blue to articulate gender-specific objects and spaces and to evoke societal fears that using toys designed for the "opposite" sex will result in a loss of status, identity confusion, and homosexuality. For discussions of how associating toys with gendered consumers and creating pink and blue zones in toy stores limit sales, see Henry Jenkins, ed., *The Children's Culture Reader* (New York: New York University Press, 1998); Pat Kirkham and Judy Attfield, "Introduction," in *The Gendered Object*, ed. Pat Kirkham (Manchester, U.K.: Manchester University Press, 1996); Beverly Lyon Clark and Margaret R. Higonnet, ed., *Girls, Boys, Books, Toys: Gender in Children's Literature and Culture* (Baltimore: Johns Hopkins University Press, 1999); and Ellen Seiter, *Sold Separately: Children and Parents in Consumer Culture* (New Brunswick, NJ: Rutgers University Press, 1993).
8. eBay, "Move In," http://thepowerofallofus.com/flash.html (accessed June 29, 2005).
9. Cohen, 35.
10. Ibid., 153.
11. Michael Moon and Eve Kosofsky Sedgwick argue that academic and popular explorations of drag tend to displace gay and lesbian positions and practices. Michael Moon and Eve Kosofsky Sedgwick, "Divinity: A Dossier, a Performance Piece, a Little-Understood Emotion," in *Bodies out of Bounds: Fatness and Transgression*, ed. Jana Evans Braziel and Kathleen LeBesco (Berkeley: University of California Press, 2001), 292–328.
12. eBay, "General Announcement Board," www2.ebay.com/aw/marketing.shtml (accessed October 25, 2004). This is eBay's ongoing explanation of category changes.
13. eBay seller Charlotte notes, "They continue to 'improve' the categories. Sadly these 'improvements' aren't helping the sellers. And from what I've heard the buyers aren't impressed either." Charlotte, "AuctionBytes Soundoff: Letters from Readers," *AuctionBytes*, www.auctionbytes.com/cab/abu/y204/m09/abu0127/s08 (accessed September 26, 2004).

14. eBay, "Policy—Items for Mature Audiences," http://pages.ebay.com/help/policies/mature-audiences.html (accessed October 30, 2004); and eBay, "eBay Help: Community Standards: Policies and Conduct: eBay Mature Audiences Information," http://pages.ebay.com/help/community/adult.html (accessed October 30, 2004).
15. Keith Obadike, "Keith Obadike's Blackness," http://obadike.tripod.com/ebay.html. For an interview with Obadike about his August 2001 eBay listing, see Coco Fusco, "All Too Real: The Tale of an On-Line Black Sale," www.blacknetart.com/coco.html (accessed November 27, 2004).
16. pisto4, "Karoll of Havana Cuba 1940s Gay Male Nude," http://cgi.ebay.com/ws/eBayISAPI.dll?ViewItem&category=1507&item=3289320493&rd=1 (accessed April 25, 2004). Many of the eBay gay interest listings referenced in these notes are no longer available. However, this does not mean that this information is not useful. References provide information about how items were titled and when they were listed, allow researchers to trace tendencies over time, and provide user IDs of eBay sellers so that readers can view current listings or contact the individuals. Additional references to listings are in the following format: eBay user ID, item title, date auction listed, and item number. Readers who require additional information on URLs may contact the author.
17. endymian, "unique vtg photo male modeling gay int c.1960," May 2, 2004, Item #3272885976.
18. cornstock28, "crusie soldier men group fix engine close up gay photo: looks like one cruises one with tongue out 8x10" press," October 10, 2004, Item #6123556349.
19. Alexandra Chasin, *Selling Out: The Gay and Lesbian Movement Goes to Market* (New York: Palgrave Macmillan, 2001), 36.
20. eBay, "Community Hub Overview," http://pages.ebay.com/community/index.html?ssPageName=h:h:over:US (accessed November 27, 2004).
21. kingoflithia, "Sexy Guy Swimsuit From Behind Gay Int.!" March 18, 2004, Item #3282137332; and pixidiom, "1940 UNUSUAL GAY INTEREST-MAN FROM BEHIND," September 30, 2004, Item #6119833757.
22. pelicancan, "Vintage Photo 2 Affectionate HANDSOME SCOUTS 1914 Gay I," February 24, 2005, Item #6157723162.
23. pelicancan, "Vintage Photo Gay Brothers Double Date In Wagons 1916," March 31, 2004, Item #3284633285.
24. pelicancan, "Vintage Photo Gay Secret Clubhouse Affectionate Frats," March 31, 2004, Item #3284633345.
25. pelicancan, "Vintage Photo NUDE SOLDIERS IN SHOWER 1944 Gay Int," November 24, 2004, Item #6134046732; and pelicancan, "Vintage Photo 2 Men Sitting Under Tree 1890 Gay Interes," November 24, 2004, Item #6134046298.

26. pelicancan, "Vintage Photo 2 Men Sitting Under Tree 1890 Gay Interes," November 24, 2004, Item #6134046298; and pelicancan, "Vintage Photo Near Nude Sailors Flex Butts On Beach Gay," November 24, 2004, Item #6134046634.
27. pedudek, "eBay Member Profile for Pelicancan," November 13, 2004; samson829, "eBay Member Profile for Pelicancan," November 10, 2004; and gll1967, "eBay Member Profile for Pelicancan," July 22, 2004, all at http://feedback.ebay.com/ws/eBayISAPI.dll?ViewFeedback&userid=pelicancan.
28. fouraker, "Five Nude Girlfriends in the Backyard," May 31, 2004, Item #3293441631.
29. vuky14, "Sexy Lady-Sheer-GRANDPA'S GIRL-Gay lesbian Interest LA," November 16, 2004, Item #6132046573.
30. Slash fiction is a form of fan production in which individuals rewrite their favorite media texts to include erotic relationships between same-sex characters. The term derives from the "/" used to articulate these erotic pairings and includes K/S (Kirk and Spock from *Star Trek*), Spike/Xander (from *Buffy the Vampire Slayer*), and Pacey/Jack (from *Dawson's Creek*). For discussions of slash fiction, see Henry Jenkins, *Textual Poachers: Television Fans & Participatory Culture* (New York: Routledge, 1992); Constance Penley, "Brownian Motion: Women, Tactics, and Technology," in *Technoculture*, ed. Constance Penley and Andrew Ross (Minneapolis: University of Minnesota Press, 1991), 295–315; and Veruska Sabucco, "Guided Fan Fiction: Western 'Readings' of Japanese Homosexual Themed Texts," in *Mobile Cultures: New Media in Queer Asia*, ed. Chris Berry, Fran Martin, and Audrey Yue (Durham, NC: Duke University Press, 2003), 70–86. For a discussion of the yaoi comics phenomenon, see Fiona Ng, "Drawn to It," *Nerve*, www.nerve.com/dispatches/ng/drawntoit/ (accessed November 24, 2004).
31. Roland Barthes, *Camera Lucida: Reflections on Photography*, trans. Richard Howard (New York: Hill and Wang, 1981), 5; and Susan Sontag, *On Photography* (New York: Penguin Books, 1977), 154.
32. Judith Butler and Biddy Martin, "Cross-Identifications," *Diacritics* 24, nos. 2–3 (1994): 3. They also argue that queering white heteronormative culture too often leaves race unexamined.
33. John Ibson, *Picturing Men: A Century of Male Relationships in Everyday American Photography* (Washington, D.C.: Smithsonian Institution Press, 2002), 154.
34. Ibid., xi.
35. Early photographs, such as cased daguerrotypes and ambrotypes, are an exception because they are more highly valued than many other photographic materials and generally garner higher prices.
36. gargantua, "1910s PHOTO! SeXY COWBOY COSTuME MAN CIGARETTE GUN! gay," May 30, 2004, Item #3294961113.

37. speakswithmusic, "eBay View About Me for speakswithmusic," http://members.ebay.com/ws2/eBayISAPI.dll?ViewUserPage&userid=speakswithmusic (accessed May 15, 2004).
38. Bruce Hershenson, "E-Mail Club Message Number 191," eMoviePoster, www.emovieposter.com/section_newsandclub/club_messages.cfm?id=193 (accessed October 3, 2004). The responses that follow are drawn from message numbers 191 and 202.
39. hansonenterprises, "VINTAGE OLD PHOTO POSTCARD TWO GAY MILITARY MEN," October 13, 2004, Item #6124516365.
40. babs-loves-b-bay, "CABINET CARD Photo~2 MEN in Tuxes, CLOSE~Gay Interest," September 29, 2004, Item #6122016113.
41. rufusworx, "Tintype Five Men Smoking Cigar Affectionate," September 29, 2004, Item #6121987906.
42. lexo206, "1940's Gay Sailors @ California Night Club," September 29, 2004, Item #6121978989.
43. Danae Clark, "Commodity Lesbianism," in *The Lesbian and Gay Studies Reader*, ed. Henry Abelove, Michele Aina Barale, and David M. Halperin (New York: Routledge, 1993), 187.
44. Some other internet settings, including graphical and text-based chat, and personal websites and profiles, provide specific information about gender and other attributes of the individual.
45. comstock28, "1927 shirtless beefy cabinet team photo men group gay," April 25, 2004, Item #3289343320; comstock28, "perfect faced wrestler man photo team gay shirtless," April 25, 2004, Item #3289353458; and unique_finds93, "OLD PHOTO CUTE MAN; SEXY LIPS & EYES GAY INTEREST#4241," September 25, 2004, Item #6121203808.
46. endymian, "GAY INT CABINET CARD GREAT DRAG X DRESS GUY," April 27, 2004, Item #3289666107.
47. endymian, "eBay Store—stonewall endymian gay photo shop," http://stores.ebay.com/stonewallendymiangayphotoshop/pages/store-policies (accessed May 2, 2004).
48. rancherhamp, "2 8x10 studio PHOTOS of Tarzan Denny Miller GAY INT!!!!" May 12, 2004, Item #3292317572; and bizzilizzit, "Cabinet Card of two gay and dandy men weird props," October 16, 2004, Item #6125129476.
49. John Elsner and Roger Cardinal, "Introduction," in *The Cultures of Collecting*, ed. John Elsner and Roger Cardinal (Cambridge, MA: Harvard University Press, 1994), 2.
50. gargantua, "GargantuaPhotos.com—Vintage Photographs and Snapshots," www.gargantuaphotos.com/whatisthisplace.html (accessed December 1, 2004).
51. gargantua, "20s PHOTO! SHiRTS OFF & SEXY HUNTiNG MEN & RABBiT! Gay," November 21, 2004, Item #6133409494.

52. gargantua, "40s PHOTO! SEXY SAiLOR MEN FiGHT then MAKE LOVE! Gay," November 21, 2004, Item #6133406507.
53. endymian, "gay int tintype 6 affectionate men overthetop," May 2, 2004, Item #3272664682.
54. Shawn Michelle Smith, *American Archives: Gender, Race, and Class in Visual Culture* (Princeton, NJ: Princeton University Press, 1999), 9.
55. Elsner and Cardinal, 2.
56. Ibid.
57. Michael Camille, introduction to "Other Objects of Desire, Collections and Collecting Queerly," *Art History* 24, no. 2 (April 2001): 164.
58. Craig Owens, "The Discourse of Others: Feminists and Postmodernism," in *The Anti-Aesthetic: Essays on Postmodernism*, ed. Hal Foster (Port Townsend, WA: Bay Press, 1983), 58.

"Cleaned to eBay Standards"
Sex Panic, eBay, and the Moral Economy of Underwear

MICHAEL PETIT

> In answer to the question "is there anything which you'd never look at in a charity shop?" we were consistently and without hesitation told "underwear" by everyone we interviewed.
>
> **Nicky Gregson and Louise Crewe,**
> *Second-Hand Cultures*[1]

Many of the underwear listings once permitted on eBay seem innocuous enough: a pair of panties worn by an attractive college coed making extra money for books, a muscled jock's heavily used workout shorts with the promise "to be cleaned to eBay standards," a pair of white Hanes briefs, size 32—"email me with any questions, suggestions or special requests." Designed to appeal to used underwear fetishists, such listings were banned permanently from the eBay site on November 21, 2000. eBay's action, justified as a response to users' complaints, provides an interesting case study of how online environments contribute to and update sex panic, a dynamic identified by Gayle Rubin in her classic essay "Thinking Sex: Notes for a Radical Theory of the Politics of Sexuality." Rubin discusses sexuality as an ideological system of values: marital reproductive heterosexual sex stands at the pinnacle of the hierarchy, and "as sexual behaviors or occupations fall lower on the scale, the individuals who practice them are subjected to a presumption of mental illness, disreputability, criminality, restricted social and physical mobility, loss of institutional support, and economic sanctions."[2] At particular moments, characterized by conditions of high social, political, cultural, or economic anxieties, sex and what constitutes its "legitimate" parameters are hotly contested and overtly politicized, with those on the sexual margins typically policed and controlled by institutional forces, often for "safety's sake." Rubin points to "the homosexual menace" of the

1950s coincidental with the height of the Cold War as one of the best documented cases of sex panic crackdown, what Christopher Castiglia defines as "the systematic assault on sexualities that diverge from the interests of the privatized and heteronormative reproductive family."[3] Yet "deviants" of all kinds may be positioned as scapegoats; the sexual system, as Rubin notes, "is not a monolithic, omnipotent structure. There are continuous battles" (25). This chapter examines one of these battles.

I historicize eBay's banning the sale of used underwear, along with the policy changes it instituted in its "Adult Only" category, in order to expose the ideological myth of eBay as a perfect market, a myth that implicitly posits the internet and information technology more generally as providing a solution to previously intractable social and economic problems. eBay's early management accepted the ideology of "friction free capitalism"; individuals conducting online transactions could avoid the biases that inhere in embodied social and political relations and that invariably influence market functionality. The company's subscription to these utopian ideals, however, is belied by its scapegoating of used underwear sellers and buyers. Although eBay states it "will not include sexual preferences or viewpoints as a factor in determining what goods or services are prohibited under the Mature Audiences Policy"[4] (clearly an attempt to suggest the company is not homophobic and thus reflective of how gay men and lesbians have made progress toward acceptability within certain neoliberal settings), the used underwear ban suggests that the same level of acceptability or even toleration does not extend to other sexual minorities who engage in specific sexual activities, heterosexual or homosexual, that challenge normative sexuality.

SEX PANIC ONLINE AND OFF

Eric Rofes notes that sex panic takes different forms depending on locale. It "looks different in urban, small city, and rural areas and will have different characteristics, contexts, and trajectories."[5] So, too, does it "look different" in online situations. The cloak of anonymity offered by an eBay user ID means that while components of an individual's identity may be excluded from the broader "community" (as used underwear sellers, buyers, and fetishists were), the effect of such policing is less destructive and less complete than the harassment and persecution of sexual minorities in the offline world—say, the arrest of men soliciting consensual sex in a known cruising area and their subsequent trial, conviction, and public humiliation facilitated by mass media reports. Both situations participate in the powerful policing cultural dynamics characteristic of sex panics—the scapegoating, shaming, and silencing of sexual minorities—yet the possibility of increased anonymity explains in part why the internet, as Larry Gross has observed, "has particular importance to sexual minority communities."[6] A sense of safety, however illusory or temporary, flows from the ability to be "out" on the internet yet still remain partially closeted as a representation or an eBay ID with nothing more concrete disclosed than an email address. Seclusion and the ability to speak with others in the relative safety of virtual spaces also allow a sense of solidarity to form, a recognition that one is not alone. This factor is important to community formation for all minorities, but particularly so for individuals highly marginalized and isolated because of their askance sexuality and interests.

That eBay became a center of exchange for sexual minorities is no surprise. Tom Rielly, who launched PlanetOut in the mid-1990s, commented, "Gays and lesbians don't have a high level of ownership of mainstream media properties. The internet is the first medium where we can have equal footing with the big players."[7] Also drawing on the mid-1990s libertarian discourse about the utopian power of the internet, eBay founder Pierre Omidyar espoused eBay as a "level playing field" where a networked "community" of individuals could connect directly to other individuals as part of contributing to a "perfect market." *All* sellers and buyers would have the same opportunity to buy and sell, with access to the same information about products and prices. However, eBay's policing and eventual elimination as personae non grata of used underwear sellers (and therefore its buyers too) debunks eBay's claims and suggests the impossibility of a "level playing field" uninflected by cultural dynamics such as sex panic.

The dynamics underpinning eBay's panic are complex and overlapping, and include factors related to long-standing hierarchical understandings of acceptable outlets for sexual expression that Rubin identifies; eBay's choice of culturally conservative Draper, Utah, as the location for its customer support operations facility; the auction site's increasing notoriety as a major source for pornography; the company's pending business alliance with Disney; the anxiety produced by the dot.com crash earlier that year; and the open question of how pornography might affect eBay's bottom line. As Rubin notes, "Disputes over sexual behavior often become the vehicles for displacing social anxieties" (4), and eBay's restructuring of its Adult Only category in November 2000 declared the "vice" of buying and selling used underwear a menace to public health, a threat to children, and detrimental to the safety of the eBay community. It was discursively positioned as a criminal act, punishable by exile from the moral economy of eBay.

In June 1999 eBay moved several employees to Draper, Utah, to train new customer support representatives, including Jim Griffith, an openly gay man known on eBay's early discussion boards as "Uncle Griff" (highlighting the communal, family-like atmosphere of the company's early days). Yet the culturally conservative climate of the largely Mormon area just south of Salt Lake City undoubtedly inflected the attitudes of eBay's customer support representatives. In his history of eBay, *The Perfect Store*, Adam Cohen tells the story of Jeffry Totland, "a clean-cut twenty-nine-year-old raised in the Mormon Church," as he monitors the "erotica queue" for violations of eBay's adult material policy, including listings for used underwear.[8] Prior to the November 2000 prohibition, eBay had allowed used underwear listings under specific conditions: items had to be "thoroughly cleaned according to the manufacturer's instructions," and sellers could offer no "extraneous" information such as describing their body or the circumstances under which the underwear had been worn. Cohen relates the kinds of subjective decisions Totland had to make under this policy: did "cleaned to eBay standards" in quotation marks on a listing really mean the item would be washed? Was there an implicit offer to "customize" an item by wearing it for an extended period before shipping? The used underwear listings raised issues that customer service representatives, according to Cohen, "dreaded," and this sense of dread arguably had an effect on the Draper facility's corporate culture. What Cohen calls the "endless line drawing" engaged in by eBay customer support staff also increased the number of complaints about used underwear listings. They came not from offended viewers who had inadvertently stumbled across the auctions, but rather other sellers who felt that since their own auction had been suspended for violating eBay's policy, they would complain about listings that hadn't been suspended. Therefore, many of the complaints that purportedly informed eBay's justification for the ban were from competitive yet disenfranchised community members rather than the eBay "community" at large.

By the late 1990s, the site already was well known as an important player in the online pornography industry; Cohen notes that eBay was "getting a reputation as one of the best free porn sites" on the Web because of the open availability of erotic images that illustrated auctions.[9] The availability of used underwear was also reported, and "Brief Stunt," an article by Deborah Picker published in the April 2000 issue of *Metro*, Silicon Valley's weekly newspaper, exemplifies how media reports rhetorically positioned used underwear as a shorthand for the vast array of sexually explicit items available on eBay and their profitability.[10] The article, structured around "the wild and whacked-out world of selling used undies online," reports that as much as five percent of eBay's profit is based on the listing of adult items: "[T]hat means up to $140 million [USD] in extra cash from Hello Kitty vibrators, remote-control butt plugs and the like." Picker provides a primer on how others might cash in, detailing how she created eBay user ID pntygrl to list her own pair of underwear. Two months before Picker's article appeared, eBay had entered into negotiations with Disney for a joint family-friendly cobranded auction site, ebay.go.com, which was officially launched on October 16, 2000; almost simultaneously, eBay announced changes to its Adult Only category. It would become the less X-rated-sounding "Mature Audiences" and have its own separate search engine, with age continuing to be verified by restricting access to those willing to provide a credit card number. It also restricted sexually graphic images, the "free porn" noted by Cohen. eBay's logic was to isolate the category from its main site like a quasi-red light district (with specific rules about permissible behavior) just as "a number of cities segregate stores selling sexually-oriented materials to certain parts of the community."[11]

eBay believed it was taking a balanced approach and steering a middle course, yet the changes were met with mixed reviews by sellers of sexually explicit material. To access the Mature Audiences category, users must navigate a series of pages, first finding an alphabetized link buried in "Other Categories" on the bottom of the main categories page, and then signing in. To continue, users must click through eBay's eleven-point "terms of use" agreement and a verification page before arriving at the auction listings and the category's search engine. eBay's justification for effectively hiding this part of its auction site and making it cumbersome to enter is the standard "This material is not appropriate for viewing by minors." This justification conforms to what Rubin identifies as "the extensive social and legal structures designed to insulate minors from sexual knowledge and experience" (4). eBay produces and polices sexual conformity by perpetuating long-standing yet unexamined beliefs that failure to shield minors through age seventeen from sexual knowledge and experience somehow intrinsically harms their growth and development. When sexual knowledge exceeds this ideological boundary, it must be sanitized, and sex panics often lead to systematic "clean-ups," whether they take the form of a crackdown on a specific part of town, such as a red light district, or they focus on eliminating visible "deviants" within the larger community. CNet News' headline reporting eBay's actions, "eBay Set to Clean Up Pornographic Auctions,"[12] trades in this use of language and illustrates how eBay operates within larger ideological social structures that categorize expressions of human sexuality according to very specific spatial and social hierarchies.

As part of its policy change, eBay banned the sale of all used underwear, even in the Mature Audiences category ("including, but not limited to, boxer shorts, panties, briefs and athletic supporters").[13] The company promised effective enforcement while threatening to increase restrictions "if the new policies are not quickly and consistently adopted,"[14] but this begs the question of why eBay, the proponent of a friction-free marketplace, believed that credit card-wielding individuals shopping in the Mature Audiences category needed such protection, particularly when minors were barred. As Rubin notes, claims to police adult sexuality for the protection of minors are typically deployed to stratify sexuality so that marital reproductive heterosexuality becomes the de facto definition of sexuality. Some internet analysts at the time directly connected eBay's changes to Disney's influence, one noting that "it's the first step toward house cleaning," and another commenting he believed eBay was embarrassed by its adult site: "Especially now that they have a partnership with Disney, they don't make [adult merchandise] easy to find."[15] Meg Whitman, eBay's CEO since 1997, had once been a senior vice president of marketing at Disney. Yet no matter what prompted eBay's move, it had the effect of sharply curtailing used underwear listings. On occasion they had reached as many as 600 plus per day; while some articles of clothing, particularly the used panties of attractive women who provided erotic descriptions of themselves and their underwear, had sold for hundreds of dollars, they were no longer to be found on eBay's "level playing field" at any price.

eBay's actions reflect a generalized anxiety within the hierarchical sexual value system about mixing sex and commerce: while using sex to sell is arguably the norm in mass media contexts, sex for sale is not. A satiric news article by robp, the editor-in-chief of furiosity.com, "a place where we ['a select group of self-professed intellectual elites from Canada'] can rage impotently against the stupidity that surrounds us," underscores how marketplace considerations dynamically inflect online sex panics.[16] robp's article, "Looming Recession Continues to Be Held Off by Online Used Underwear Industry," posits that only people selling "stanky old underwear" are keeping the economy afloat:

> This proves my long-standing theory that something is fundamentally wrong with people. What kind of depravity does it take to purchase someone else's used underwear, sight-unseen, over the internet? Or *at all*, for that matter? And as disturbing as that thought is, consider for a moment that these social deviants are actually *trying to outbid one another* in an attempt to win the coveted undergarments. It's clearly the end of civilization, as we know it.

Expressing "innate revulsion" at the idea of wearing some stranger's underwear, while also considering the possibility of selling an unused vintage pair himself, robp concludes it would be better to "bring on the freaking recession, baby," than continue the unsavoriness of the used underwear market. Rather than applaud eBay's ban, however, he suggests it does not go far enough. His language is steeped in the rhetoric of sex panic. It calls on the sacred coupled with threats of violence:

> I personally would have been a lot more reassured if they'd have released a statement like "in the name of all that is **decent** and **holy**, eBay will no longer sanction the sale of used underwear through its online service and violators will be publicly beaten about the head until they regain their senses and/or come into compliance with the new policy. That is all."

A hybrid mix of scorn at buyers of used underwear and awe at the power of the market is a consistent theme in responses to eBay's used underwear market. One respondent to slate.com's book club discussion of Cohen's *The Perfect Store*, for example, writes, "I knew about used underwear, and for fetishists, it makes perfect—if twisted—sense. What was more surprising was that people complained about finding sex toys when looking for used underwear for legitimate daily use! Let's see—underwear drawer empty. Better get online and buy some used ones on eBay. Now that's sick! What does this tell me? Buy eBay stock, now."[17]

The website "Idiotic eBay Underwear ADS!" also exemplifies the peculiarly American response to the sale of sex and sexuality-related materials: puritan shock, prurient titillation, and esteem for eye-popping profits. The site, updated periodically since it began to track eBay's used underwear market in October 1999, purports to expose this "open secret":

> **Do you know where you can buy ripe undies sealed in plastic bags??**
>
> **Not even Times Square porn stores sell this stuff!**
>
> **In fact, a woman CAN'T return underwear once it's bought for health reasons!**
>
> **But for years, eBay had used underwear ads running, legally, ALL OVER THE WEBSITE**[18]

The writer labels the practice "bizarre" and "a menace," and refers to buyers of used underwear as "sick-o." Just as exposure of a "perversion" ironically gives voice to it, the owner of this Web page, in a manner that parallels

Picker's "Brief Stunt" primer on how to cash in, offers advice on how viewers can find the offending auctions and presumably achieve the same level of incoherent moral outrage and titilation: "Just type in 'used panties' or some such word and see if you get something like this… ." The writer provides a screen shot of an auction that offers a cache of used panties discovered by "Meg" at a girls' weekend basketball camp and another eBay listing entitled "Traci's 'Worn' used silk red panties." Certain that eBay will fail to monitor its site adequately to "prevent abuse from sellers" (just how auctions offering used underwear might abuse others is never discussed), the writer provides screen shots of other auctions that feature attractive women and also one from "Dennis" "wearing a pair of white cotton panties, size 6," with the notation "Even men have tried it!" The writer encourages readers to search eBay for themselves, despite the ban, noting that "it could be profitable." Ultimately moral outrage, performed American style, yields to a focus on profit and the writer's most trenchant point: "What can you do? Nothing, except START STRIPPING!! It can MAKE YOU SOME EXTRA BUCKS!!" Purported moral outrage inflected with ironic humor and the attempt to be funny is the lofty ground allowing the writer to remain aloof and superior to the supposed sick-os he or she critiques, even as this tone of superiority is the platform allowing him or her to promote the idea that "those of us" who find this "sick" can nevertheless make money selling to moral defectives. There is a recognition here, lodged within a highly mediated visual culture awash with advertising reliant on the association of sex with any and all manner of commodities, that since the fetish exists, why not cash in? While this attitude could be argued to accord with eBay's "level playing field" discourse, ultimately eBay, as the site's de facto government, ignored its own libertarian origins and strictly policed a very specific segment of its community—sexual outsiders easily identifiable, made disreputable by their sexual practices, and therefore subjected to lasting social and economic sanctions.

It's important to note that eBay's actions specifically targeted sellers and buyers of used underwear while continuing to allow other fetishists access to the site as a trading space—including the main site and not just the Mature Audiences category. Auctions designed for transvestites and other cross-dressers number in the hundreds, and a search on "adult baby," for example, yields pages of listings for merchandise aimed at those interested in infantilism and other age play-related paraphilia. Likewise, eBay did not prohibit the selling of used footwear and does not remove listings aimed at individuals with a sexual interest in shoes (though used socks are prohibited). A June 2005 search in Mature Audiences on the term "fetish" yielded 1,097 hits. The same search in the main part of the site, however, yielded almost six times as many, 6,126. "Leather fetish" in the main site produced 800 hits for merchandise related to s/m practices. In these thousands of examples, we see at play the libertarian community ideal of Omidyar, yet eBay's decision to not restrict such listings again raises the question "Why go after used underwear?" One answer, as I have argued, is that used underwear received the lion's share of titillating yet scolding mass media publicity and was seen by the company as detrimental to its partnership with Disney and plans for expansion. Thus, those interested in used underwear became a scapegoat for eBay's corporate anxiety over how its vastly broader pornographic listings would affect its future bottom line, particularly in the context of the 2000 stock market crash and unknowns about how the bursting of the dot.com bubble might affect the company.

Of course, eBay is within its rights to draw parameters around what is "fit" for sale on its site. eBay believed that guns and ammunition put the corporation in a potentially litigious situation and ended their trade, despite strong protest from members of that community. Wine and alcohol sales were curtailed; conflicting U.S. state laws meant that eBay might be found to facilitate illegal interstate commerce. Clearly, however, no such rationale exists concerning the sale of used underwear: it is neither a particularly litigious product nor one singled out in interstate commerce law. As Jen Hassler, an eBay seller of used clothing, stated in response to the ban, "I gather what they are really trying to prevent is strange fetish listings… . They're limiting something that doesn't seem to skirt the edge of legality. It's a moral issue as opposed to a legal issue."[19] Yet eBay continues to justify its action as part of "urg[ing] its sellers and buyers to comply with all governmental laws and regulations." Perhaps recognizing the specious nature of this justification, eBay adds, "Furthermore, due to hygiene concerns, eBay does not permit the sale of used underwear … [s]ince the sale of used underwear or unwashed clothing may cause harm to eBay or its members."[20] This justification may seem to have a patina of logic, but only if one assumes that worn clothing is in and of itself "dirty," and that those who seek it out are themselves unhygienic or illegal and may (implicitly) "cause harm." Cultural issues beyond those of the marketplace are at play here, and a brief examination of possession rituals in the buying of secondhand items offers a deeper understanding of reasons underlying sex panic on eBay.

***

In *Second-Hand Cultures*, a study of buying practices in charity shops and other bricks-and-mortar secondhand venues, Nicky Gregson and Louise Crewe discuss how the value of secondhand commodities is in constant motion, actively negotiated, and (re)created by consumers who engage in various rituals to make used items their own (see also chapter 2 of this book). In recovery rituals, for example, "[M]eanings and traces of ownership are retrieved, recaptured, and reimagined"[21] by purchasers. This dynamic is also at play for buyers of used underwear who rely on the material object to imagine an engagement with the former wearer. tpaul5, a seller on eBay before the ban, reports, "It's something I always thought was sort of sexy—like you're at the gym and, I don't know, you see a pair of underwear just laying there, I think that's very sexy … the imagination of thinking that somebody had that on."[22] For tpaul5, reimagining a trace of the body activates desire, which also explains why sellers before the ban often provided elaborate descriptions of themselves and how the underwear on offer had been worn. Some sellers also linked their listings to evocative poses of themselves along with personal details on their "About Me" eBay pages. eBay, by facilitating connection among interested parties, encourages an imagination-inflected experience and therefore attaching a premium to such clothing. The virtual space of eBay, more so even than a traditional secondhand clothing store in a major metropolitan area, enables buyers to capture a sense of the authentic that is then actualized in the material object that arrives in the mail. As Gregson and Crewe write, "[T]he consumer's work here involves recapturing these former traces of ownership in order to, quite literally, produce meaning" (144).

The possibility for reimagining and making meaning is present in the acquisition of all manner of used clothing, as Katalin Lovász indicates in chapter 18. Gregson and Crewe report that one of their correspondents, Rupert, "enjoys thinking about and romanticizing the person who wore the clothes before him" (153). Yet while all secondhand clothing may carry traces of the body, used underwear in particular is susceptible to "too much bodily presence, particularly a presence associated with visual and/or olfactory leakiness" (157). In a bricks-and-mortar charity or thrift shop, such "leakiness" works to render *any* garment valueless, and so purchasers of secondhand clothing examine it carefully before donning it; once an item is purchased, they generally engage in "divestment rituals" (144)—the cleansing, purification, and personalization of the clothing so as to make it their own by expunging traces of previous ownership. Used underwear buyers do not engage in such divestment rituals, as visual and olfactory leakiness may be the very attributes they seek in the material objects they purchase; indeed, many are willing to pay a premium for it. Picker quotes one buyer who told her, "I took a gamble and bought some panties… . They arrived wet, smelly and with a few stray hairs. I was quite happy."[23]

Used underwear buyers may seek out such clothing because it contains the bodily trace of its wearer, but the broader group of people who purchase vintage and other used clothing on eBay, as the epigraph at the beginning of the essay suggests, find buying—let alone wearing or using—used underwear unthinkable. And given the near universality of divestment ritual practices in the purchase of secondhand clothing such as cleaning before wearing, it is highly unlikely that should nonfetishists purchase used underwear, they would fail to clean it. This points out that eBay's claim that used underwear "may cause harm" is a displacement of other fears, anxieties, and concerns. To accept the company's logic unexamined is to participate in sex panic—to scapegoat a sexual minority as a menace to public health and safety on the flimsiest of corporate pretexts. As Rubin notes,

> In Western culture, sex is taken all too seriously. A person is not considered immoral, is not sent to prison, and is not expelled from her or his family, for enjoying spicy cuisine. But an individual may go through all this and more for enjoying shoe leather. Ultimately, of what possible social significance is it if a person likes to masturbate over a shoe? (35)

eBay in effect tried to impose divestment rituals on used underwear sellers and buyers through its "cleaned to eBay standards" policy, and when this failed the company instituted the ban, divested itself of the listings, and continues to do so from its Draper, Utah, facility. The focus on cleaning suggests the company responded to what it saw on the part of some buyers as a compulsion or fixation on bodily leakage and the discomfort that implies. The complaints of some eBay members provided justification enough to censure such fetishists, despite eBay's neoliberal articulations of "community" to a "perfect market" and "level playing field." Sellers who bought into Omidyar's ideology that the internet would provide a "friction-free" marketplace were caught off guard by the ban, undoubtedly surprised when eBay followed through and actually policed the site for used underwear listings. During a two-month period of observation in early 2005, searching weekly on the terms "used underwear" and "used panties," I spotted only occasional listings that were inevitably pulled before the auction could be completed. Rubin notes that sex laws, once in place, are extremely difficult to dislodge, even when their enforcement comes to seem irrational. In May 2005, the company made news headlines when it enforced its used underwear policy by pulling a listing offered by a U.K.-based nightclub for the black, girdle-style underpants Madonna wore in the Uli Edel film *Body of Evidence* (1993).[24] The bid had reached 1,000 GBP.

SEX PANIC AND MEMORY

Castiglia observes that "sex panics cannot take place without a systematic assault on memories that associate sex and subjectivity in ways that challenge normative regimes."[25] Like sex panic itself, the formal structure of eBay as an ever-changing virtual archive contributes to this assault on memories. Although most transactional feedback on completed sales remains part of the site in perpetuity, with item numbers preserved in ghostly gray, listings automatically delete sixty days after an auction closes, and auction-related images vanish even sooner. While freeing up space on its servers is important, this continual deletion indicates how eBay has designed into its technological structure the marketplace ideology of "out with the old, in with the new." Though perhaps unremarkable as such, this process works in tandem with sex panic to erase the histories of outsider sexualities, to render them invisible, unknown, and thus forgotten—and in the process to reify normative modes of sexual expression. On the eBay site itself, the policy statement prohibiting used underwear is all that remains, a fossil record that preserves the result of the eBay sex panic but not the historical and social contexts informing this exercise in ideological power. Memory lives in the details, and Michel Foucault articulates the stakes: "[I]f one controls people's memory, one controls their dynamism. And one also controls their experience, their knowledge of previous struggles."[26]

Few of the many used underwear listings that appeared on eBay have been reproduced digitally elsewhere on the Web, and this highlights the easy disposability of memory in market-driven online situations.[27] If used underwear sales have ended on eBay, they have undoubtedly migrated to other parts of the Web—private Web pages, the adult auction site naughtybids.com—though sellers of erotic materials banned on eBay soon discovered there were few viable options outside eBay.[28] The used underwear fetish community, though fractured and certainly not as visible as it was before the ban, may still use the site to facilitate trading. ebulges.com, for example, has an extensive gallery of images collected from ongoing clothing auctions listed in eBay's main site that show the outline of male genitalia. Adding the term "gay interest" (see chapter 16) to searches in male underwear and "fetish" to searches in women's intimates brings up ambiguously worded descriptions for items, the sellers of which may be open to private requests to "personalize" their wares. lucidlingerie "invites you to bid on this latest auction, these are our newest and most gorgeous panties yet … please email us if you have any questions," and the muscular seller pictured wearing boxer briefs notes they are "COMFY! Hot."[29] The persistence of such listings suggests that while forms of human sexuality may evolve, including heteronormatively sanctioned ones, human sexuality as a drive persists across many permutations and is at least as tenacious as the ideologically driven moral crusades to police and bound it.

Implicit in eBay's sex panic is that the parts of the body that touch underwear are intrinsically inferior, even dirty. This sex- and body-negative attitude resonates with other utopian discourses about how the internet and other information machines such as virtual reality would allow individuals to escape bodily limitations—to leave behind their "meat" or "wetware" and float free as "pure" disembodied information.[30] Sex panics take place across a variety of scales, and the online eBay case discussed here clearly does not have the same heft and consequence of embodied sex panics such as McCarthyism, or the scapegoating and subsequent extermination of thousands of homosexuals in Nazi concentration camps. Nevertheless, as Rubin notes, analyses of sex panics reveal overarching patterns of harassment, and they are important to interrogate for the subtle and not-so-subtle ways they work to delimit human erotic possibilities—for, as this case study reveals, even on eBay, it's not always just about the bottom line.

NOTES

This essay is dedicated to Terry Rollins and Nicholas Newman, who have their own battle stories to tell.

1. Nicky Gregson and Louise Crewe, *Second-Hand Cultures* (Oxford: Berg, 2003), 158.
2. Gayle S. Rubin, "Thinking Sex: Notes for a Radical Theory of the Politics of Sexuality" (1984), in *The Lesbian and Gay Studies Reader*, ed. Henry Abelove, Michele Aina Barale, and David Halperin (New York: Routledge, 1993), 12. Additional page numbers of this reference are cited parenthetically.
3. Christopher Castiglia, "Sex Panics, Sex Publics, Sex Memories," *boundary 2* 27, no. 2 (Summer 2000): 150.
4. This language is from the "Mature Audiences Policy" of PayPal, an eBay company, www.paypal.com (accessed June 27, 2005).
5. Eric Rofes, "The Emerging Sex Panic Targeting Gay Men," speech given at the National Gay and Lesbian Task Force Creating Change Conference, November 16, 1997, San Diego, California, www.managingdesire.org/sexpanic/rofessexpanic.html (accessed April 8, 2005).
6. Larry Gross, "Forward," in *Getting It On Online: Cyberspace, Male Sexuality, and Embodied Identity*, by John Edward Campbell (New York: Harrington Park Press, 2004), x.
7. Quoted in Gross, x–xi.
8. Adam Cohen, *The Perfect Store: Inside eBay* (Boston: Little, Brown, 2002), 292. Details in this paragraph are drawn from Cohen's account, 292–95.

9. Ibid., 276.
10. Deborah Picker, "Brief Stunt," *Metro*, March 30–April 5, 2000, www.metroactive.com/papers/metro/03.30.00/panties-0013.html (accessed April 8, 2005).
11. eBay, "Mature Audiences," http://pages.ebay.com/help/policies/mature-audieces.html (accessed June 27, 2005).
12. Troy Wolverton, "eBay Set to Clean Up Pornographic Auctions," *CNet News*, October 20, 2000, http://news.com.com/2100-1017-247381.html?legacy=cnet (accessed June 27, 2005).
13. "Mature Audiences." eBay's non-U.S. sites also prohibit listings for used underwear. Among its English-language sites, eBay India provides the most comprehensive list and forbids "boxer shorts, panties, briefs, lingerie, girdles, brassieres, swimwear, leotards, and athletic supports."
14. Quoted in Wolverton.
15. Quoted in Picker.
16. www.furiosity.com/feature.php?fid=4 (accessed April 8, 2005).
17. "The Book Club," *Slate*, http://slate.msn.com/id/2069611/entry/2069727/ (accessed April 8, 2005).
18. "Idiotic eBay Underwear ADS!" www.geocities.com/Hollywood/Academy/8135/ebayunderwear.html (accessed October 5, 2004). Caches of previous versions without images from which this account also draws are available through Google.
19. Quoted in Wolverton.
20. eBay, "Used Clothing," http://pages.ebay.com/help/policies/used-clothing.html (accessed June 27, 2005).
21. Gregson and Crewe, 144. Additional page numbers of this reference are cited parenthetically.
22. Quoted in "eBabes 2001," www.bananaguide.com/features/novunderwear2.htm (accessed June 26, 2005).
23. Quoted in Picker.
24. "Madonna's Knickers Removed from eBay," *Fazed*, www.fazed.com/musicnews (accessed June 27, 2005). Ironically, in late 1999 eBay argued that under the 1998 Digital Millennium Copyright Act it might be open to lawsuits if it too aggressively monitored transactions on its site. See Matt Richtel, "eBay Says Law Discourages Auction Monitoring," www.nytimes.com/library/tech/99/12/cyber/articles/10ebay.html (accessed July 11, 2005).
25. Castiglia, 150.
26. Quoted in Castiglia, 168.
27. In this chapter I attempt to recover a history that otherwise would be lost. At times, the internet can facilitate the recovery of memory. Searching sites other than eBay yielded information crucial to my account.
28. Naughtybids announced beginning June 1, 2005, it would no longer accept listings for soiled clothing of any kind, though access on July 11, 2005 provided dozens of supposedly banned items. The site offers no explanation for

this change, but it may be in response to eBay's "Links" policy, which states that sellers can only link to sites outside of eBay that conform to eBay policies, including those outlined in Mature Audiences.

29. lucidlingerie, "Silky satin cute panties fetish white and black 8-10," item #5406878939, ending July 14, 2005; and queeniemmm, "CHAPS blue Briefs-SZ L_gay interest," item #8317022419, ending July 12, 2005.
30. See Marvin Minsky, *The Society of Mind* (New York: Simon & Schuster, 1986); and Hans Moravec, *Mind Children: The Future of Robot and Human Intelligence* (Cambridge, MA: Harvard University Press, 1988).

18

Playing Dress-Up
eBay's Vintage Clothing-Land

KATALIN LOVÁSZ

It is not recommended research practice to seek physical identification with the subject of one's research. I've just never been able to compartmentalize myself: I generally find my research echoed in the bits and pieces of my daily life, the patterns of my thoughts overlapping with patterns I discern in physical and social spaces around me. Shopping on eBay makes real the dissolve between my private and professional selves, and this chapter can be read as a case study of how eBay enriched an academic's understanding of her research practice.

When I receive in the mail a vintage dress from 1939 or a 1934 copy of *Cosmopolitan* won at an eBay auction, historical objects enter my life in the same ways contemporary ones usually do. Just think: we receive magazines and the clothes we shop for in catalogs, both printed and online, in the mail every day. But when the package at my door contains a dress that another woman wore in 1939, the sense of discovery, of excitement at my acquisition is accompanied by something else: a mysteriously personal union with the past and history. After I open these packages, I proceed to do the same things that women in the past did: I try on my new dresses, flip through the pages of my new-old magazines, just as I do with contemporary dresses and magazines. I thereby overlap the past habits of these women with my present ones, collapsing the distinction between the past and the present. An eBay seller of vintage items is a bit like the operator of a time machine, disengaging the buyer from her immediate surroundings and transporting her into the world inhabited by the first owner of the item on which she's bidding. My (real) present overlaps with the (imagined) past of someone else, and in this way I live, briefly, a part of the past I theorize and imagine in my research.

This isn't quite as fantastical as it first sounds. My work involves representations of women in 1930s screwball comedies.[1] Hollywood then was entertainment as Hollywood is now, but it was also a shop window for clothing lines that had just hit department stores nationwide. Because of strong product tie-ins between the movie and fashion industries, the costumes worn by stars such as Carole Lombard and Joan Crawford were sold as ready-made fashions in Macy's and other department stores. This means that the stories acted out on-screen by the stars wearing these kinds of clothes trickled over into physical reality to an extent not since repeated.[2] American women in the 1930s would look at how actresses wore the clothes advertised to them onscreen, identifying with their heroine and her (most often) triumphantly subversive story of social change. They could then go home and identify with their favorite stars and movie fantasies in an entirely physical way. When a woman bought and then wore a replica of the outfit that Claudette Colbert wore in Frank Capra's *It Happened One Night* (1934), Colbert's character of the rebellious heiress who questions the class divisions of 1930s society spilled over into the dress wearer's physical reality. The woman who bought the department store replica of that dress imbued her daily life with a trace of the rebellion that Colbert acted out on the movie screen and could become a participant in the movie's subversive rewriting of the rules of feminine behavior.

When I shop on eBay, I am much like the woman who "shopped" on film for new fashions in the 1930s. I first see a dress as a representation, though the movie screen has been replaced by a computer screen. A story often accompanies items sold on eBay: I bought one blue silk velvet dress that, according to its seller, was worn to a wedding in 1939 (in Figure 18.1, I model the vintage dress). It is a striking, soft dress I slip into as easily as if it had always been mine. I move easily in it too: the cut, almost elastic, fits snugly at the waist but without constricting my torso and flows freely as I walk. The color and texture are luxurious, the shape straight off a movie screen. Wearing this dress, I feel like I am one of the rich New York socialites in George Cukor's *The Women* (1939) who live out intrigues, divorces, new marriages, and childbirth in between dropping off their dogs at their spa's doggy day care and picking out a ball gown at a department store fashion show. So decadent, so posh, so far removed from the everyday concerns of the not-so-rich, not-so-free to explore, make fun of, and play with the most extreme stereotypes that make up the social construct of Woman. Wearing this dress I feel connected to the everyday lives of women in the past who sat in theater audiences, who bought and wore knockoffs of the dresses they had seen on-screen, and who could, like the heroines they watched, subvert that construct but do so without tearing down the institutions of which it is a part.

Figure 18.1 Katalin Lovász in a 1930s dress. Photograph by Andrew Moore.

But it's more than just fantasizing I'm a wealthy woman living in glamour and luxury, or, alternatively, an actress in a movie. There is also something subversive about wearing a vintage dress. One feels one is cheating the fashion industry, one-upping it even: a quality dress worn outside its time marks its wearer as either a fashion pioneer (if one gets it right) or an eccentric (a less desirable but nevertheless successful attention-grabbing effect). Either way, one has done something that stands convention on its head, perhaps ridiculously so at times, but in ways that resemble the 1930s screwball comedy heroine's attention-grabbing antics. In the case of my blue dress from 1939, the seller's story had made this kind of identification all the more real: there had been an actual real-life person living in a real-life story that I can imagine myself half-living as well whenever I wear the dress. And over time I have come to realize there is an interesting message about my research in this kind of physical identification with the past.

But let me backtrack and first explain how I began to buy clothes on eBay. A few years ago, 1950s styles started to become fashionable once again and I purchased dresses from the period simply because I wanted to save money. In 2001 one could get a vintage dress on eBay for less than 20 USD that was very similar to dresses appearing on the runways of designers like Marc Jacobs, later knocked off by Banana Republic and sold in stores for well over 100 USD. Unlike Banana Republic dresses, the vintage ones I bought on eBay weren't clearly brand recognizable and didn't look exactly like the dress everyone else in town bought this month (which is, for some of us, a fairly important consideration).

Going about my day in my new-old purchases, I became very conscious of how I felt, physically, in these dresses. The ones made in Dior's New Look style, with wasp-waists accentuated by billowing skirts and tailored bust-lines, constrained my body in very specific and, to me, unexpected ways. The bodices didn't allow my upper body to move as freely as the loose-fitting or stretchy tops fashionable today. The tight waists restrict breathing to the top part of one's chest (and we of the twenty-first century are used to breathing through our whole lungs), and the narrowly tailored three-quarter sleeves hold one's elbow in a perpetual slight bend, which also made me think it isn't accidental that Barbie's arms bend exactly at the angle they do to this day: Barbie was born in 1959.

In other words, a very clear and physical definition of the female social self was stitched and sewn into 1950s dresses. I could feel myself defined and restricted by these dresses, the gender ideologies of the 1950s repeating themselves to me on my very own body in potentially unironic ways, if I paid attention. Suddenly the constrained female characters of, for example, Alfred Hitchcock's *Vertigo* (1958) began to make sense to me in an entirely new way. I realized that there was a very physical choreography of gender identity played out on-screen in *Vertigo* (and most other 1950s movies), one that placed strict boundaries on not only how women moved in space but also how they could move in society. On the other hand, there was no way I could have experienced this without actually wearing these dresses and doing so in my daily life. And I suspect I would not have felt quite at home in these dresses had it not been for the particular economy of shopping on eBay: the way each item I purchased came into my life in the same way a newly purchased J. Crew catalog item comes into it. At the same time, the dresses I bought on eBay carried traces of past wearers: a 1950s metal zipper replaced by a contemporary plastic one, an address scribbled on a scrap of paper forgotten in a pocket. (Surprisingly, while these wide-skirted 1950s dresses need attending to at all times so as to not knock things over when moving in narrow spaces, they are more practical than one might think: every single one I bought has pockets big enough to hold keys, some change, tissues, lipstick—and forgotten old notes.)

I became more and more interested in the idea that there's a difference between knowing about something from the inside, by feeling oneself immersed in it and letting it take shape on one's body, as opposed to encountering its traces and signs at a physical remove. As much as I love reading gender theory, I've always felt the attempt to decipher only the external markers of social constructions of gender somehow occludes the subversive potential that people invariably find in the constraints of their lives. And I suspect there is virtually no way to know these secret spaces of rebellion except by immersing oneself in the world that produces them: they are not visible from the outside. I am not proposing that such secret subversive acts are enough to liberate women from patriarchal constraints. What happens instead is that small, deliberate, and devious acts of subversion allow women to hold on to parts of themselves that escape social constraints, and to do so in tactical ways that keep them safe from the potentially negative repercussions awaiting those who transgress openly.

However, the fact remains that 1950s clothing constrained women's bodies, and these constraints were visible in the choreography of femininity on movie screens in a way that (I realized) was not the case in 1930s movies, the period I was researching. Up to this point, I'd been buying clothes on eBay for fun and thrift and hadn't really looked for items from the 1930s. But I was becoming curious about what it would feel like to wear and move in clothing that marked one as woman with that decade's particular signs of femininity.

I already had the idea of clothing as a potentially subversive element because of my earlier forays into eBay vintage clothing-land. Now I wanted to see if the 1930s incarnation of this screen between one's physical body and social spaces might account somewhat for that mobile, chaotic, and often even experimental definition of gender identity characteristic of most 1930s screwball comedies. Says Judith Butler, "If the ground for gender identity is the stylized repetition of acts through time, and not a seemingly seamless identity, then the possibilities of gender transformation are to be found in the arbitrary relation between such acts, in the possibility of a different sort of repeating, in the breaking or subversive repetition of that style,"[3] in which case the actual bodies' actual movement in spaces both physical and social needs consideration: the choreography of gender and social identity created, in part, by the particular constraints and freedoms inherent to the clothing one wears.

On eBay, I found dresses nearly identical to dresses worn in the movies I was writing about and, wearing them, realized there is one type of tailoring common in the 1930s whose approach to the clothed body significantly differed from tailoring in the 1950s, and which virtually disappeared after the 1930s. This is the bias cut, in which the strands in woven fabric are positioned diagonally on the body (as opposed to vertically and horizontally). This positioning produces a large amount of give in the fabric that makes clothing cut on the bias almost elastic. In the Renaissance, before the invention of knitting, turning woven fabric onto the diagonal was used when making the tight-fitting stockings worn by noblemen. However, no one had constructed skirts or dresses using fabric in this way until Parisian designer Madame Vionnet created her first prototype in 1927. This more body-conscious dress construction allowed for a far wider range of motion than any women's clothing preceding it (or, for that matter, afterward during the post-World War II backlash against women's emancipation). The bias cut reverses the relationship between body and clothing so that the body's comfort and ability to *move* are foregrounded. (I am, of course, leaving aside any consideration of undergarments, which were still rather more confining in the 1930s than those worn today, though not nearly as confining as undergarments worn in the 1950s.) Bias-cut clothing lets the wearer define herself through motion rather than the carefully sculpted and embellished, immobilizing shapes common to women's clothing before the 1920s (the decade of loose-fitting shift dresses and chemises) or after World War II.

Bias-cut dresses clothe a self as changeable as motion itself. Unlike the static constraints of 1950s dresses that tailored patriarchal ideology into clothing, a woman of the 1930s could wear clothing that exploited the destabilization of gender roles caused, in part, by social upheavals during this period of U.S. history, including the economic trauma of the Depression and the end of Prohibition. Young women entering adulthood in the 1930s formed the first generation of American women growing up as full citizens in possession of the right to vote. The 1930s was a moment in time when a woman could, however briefly, renegotiate the bounds of accepted social norms, define herself as a self in motion, and explore physical, social, and mental spaces for herself rather than allow herself to be confined passively in them. Both clothing and movies in the 1930s—albeit indirectly and in ways not always openly verbalized—actively questioned patriarchal ideology.

The idea that people's motion in physical spaces reflects how they negotiate their social environment became central to my research. While surfing for clothing on eBay, I discovered listings for a few intact 1930s copies of *McCall's* magazine, with the address labels of original subscribers still attached. Magazines pervaded women's lives at that time as they still do for many today. I began to search eBay for vintage magazines such as *Cosmopolitan*, *Woman's Day*, and *Pictorial Review*. These publications targeted lower-middle-class and middle-class moviegoing women and often featured movie-stars-as-regular-people articles (as the first two still do today). I first bought copies out of fascination but quickly realized that advertisements and articles—whether on clothing, cars, kitchens, bathrooms, or other living spaces—often featured women's bodies in motion. Except for high-end glossies such as *Vogue*, libraries rarely collected women's magazines, but with eBay this research obstacle vanished: thousands of magazines from exactly the period and of exactly the kind I was looking for were auctioned daily. And I did not have to sit with them in a library reading room or read through the distancing mechanism of a microfilm reader. A vintage magazine delivered through the mail and read at home is no longer only a historical artifact assumed to have little, if any, direct contact with everyday life; it becomes the everyday. I could not buy all the magazines I wanted, however much I would have liked, but I was able to purchase enough to make observations about perceptions of motion in 1930s popular culture in my dissertation.

There is something almost magical about eBay's ability to bring together people and objects far apart from one another in space and time. Buyers and sellers connect from distant places by way of a bid placed and an auction won, forming temporary partnerships with unknown people whose unheard voices speak to them from the item description and in postauction email exchanges. These personal relationships are nurtured through eBay's ideology of "community," which is supported by a site design that works to equalize the most disparate of listings and by a reputation-based structure that governs every transaction. And yet as one surfs vintage auctions, one is also struck by the multitude of stories and distinct personalities that emerge. Each listing—the colors and fonts chosen, how the images of the item listed are structured and presented, the language of the description, and the terms of sale—seems to tell as much about the history of the seller as the history of the item sold.[4] Shopping for vintage items in this way is something of an escapist fantasy: in the virtual reality of the eBay marketplace, one is invited to enter an imagined and imaginary community[5] and shop for the past in much the same way as one would shop any online catalog.

The dynamic of this escape into imagination resonates with Virginia Postrel's description of why we fantasize about wireless technology: "It bestows on ordinary mortals the power to pluck from the atmosphere unheard voices and unseen images, whether broadcasted or recorded. [It] creates the illusion of proximity, immediacy, even intimacy. It transports us from our real surroundings."[6] This dynamic encourages us to see eBay and the Web itself as an alternate reality, an escape from the fragmentation of our real lives, yet in so doing to forget about and naturalize the web of computers and software, the processors and circuit boards, the infrastructure on both micro and macro levels, and the countless thousands of miles of wire and optical cable upon which both rely. This is an escapist fantasy particular to the twenty-first century within a culture ironically dependent on its infrastructure of information technology, a fantasy that says there's not much there, really, in all those wires unless it's to meet up with the people who imagine communities with and within them, a fantasy that springs more purely from our imagination than many others and yet has become a technological reality: friendships and marriages and eBay are made of it.

I am reminded again of the address labels bearing the names of women from the 1930s still affixed to the magazines I received in the mail. The eBay marketplace partakes of imaginariness-made-real; real items from the past come to my home through the mail, just as they would have in the past, and I reenact the same ritual of turning the pages those women enacted, see the same fashion advertisements, and read the same articles on Hollywood stars and glamour. Perhaps this is what connects us:

> Glamour isn't only about movie stars or sex appeal. The theatrical imaginative process we now call glamour thrives wherever something evokes an audience's desires and makes them seem attainable, or at least imaginable. Through a special combination of grace, mystery and seeming perfection, a glamorous person, setting or object leads us to project ourselves into a better world. Glamour's idealism and ease offer escape from the limitations of our own lives.[7]

The documented trace of the address label increases the sense of connection that I, the researcher, feel with the past I seek to reconstruct, interpret, and fashion: it is a sign that a story waits to be told. The historical magazine-reading woman is real. I know her name, her address, know where she folded the magazine back on itself as she read, the creases I find perhaps made by her hand. The woman I imagine in my research becomes as real as my own self: I am the magazine-reading woman of both (and perhaps all) times then, existing within *and* outside history. It is the imaginary made real, the virtual actualized, via the eBay transaction. The sale creates a multihistorical moment: seller and buyer inhabit the present while the vintage item changing hands retains its connection with the imagined, untouchable past.

Most of the vintage dresses I buy on eBay carry traces of the bodily self of the women who first wore them: a whiff of perfume, small thinned-out spots caused by repeated movements, faint perspiration stains in the lining.[8] When I wear such a dress, my body becomes the site upon which the story of that other woman can be acted again: the story of how women like her acted out their social identity, of how their physical appearance came to mean, even to seem to be, "Woman." I thereby dissolve the conventionally static barriers among researched, imagined, and real and make of them something organic, mobile, and changeable, something that escapes the constraints of the traditional segregation of the researcher and her subject.

In 1904 Georg Simmel defined fashion as the ever-shifting meeting point between the conflicting desires for individuation and conformity. In Simmel's schema, change is constant and the seeking out of ever-newer forms of subversion a necessity. With fashion, he says, "[W]e have always to deal with the same fundamental form of duality which is manifested biologically in the contrast between heredity and variation. Of these the former represents the idea of generalization, of uniformity, of the inactive similarity of the forms and contents of life; the latter stands for motion, for the differentiation of separate elements, producing the restless changing of an individual life."[9] Simmel, importantly, casts fashion's changes in biological terms, as an organic kind of change not unlike the kind of tactical subversion of social norms I describe above. When I infuse my research with the little acts of my everyday life (and vice versa), as eBay allows me to do, I set myself in motion against the paradox upon which a researcher's life is predicated: the need to say something new and yet say it only using well-established methods and words—the duality of individuation and conformity noted by Simmel. Scholarly research is supposed to come to structured conclusions built systematically upon the preexisting foundation of others' already accepted, cataloged, learned, and even canonized ideas. But what happens when ideas vary? American academia today is a series of winner-take-all competitions that determine who gets the jobs, who gets to teach which courses, and therefore whose ideas get taught. The ideas, stories, and histories of those who resist this conformity are systematically erased from academic discourse.

Yet when I read a magazine or wear a dress from another lifetime that I bought on eBay and subsequently let the experience seep into my research, my life and body become the physical site of my academic work. I thereby resist the conventional erasure from academic discourse of unconventional research methods and ideas by allowing myself to become the embodiment of my research. In letting my research take shape on my body, I resist the distance that one is expected to create between the past one researches and one's life. My body is the transition between the here and now that I inhabit while imagining the past, and the past I imagine. I become the bridge across the gap between my bodily self, engaged in fantasizing, and my mental self, the one imagining what I would have felt and thought in the past from which the clothing I buy on eBay and then wear is the envoy. By wearing a dress from the 1930s, I become the act of imagining, and I embark on a bodily engagement with the reconstruction of the past. It is in this way that using eBay for research lets me diffuse the painful dichotomy of having a thought-life that is supposed to be distinct from my lived and felt experiences: it allows me not to compartmentalize myself and instead to *move*, as if at one with the bias cut.

NOTES

1. Screwball comedy grew out of the slapstick comedy silent film genre and was characterized by wisecracking dialogue, fast pacing, some visual burlesque, and plots that invariably include a couple in a strange predicament. See, for example, *It Happened One Night* (1934), *My Man Godfrey* (1936), *Nothing Sacred* (1937), *Bringing Up Baby* (1938), *His Girl Friday* (1940), and *Woman of the Year* (1942). For more information, see David A. Cook, *A History of Narrative Film* (New York: W. W. Norton, 1990), 294–95.
2. Fashion photography did not exist as advertising for clothing in the 1930s as it does today. Women's magazines hired professional illustrators for their fashion segments and presented the clothes advertised as drawings that looked like designer sketches. The only places where women could see how a dress looked on a model was at the movies or fashion shows, but fashion shows were the domain of the rich and the average woman never saw them, except in movies such as *The Women* (1939), a black-and-white film that presents a Technicolor fashion show in its middle section. For a discussion of Hollywood's role in product and fashion promotion, see Charles Eckert, "The Carole Lombard in Macy's Window," in *Fabrications: Costume and the Female Body*, ed. Jane Gaines and Charlotte Herzog (New York: Routledge, 1990), 100–22.
3. Judith Butler, "Performative Acts and Gender Constitution: An Essay in Phenomenology and Feminist Theory," in *Writing on the Body: Female Embodiment and Feminist Theory*, ed. Katie Conboy, Nadia Medina, and Sarah Stanbury (New York: Columbia University Press, 1997), 402.
4. For a discussion of eBay sellers constructing their own histories through the objects from the past they list for sale, see chapter 5.
5. For a seminal account of the idea of imagined community, see Benedict Anderson, *Imagined Communities* (London: Verso, 1983).
6. Virginia Postrel, "Gadgets and Glamour: Let's Make Some Magic, with No Strings Attached," *New York Times*, May 4, 2005, www.nytimes.com (subscription required; accessed June 25, 2005).

7. Ibid.
8. eBay's requirement that all used clothing items be cleaned allows for such traces in vintage clothing, so long as they are accurately described. For a discussion of eBay's policy, see chapter 17.
9. Georg Simmel, "Fashion," in *On Individuality and Social Forms: Selected Writings*, ed. Donald N. Levine (Chicago: University of Chicago Press, 1971), 294.

Contributors

Lisa Bloom writes and lectures on the intersections among gender, technology, and visual culture. She is author of *Gender on Ice: American Ideologies of Polar Expeditions* (University of Minnesota Press, 1993) and editor of *With Other Eyes: Looking at Race and Gender in Visual Culture* (University of Minnesota Press, 1999, also translated into Japanese). Her forthcoming book is titled *Ghosts of Ethnicity: Jewish Identities in American Feminist Art* (Routledge, 2006). Lisa has been an eBay Power Seller since 2003.

James Leo Cahill is a doctoral student in critical studies at the University of Southern California School of Cinema-Television. His work focuses on experimental and scientific cinema and critical theory. He first used eBay in 1998 to find a copy of *Mrs. Miller's Greatest Hits* (Capitol Records, 1966), but since becoming a graduate student he has limited his collecting to eBay images. His eBay user ID is corndoggin.

Daniel Mudie Cunningham is a writer, curator, and lecturer specializing in contemporary art, design, and cinema. Based in the Blue Mountains, Australia, Daniel completed his Ph.D. on "white trash" film cultures at the University of Western Sydney in 2004. He lectures in the School of Communication, Design, and Media at the University of Western Sydney. An avid eBay user since 2001, Daniel's eBay ID is show_pony, and his user rating was 153 (100 percent positive feedback) at the time of writing.

Mary Desjardins is associate professor of film and television studies at Dartmouth College, Hanover, New Hampshire. Her book, *Recycled Stars: Female Film Stardom in the Age of Television and Video*, and her coedited volume on Marlene Dietrich are forthcoming from Duke University Press. Several years ago, Mary's friend Barbara Hall introduced her to eBay by showing her pages of Mrs. Beasley dolls that were proudly advertised as having "no bites." She's been fascinated by eBay seller codes and protocols ever since.

Rebecca Ellis and **Anna Haywood** are researchers at the University of Essex, United Kingdom. They are undertaking a two-year project on eBay, funded by the United Kingdom Economic and Social Research Council (ESRC), titled *Virtually Second-Hand*. Rebecca has a Ph.D. in human geography from the University of Sheffield, and Anna has an M.Sc. in ergonomics and human computer interaction from University College London. Both became eBay members in 2000, and they remain fascinated by the site from both personal and academic perspectives. Rebecca is one of the very few female vintage radio collectors and has used eBay to buy rare sets and sell surplus parts from her collection. Anna uses eBay as a first port of call when interested in buying almost everything, particularly kitsch items.

Nathan Scott Epley is assistant professor in e-media at the University of Northern Iowa, where he teaches media production and criticism. His research on digital cultures explores the cultural, political, and labor practices of "no-collar" professionals and the mobilization of everyday life under contemporary capitalism. For several years, "My eBay" has been second in his browser's bookmarks.

Eric Gardner is associate professor of English at Saginaw Valley State University, University Center, Michigan, and editor of *Major Voices: The Drama of Slavery* (Toby Press, 2005). He has authored articles on Harriet Wilson, Frank J. Webb, and Mary Webb, and recently won a National Endowment for the Humanities Summer Stipend for work on the St. Louis freedom suits. He is beginning a study of the representation of African American fortune-tellers in early American texts and has been an eBay user since late 1999.

William Gibson has written novels, short stories, and screenplays. *Neuromancer* (1984) won the Hugo, Nebula, and Philip K. Dick awards for best novel. Other novels include *Count Zero* (1986), *Mona Lisa Overdrive* (1988), *Virtual Light* (1993), *Idoru* (1996), *All Tomorrow's Parties* (1999), and *Pattern Recognition* (2003). With Bruce Sterling, Gibson coauthored *The Difference Engine* (1991), and he wrote the screenplay for the film *Johnny Mnemonic* (1995). Gibson coined the term "cyberspace," which first appeared in *Neuromancer*. Credited with developing the subgenre of science fiction known as cyberpunk, Bill hasn't used a manual typewriter since 1985.

Ken Hillis is associate professor of media studies in the department of communication studies and adjunct professor of geography at the University of North Carolina–Chapel Hill. He has published in several anthologies and in such journals as *Cartographica*; *Ecumene*; *Progress in Human Geography*; *Space and Culture*; *The Velvet Light Trap*; and *Culture, Theory, and Critique*. His work has been translated into Dutch and Portuguese, and his book, *Digital Sensations: Space, Identity, and Embodiment in Virtual Reality* (1999), is published by University of Minnesota Press. Ken is currently preparing his next book, *Rituals of Transmission*, for publication, and he hates being sniped.

Kylie Jarrett is employed in the School of Communication, Information, and New Media at the University of South Australia. Her doctoral thesis, completed in 2003, explores the discursive construction of consumer empowerment in e-commerce. Her particular fascination with eBay stems from a battle of wills between a friend buying motor scooter parts and a shill-bidding grandmother from Germany. It was here that notions of individuated yet communal disciplining first crystallized for Kylie, culminating in the analysis included in this book.

Jon Lillie is assistant professor of new media and online journalism at the University of Hawaii–Manoa. He applies a critical cultural lens to explore questions of how and why Web-based phenomena, mobile phones, and other information and communication technologies (ICTs) are narrativized in popular culture. He also is interested in how commercial technologies mediate modes of social and cultural interaction in everyday life. Jon has bought and sold a small number of items through eBay over the last five years and can be contacted at lillie@hawaii.edu.

Katalin Lovász was born in Hungary and studied at Budapest University of Economics before receiving her B.A. from Rutgers University, New Brunswick, New Jersey in English and comparative literature. A doctoral student in Princeton University's comparative literature department, Katalin focuses on film and popular culture. She is a founder of Princeton's /@rts (pronounced "slash arts") lecture series, which features speakers working at the intersections of technology and the arts and humanities, and she is a founder of Princeton's Art of Science Competition, which recently gained widespread recognition via digerati publications such as boingboing.net and *Wired News*.

Susanna Paasonen is assistant professor of digital culture at the University of Jyväskylä, Finland and adjunct professor of media culture at the University of Tampere, Finland. Her publications include *Women and Everyday Uses of the Internet: Agency & Identity*, edited with Mia Consalvo (Peter Lang, 2002), and *Figures of Fantasy: Women, Internet, and Cyberdiscourse*

(Peter Lang, 2005). She is currently working on affect and online pornography. With a passion for kitsch and popular culture, Susanna browses regularly both online and at flea markets.

Michael Petit is a Mellon postdoctoral fellow at Duke University, where he teaches critical thinking through critical writing in the university writing program. His Ph.D. is in eighteenth-century British literature, and his research interests include writing pedagogy, writing across the curriculum, and the intersections of popular culture and new information technology. His book, *Peacekeepers at War* (1986), is published by Faber and Faber. Michael uses PayPal to maintain his "A+++++ grrreat ebayer!!!" 100 percent positive approval rating.

Laura Robinson is a Ph.D. candidate in the in the department of sociology at the University of California–Los Angeles. Her research applies sociological and interpretative methods of analysis to explore the processes through which participants in virtual community forums generate dominant and dissident framings of highly charged issues. Laura's dissertation takes a comparative approach to contrast an American forum with similar French and Brazilian forums devoted to 9/11. Her publications have focused on digitization and the arts, discourses of the cyberself, and a comparison of eBay USA and eBay France.

Zoe Trodd teaches in the department of history and literature at Harvard University, and has degrees from Cambridge and Harvard Universities. She has published on American literature, visual culture, and "people's history." Her book, *American Protest Literature*, is forthcoming from Harvard University Press. With John Stauffer, she has also published *Meteor of War: The John Brown Story* (2004). Her first eBay bid was for a "beautiful and authentic hair from John Brown's head."

Lyn M. Van Swol is assistant professor of communication studies at Northwestern University. She received her Ph.D. in social psychology from the University of Illinois–Urbana/Champaign in 1998. Her research interests include the effects of regulation on trust and the establishment of reputation and trust in e-commerce settings. She has published in such journals as *Basic and Applied Social Psychology*, *Behavior and Human Decision Processes*, *Communication Research*, and *Organizational Behavior and Human Decision Processes*. She maintains a gold-star reputation on eBay.

Michele White is assistant professor in the department of communication at Tulane University, New Orleans, Louisiana. Michele's first book, *The*

Body and the Screen: Theories of Internet Spectatorship, is forthcoming from MIT Press. She is currently writing a second book, *Buy It Now: Lessons From eBay*. Other recent publications include "Too Close to See: Men, Women, and Webcams," *New Media & Society* 5, no. 1 (2003); and "The Aesthetic of Failure: Net Art Gone Wrong," *Angelaki* 7, no. 1 (2002). She can be contacted at mwhite@michelewhite.org.

Index

A

Abelove, Henry, 279
Adler, Jerry, 41
Advertising, 6, 92–93, 95, 103, 169, 170, 256
- "Belief," 92
- "Clocks," 247
- consumption, 103
- corporate strategy, 112, 132
- "Maze," 247
- "My Way," 92
- "Power of All of Us, The," 40–41, 87, 92, 167, 196, 247, 259
- "Toy Boat," 167, 170
- truth, 175, 183

Affect, 1,12, 212
African American, 9, 63, 65–66, 70
- collectors, 64
- women as readers, 84

Afro-Americana, 63, 64, 65, 66, 67, 68, 70
- racism, 69

Agamben, Giorgio, 208, 209
Agnew, Spiro, 25
Americana, 203
- eBay folklore, 203

Ahmed, Sara, 212
Alcott, Louisa May, 88
Aldrich, Robert, 35
Anderson, Benedict, 104, 292
Andreessen, Marc, 167, 179
Anonymity online, 5, 129, 133, 227, 243, 238
AOL, 96, 99
Apparitions, 14, 2–3, 204
- as fetish, 208–209

Archive, the, 10, 15, 80, 83, 86, 185
- auction, 80
- digital, 15
- domestic space, 87
- ephemeral, 193
- fabrication of history, 10
- forgetting, 193
- image, 80
- image-repertoire, 13
- museum and auction, 87–88
- narrative, 10, 78

Argentina, 16
Art culture system, 207; *see also* High art/low art
- and mass culture, 207

Artfact.com, 232, 235, 238
Artnet.com, 232, 235, 238
Art practices on eBay, 3–4, 13
Artprice.com, 235
Askart.com, 235
Attfield, Judy, 261
AuctionBytes.com, 261
Auctions
- archive, the 80
- cyber, 32, 40
- "Dutch," 27, 162
- "English-style," 154–155
- exceptional, 201–203
- experience economy, 3
- format and incentive to bid, 154
- format of, 12–13
- high risk, 146
- history of, 3
- humanization, 34
- internet, 43
- live, 234
- media friendly, 168, 171
- price, 12, 152
- racist language, 69

reserve, 123, 125–127
second price sealed bid, 154
AuctionWeb (eBay precursor), 1, 92, 110, 169, 179, 180, 232
Auster, Paul, 82
Authenticity, 14, 38, 52, 113, 146, 171, 179, 192, 221, 276; *see also* Value
art, 203
commodification, 169
narrative performance, 175
as ultimate fetish, 210
Avatar, 179

B

Ba, Sulin, 139, 145
Bacon, Francis, 79
Baldwin, Rosalinda, 241–242
Balzac, Honoré de, 81
Barale, Michele Aina, 279
Barlow, John Perry, 94
Barnum, P.T., 79, 81
Baron, David, 107, 113
Barthes, Roland, 7, 13, 17, 185, 190–191, 193, 194, 222, 223, 253
image-repertoire, 193–195
punctum, 190–191, 222, 223
Basbanes, Nicholas, 65
Bassett, E.H., 178
Baudelaire, Charles, 87
Baudelaire's man, 87
Baudrillard, Jean, 32, 34, 42
Bauman, Zygmunt, 118
Becker, Carl, 83
Belk, Russell, 7, 37, 41, 47
Benjamin, Walter, 7, 70, 82, 85, 87, 88, 89, 170, 175, 177, 204, 217–218, 220, 221, 227
Bentham, Jeremy, 108, 116, 118
Berger, John, 84
Berry, Chris, 263
Bidding practices, 23–24, 37, 119, 205; *see also* Bid stalking; Buying and selling practices; Reserve bidding; Sniping
"auction fever," 3, 144
bid history, 154
buyer vulnerability, 136
hybrid auction format, 155–157
identity, 35
as production and consumption, 171–172
purchaser promiscuity, 12, 142
retaliatory feedback, 130–131
"tourist bidders," 132
Bid stalking, 156
"Black Friday," 11, 123–124, 125, 129, 134, 135
Blockson, Charles, 65
Boltanski, Christian, 197
Bolter, Jay David, 224
Boot sale, *see* Car boot sale
Branding 2, 5, 99
of authenticity, 168; *see also* eBay, as brand
Braziel, Janna Evans, 261
Bricks-and-mortar retailers/outlets, 98, 100, 144, 153, 236, 242, 275
and flipping, 142
Bruneau, Carol, 142
Bulletin Board, 93, 94
Business model, 91, 95, 234, 241
importance to neoliberal political economy, 118–119
as neoliberal, 91
Butler, Judith, 253, 287
Butterfield & Butterfield, 232
Buying and selling practices, 32, 55–56
"Buy It Now," 153

C

Camille, Michael, 259
Campbell, Colin, 43
Campbell, John Edward, 279
Canada, 145, 247
Cannon, Joseph, 138
Capra, Frank, 284
Car boot sale, 9, 53–54, 58; *see also* Markets

Cardinal, Roger, 257, 259
Cartes-de-visite, 10, 77, 79
history of 79–80
as mass produced photography, 77
Castells, Manuel, 91, 96, 103; *see also* "Network society"
Castiglia, Christopher, 268, 278
Category system, 67–68, 78–79, 161, 228, 245, 248–249, 261
"Adult Only," 15, 26, 268
"gay interest," 15
as heteronormative, 15
"Mature Audiences," 248, 268, 271, 272, 274, 280
resistance to, 248
Chasin, Alexandra, 249
Cheney, Dick, 102
Child, Lydia Maria, 88
Christie's, 15, 231, 233, 238
Cisco Systems, 96
Citizenship, 11, 109
as citizen consumer 99
relationship to neoliberal community, 110
Clark, Beverly Lyon, 261
Clark, Danae, 256
Cohen, Adam, 107, 110, 124, 151, 152, 249, 270, 271, 273
Colbert, Claudette, 284
Collectibles, 2, 19, 31–32, 87
death, 223
distribution networks of, 47, 57–58, 64–65
narratives, 52
virtual, 43, 175
Collecting, 6, 9, 170
acceleration of, 47
and the everyday, 6
globalization of, 54–55
implications of, 257
politics of, 84
practices, 47–48
seriality of, 37
space of, 59
Collecting communities, 9, 156, 232
Collecting culture(s), 153, 159
and material geography, 9
nineteenth century, 84
Collecting rituals, 45; *see also* Ritual
challenges to, 50, 51, 53, 56
defined, 51
and geographic space, 52–54, 54–55, 57–58
Collecting subcultures, 152
expertise, 158–160
price, 156
subcultural capital, 159, 164
Collections, 45, 88, 170
defined, 45
Collectors, 6, 9, 23–24, 36, 45, 50, 53, 55–56, 57, 60, 85–86, 160–161, 217–218, 237
of Afro-Americana, 71
book, 64–65, 66, 217–218
coin and stamp, 46–47
as heart and soul of eBay, 31, 158, 168
Collins, Joan, 192
Commodification, 4
of authenticity, 169–171, 169
and experience, 36, 169
of experience, 181
of memory, 1, 70, 169
of self, 2, 36, 181
Commodity exchange, 38, 169
Commodity fetish, 83
Commodity fetishism, 168, 170, 182, 208
Community, 11, 31, 33–34, 91, 92, 93, 94, 95, 98, 103, 107–108, 209, 242
collective imaginary, 93
commercial advantage, 108, 269
construction of norms, 11
"consumption literacy," 103
dialogue, 94; *see also* Bulletin Board *vs.*
eBay administration, 127–128
face-to-face, 46, 53
ideology of, 289
imagined, 104
as master narrative, 94–95, 107
membership, 93
as neoliberal, 11

relationship to buying and selling, 250
rhetoric of, 10, 11, 100, 114, 119, 125
values, 92–93, 103–104, 111
vintage radio, 46
virtual, 10, 46, 95, 98
Competition 33, 34, 41, 67, 69, 154, 156, 182
academic, 291
Consumer, 114, 242
choice, 113
culture, 205, 208
values, 204
Consumerism and religious experience, 204
Consumption
chain of, 66
culture of serial, 168
cycle, 3, 38
literacy, 103
work and play of, 101
Convoy, Katie, 292
Cook, David A., 292
Cope, Walter, 78
Costco, 100
Crafts, Hannah, 65, 71
Crawford, Joan, 35, 284
Crewe, Louise, 60, 276
Critical theory, 6
Csikszentmihalyi, Mihaly, 34, 42
Cukor, George, 284
Cultural capital. 96, 140, 159, 160, 221, 238
Culture industry, 6
Cyberspace, 3, 23, 26, 94–95

D

Davis, James, 138
Database, 47,179
Debray, Regis, 17, 170, 175, 176
Deleuze, Gilles, 7, 169
Democratization, 3, 9, 19, 64, 66, 70, 102, 152, 161–162, 189, 232, 234
book collecting, 9, 66
competition, 237
fine arts and antiques, 14–15
Derrida, Jacques, 13, 185, 193, 183
Desire, 1, 2, 15, 38, 161, 169, 176, 178, 180, 195, 241, 245, 252, 254
fetishized, 168
queer, 253
and vicarious experience, 172
Dholakia, Utpal, 135
Diebenkorn, Richard, 60
Dietrich, Marlene, 211
Digital trace, 181; *see also* Trace, the
Disney, 15, 269, 272, 275
Doney, Patricia, 138
Dot.com crash, 11, 124, 235, 275
and boom, 232
Douglass, Frederick, 66, 70–71
Doyle's auction house, 234
Dreyfus, Hubert, 169
Duchamp, Marcel, 208
and the readymade, 208
"Dustbin of history," 87
Duyser, Diana, 201, 204, 206, 207, 208, 210, 211, 212
and the sublime, 206

E

Eastlake, Lady Elizabeth, 86
eBay
as arbiter of price, 153
as archive, 80
Australia, 107
as brand, 32, 110,112, 168; *see also* Branding
as cabinet of curiosities, 79, 83, 88
China, 16
as civic-minded community, 239
collectors as heart and soul of, 31, 158, 168
as discursive formation, 108
as entertainment, 168
as ephemeral archive, 171, 180
as ephemeral community, 33
as experience economy, 2, 5, 169
as global brand, 3
as heteronormative, 250

as hybrid auction format, 154
as hybrid commercial entity, 91
as hybrid new economy enterprise, 95
as ICT, 94–95
as information machine, 169
as marketplace, 189
as "media friendly" auction, 168, 157
as memory machine, 81, 218
as neoliberal ideal, 96, 118–119
as renewable history, 88
as virtual archive, 167
as virtual place, 21
as virtual reality, 289
as virtual space 178, 276
as virtual stage 1, 169
as virtual town square 137, 143
eBay Buyer Protection Program, 114
eBay "Great Collections," 232, 233
eBay Motors, 97, 168, 245
eBay Picture Services, 179, 190, 198
eBay Premiere, 233
eBay University, 188
eBulges.com, 278
Eckard, Charles, 292
Economics, 1, 6, 40, 101, 236; *see also* Business model
and efficiency, 231, 233
and gender, 238
and neoliberal, 10
Economy, 10, 268, 286
entertainment, 17, 168
experience, 2, 5, 169
of fun, 169
moral, 269–270
and sub-economy of small businesses, 31
Edel, Uli, 277
Elsner, John, 257, 259
Emblem, 175, 179
Emotion, 1,12
Ephemera, 6, 9, 19
defined, 32–33
film related, 8, 34, 37, 255
and Hollywood, 32, 34
human, 219
and the relic, 38
sellers of, 36
and technical form, 40
Ephemeral, 6
community, 33
interactions, 33
moments of viewing, 33
placeholders, 196
and the trace, 39
Equiano, Olaudah, 66
Evans, Gerald, 142
Everyday, 6–7, 79–80, 98, 161, 162, 188, 190, 206, 221, 284, 289, 291
and Hollywood films, 39
and market ideology, 152
Exhibitionism, 41
Experience, 2, 13, 168, 181; *see also* Value
mediated, 36, 176
and price, 276

F

Fame, 33
Fan culture, 7
Fandom
and self-identity, 35
theories of, 33–35
Fan practices, 33–34
Fashion, 286, 291
photography and film, 292
and vintage clothing, 285
Feedback Forum/feedback, 2, 11, 12, 24, 93, 108, 110, 115, 117, 124, 129–131, 132, 133, 134, 136, 137, 139, 140–141, 144, 147, 157, 182, 231, 240
as disciplinary mechanism, 119
ethical framing, 115
explanation of, 140
failure to police, 130
Panopticon, the, 119
reputation, 142
reputational gossip, 143
as self-policing, 11, 114, 116
surveillance, 11
transactional, 140

Fernback, Jan, 92–93
Fetish, 6, 195, 210, 274, 275
as apparition, 209
virtual object as, 169
Fetishism, 210
logic of, 37
theories of, 170
Fetishization of trivia, 176
Fetishized objects, 6, 38, 167
and reclaiming the past, 6
Fine art and antiques, 2, 15, 231, 240
and online auctions, 232
Fiske, John, 36, 42
Foote, Julia, 66
Ford, Henry, 87
Foster, Hal, 263
Foucault, Michel, 7, 108, 116, 117, 278
France, 145
Fraud, 11, 47, 100, 114, 133–134, 128, 139, 140, 142, 146, 240–241
and disreputable practices, 119
"Friction free" (capitalism), 15, 169, 173, 183
Freund, Karl, 37
Freyer, John, 3

G

Gaines, Jane, 292
Gaitenby, Alan, 139, 145
Gates, Henry Louis, 65–66, 70, 71
"Gay interest," 15, 245, 278; *see also* "Lesbian interest"
and narrated histories, 250–252
political significance of, 255–256
and vintage photography, 259
Gender, 14–15
and the book, 85
choreography of, 287
and economics, 237
and heteronormative narrative, 246
and Hollywood, 290
and identity, 287
and reading, 83–86
and resistance, 287
social construction of, 284
and ways of looking, 85
Germany, 145
Getty, Paul, 63
Gilmore, James, 2, 3, 17
Giuliani, Rudolph, 207
Global, 1, 7, 16, 59, 93, 96
Globalization, 47
and knowledge, 54–55
GoldenPalace.com, 201, 208, 211, 212, 213, 214
Goncourt, Edmund de, 87
Google.com, 96, 235
Gramsci, Antonio, 7
Greenberg, Clement, 209
Greenblatt, Stephen, 220, 221, 225
Gregson, Nicky, 60, 275, 276
Griffith, Jim ("Uncle Griff"), 93, 247, 270
Gross, Larry, 269
Grusin, Richard, 224
Guattari, Félix, 7
Guernsey, Lisa, 41
Guilelessness, 173, 211; *see also* Value
and authenticity, 173
and syntax and spelling errors, 173, 211

H

Halperin, David, 279
Hardin, Russell, 138
Hardt, Michael, 97–98, 102
Hassler, Jen, 275
Heft, Miguel, 41
Hegemony, 5, 11, 15, 64, 176, 182
and neoliberalism, 109, 119
Heimer, Carol, 141
Hepburn, Audrey, 37
Hershenson, Bruce, 255
Herzog, Charlotte, 292
High art/low art, 2, 14, 15, 152, 207, 208, 221, 232
destabilization of categories, 221
Higonnet, Margaret, 261
Hills, Matt, 41, 43
Hine, Christine, 59
History, 14

as affective entertainment, 175
biodegradable, 87
and eBay, 79–80
as junk, 87; *see also* Junk
and media formats, 221, 222
people's, 81
personal, 14, 16, 218, 220, 223
value of, 82
women's, 80
History of eBay, 15, 27–28, 85–86, 124, 189, 232–233, 236–237, 268, 270
and PEZ founding myth, 112, 151, 161, 189, 232, 245
Hitchcock, Alfred, 286
Hoffman, Donna, 137
Holden, Greg, 160
Holmes, Oliver Wendell, 80
Holt, Douglas, 192
Hong Kong, 24
Howard, Richard 194
Hypertext, 113

I

ICT, *see* Information technology (IT/ICT)
Identity, 1, 3, 5–6, 9, 15, 16, 31, 34–35, 38, 106, 114, 200, 238, 245; *see also* Self
and buying and selling history, 256
and community, 87
and consciousness, 34
gay and lesbian, 15, 256
neoliberal, 103
performance of, 50
relationship of history and the past to, 40–41, 255
and self-steering self, 109
IGavel.com, 242
Image
ambiguity of, 2
digital, 168
and narrative, 79
Image-repertoire, 185, 195–196, 197
India, 16
Index, idea of the, 13, 177
Indexicality, 177, 178, 190, 191
Information asymmetry, 12, 157, 160
Information technology (IT/ICT), 8, 20, 91–92, 93, 98, 100, 103
literacy, 101
Internet Relay Chat (IRC), 180

J

Jacobs, Harriet, 66, 71
Jacobs, Marc, 286
James, Henry, 88
Japan, 16, 138
Jenkins, Henry, 42, 261, 263
Jenner, Brian, 45, 49
Jim Crow Museum, 71
John Paul II, 181
Junk, 80, 88, 167
as collectible, 80
collector, 82
as counter history, 88
as history, 87; *see also* History

K

Katsh, Ethan, 139, 145
Kauffman, Robert, 142
Kelley, Mike, 221
Kerr, David, 111
Kirkham, Pat, 261
Kitsch, 2, 6, 14, 88, 209–210
defined, 209
relationship to beauty and the sublime, 209
Kollock, Peter, 139
Kopytoff, Igor, 61
Kracauer, Siegfried, 86
Krips, Henry, 176
Kuhn, Annette, 39, 43
Kunstler, James, 175

L

Labor, 91, 236; *see also* Value
affective, 10, 97–98, 102, 151
immaterial, 97

physical, 100–101
value, 170
Lacan, Jacques 194
and Lacanian Imaginary, 194, 195, 199
Lack, 177, 191, 192
Lacy, Robert, 233
Lahno, Bernd, 142
Landy, Michael, 87
LeBesco, Kathleen, 261
Lefebvre, Henri, 188
Lesbian and gay studies, 253
"Lesbian interest," 252–253; *see also* "Gay interest"
Levine, Donald N., 293
Libertarian ethics, 231; *see also* Omidyar, Pierre
betrayal of, 274
Listing practices, 171–175, 256
and marketing, 255
Listing/transaction fees, 125, 126–128, 236–237
Lombard, Carole, 284
Long, Lisa, 32, 40, 41
Lourdes, 203
Lurkers, 59
Lyotard, Jean-François, 207

M

Madonna, 277
Maes, Nicolaes. 86
Malaysia, 16
Markets/marketplace, 10, 13, 19, 114, 162, 182; *see also* Car boot sale; Swap meet
digital, 242
flea, 26–27, 66, 102
"friction free," 169, 277
humanization of, 32, 36
slave, 10, 64, 70
virtual, 32, 39, 153
Martin, Biddy, 253
Martin, Fran, 263
Marx, Karl, 7, 169, 170, 208, 212
Material culture, 34
Material objects, 276
condition of, 38
as souvenirs, 38
status of, 89, 158
and the virtual, 176
Mayer, Roger, 138
McClintock, Anne, 180
McCracken, Grant, 35, 38, 51, 61
McSpadden, Kevin, 103
McWherter, Dustin, 243
Medina, Nadia, 292
Memory, 39, 158–159, 218; *see also* Value
access, 169
auctioning of, 71
and chaos, 218
as competitive process, 182
disposability of, 278
objects, 167, 170
and passion, 218
and the past, 167
poetics of, 218
and price, 158
and race, 74–75
and technology, 209
Metsu, Gabriel, 85
Mexico, 16
Micropolitics, 109, 182
Mineo, Sal, 255
Minsky, Marvin, 281
Moon, Michael, 261
Moore, R. Laurence, 204
Morality, 112
Moravec, Hans, 281
Morgan, David, 42, 195
Morrison, Toni, 88
Mother Teresa, 188
MSN, 96
Museum for Moderne Kunst, 4

N

Narratable self, 84
Narrative, 2, 13, 39, 52, 83, 189, 195
of acquisition 68
and the archive, 83
of divestment, 38
effect, 168–169, 171
and image, 79
and memory, 159

as people's history, 81–83
personal, 170
Naughtybids.com, 278
Negri, Antonio. 97
Neoliberal/neoliberalism, 7, 10–11, 98, 101, 150
business model, 91
capitalism, 109
democracy, 110
discourse of "perfect" community, 108–111
ethics, 110
ownership society, 151
relationship to community and society, 110
subject, 167, 182
Nerve.com, 263
NetLingo.com, 246
"Network effects," 107, 118; *see also* "Virtuous circle"
"Network logic," 90–91
"Network society," 85, 92, 96, 103
Cisco Systems, 96
eBay, 96–97
Ng, Fiona, 263
Nicolette, Gianluca, 181
Nonnecke, Blair, 59
Nostalgia, 19, 101, 182, 218, 220, 223
Novak, Thomas, 137

O

Obadike, Mendi and Keith, 3, 4, 248, 262
Ockenfels, Axel, 155, 157
Offili, Chris, 14, 207, 212
Olalquiaga, Celeste, 209–210
Olsen twins, 192
Omidyar, Pierre, 1, 3, 92, 93, 98, 99, 101, 107, 108, 110, 119, 124, 126, 128, 134, 140, 151, 152, 157, 169, 246, 269, 275
and libertarian ideology, 92, 99, 100, 152, 155, 277
"Organization of coincidences," 6, 53, 54, 59, 60
O'Riordan, Kate, 178
Ottaway, Thomas, 142
Owens, Craig. 259

P

Panopticon, 116, 118; *see also* Surveillance
and neo-Panopticon, 116
Past, the, 6, 8, 10, 32, 159
as commodity, 289
imagined, 290
and relationship to history, 39, 283
Patriarchal ideology, 288
Pavlou, Paul, 139, 145
PayPal, 94, 96, 178, 239, 279
Peer-to-peer (P2P) exchange, 11, 54, 91, 100, 103, 203
Peirce, C. S., 13, 177, 178
Penley, Constance, 263
Pensky, Max, 43
People's archive, 10
People's history, 10, 80
Peralta, Marcos, 137
Perfect community, 107
"Perfect market"/"perfect price" discourse, 12, 16, 99, 151–152, 157, 159, 161, 246, 269
"Perfect store," 99
Performance, 2, 3, 36, 41, 48, 158
and narrative effect, 169
Persona, 2, 36, 139; *see also* Self
Philippines, 16
Photograph, 37, 191
amateur, 187, 191
and death, 204–205
Photographer, amateur, 185, 191
Photographer, role of, 82, 85
Photography, 13, 14, 15, 180, 236, 259; *see also* Technological form
amateur, 185, 187, 189, 190, 191, 195
amateur commercial still life (ACSL), 13, 185, 186, 187–188, 189, 190, 191, 192, 193, 194, 197

ambrotype, 263
and the book, 84
and collecting and gay identity, 259
and consumer culture, 208
daguerreotype, 222, 263
and death, 222
digital, 55, 180–181
fashion and film, 292
"gay interest," 15, 245, 254–255, 259
historical importance of, 80
and hypermediacy, 206
and immediacy, 206
and metaphysics, 180
misrepresentation in, 47
and reading women, 77
slide show, 203
and the trace, 180, 253
and truth claims, 181, 185, 191
vernacular, 220, 228, 253, 254; *see also* Amateur photography
vintage, 15, 245
and ways of looking at, 84, 85
and women's bodies, 84
Picker, Deborah, 270, 271, 274, 276
Pilgram, David, 71
Pine, Joseph, 2, 3, 17
PlanetOut.com, 269
Plath, Sylvia, 77
Plato's Cave, 179
Platter, Thomas, 72
Pleasure, 2, 52, 156, 176, 178
Poiesis, 208
and technics, 208
Policy, 11, 74, 123, 125, 127, 139
on adult material, 270
and corporate discourse, 108, 111–112
on offensive items, 68
on used underwear, 275
Political economy, neoliberal, 108, 119
Popular culture, U.S., 32, 101, 152, 187, 212, 232, 289
and religion, 204–205
Pornography, 269, 270–271, 275
Postmodern, 6, 42, 103, 221
Postmodernity, 39
Postrel, Virginia, 289
Power, normative, 259
Power Sellers, 14, 102,141, 146, 152
and "high risk" auctions, 146–147
Preece, Jeny, 59
Price, 3, 13, 22, 46, 53, 55, 56, 87, 152, 235
eBay's effect on, 152, 157
as "fair market value" on eBay, 153
market, 152
and memory, 158
and reputation, 153, 157
unpredictability of, 48

Q

Queer Nation, 260
Queer/queering, 260
Queer theory, 260

R

Race and racism, 3, 9–10, 64, 67, 69–70
"Rare"/rarity, 9, 37, 51, 56, 62, 158, 160
Reality TV, 175
"Reflectoporn," 192, 199
Reich, Robert, 97
Relics, 37, 79, 184, 302, 214
Religious iconography, 207
Remediation, 14, 80, 224–225
of magic lantern, 224
of slide photography, 224–225, 226
Reputation, 5, 12, 115
and price, 153, 157
Research practices, 16, 35, 63, 67–69, 292
Reserve bidding, 20, 115; *see also* Auctions, reserve; Bidding practices
Resistance, 7
Rheingold, Howard, 94

Richardson, Elvis, 14, 217, 218, 219–220, 221, 222, 223, 224, 227
Rielly, Tom, 269
Rifkin, Janet, 139, 145
Ritual, 35, 38, 45, 51, 290; *see also* Collecting rituals
  acquisition, 45, 51, 53
  exchange, 51
  new forms of, 46
  possession and bidding, 159
  possession and divestment, 9, 35–37, 38, 159, 172, 275–276, 277
  practices, 9, 36
Rivlin, Gary, 16
Robins, Kevin, 98
Rofes, Eric 268
Romanyshyn, Robert, 172
Rose, Nikolas, 108–109, 110
Ross, Andrew, 263
Roth, Alvin, 155, 157
Rubin, Gayle, 15, 267–268, 269, 271, 272, 277
Russel, Chloe, 63, 68, 69, 70, 71
Russell, A. B., 188–189

S

Sabucco, Veruska, 263
Sacred and profane, 6, 14, 206–207, 209, 211, 213
Schomburg, Arthur, 65
Schoorman, David, 138
Screwball comedy, 16, 283, 285, 292
Search practices, 9, 54, 57, 67–68; *see also* Category system
Searle, John, 112
Sedgwick, Eve Kosofsky, 259
Seiter, Ellen, 261
Sekula, Allan, 80
Self, 34–35, 36, 118, 150; *see also* Identity; Persona
  employment, 1, 100–101, 128
  and the interface, 260
  policing, 114, 116
  and self-construction, 258
  and self-object relations, 16, 38
  steering self, 109
  technologies of the, 109
Serrano, Andres, 14, 207, 212
Sex and commerce, 272
Sex panic, 16, 268, 268–269, 271, 273, 275, 277, 279
  and McCarthyism, 279
  and memory, 278
Sexuality, normative, 15, 268
Sherman, Cindy, 221
Shields, Rob, 178
Simmel, Georg, 291
Simulacra, 19, 32, 179
Sinatra, Frank, 92
Singapore, 16
Slash fiction, 263
Slate.com, 273
Slave economy, 71
Slide projector, 222, 224, 229
Slide transparency, 14, 218–219, 220–221, 222, 223–224, 228–229; *see also* Photography
  and personal history, 219
Super 8 film, 228
  technological form, 15
Smith, Shawn Michelle, 259
Sniezek, Janet, 139
Sniping, 21, 27–28, 54, 68, 124, 153–156; *see also* Bidding practices
  definition of, 153–154
  and expertise, 157
Social Darwinism, 169
Social science research on eBay, 12, 137, 147–150
  and coin and stamp auctions, 163–164
  and ethnography, 59
"Society of the spectacle," 174
Sociolinguistics, 108, 120
Song, Mary Lou, 151, 152, 261
Sontag, Susan, 7, 88, 180, 191, 253
Sotheby's, 15, 22, 152, 231, 232, 233, 234, 236, 238
SothebysAmazon.com, 232
Sothebys.com, 232, 233, 234, 238, 242

South Korea, 16
Space,
of buying and selling, 67
postmodern, 5
of productive consumption, 45, 58
and sight, 181
and virtual public sphere, 89
Space, geographic, 46, 54–55, 56, 57–58, 95, 179
and collecting, 47
influence of location in, 46, 56, 57
Space, virtual, 13, 48, 51, 60, 178
global, 235
influence on geographic space, 80, 95, 289
and online trace, 178
Spatial metaphor, 178
Stacey, Jackie, 42
Stackpool, Peter, 37
Stallybrass, Peter, 170. 173
Stanbury, Sarah, 292
Stanwyck, Barbara, 34
Star, Susan Leigh, 95
Sterling, Bruce, 296
Stewart, Susan, 37
Stone, Sandy, 243
Sublime, 6, 14, 206
and gender, 207
and visual arts, 207
Superfluity, 168
Surveillance, 84, 108, 117
and the Panopticon, 118
politics of, 84, 118
Swann Galleries and catalog, 65–66, 69, 74, 234
Swap meet, 9, 46, 48, 53, 56, 57; *see also* Markets
"Switching costs," 107

T

Taiwan, 16
Tamagotchi gesture, 21, 22
Taper, Louise, 65
Taste, 150, 207, 209, 213
community of, 36
and kitsch, 209
Taxonomy, 86
Techno-communitarian discourse, 98–99
Technological form, 7, 40, 94, 168, 178–179, 180; *see also* Photography
and desire, 180
and history, 87
influence of, 176, 219, 235–236, 247, 278, 290
and memory, 180
and social change, 87
Telepresence, 175, 180
and the trace, 175
Temple, Shirley, 211
Tiffany & Company, 240
Time, 19, 34, 223
defeat of, 223
and futurity, 29–30
Totland, Jeffry 270
Toys-R-Us, 101
Trace, the, 13, 175–179, 187–188, 200, 276, 286, 287, 290
and digital images, 181
and the ephemeral, 37
and experience, 177–178
of history, 83
and memory, 201
and photography, 253
relationship to space, 177–178
and telepresence, 176
Trachtenburg Family Slide Show Players, 228
Tradescant the Elder, 78
Trilling, Lionel, 175, 176, 181
Trotsky, Leon, 87
Trust, 11, 12, 127–128, 129–131, 133, 134 157
and anonymity, 138–139
and deregulation, 139
and face-to-face interactions, 139
and networks, 137
online, 137
and regulation, 139
and reputation, 141–143

and the "responsible user," 114–115
and risk to self, 138
and technical breakdown, 126
and virtual interactions, 139
Turner, Victor, 169

U

"Uncle Griff," *see* Griffith, Jim
"Unknowingness," 45–46, 48–50, 54, 59, 60; *see also* Value
and the archive, 54
Uruguay, 21
User ID (eBay), 26, 40, 58, 66, 115,129, 137, 139, 231, 234, 242
and anonymity, 242, 268
explained, 140
and identity, 5

V

Value, 2, 3, 9, 13, 14, 159, 177, 178; *see also* Guilelessness; Labor; "Unknowingness"
affective, 3, 158, 163, 169, 212
and authenticity, 2, 175
common, 157
and cultural capital, 152
estimation of, 152, 156
exchange, 168, 182
and experience, 2
"fair market," 141
of history, 82
labor, 170
and memory, 2
and misidentification, 160
and misspelling, 48–50, 160
and performed histories, 158
private, 154, 157
sexual, 272
and sniping, 145
and stable identity, 5
use, 88, 167, 172, 173, 177
Vintage clothing, 283
bias-cut dress, 288
and body movement, 286
and gender, 286;
and subverting fashion, 285
and the trace, 293
Vionnet, Madame, 288
Virtual and the actual, 176, 178, 290
Virtual reality, 279
Virtual space, *see* Space, virtual
"Virtuous circle," 95, 96, 99, 212; *see also* "Network effects"
Vishwanath, Arun, 138, 145
Visual culture, 245

W

Wal-Mart, 100
Webster, Frank, 99
Wharton, Edith, 64
White, Hayden, 79
White, Richard, 206
Whitman, Meg, 33, 112, 134, 272
Wikipedia, 102, 260
Wilder, Laura Ingalls, 88
Wilson, Catherine, 179
Wilson, Edward, 77
Wilson, Harriet, 71
Witkin, Joel-Peter, 85
Wolf, Michael, 17
Women,
as art objects, 87
and the book, 86
as consumable goods, 87
Wood, Charles, 142
Woolf, Virginia, 77
Woolson, Abba Goold, 89
"World's Online Marketplace" (eBay), 152
World Wide Web, 91
as space, 178

Y

Yahoo!, 96, 213
Yue, Audrey, 263

Z

Zukin, Sharon, 41, 52, 169